The Rise and Fall of California's
Radical Prison Movement

THE RISE

AND FALL

Eric Cummins

STANFORD UNIVERSITY PRESS

OF CALIFORNIA'S

RADICAL

PRISON MOVEMENT

STANFORD, CALIFORNIA 1994

Stanford University Press, Stanford, California
© 1994 by the Board of Trustees of the Leland Stanford Junior University
Printed in the United States of America

CIP data appear at the end of the book

Stanford University Press publications are distributed exclusively by
Stanford University Press within the United States, Canada, and Mexico;
they are distributed exclusively by Cambridge University Press
throughout the rest of the world.

To Nightcrawler

PREFACE

This is a history of California prisoners from 1950 to 1980, focusing on the San Francisco Bay Area's San Quentin State Prison. The book opens with the Caryl Chessman years (1948–60) and closes with the trial of the San Quentin Six (1975–76) and the passage of California's Determinate Sentencing Law (1977). This was an extraordinary era in the California prisons, one that saw the emergence of a highly developed radical convict resistance movement inside the prison's walls. This inmate groundswell was fueled at times by such remarkable prisoners as Caryl Chessman, Eldridge Cleaver, and George Jackson, at other times by groups of inmates such as the Black Muslims, the San Quentin chapter of the Black Panther party, and members of what would become the Symbionese Liberation Army or the Black Guerrilla Family. But most often the resistance grew from much wider sources and in quieter corners: from dozens of secret political study groups springing up throughout the prison; from a secretly published underground San Quentin newspaper; and from covert attempts at organizing the nascent California Prisoners' Union. This book traces the rise and fall of the prisoners' movement, ending with the inevitable bloody confrontation between prisoners and the state and the violent crackdown that followed on the part of the prison administration. It surmises that the tremendous recent expansion of the use of imprisonment in California, coupled with the introduction of cruel, new, high-tech "maxi-maxi security" prisons, is likely to bring more, not less, California convict struggle behind the walls and perhaps more violence on the streets as well, as prisoners are released into the community.

No prison exists in isolation from the surrounding community, and this was particularly true for San Quentin from the late 1940's to the late 1970's. During this period, San Quentin's walls became permeable in critical ways and Bay Area outsiders became intensely involved in the prison. But the greater San Francisco community was badly fractured along ideological and moral lines, split by a deep and bitter conflict between differing notions of community and crime, where crime originated, and what it signified. During the height of prison activism, huge numbers of citizens, not all of them "radicals" by any means, would come to support prison strikes and agitations with massive street demonstrations, lobbying campaigns, court actions, defense committees, teach-ins, lecture series, letter-writing campaigns, and massive media coverage. The majority sought simple, though far-reaching, prison reforms and civil rights for inmates. But many also lionized ex-convicts as revolutionary heroes and looked to them for political leadership, sometimes challenging the legitimacy of state punishment itself. The more radical participants in the movement believed violence was an inevitable part of a coming revolution. Some came to see violence as a self-actualizing and ennobling activity. A few planned and participated in inmate escapes. Others joined escaped convicts in acts of urban terrorism. To San Quentin administrators, local citizen involvement in prison issues seemed so potentially violent in the early 1970's that the prison prepared for a "storming of the Bastille" and drew up plans to close access roads to the prison and even to direct prison tower gunfire outward, for the first time in history, onto any group attempting to break *into* the prison. Ultimately, conservative forces in both the California state and the federal governments harshly tightened prison rules in the late 1970's and put an end to prison activism.

Inmates' expanded contact with the public, which began in the early 1960's, was accompanied by a virtual explosion of inmate reading and writing, often fueled and ignited by interested groups of outsiders. The result was the slow emergence of a prisoner intelligentsia that would build the ideological foundation for resistance. What quickly followed was a critique of prison itself and, in much writing from San Quentin inmates, a rejection of the penitential self-image of the traditional American convict autobiography. For a short time, for some inmates, among them some of the more powerful and articulate, the new self-image was that of the urban guerrilla revolutionary, vanguard of a longed-for American people's revolution. No longer a remorseful penitent, the male California convict-author began to see himself as a cultural hero and leader, in writings sometimes openly celebratory of crime. The public, too, embraced this new image when some of these writings, like Chessman's *Cell 2455*, or Cleaver's *Soul on Ice*, or Jackson's *Soledad Brother*, reached far beyond the prison's walls to become national best-sellers. Upon release from prison, some celebrity inmates quickly stepped into roles of leadership in radical political organizations at a time when, with the Vietnam War winding down, the Left was turning to domestic issues. For a few short years in the early 1970's, prison issues became such a major concern in Bay Area politics that a small number of ex-convicts from San Quentin came into positions of considerable political influence. Sadly, the role of prisoner as cultural hero and revolutionary vanguard leader was one to a great degree invented for prisoners by the Bay Area radical Left. The culture simply substituted one role for another; the age-old "penitent criminal convert" was replaced by the "guerrilla people's revolutionary leader." Neither script fit the real California prisoner very well, and this naive casting of prisoners as society's potential leaders would become one of the fatal mistakes leading to the demise of radical politics in California in the 1970's.

This book is very much a product of my personal life. In Ann Arbor at the end of the Vietnam War, when the Left was casting about for new issues to recharge its flagging campus support, I chose to ally with the emerging prison movement. For myself and many others, when 1971 brought Angela Davis's arrest and trial, George Jackson's death, and the massacre at Attica, prison issues assumed a major political importance. We told ourselves that the leadership of the coming revolution would surely soon emerge from the prisons, which were to be our universities of revolution. Their resisters would be our leaders. I was swept along into a community organizing activism that finally led me to live in and manage a group of three halfway houses for pre-parole male prisoners coming out of Michigan's Jackson State Prison. It was while living with these men that I first began to reexamine some of the ideological baggage I had brought into the prison movement. At the time Angela Davis, Eldridge Cleaver, and George Jackson were my personal heroes. I had arrived at the halfway house naively expecting to find more just like them. Soon I was sorely disappointed to discover that these Michigan prisoners were not revolutionary heroes of the coming struggle as Davis, Cleaver, and Jackson had seemed. These prisoners were, more rightly, simply the nation's beaten-down victims. These were broken men. Even if the revolution was fought in their name, it would not find its leadership among them. I was not alone in my disillusionment at this revelation, but many more in the Left chose to remain naive. Sometimes, as in the case of the Bay Area, this naïveté was to have disastrous consequences. Eventually I came to feel that my leftist radical stereotype of male prisoners—as political captives, revolutionary brothers engaged in a political struggle against the corrupt state—had been an oversimple one. It was of no help to the real prisoners, either.

The history of these stereotypes is one subject of this book. As ever, my sympathies are with the prisoners themselves. What follows here is a critique of the Left's role in the California prison movement because that is what I am closest to and know best. This need not make me seem an apologist for the prisons, however, or a special pleader for the Right. If this book can help the prison movement Left recover from the failure of the romantic vision of prisoners that contributed to its demise, it will have accomplished its goal. And if it can contribute in some way to a rebirth, a new movement founded on a more realistic, and therefore more helpful, attitude toward prisoners, then the California Left of the future may ensure prisoners more lasting reforms.

It is to the California prisoner, who has been stereotyped by both the Right and the Left, misused by each side in an ideological struggle and then conveniently forgotten, that I dedicate this book.

A book that deals with so broad a range of events and materials and as difficult an institution to study as this one owes a multitude of debts. First, to the prisoners and former prisoners, unionists, legislators, and staff and family of San Quentin, Soledad, Vacaville, and Deuel prisons who consented to interviews I owe the heart of the book: Ernie Bradford, Terry Cuddy, Byron Eshelman, William Hankins, Nate Harrington, Keith Hayball, William Malin, Ray Martin, James McHenry, Mary Mims, Robert Minton, Joe Morse, Louis Nelson, Richard Nelson, Dorsey Nunn, James Park, Fred Persily, Michael Snedeker, John Spain, Edna Spector, Luis Talamantez, Harlan Washington, Paul Comiskey, Vernel Crittendon, John Irwin, Ted Davidson, Charles Garry, Jay Halford, Rowan Klein, Alan Sieroty, James Smith, as well as those who must remain anonymous. Thanks to San Quentin State Prison and its warden Dan Vasquez for allowing me to do this project. Special thanks for long hours of help from the archivists of the Social Protest Project at Bancroft Library, University of California, Berkeley, and of the California Department of Corrections at the California State Archives in Sacramento. I am grateful as well to the Pelican Bay Information Project for access to its interviews of prisoners at Pelican Bay State Prison, and to Dr. Corey Weinstein, especially, for his insights into contemporary California prisons.

I want to express my sincerest thanks to Murray Murphey and Janice Radway who put long hours into reading early drafts of the book and asked me hard questions. To Michael Zuckerman who read and critiqued every chapter, every word, and pounded the table and then finally seemed to believe in the book even before I did myself, I owe my deepest gratitude. I couldn't have done this without you. Special thanks as well to Norris Pope at Stanford University Press who agreed we were on to something, and to my editor Karen Brown Davison for her care. To my manuscript editor Trudie Calvert for helping my sentences up onto their feet, I owe whatever grace the book manages to achieve. All these people and more punched and polished this book from its roughest stage. The errors that we missed are mine. I invite any comments or corrections.

Wanda, Lucille, Xiao-poo, Doris, and Vicki, thanks for hanging tough. And to my father, who led me to the struggle, my love and fondest memories.

E.C.

CONTENTS

1 The Gates Open Up and the Experts Pour In 1

2 Bibliotherapy and Civil Death 21

3 Caryl Chessman and the Roots of Convict Resistance 33

4 Taking the Yard, Freeing the Mind: The Black Muslims 63

5 Eldridge Cleaver and the Celebration of Crime 93

6 Crime Fetishism in the Radical Left 128

7 The Construction of George Jackson 151

8 Prisoner Unions and the "Imprisoned Class" 187

9 "Foco" Terrorism in the SLA 222

10 The Force of Imprisoned Words 252

Notes 281

References 303

Index 313

Photographs follow pp. 84 and 178

THE RISE AND FALL OF CALIFORNIA'S
RADICAL PRISON MOVEMENT

1

The Gates Open Up and the Experts Pour In

On a humid Thursday evening, August 17, 1950, 240 convicts surged toward their guards in the San Quentin prison mess hall, hurling plates, trays, and cups and shouting insults. Shots were fired over their heads by gunrail officers on the catwalk above, and the prisoners fell back.

Warden Clinton Duffy, who was vacationing in Carmel, was summoned immediately by duty officer Dr. Leo Stanley. Friday night brought more rioting. Eleven convicts were injured. Warden Duffy sent eleven more to solitary confinement on a bread and water diet. On Saturday night more booing and hooting accompanied the evening meal. This, too, was answered by gunshots from the guards.

San Quentin's warden lashed out at what he labeled an "outbreak of hooliganism." Duffy could see no obvious cause for the disturbances. No demands had been published. No complaints had been forthcoming. There had been no hint of trouble from "sources" in the prison grapevine. The warden went on radio KSQ, the direct communication link to headphone sets in all the cells: "You men know the rules must be obeyed. Any other course of action means loss of privilege. Baseball, movies, canteen—these are a privilege, not a right. I'm accused of being lenient. I want to give you all a break, but I'll tighten up this place more than you ever thought possible if there's another outbreak. Think it over, fellows."[1]

By Tuesday, calm was restored to the prison. Disciplinary hearings were ordered for those found responsible for inciting the riots. The matter was assumed closed. But Duffy remained anxious. What had caused these outbursts? Duffy's was a popular reformist administration that had overseen a decade of unparalleled calm. Why were the prisoners so volatile?

On October 31, 1950, a mere two months after the mess hall riots, trouble returned to San Quentin. Thirteen of the sixteen condemned men on Death Row staged a sit-down strike, refusing to return to the cell block after their exercise period. After one hour they were forcibly removed. One was later treated for a head wound inflicted by a billy club. Three others were put in solitary confinement. The story made the front page of the *San Francisco Chronicle* with the banner headline QUENTIN GUARDS BREAK UP KILLERS' SIT-DOWN STRIKE, a headline that conveniently ignored the fact that several of the condemned, most prominently Caryl Chessman and Wesley Robert Wells, were scheduled to die for crimes other than murder. Chessman and Wells appear to have been the instigators of this strike. They demanded fountain pens to replace the ballpoint pens currently in use; lights on all night (the lights went out at midnight, a recent improvement over 10:30 P.M.); better screens on the Death Row windows so birds could not fly in; longer exercise periods; and better food. The last three were housekeeping demands common to any protest. But the first two demands were a surprise. Why did the prisoners want pens and light? Warden Duffy dismissed the requests as nonsense and ordered disciplinary hearings. The *Chronicle*, too, sniffed about the prima-donna "killers" who should be grateful for anything they got.

But Clinton Duffy might have done well to look more carefully for the motive behind these demands from Death Row. Chessman and Wells were soon to become principal actors in an unfolding drama that would spread through the general inmate population. It would attract the attention of the Bay Area public, and at times the world, to San Quentin prison, ultimately launching a community movement that would threaten to tear down the very walls of the prison. The celebrity of the Caryl Chessman and Bob Wells cases, and the prison activism that their cases inspired, would feed into a whirlwind of prison revolt in the 1960's, much of it centered around demands for inmates' rights to unrestricted communication, reading, writing, and association, all necessary for organizing a political movement inside the prison.

Not by coincidence, in the 1950's the Bay Area public was also becoming sensitized to issues of free speech. In the late 1940's state senator Jack Tenney's Fact-Finding Committee on Un-American Activities had charged numerous Bay Area university faculty members and legislators with having "tainted," un-American thoughts. In 1949, in the same spirit, the University of California instituted loyalty oaths and fired any faculty who refused to take them. Those accused found little protection under the law. Although the university's loyalty oath was invalidated by the state supreme court in 1951 and the fired faculty members were reinstated, the mood of repression remained. In the anticommunist panic that was sweeping the nation, even the highest courts were turning their backs on the Constitution. The Supreme Court in 1951 (*Dennis* v. *United States*) ruled that the First Amendment did not protect the subversive language of those calling for radical changes in the structure of the U.S. government, and the Communist Control Act of 1954 outlawed the nation's Communist party. Radical trade unionists active in San Francisco since the 1930's, such as the International Longshoremen's and Warehousemen's Union (ILWU) president Harry Bridges, came under attack for their Marxist rhetoric and were accused of being communists. The growing spirit of repression unfairly silenced many. Bay Area listeners to Berkeley's fledgling KPFA, Pacifica Radio (established in 1949), which had aired interviews with communists, felt particularly threatened. In the late 1950's local academics would again come under attack by the House Un-American Activities Committee in its visits to San Francisco, and students in groups like UC Berkeley's SLATE quickly began to realize that they had little right to political expression on campus.[2]

The Bay Area was not alone in this experience. All across the nation, constriction of freedom of thought and speech was becoming a galvanizing issue for the emerging New Left movement. The plea of San Quentin inmates Chessman and Wells for light and writing materials that day in 1950 was soon to become a common refrain of California prisoners generally, and it was one that would strike an immensely sympathetic chord with the American public. Clinton Duffy's prison was about to play a central role in invigorating the New Left in the Bay Area, now catalyzed by demands for intellectual freedoms both within the prisons and without.

But the prisoners had much more in mind. The goals of California inmates did not end with simply establishing First Amendment rights for prisoners. They had actual freedom in mind. The new behavior modification program of the California prison system, a product of the "treatment" medical model of criminal deviancy popular in the 1940's and 1950's, claimed that if the causes of criminal behavior could be diagnosed, such behavior could be cured. Chessman and Wells's plea was the first sign that inmates were about to use the rehabilitation rhetoric of the prisons to subvert their own imprisonment. At the center of the maelstrom was an unrecognized contradiction in the

design of the rehabilitative prison, which insisted that prisoner reform and long-term prisoner custody were compatible. They were
not. The notions of prisoner rehabilitation and continued custody
were ineluctably at odds—a prisoner's reform by definition required
his release. And California prisoners, who were the first to grasp the
seriousness of this ideological contradiction, would soon use proof of
their own rehabilitation to dispute the need for their continued custody. Both these forces were about to converge fatally at San Quentin
prison: demands for intellectual freedom for convicts and calls for
their release by reason of rehabilitation.

In 1950 Warden Duffy called Chessman and Wells's plea for pens
and light "nonsense," but Caryl Chessman was about to teach Duffy
a lesson in his own prison's history and in the heritage of American
imprisonment in general. It was as though Chessman realized better
than the warden that his treatment-model prison functioned in part
by close control of inmate thought and communication. At San Quentin in 1950 this form of prisoner control became more crucial than it
had ever been.

The modern behavior-modification prison prominent in California
in the 1950's was an institution returning to its roots. At the time of
the creation of the American penitentiary, in eighteenth-century Philadelphia, solitude—the absence of any inmate communication whatsoever—was envisioned as the paramount cure for criminals. Even
labor was seen as secondary to solitude, and, in the perfection of the
early American inmate's quiet, one of the more spectacular instruments of "correction" was the iron gag, a device fixed to the head and
shoulders of an inmate with an attachment that gripped the tongue.
Long a valued implement in the repertoire of torturers, the iron gag
was one of the few sanguinary punishments the Philadelphia inven-
tors of the prison preserved from the past, intending it for use on
prisoners caught talking to each other—to punish the simple offense
of speaking. These early "treatment"-prison ideologues envisioned a
penitentiary designed in significant part to control prisoners by controlling their communication and thought, prisons well-supplied with
devices such as this one, working in tandem with the crowning invention of the solitary cell.[3] Early prison communication control could be
severe. Laughing, singing, and shouting were forbidden at Philadelphia's first prisons. But early prison advocates such as Benjamin Rush
went even further in their attempts to mold the inmate mind, calling
for forced attendance at prison religious services and a strict diet of

sacred reading, dominated by the Bible. Other books were expressly forbidden.

Rush had particular reasons for wanting to limit a prisoner's reading to sacred texts. As a medical doctor, he had a strong belief that criminality must have a physical, biological cause and that eventually a physical cure for the disease would be found. Rush's line of reasoning led him to the conclusion that criminality was the product of disordered, overactive sensation and that medicines might be discovered to treat this condition. But in the meantime the doctor felt obliged to treat criminality with the one sure cure he knew to reintroduce harmony to the senses—the Bible. In his *Medical Inquiries and Observations upon the Diseases of the Mind*, Rush compared the Bible to "an apothecary's shop, in which is contained remedies for every disease of the body."[4] According to this logic, in the hands of a skilled practitioner a prison library of sacred texts could serve as a kind of intellectual pharmacy. By prescribing particular passages out of the Book, the diseased excitement of criminality could be treated and equilibrium restored. The Bible was the ideal meditation for criminals, and the solitary cell was the perfect place for a convict's disordered senses to be reconstituted by its agency. The convict would fix his mind on God.

Benjamin Rush was the first of many American prison theorists to suggest the almost magical rehabilitative power of books and to insist that prisoners read carefully selected sacred texts under close supervision. But Rush was only articulating his own variant of a notion that had already gained rather wide currency throughout the nation.[5] After Rush's time this idea was picked up and recirculated elsewhere. By the mid-nineteenth century it was well accepted nationwide that close control of an inmate's reading and writing was central to his reform. Enoch Wines's *The State of Prisons and of Child-Saving Institutions in the Civilized World* recorded in 1880 that amazing physical and spiritual changes in convicts were commonly attributed by wardens to reading.[6] Consequently, the nineteenth-century American prison became a place engineered as much to control and reform thought as to maintain custody or to punish an inmate's body. At Pennsylvania's Eastern Penitentiary, for example, from the instant inmates entered the prison they never saw, spoke to, or received letters from anyone but prison officials and the Society for Alleviating the Miseries of Public Prisons, a select group of prison advocates that at one time counted Benjamin Rush as a member. Prisoners' cells were lit by one small, eight-inch "dead-eye" in the ceiling, and their meals were de-livered through a feedhole in the door. They exercised and worked alone for the duration of their terms. If they had to be taken into the hallway, a black hood was draped over them. On Sundays they knelt by the door and listened to a sermon being delivered in the hallway. Both work and books were given "as favors," since at first inmates were not permitted them. When the inmates at last begged for read-ing, they were given the Bible or other moral tract literature.

Programs of convict reform that included strategies of communi-cation and thought control developed slowly in the nation's nine-teenth-century prisons, the evolutionary thread toward treatment broken countless times by reversions back to simple, brutal retribu-tive punishment. The prisons, however, did change. And at each stage in their development, while some prison designers were devot-ing their energies to prison architecture, reordering space so that the convict might be more closely examined and brought under stricter physical control,[7] others were attempting to augment this physical reformative technology with more effective means of correcting the moral "sensibilities," through education, reading, and the control of inmates' thought and communication.[8]

As the nineteenth century progressed, criminological writings in-creasingly identified ignorance and lack of education as the main source of crime. By 1840 almost all American prisons had some type of library for prisoners.[9] The librarian was almost always the prison chaplain or "moral instructor," who closely supervised convicts' read-ing and writing. Until the mid-nineteenth century, most prison librar-ies were stocked exclusively with religious and temperance works, some with only Bibles and prayer books.

California was no exception to this pattern, although at its first state prison, San Quentin, the eastern rhetoric of the "moral reform" penitentiary movement got a later start than at most prisons and took many years to implement. The prison's first years were marked by unrelieved brutality. San Quentin prison originated in 1852, when the brig *Waban* was towed across San Francisco Bay and moored at Point Quentin to become California's first state penitentiary. Construction of a more permanent facility began almost immediately, and by 1854 the first cell block was completed, loosely modeled on the Auburn system, with congregate dining and labor.* In 1855, behind each of

---

*The Auburn system of imprisonment, named for the New York State prison at Auburn, its place of first use, and sometimes called the "association system" or the "congregate system," was a prison regimen in which inmates slept in single cells but

the cell block's forty-eight solid-iron doors, each with a "Judas hole" for air supply and guard observation, sat four prisoners furnished with wood bunks and a night bucket.* Convicts at mid-nineteenth-century San Quentin were "reformed" with rawhide floggings, strait-jackets, or gas from chloride of lime spread in their cells. Sometimes they were treated to the "derrick," a block and tackle from which the prisoner was suspended by his handcuffed wrists. Especially stub-born inmates got the "ladder," a device to which they were strapped while a high-pressure stream of water was directed at them.

But in 1858, when Governor John B. Weller included in his list of prison rules a directive to the warden of San Quentin to provide Sun-day services for his prisoners, almost a century of slow and halting, but nonetheless certain, movement away from physical torture and toward inmate reform through "moral education" began in the Cali-fornia prisons.[10] An 1861 legislative committee report expressed re-grets that at San Quentin "no prayer is heard, no Bible is read, no exhortation to repentance is heard."[11] This situation was soon to change. In November 1868 captain of the yard R. G. Gilchrist sug-gested that a prison school might help San Quentin put to use the "regenerative power of the word of God" in the reformation of its prisoners,[12] and in 1870 former Mendocino County school superinten-dent C. C. Cummings was appointed the prison's first moral instruc-tor. That same year California sent a representative to Cincinnati for the first meeting of the Congress of the National Prison Association, where speaker after speaker called for the "moral regeneration" of prisoners rather than the "infliction of vindictive suffering" and rec-ommended the release of the prisoner when the "moral cure" had been effected and "satisfactory proof of reformation" was obtained.[13] Many of these recommendations of the congress were not to be im-plemented in California until 1944, but in small ways new convict treatment strategies began slowly to creep into the California prison system. In the mid- to late 1940's, however, at San Quentin, Folsom, the new California Institution for Men at Chino, and the Correctional Training Facility at Soledad, a truly rehabilitative rhetoric of reform

---

worked together in enforced silence with downcast eyes. This became the more com-mon type of imprisonment after the Pennsylvania "separate system"—in which pri-soners remained totally separate at all times—was demonstrated in the 1830's to drive inmates to insanity.

*A "Judas hole" was a peephole in a cell door through which guards could ob-serve prisoners without their noticing, in order to catch them at any of their Judas-like betrayals of the rules of civil society. The term originated in the mid-nineteenth century.

would be fully embraced, and behavior modification technology would finally be widely applied to inmate correction.

When Dr. Leo Stanley called Warden Duffy back from Carmel to handle the mess hall riots of 1950, the warden was at the seaside resort town autographing copies of his just-published book, *The San Quentin Story*. "Today," the warden had written, "the once bloody battle ground where brutality was the rule . . . is a huge, modern laboratory for the study of criminals and crime." Duffy sang the praises of his new prison Guidance Center, where incoming prisoners were screened, tested, and classified by teams of psychologists, sociologists, medical doctors, religious advisers, and educators to "examine their crimes and plan their future with us." [14] The age of the expert had come to San Quentin. Guards were henceforth to be known as "correctional officers" and dungeons as "adjustment centers." Teams of social scientists and medical personnel were to provide the convict with opportunities for self-understanding and improvement. All the behavior modification technologies of modern social science would be brought to bear on the convicts.

A prominent part of his new prison, the warden promised, would be "a larger library [and] expanded educational and religious programs." He referred to the Education Department as part of psychiatric treatment. Duffy assumed total control over inmate communication, movement, association, and outside contact. Of an inmate's personal correspondence with family and friends, for example, he wrote:

We keep a careful record of every letter written or received by the inmates, and our censors read every line. This is a prodigious book-keeping job, but in the long run it benefits the men themselves. Letters are clues to a man's thinking and emotions—they show progress or despair; they reveal an unreported illness, a family crisis that has affected a man's behavior, or even evidence that may be vital to his chances for parole. [15]

These letters could also reveal escape plans or resistance. Letters containing criticism of the prison or any other government or law enforcement authority were strictly against the rules and were rigidly censored. The writer could be brought before a disciplinary committee to receive loss of privileges, extension of sentence, or time in isolation. The inmate newspaper, too, was strictly censored and was actually a vehicle to disseminate administrative opinion.

All across the nation in the 1950's social and behavioral scientists were gaining unprecedented prestige, and while radical subversives were being exposed across the land and the American public safe-guarded from their "tainted" deceptions, San Quentin not coinci-dentally began to portray itself as a machine designed for altering minds rather than punishing bodies, as the penal operation, in Michel Foucault's words, took on "extra-juridical elements and personnel . . . a whole set of assessing, diagnostic, prognostic, normative judge-ments concerning the criminal . . . lodged in the framework of penal judgement." At San Quentin, again in Foucault's words, the way was opened up for a displacement of the punishment "to the soul . . . the thoughts, the will, the inclinations."[16]

At the same time, a shift was taking place in the conception of language in American culture that was to have far-reaching conse-quences for prisoners. Since 1919 the accepted definition of "subver-sive language" had required that it constitute a "clear and present danger." It was in this context that Justice Oliver Wendell Holmes had declared that "one could not shout fire in a crowded theater if there was no fire." But in 1951 the Supreme Court reshaped the doctrine of "clear and present danger" in *Dennis* v. *United States*, ruling that the First Amendment did not extend to those who conspired to advocate the overthrow of the American government. In its decision the Court "shift[ed] the test from the relation between language and the world to the *intention* of the language itself. . . . Justice Harold Medina instructed the jury that 'words may be the instruments by which crimes are committed.'"[17] Not only were words now seen as weap-ons, but to a nonexpert insidious words could seem totally innocent. Stefan T. Possony, a language expert on the faculty of Georgetown University, testified before the House Committee on Un-American Activities in 1959 that "every Communist communication" contained two messages: one designed to activate communist revolutionaries and another to paralyze those opposed to communism. Communists achieved this effect by a conscious perversion of meaning and a sys-tematic transposition of terms. Possony warned against taking lightly even the most innocuous-seeming statements made by subversive elements.[18] On the tongues of outspoken crusaders such as Whittaker Chambers and J. Edgar Hoover, the word "communist" encompassed "fellow travelers" and "duped sympathizers" alike. As Chambers wrote in a *Reader's Digest* article in 1953, the list of those who deserved mistrust included many union members, "doctors, scientists, engi-neers, artists, economists, [and] teachers—a surprising number from top American universities."[19]

At San Quentin, wardens, librarians, educators, and even cell-block guards—especially cell-block guards—were soon taking it as their personal responsibility to inspect all prisoners' mail, magazines, newspapers, library books, and writings for telltale signs of subversion. Prisoners' mental hygiene was scrutinized to an even higher degree. The library record of each inmate had to be "cleared by the associate warden [of] custody, before release to a camp, to another institution or before parole or discharge." This record became "part of the inmate's official history . . . contained in the Cumulative Case Summary." When the inmate left prison he was "given a list of books suitable to his tastes and interests." The senior librarian served on the Classification Committee "upon request of the associate warden for care and treatment, [and could be required to] report upon the reading accomplishments of individual inmates." [20]

The man who first claimed to have raised San Quentin to this height of treatment-model thought control was Clinton Duffy. Duffy had come to the warden's office at San Quentin riding a wave of reformist zeal after a scandal in the previous administration. His predecessor, Court Smith, had been forced to resign in 1940 after alleged inmate beatings and horrible abuses had been revealed in the newspapers and in the hearing rooms of Governor Culbert Olson. On the occasion of a mere rumor of an inmate strike in February 1939, Smith had peremptorily sent 27 suspected agitators to "Siberia," a group of cells in which the temperature could be lowered to a bone-numbing chill. Inmates in the cold cells were treated during the day to the "Spot," a painted gray circle two feet in diameter in front of each of the Siberia cells, where the prisoners were forced to stand for two four-hour shifts each day. No movement was permitted while on the Spot, not even a shift of weight. The convict was allowed two two-minute toilet breaks. On this February day in 1939, however, Siberia was already full, and the prisoners had to be "double-celled" and doubled up on the Spots. Instead, the men sat down in protest. During the ensuing investigation ordered by Governor Olson, a San Quentin guard confessed to having taken part that day in a mass beating of the prisoners, using "loaded" hoses, canes, and clubs. Evidence also showed that the prisoners were being served rancid food containing "putrid and decomposed animal substance," and that the old dungeon was still in use.

Duffy changed all that. On taking office in 1940, he fired the guards who participated in the beatings. He had the Spots painted over and the huge iron doors torn off the old dungeon, converting it to a storeroom. Clinton Duffy had plans for a different kind of prison at San Quentin. He had a deep faith in convict rehabilitation. He put his efforts into education, sports, religion, and psychiatry and set about immediately to expand the Education Department.

Duffy couldn't do it alone, but fortunately he didn't have to. A spirit of prison reform was in the air. When Earl Warren won the governor's race in 1942, he immediately ordered an investigation of the state's entire prison system. He released the report to the press, and the anger it aroused in the public enabled him to call a special session of the state legislature on January 27, 1944, to ask for a complete reorganization of the prison system. Warren got much of what he wanted. The result was a penal system designed expressly to put to the test those strategies of treatment that the first Congress of the National Prison Association had advocated with such fervor in 1870 but that had never been fully implemented. For the first time at San Quentin, a truly rehabilitative technology would be applied to inmate correction.

Governor Warren's new penal system started by reinvigorating the 1917 California Indeterminate Sentence Law, by which each inmate was sent to prison for an indefinite time period. It would remain up to the prisoners to demonstrate through reformed behavior that they were ready to leave. This much was nothing new. The new law would be administered by the Adult Authority (AA), or parole board, but this was to be a radically changed parole board, a panel of experts that was to include educators and sociologists in addition to attorneys and law enforcement personnel. The board would travel from prison to prison, periodically reviewing each inmate's progress toward rehabilitation.

Warren chose Richard A. McGee to accomplish his reforms. A former college administrator, McGee had recently been the director of education for the U.S. Bureau of Prisons. The governor recruited McGee as director of the California Department of Corrections and put him in charge of the Adult Authority as well. McGee was a master politician, a master of the art of the possible. He put together a penal system founded on an innovative-sounding philosophy:

The policy of the California State Board of Prison Directors is based upon the concept that there can be no regeneration except in freedom. Rehabilitation, therefore, must come from within the individual, and not through coercion. With this principle in mind, the rehabilitation program of the State Board of Prison Directors contemplates not only important educational and vocational factors, but also, by and through classification and segregation, a gradual

release from custodial restraint, and corresponding increase in personal responsibility and freedom of choice.[21]

The new Correction Department's rhetoric of regeneration in freedom
set San Quentin and other California prisons on a course away from
the manipulation of inmate behavior by threat of physical harm and
toward a loosening of the rules. The new prisons would be designed
to provide more freedom, and with the aid of teams of social scientists
and medical personnel they would provide the convict with more opportunities for self-understanding and improvement. McGee pressed
California prison wardens to hitch their inspirational but archaic penal philosophies to the behavior-modification technologies of modern social science. The gates opened up, and the experts poured in.

An era of calm came to San Quentin. In retrospect, this was probably more a product of wartime patriotism among the inmates than
anything else. But the new treatment rhetoric had pulled off a public
relations coup. The public began to see the prison as a model community in which shattered lives were being remade. When war was
declared in 1941, Duffy's convicts seemed to shine with civic responsibility and public-spiritedness. Fourteen men volunteered to become
human torpedoes in the wartime effort and had to be politely turned
down. Others gave blood, bought bonds, and saved fat. The prison
jute mill was converted to the production of camouflage netting, and
prisoners made submarine nets, ammunition cases, and other war
products. Duffy was elected vice president of the American Prison
Association and president of the Wardens' Association.

The triumph of San Quentin did not go unnoticed in the press.
The *Saturday Evening Post* in November 1941 swept Duffy into the
national limelight. Over the years he would receive lavish praise for
his reform philosophies, his preference for treatment rather than punishment. *Life* (1947) went so far as to claim that prisoners "regard him
more as a friend than a keeper,"[22] a conclusion also reached by *Reader's Digest* (1946). In a 1946 movie called *San Quentin*, a congenial Warden Kelly portrayed the romantic public image of Clinton Duffy.

A comprehensive prisoner rehabilitation apparatus was being put
in place in California by the mid-1940's. Group counseling had been
established in 1944, "bibliotherapy" in 1947. At the California Institution for Men at Chino, family picnics were encouraged and relatively
free visiting practices were allowed, outgrowths of the radical notion
that more, not less, contact with the outside world was the answer to
curing criminal misbehavior.[23] The call went out for more "program"

in the prisons, and the prisoners became juridically paradoxical crea-
tures: on the one hand, they were viewed as enemies of society,
thought to have consciously rejected the social contract; on the other,
they were presumed to want to belong to society and to achieve the
conventional goals of the culture. Undergirding this paradox was a
new faith: opportunity theory. American sociologists had been developing new rationales to explain the origin of crime in juveniles, arguing that everybody wanted to be part of law-abiding society; it was the
discrepancy between aspirations and legitimate chances for achieve-
ment, the lack of opportunity, that caused juveniles to descend into
crime, not that the criminal subculture had rejected conventional cultural goals.[24] It had, in fact, internalized them too well. The redemp-
tion of criminals, then, would be a simple matter of offering them
more opportunity to conform. As a consequence, as the new rehabilitative technology came into place, prisoners of the 1950's would be
made to reaffirm civitas by participating in their own punishment.
They would do this by "programming," by becoming willing participants, or acting like such, in any program their keepers required. The
prison seemed to come alive with a new sense of purpose, the reform
of its inmates via "program."

The newly arriving prisoner entered the treatment-era California
men's prison by way of a Reception-Guidance Center. He stepped out
of a sheriff's van in a suit of prison whites and belly chains, and while
the deputy who brought him in was given a "body receipt" to cer-
tify his delivery, the "fish" convict was skin-searched (ears, mouth,
armpits, rectum, and toes examined), showered, and fingerprinted.
Then he started answering the battery of questions that made up his
initial psychological evaluation. This would determine in which of
California's prisons he was to serve his time. Letters were sent to the
convict's wife and family, his high school principal, and his county
jailer: Was this man a good mixer? What was the subject's attitude
toward schoolwork? Do you plan divorce? The psychiatric workup
and the results of a battery of tests went into the inmate's cumulative file, his "jacket" as prisoners termed it, which could contain a
great range of information, including notes on prior arrests and a
statement written by the convict in his own words explaining why he
had committed his crime. As the years of his sentence passed, his
jacket would record his progress or lack of progress toward rehabilitation. Its contents would be used by the Adult Authority to deny or
grant parole.

The centerpiece of San Quentin's program was its psychologically based group counseling. Group counseling, which had been developed in army mental hospitals early in World War II, was introduced in the California prison system in 1944 by the deputy director of corrections, Dr. Norman Fenton. "Essentially," Fenton wrote, "we are told that a therapeutic technique called group counseling, involving periodic meetings of staff and inmates to talk over matters of concern, has certain consequences for the participants—consequences that are rehabilitative. . . . Operationally, group counseling means that ten or twelve inmates meet one or two hours a week under the guidance of a lay group leader." [25] Fenton took up Clinton Duffy's metaphor of the prison-as-laboratory and extended it to a vision of the prison-as-hospital:

The treatment program for the inmate in the prison [is] planned in terms of an understanding of him as a person. . . . Human kindness pervades the things that are done in attempting to help him in the prison. . . . With understanding help in an atmosphere of kindness this purpose can best be accomplished. . . . [The prisoner's children should be told that] their father is there because he needs the help he can receive. . . . The prison, the children may be informed, is like a hospital—only the kinds of troubles treated there are not physical illnesses but personal troubles. . . . Nothing which the families can do is more important than to try to change their loved-one's attitudes toward the prisons and to try to accept them as places for treatment not unlike hospitals. [26]

Rhetoric aside, San Quentin remained a grim, punishing place. Maybe only the prisoners who did time there in this period can sense the irony in the institution's comparing itself to a hospital. James Park, a clinical psychologist in the California prisons of the early 1950's and later an associate warden of San Quentin, describes Duffy-era San Quentin as "a fairly brutal, old-fashioned behind the times system. Duffy . . . got an awful lot of publicity, [but] people were still being beaten to death under Duffy's regime. He was not the great fucking savior that his own press agent built him up to be." [27] Basically, the California prisons' devotion to treatment rather than punishment was hollow, substanceless rhetoric. As before and since, the first function of the prison remained custody, control, and punishment.

But despite the seeming irony, San Quentin treatment staff—counselors, chaplains, educators, librarians—took the word "treatment" seriously. In group therapy they began sincerely attempting to use group dynamics and peer pressure to counter the force of the inmate criminal subculture and change the values of participating inmates. In the inmates' eyes, however, adopting a treatment model of criminal deviancy had unforeseen consequences that transformed the treatment staff into custody officers of sinister, Orwellian character. As political scientist Ronald Berkman has pointed out, couching the definition of criminal offense in terms of organic-functional disorders, as Fenton's system did, legitimized the indeterminate sentence.[28] If prisoners, all prisoners, were mentally or emotionally sick and their keepers were psychological experts, then it seemed natural to leave to the experts the decision of when, if ever, a particular prisoner should go free. But the same principle held out a tremendous opportunity to the prisoners: if convicts were in prison to be cured, it made no sense to continue to punish them with beatings, solitary confinement, and severe deprivation. And when their cure had been effected, it made no sense to keep them in prison one minute longer. The inmates would put this glitch in the treatment model to wonderful advantage, for it was the prisoners themselves more than anyone else who had faith in convict reform, or at least it was they who pressed treatment ideology to its breaking point. During the period of judicial prisoner rights activism in the 1960's, California prisoners en masse would bring the courts to the collective revelation that the "adoption of the principle of rehabilitation [had] undercut the traditional notion of punishment which shaped the severely authoritarian system of governance within the prison."[29] This led inevitably to many court decisions against the prison system and to the expansion of civil rights for prisoners. Louis Nelson, who first came to San Quentin in 1951 and served as its warden from 1967 to 1974, comments on 1950's-era treatment ideology:

We expounded the virtues of the treatment system. We knew we could cure. The only people that knew we couldn't cure were the convicts themselves, and they got onto it a lot faster than the staff did. We preached the gospel that we were the great physician. So just cast all your troubles onto our shoulders and you will be healed. Well, after about seven trips to the prison by the same convict and going out on the street and being returned, they found out we didn't have a cure at all. We didn't have the slightest idea what the hell we were talking about.[30]

The prison itself may have been in the dark, but its prisoners were not. The treatment-era California prison had introduced reforms it could not fulfill and probably had never intended to. Instead it had created a reform rhetoric that could be manipulated for other purposes.

Prisoners were promised expert help with their problems. They were told they would receive an education, learn a trade, and get psychological help. Teams of correctional counselors, psychiatrists, educators, chaplains, and even surgeons were at their service at the prison, they were told, waiting to help them. In reality, San Quentin's ratio of treatment staff to custody staff remained low and counselors had impossibly large caseloads, so the guards were still the ones who had the most contact with and control over the prisoners, and the ones whose reports were most important to the Adult Authority. Nonetheless, accolades for the treatment continued to spew forth from the prison system. California Corrections Department pamphlets of the day included photos of classrooms, counseling offices, and even modern operating rooms at San Quentin, where it was promised physical disfigurements and deformities would be corrected, scars and tattoos removed, and other unseemly facial features changed. This modern correctional facility was to be capable of altering any physical or psychological defect that produced feelings of inadequacy leading to antisocial tendencies.

Small group counseling sessions took place in many departments of the prison. In the chapel, for example, which had long since separated from the Education Department and prison library, Protestant supervisor of religious activities Byron Eshelman ran the "Yoke-fellows" once a week, as well as the prayer therapy group. He also taught a course titled "Character Growth Through Religion and Psychology." Eshelman, who served as supervising chaplain of the Department of Corrections and San Quentin resident chaplain from 1951 to 1971, recalls running as many as twelve sections of prayer therapy at once, involving approximately 150 inmates:

They were trying to get every inmate in some form of group counseling. It was basically a matter of sharing feelings about oneself, being personal, confessing one's own problems and "sins" as we used to say. . . . We submitted regular forms on any inmates that were active in our programs to go in the [cumulative] file. Form #118 they called it. And we'd do that for any inmate that was coming up before the board if we had any information in our file. We had a file on every inmate in our chapel and these classes that they took and so on, we'd keep a record of that. And if we knew them personally from conversation, if they sang in the choir or ushered or had a staff role, we would report that for the records so the Adult Authority would have that information.[31]

Eshelman saw his role as helping the inmates to achieve true and lasting religious transformation, though the prison put him in the awkward position of using their religious behavior as a measure of reform. Prison officials insisted that he serve as a member of the Classification Committee until 1961, participating in hearings to determine prisoners' custody level.

The San Quentin library, run by senior librarian Herman Spector from 1947 to 1968, joined eagerly in the group therapy effort, conducting goal-directed reading programs, group discussions, special study groups, writing groups, and group forums. The librarian's central role was to select books appropriate for group therapy objectives, to highlight certain passages, and to conduct small group discussions, eliciting personal insights that might foster moral growth and maturation. Spector came highly recommended. He had been recruited by Warden Duffy in New York, where he was serving as librarian at the Penitentiary of the City of New York and chief librarian of the New York Department of Corrections. He had studied at Columbia University. More important, Spector was known for his staunch integrity and feisty determination. He was young, energetic, and zealously devoted to bringing the regenerative power of books to the service of inmate rehabilitation. He had already been offered the job of warden at prisons in Atlanta and Puerto Rico. Duffy offered Spector the position of assistant warden, but Spector turned it down in favor of the library post, which would enable him to avoid the politics of the front office and be in the best position to test his theories of bibliotherapy. Herman Spector was burning with enthusiasm, fired by the marriage of science and penology, and eager to initiate a statistical study of the moral effects on a large inmate population of prolonged exposure to the eternal verities of classical literature.[32] Warden Duffy would give him that chance.

Periodically, usually once a year, each San Quentin inmate convicted under the Indeterminate Sentence Law went before the Adult Authority to be granted or denied parole. At that time the inmate's cumulative file, including his reading record, provided the AA with comprehensive information on the inmate's crime, his current attitude toward it, his involvement in rehabilitative programs, and any "beefs" or misconduct citations he had. The California Penal Code required that the board include educators and social scientists: "Insofar as practicable members shall be selected who have a varied and sympathetic interest in corrections work including persons widely experienced in the fields of corrections, sociology, law, law enforcement, and education."[33] In 1953, however, this paragraph was deleted from the code, and the board was subsequently composed almost exclusively of law enforcement and corrections personnel. In 1971, for example, the board included "one individual with a police department background; one with an FBI background; a former assistant U.S. attorney; a parole agent; a D.A.; a police chief; and a correctional officer."[34] The absence of behavioral "experts" on treatment-era parole boards indicates a serious turning away from the stated principles of the treatment prison.

Although the parole hearing was an attempt to assess an inmate's rehabilitation, few today would claim the process was fair or successful. The Adult Authority hearing required attendance of one AA member, one hearing officer, and the inmate. Witnesses were often called from San Quentin staff and customarily included a correctional counselor. Hearings averaged ten minutes. There were no published rules for how the hearings should be conducted, and if the prisoner was denied parole he was not told the reason. No attorneys were permitted at hearings, prisoners were not allowed to cross-examine witnesses, and no transcript was made. Official criteria for denial or approval of parole included the "subject's attitude toward [his] offense," his "social and psychological history," and his "response to institutional program in terms of participation and accomplishments." The goal of the AA hearing committee, its chairman, Henry Kerr, said in testimony before a House of Representatives subcommittee inquiry into California prisons in 1971, was to assess "the individual's behavioral and emotional problems, his degree of understanding and insight and his plans, if any, for modification and self improvement."[35]

After completing what inmates called the "cop-out" sheet, filling in information on what programs the inmate had participated in, how he felt about his crime, what religious faith he belonged to, and his plans for the future, the San Quentin convict waited for his parole hearing in a foyer on the second floor of the prison's administration building. When a buzzer sounded in the tiny room, an officer waved the man into an oak-paneled room where one Adult Authority member and a hearing officer were seated in high-backed leather armchairs behind a long, polished table. Then the hearing commenced. "What is important," wrote Walter Burckhard, a prisoner sent to San Quentin in the 1960's for possession of marijuana,

is how near your guilt can make you to a replica of their version of you—your productivity, your religious character, your obeisance to them and the facticity of the law, your by now rather severe respect for the society you have offended through a narcotics officer . . . , your love of family, your knowledge of your psychological patterns no one has defined for you, your demonstrable commitment to every fashion of social compliance. And their beaks will

snatch at the subtlest scurry of falsity. Then you will have to stay for another
year. This is what your guilt entitles them to. You are no longer judged for
your act. Your act is merely a lever for the judging of your every aspect. Your
guilt must always be reproven.[36]

San Quentin's pretense of thoroughly examining an inmate's every
aspect in preparation for parole hearings had the effect of making
daily prison life a game. It was the "rehabilitation game." "Dig," a
black inmate in 1971, said: "I go to my counselor and he wants to
know am I guilty of my crime. I told him I was, and he gets out this
Bible and asks me if I'd like him to read from it. I figure that's his trip,
so I shine him on and let him do it, man, because I'll do anything that
will help me get out of here."[37] Treatment staff were at the heart of
the game because progress in treatment programs was essential to
getting parole. This made the pencils of librarians, educators, chaplains, and counselors perhaps even more lethal weapons than those
of the gunrail officer. A survey of seventy California parolees in the
summer of 1966 (many of whom had been in the system since the
1950's) showed that few inmates put any faith in treatment programs:
57 percent regarded treatment programs as ineffective, 55 percent
believed the programs were intended by the Corrections Department
simply to get more state monies, and 28 percent thought they were
devised to control inmates.[38] Though group counseling and various
other treatment programs were to continue through the 1960's and
into the 1970's, by the mid-1960's fewer and fewer staff, and even
fewer prisoners, believed in their value. A white inmate who was on
San Quentin's Death Row from 1962 to 1972 and is now in the mainline prison population recalls 1960's-era treatment strategies: "They
had different small group therapy sessions and so forth. Group
counseling. Some of that was a shuck to pacify the board. . . . The
word was 'program.' You had to comply with all board requests,
whether it was group therapy, academic, vocations, whatever, Alco-
holics Anonymous, church, could be any of a number of things. And
you had to comply in order to get out."[39]

According to former 1950's-era Soledad prison inmate John Irwin,
a recently retired sociologist from San Francisco State University, as
coercive as the "chickenshit routines" of the rehabilitative San Quentin had been, "rehabilitation inadvertently contributed to mounting
criticism of itself by promoting a prison intelligentsia. Partly because
of the expanded possibilities and the encouragement stemming from
rehabilitation, more and more prisoners began educating themselves.

Once we freed ourselves from the narrow conceptions contained in the rehabilitative philosophy, we began reading more and more serious literature."[40] In a similar vein, Malcolm X, another product of the treatment-era prison system, said of his own experience with the library at Norfolk Prison in 1948: "No university would ask any student to devour literature as I did when this new world opened to me, of being able to read and *understand*."[41]

It is the slow rise of this prisoner intelligentsia and its relation to the community outside San Quentin prison that we will look at now, for in the end what became most important was not the failure of the California treatment-era prison to live up to its own reform ideals, or even its failure as social control, but how it allowed inmates to manipulate and subvert this reform rhetoric, ultimately spawning a radical prison movement in the Bay Area.

Trouble was already brewing at San Quentin at the beginning of the 1950's. In April 1951, the prison's jute mill burned to the ground, putting almost a thousand men out of work and adding the monotony of unemployment to an already volatile situation. Warden Duffy resigned soon afterward, perhaps wisely, leaving Harley O. Teets to succeed him as warden in December, just in time for one of the most tumultuous periods of U.S. prison history. A major wave of prison riots swept the nation in 1951–53. One expert estimated that during the eighteen months from April 1952 through September 1953, "thirty prison riots or other major disturbances" had occurred—more than had taken place in the entire preceding quarter-century.[42] In California there were riots at Soledad, Alcatraz Island Federal Prison, San Quentin, and Folsom. In stark contrast to previous eras, however, in the 1950's California would respond to this disorder by weakening, not strengthening, the ideological systems of punishment, an administrative decision that would eventually have the unforeseen effect of pushing the prison population even further toward political protest.[43]

2

BIBLIOTHERAPY AND CIVIL DEATH

Herman Spector, who avidly followed developments in his field, eagerly moved to make his library a modern-day site for bibliotherapy. He followed the advice of the journals in his field and took university courses in criminology, psychology, supervision of social casework, and administration of correctional institutions. He began conducting small-group therapy, using discussions in a Great Books class with bibliotherapeutic goals in mind. Spector also ran therapeutic creative writing sessions and became co-sponsor of the Seekers, an inmate self-improvement discussion group. He supplied books and recommended reading lists to other treatment staff. And he kept detailed files of each inmate's reading record, preferences, and needs. Spector soon established a strong reputation in the prison library field. His library became renowned as possibly the best prison library in the land, partially owing perhaps to Clinton Duffy's public relations success. By 1955, when he was appointed supervising librarian of the entire California Department of Corrections, Spector had also established a reputation as an author on the male criminal and his remediation and as an editor on penal subjects generally.*

*Spector served as the assistant managing editor of *Prison World*, the official organ of the American Correctional Association, and as editor in chief for the *Correctional Library Manual* of the American Correctional Association and *Correctional Recreation*. He compiled bibliographies on penology, criminology, and juvenile delinquency and wrote on prison libraries for the *Encyclopedia of Penology* and for numerous journals. Spector reported before the California Crime Commission in 1948 on the causes of crime and served as in-service training lecturer on prison education and libraries for the United States Naval Training Command from 1949 to 1952. He spoke many times before professional groups and organizations on the topic of bibliotherapy in the prison and served as chairperson for the American Correctional Association's Committee on Institution Libraries and as president of the California Library Association's Association of Hospital and Institution Librarians. The titles of some of his publications are sug-

Library journals were proclaiming a new dawn in bibliotherapy with the advent of psychiatry and a new function for the prison library. Large inmate populations made individual psychiatric treatment impossible, they argued, and even a few hours a week in group therapy could work only small changes on prisoners' attitudes. The inmates would have to "undergo more extensive and broader reconditioning than possible with present methods of group-therapy," an article in the *Wilson Library Journal* observed in 1952. A "continual intellectual atmosphere" had to be created:

It is at this point that the prison library can make a decisive contribution by tying up with the group therapy efforts. . . . The library . . . can help to realize the ideal of group therapists in that it can surround the inmate with a perpetual intellectual atmosphere of the type which is necessary to bring about a definite change in his behavior patterns.[1]

Spector's faith in bibliotherapy and his conviction that the San Quentin library should be at the very center of the prison's treatment strategy was not shared by the prison's administration or even necessarily by other treatment staff. Custody staff as well were skeptical of any treatment strategy, and the idea that reading books would reform hardened criminals was laughable to many San Quentin officers. Besides, the California prisoners deemed truly salvageable were being sent to the new California Institution for Men at Chino. The incorrigible worst remained at Folsom and San Quentin. Nonetheless, administrators were increasingly at least giving lip service to the usefulness of books in convict reform even at these prisons. At the 1940 Congress of the American Prison Association in Cincinnati, even the aging James A. Johnston (San Quentin's warden from 1913 to 1925) had told the Committee on Institution Libraries that "the written word is so powerful an influence in all of our lives, [that] the use of the prison library should be regarded as a potent agency in the training of prisoners."[2]

Another speaker on the same occasion, Dr. C. V. Morrison, in an address titled "Prison Library Book Prescriptions," called for "the close cooperation of psychiatrist and trained librarian." Finally, James A. Quinn addressed an issue of great concern to the growing number of prison librarians who were committed to a more active treatment role: how to measure inmate reform through bibliotherapy. Quinn rec-

gestive of Spector's faith in bibliotherapy: "The Prison Library as an Educational Agency"; "What Men Write in Prison"; "Triumphant Confidence."

ommended administering "scales" tests before and after bibliotherapy. "Differences," he said, "between the later and earlier responses [would] indicate what changes in attitude [had] actually occurred." Quinn suggested the following test as an example:

1. I believe the church is the greatest institution in America today.
2. I think the church is a divine institution and deserves the highest respect and loyalty.
3. I believe the church keeps business and politics to a higher standard than they would otherwise maintain.
4. The church does not interest me now, but sometime I expect I shall find it worthwhile to join.
5. I go to church occasionally but have no special attitude toward it.
6. I do not think the church is essential to Christianity.
7. I get no satisfaction from going to church.
8. I believe the churches do far more harm than good.
9. I think the church is a parasite on society.[3]

Subjects were to check the item on the scales that most fit their beliefs. It was hoped that following bibliotherapy their attitudes would conform more closely with cultural norms represented by the "correct" scales-test responses—those of the bibliotherapist acting in the role of cultural spokesperson and trained in criminology and mental hygiene.

The *Wilson Library Journal* urged prison librarians to begin "furnish[ing] books as a basis for group therapy sessions" and to follow up "each therapy session with special reading lists properly explained to the reader." Each librarian should first "digest a number of books and classify them with reference to the possible role they might play in group therapy" and mark "certain passages and sections of a book . . . [for] meaty and significant material." The publication called this process "separat[ing] the wheat from the chaff" to "save work for the inmate reader who is as a rule not very well trained to read." No note was taken of the political implications of telling readers what was important in their reading. The librarian "provides the medicament," the article asserted, advising prison librarians henceforth to "receive a certain amount of training in both criminology and mental hygiene, in addition to library preparation."[4]

Beyond the reaches of the library the California Department of Corrections aided Spector's efforts by forbidding inmates access to ideas deemed dangerous that might sneak in from outside the walls. This meant thoroughly censoring prisoners' correspondence as well as books, magazines, and newspapers. Television was still rare in the cell blocks. In-cell radio was limited to two institutional channels broadcast as KSQ. The 1954 *Director's Rules* declared that "no inmate shall be permitted to send or receive a communication or a package of any nature until he has signed the required form consenting to the opening of same and examination of the contents." No inmate was permitted to correspond with persons whose names did not appear on the "approved correspondents list." This list could include a maximum of ten correspondents whose relation to the inmate had been investigated by the department. Prison staff were directed to "keep a permanent record of all outgoing and incoming correspondence and packages . . . [and] familiarize themselves with the institutional program so that they may be able to recognize any information which might affect the emotions of the inmates or disturb the normal routine of the institution."[5] Though the prison's official censor was the associate warden for care and treatment, the actual work fell to Spector. Except for mail, which was read in the cell blocks or the mail room, the senior librarian censored all writing by inmates that left the prison and decided what publications would be purchased for the library. He reviewed all manuscripts that inmates wished to submit to outside publishers, kept meticulous records of them on file, and rooted out those he found improper. In this role Spector was certainly not alone in believing in the power of the word. The California Department of Corrections provided the librarian with explicit censoring guidelines. He was to stop any writing that was libelous, pornographic, or critical of the Department of Corrections or other law enforcement authorities, glorified crime or drug use, or might be offensive to any race, religion, or organized group.[6]

Confiscating and destroying inmates' writing was a task the librarian apparently performed without qualms. He apparently accepted the state's simple logic, which it argued many times in court against inmates who tried to regain their confiscated writings, that because prisoners were technically "civilly dead" anything they produced, including their ideas, was the property of the prison. Since 1871 California prisoners had been deemed civilly dead slaves of the state. Following the Supreme Court case *Ruffin* v. *Commonwealth*,[7] the California Penal Code had been amended to read:

673 CIVIL RIGHTS OF CONVICT SUSPENDED
A sentence of imprisonment in a state prison for any term less than for life suspends all the civil rights of the person so sentenced, and forfeits all public offices and all private trusts, authority, or power during such imprisonment.

674 CIVIL DEATH
A person sentenced to imprisonment in the state prison for life is thereafter
deemed civilly dead.[8]

According to these two provisions, persons imprisoned in California
had no legal identity. As a consequence, authorship and the possession of copyright were not possible for inmates. Even when their liberty was restored after release from prison, convicted felons in California had no right to vote, hold office, make contracts, own property,
or compose a will. Those rights, and more, remained forfeited to the
state. In 1919 the Penal Code was again amended to restore certain
rights on parole, but at the discretion of the Board of Prison Terms,
the parole board.[9] The reduced civil status of prisoners was reaffirmed
in 1941 in a section of the penal code titled "Civil Death," penal code
2600–2601.[10] As a consequence of the Civil Death statute, the California Department of Corrections regarded all writing produced by state
prisoners as state property, just as a chair or table made in prison
industries belonged to the state. With certain exceptions (between
1954 and 1968 Death Row inmates were not permitted to write), the
right to ownership of written manuscripts was customarily restored
to inmate authors, but as a favor revocable at any time. It was against
the background of this legal history that the destruction or confiscation of inmate manuscripts went forth with such alacrity at San Quentin in the 1950's.

Although as senior librarian Spector seems to have had no reser-
vations about censoring and confiscating inmates' writing, he publicly professed a distaste for censorship of reading. Nevertheless, it too
was an everyday fact of his life at San Quentin. All book acquisitions
had to be officially approved by the prison administration, and until
the late 1960's this gave wardens and the librarians who performed
the actual task formidable powers of censorship. The American Prison
Association's 1950 *Library Manual for Correctional Institutions* published
the following recommendations regarding book acquisition: "Books
which emphasize the morbid, sex, anti-social attitudes, ways of committing crime, disrespect for the law, religion and government and
such types as anatomical works, federal and state laws, as well as
magazines of the confessional, sensationally pictorial and pulp type
should be omitted."[11] Spector stated his own censorship policy as follows: "Those which emphasize morbid or antisocial attitudes, behavior, or disrespect for religion or government or other undesirable materials are not purchased."[12] Like most other prison librarians of the

treatment era, Herman Spector gave little thought to the danger of political, class, or cultural bias implicit in his prison censorship policies, and he wasted no time worrying that denying prisoners law books might be unfair or even unconstitutional. Books that gave inmates access to the law were to be confiscated at the gates. Books that criticized church or state were seditious.

But Spector saw his role as much more than that of a mere censor; his library, having been weeded of "undesirable materials," was a repository, he believed, of the eternal truths of mankind. He envisioned the enduring values of Western civilization prevailing over criminal deviancy by means of bibliotherapeutic techniques and a free interplay of ideas in the prison library. He had utter faith in the process. "We have the opportunity," he wrote, "to translate such a situation into a most meaningful weapon of bibliotherapy."[13]

Herman Spector served as San Quentin's senior librarian for almost three decades, doggedly persisting in his quest to reform convicts with "the inextinguishable light and wisdom," the "translucent truths" contained in his library.[14] Books, for him, were "the deathless weapons of progress" by which prisoners could be "paroled into the custody of their better selves . . . by feeding on hallowed thoughts." "The hermitage of a small, dank cell," he wrote, "if provided with books, can yield a rich harvest of sheer delight and practical values."[15] His library was a "hospital for the mind,"[16] an open-shelf facility of 33,000 books at its height in the late 1950's to late 1960's, operating long hours, sometimes seven days a week. Spector was indefatigable. Use of the library was a privilege, not a right, however. Prisoners could visit the library once a week and borrow up to five books, but only if they had a privilege card, granted for good behavior. Because access to radio and television was severely limited, this was an ardently sought-after privilege.

The centerpiece of the library was Spector's Reader's Advisory Services and his Great Books and group counseling classes. He kept "an individual record of the use of the library by each inmate, . . . an official departmental record of the man's participation in the rehabilitation program," and he made reports to other staff of "especially profitable activities by inmates,"[17] in addition to serving on the Classification Committee and often attending Adult Authority hearings. In his Great Books classes, Spector allowed the men to choose one of the "classics" (*The Iliad*, *The Odyssey*, and the novels of Thomas Hardy were his personal favorites) and then tell "how the book played an important part in their lives":

New ideas, and clearer concepts of "old" ideas can become a part of one's very psychic fiber. . . . Naturally, we are trying, primarily, to ascertain what poignant episode in any book became the meaningful turning-point in the inmate's own philosophy of life, in his determination to make a change for his own improvement and growth.[18]

Following these classes, the librarian often had the prisoners write on the Great Books. These selections, Spector wrote, "may yet be the deepest and truest responses of the inmate's attempt at describing their resocialization." There is no evidence that Spector used scales tests to measure the success of bibliotherapy. Participants in his group counseling class were drawn from the inmate group assigned to the library as a workplace, a group that ranged in size over the years from three to ten inmates:

Here the men who work in the library are encouraged to discuss their individual, personal problems and try to work out an intelligent solution to them. The librarian acts as guide and mentor to this group. . . . At first, a man is rather diffident about airing his personal problems but later realizing that he is not alone in his difficulty, he finds himself willingly discussing things that he has perhaps kept buried deep in his subconscious for many years.[19]

A major preoccupation of the senior librarian was his desire to gather statistics on what was actually being read at San Quentin, numbers that might be used to measure the success of bibliotherapy.[20] Spector refers in his writings to the desirability of such a study, though he never produced one.[21] In an article titled "Library Statistics: Their Meaning and Significance to the Librarian and to the Administrator" in the American Prison Association's 1950 *Library Manual for Correctional Institutions*, Spector compared the usefulness of prison library circulation statistics to medical records in a hospital and suggested that "maintain[ing] accurate records of both individual readers as case histories and of the institutional population as mass readers" might provide evidence of the success or failure of the prison's treatment program.[22] He was confident that such a study would reveal books to be powerful tools of convict reform. He noted a 1944 Michigan study that "was able to report—because of the availability of library statistics in the communities studied—that 'only the number per capita of volumes in district and township libraries shows a negative correlation with delinquency rates.'"[23]

Spector took this conclusion as powerful proof of reading's civilizing influence. It had only to be established statistically at San Quentin prison. To this end, the librarian insisted that "library circulation records must be kept daily" and that "they must be accurate." Separate entries were to be kept for each administrative unit of the prison because different units housed different classifications of prisoners and the "psychological interests of the inmates may be revealed by the type, variation, and amount of circulation realized in different units. . . . Each book, each type of book, can be better evaluated for its usefulness when the records of separate blocks are accounted."[24]

Spector set out to collect his data. In 1956 he reported 33,420 books on his shelves. The San Quentin prisoners were reading at the rate of 98 books per man per year.[25] In 1957 he wrote that he was heartened because almost 90 percent of San Quentin's inmates used the library, whereas only 18 percent of the free American public used lending libraries. The prisoners, he reported, were borrowing from 45 to over 100 books a year.[26] Surely this exposure would have powerful moral effects. By 1960, though he had reached no conclusions on the success of his efforts at bibliotherapy, Spector had noticed one interesting trend in prisoner reading. Convicts' choice of nonfiction was showing a dramatic rise. Whereas it had constituted only 16 percent of total library circulation in the late 1940's, it made up a full 30 percent by 1960.[27] By 1962 it had climbed to 42 percent.[28] Data for later years are not available. Spector's statistics on books and magazines that San Quentin inmates purchased by mail show that the customary prison reading staple of fiction was being rapidly replaced by a wide range of nonfiction subjects, including religion, history, social science, and psychology.* Spector did not speculate on the reasons for this apparently radical change in convicts' reading interest.

What little remains of the librarian's data suggests another trend accompanying this change in inmates' reading habits. The number of inmate-written manuscripts coming to Herman Spector's desk for clearance increased dramatically. In 1947, Spector's first year on the job, 395 manuscripts had come to him for approval. By 1961 there were 1,989 submissions—a five-fold increase—and the number stayed about this high for at least as long as the librarian continued to collect his data (through 1967),[29] even though the prison's inmate population remained constant at roughly 5,000 during these years. Similar data for subsequent years are lost, and it is possible only to speculate that the trend toward more inmate writing continued, and probably esca-

*In 1962 Spector noted that 288 men had purchased 388 books from outside publishers: 17 reference books, 18 psychology texts, 22 volumes in religion, 13 in social science, 59 in languages, 19 in science, 45 in practical arts, 69 in fine arts, 14 in literature, 2 in civilization, and 1 in travel (Spector, " . . . Nor Iron Bars a Cage").

lated, as public interest in prison issues created a ready market well into the 1970's for works written by inmates.

Year after year, Spector dutifully fed his raw data to the warden's office. And as administration succeeded administration, wardens became increasingly confused about what the aging librarian meant to prove with all his numbers. Although Spector seemed obsessed with record-keeping, and created voluminous files, he never analyzed what the data proved for bibliotherapy at San Quentin. Instead, in his later years at the prison, the senior librarian confined himself to proclaiming, as though he were enraptured by the sheer force of the numbers, that he had circulated "a total of 3,096,377 books" since his arrival in 1947.[30] Spector never achieved his dream of statistically confirming bibliotherapy's usefulness at the prison, and he retired from the San Quentin library a disillusioned eccentric. After he was gone, the prison promptly destroyed his life's work, all the files of reading and writing data on three decades of San Quentin prisoners.

Spector may have abandoned his research plans, but in his daily contact with inmate readers and writers there can be little doubt that the librarian continued to the end aggressively attempting to change their lives by controlling their reading and writing. And most of the inmates were eager to please him, though this did not necessarily signify real character change. One inmate on Death Row from 1962 to 1972 who had manuscripts cleared for submission to publishers in Spector's last years in the library reports:

I had about twelve publications. . . . For a while I was even writing anti-drug crap for teenybopper magazines. I'd have to get loaded to write it, it was so nauseating. I found a format for anti-drug articles for teenage magazines that you couldn't stop. I had the perfect combination: "I used drugs and it put me on Death Row." They were eatin' that stuff up! They loved it! [laughs][31]

Although this inmate pleased the librarian-censor with the penitent tone of his works, his authorial persona was clearly a pose. He found selling articles to outside magazines an easy way to earn canteen money, which could provide items that might be bartered for drugs, sex, or other contraband in the sub-rosa inmate economy, and he took a perverse pleasure in marketing a penitent persona to the public. Spector's figures for 1964 show that he approved 80 percent of the manuscripts he read that year, and many may have been of this nature.[32]

A more celebrated San Quentin inmate writer has given us his impressions of Herman Spector's bibliotherapy program in *False Starts: A Memoir of San Quentin and Other Prisons*. Malcolm Braly's first published novel, *Felony Tank*, was written at San Quentin and received the Mystery Writers of America scroll for runner-up as the best first mystery novel of 1961. A later novel, *On the Yard*, was also begun while the writer was in prison. Braly went on to write the screenplay for a film of the same name in 1979.

Malcolm Braly first arrived at San Quentin in 1948 on a burglary conviction, just a year after Herman Spector and at the height of the treatment era. He stayed three months at San Quentin's Guidance Center, where, he writes, "we quickly learned we were expected to view this journey through prison as a quest, and the object of our quest was to discover our problem." Braly joined a therapy group run by a young psychologist because "almost everyone in the joint was taking the line that they had come to this because of their neuroses. . . . The one thing we were truly seeking here was not an understanding of our problem, but the appearance of the search." "We knew which programs to try to associate ourselves with and we knew which ploys were now exhausted." "In the library an inmate clerk checks your card to tell the Adult Authority what you've been reading, and in the chapel of your choice someone writes a brief report on your religious participation." Braly describes Herman Spector as "a strange obsessive man, who was a filing freak. He had an office staff of three inmates who did little more than maintain his filing system. Everything, every scrap of paper that passed through the library, was copied and filed. When he spoke to you on interview he made notes of the meeting and these notes were filed."[33]

After three "jolts" in prison, three separate periods of incarceration, Braly decided to try his hand at writing. But Braly had no intention of writing within the penitential guidelines of the Corrections Department. Because writing about crime was expressly forbidden by the Department of Corrections censorship guidelines, Braly had to spend considerable time readying his work for the eyes of his keepers. A convict friend told him: "Make him an outline for his files. He loves that. You can slant the outline away from the rough stuff, particularly the sex and drugs. Then, if you're lucky, he'll only read the outline. Meanwhile, he's on your side because you've fed his obsession." The author decided to take his friend's advice: "I wrote a careful outline, and consigned my book to its fate." Braly had been careful in the past to cultivate a good relationship with Herman Spector:

This strange man had always liked me from the Sunday afternoon during my first jolt when I had stood up in a Seekers' meeting to read a thousand-line poem on the mystery of evolution. I had made him a copy for his file. He had often helped me order special books from the state library at Sacramento, and was only disappointed I had avoided his Great Books Discussion Group which met monthly to chew over Plato, Augustine, Aquinas and other heavies.[34]

The ruse worked, Braly got clearance to submit his manuscript to an outside publisher, and soon he received his first publishing contract. He informed Herman Spector of his success:

He was delighted. "Now I can start an active file on you. I have files on every man who has published here. Would you like to see them?" He brought a half-dozen folders and I went through them carefully. . . . As I studied these files, the librarian typed my name on an index label and glued it to a new folder. When my advance check came—five hundred dollars—he asked me for a copy of the check record, which I typed out for him, even copying the bank's identification numbers, and when the money was on my books, I ordered a typewriter, an Olympia portable, through the inmate canteen. I was free.[35]

Inmate Braly had successfully escaped both Spector's bibliotherapy net and the civil death statute of the law.

Herman Spector must have felt himself the subject of ridicule, his deep faith in bibliotherapy mocked by official prison policy and inmates alike. By and large, San Quentin's administration declined to stand behind the librarian's bibliotherapy, preferring to cling to an older, largely passive communication control strategy. Although the staff of the library and education departments at San Quentin firmly believed in the efficacy of bibliotherapy, the California Department of Corrections kept to its older practice of simply censoring what came and went through the gates. Prison administrators seemed unable to grasp, or unwilling fully to endorse, Spector's aggressive brand of reading and writing control. Scheming inmates, too, made Spector's efforts ridiculous. The senior librarian may have realized, finally, that the legal notion of civil death, about to become an issue of hot contention in the 1960's, was hopelessly at odds with his goals of bibliotherapy. It separated prisoners from the power of their own words rather than connecting them to it, and it ran the risk of teaching an inmate that words have no power. Spector may have been laboring single-handedly against San Quentin prison policy, opposed by inmates and administration alike; even so, the underlying assumptions of bibliotherapy would soon have a tremendous influence on the lives of certain of the brightest of San Quentin's inmates, for they would take the notion of reform through reading and writing, the foundation of Herman Spector's faith, as their own first principle. And they would then use that principle to turn the notion of civil death for prisoners on its head, reconnecting themselves to the power of words previously denied them. Nowhere was this more true than in the case of the "King of Death Row," Caryl Chessman.

3

CARYL CHESSMAN AND THE ROOTS OF
CONVICT RESISTANCE

When Caryl Whittier Chessman came to San Quentin's Death Row in May 1948, he was penniless, condemned to death, and alone. Twelve years later, when he finally took the elevator from the top tier of North Block to the first floor and walked the 13 steps from the Death Watch Cell into the green-painted gas chamber, he had won (and spent) a fortune with his writing, employed a staff of professional lawyers to work on his case, and orchestrated an international mass movement to spare his life. It would be hard to imagine a prisoner of greater renown or one who left a greater legacy of civil rights for the imprisoned. His execution day, May 3, 1960, and the protests of outrage it inspired mark the beginning of 1960's-era radical prison movement politics in the Bay Area. And within the prison, the changes he forced in San Quentin's policies toward inmates' reading and writing were to provide the expanded freedoms of speech, publication, and study that inmate radicals would need in the impending prison movement. Ironically, immediately following Chessman's execution, the rights of San Quentin inmate readers and writers would be suppressed to a greater degree than they had been since the early 1950's, as California tightened its communication control of prisoners—more for alleged prison security or for openly political reasons than to achieve any bibliotherapeutic goal. Much of the 1960's-era San Quentin history from the inmates' point of view is the story of retrieving and extending to all prisoners the rights granted to Caryl Chessman as early as 1952.

Caryl Chessman came to San Quentin for the first time in 1941, at the age of nineteen, on an armed robbery and assault conviction, following two periods as a teenager in California's Preston School of

Industry for auto theft and other, lesser crimes. An obviously intelligent young man who likely could have been successful at anything he tried, Chessman was an enigma to prison staff from the outset. By 1942 he was a trusty working in the warden's office. He was soon transferred to the California Institution for Men at Chino, an honor facility, from which he escaped. Chessman was rearrested, returned to San Quentin, and paroled in December 1947. One month later, Los Angeles newspapers began to report a mysterious series of crimes by a "Red Light Bandit." Masquerading as a policeman with a red spotlight on his car, the Red Light Bandit preyed on couples parked in lovers' lanes, sexually assaulting the women. In two instances, the bandit dragged women from their cars. At the time, this technically constituted kidnapping under the "Little Lindbergh Law" (ruled unconstitutional by the U.S. Supreme Court in 1968), the penalty for which was death. On the night of his arrest, Chessman was apprehended driving a car that matched the description of the bandit's automobile. A high-speed chase ended with Chessman in handcuffs. He confessed to the Red Light crimes but later said the confession was beaten out of him. At trial, Chessman defended himself without legal help against J. Miller Leavy, an aggressive prosecutor with a long string of convictions, in the courtroom of Judge Charles Fricke, who had already sentenced more people to death than anyone in California history. Not surprisingly, Chessman was convicted of seventeen counts of robbery, sex perversion, and attempted rape and sentenced to die in San Quentin's gas chamber. The trial, however, was plagued by irregularities. Soon after Chessman's conviction the court reporter who had made the trial transcript died. When Chessman's case entered the appeal stage, which all capital cases automatically go through, it became obvious that the bulk of the trial transcript, hundreds of pages of notes, was scribbled in such an indecipherable hand that nobody could read it. Because legally an appeal cannot be made without a transcript of the proceedings, a trial transcript had to be pieced together by guesswork. Prosecutor Leavy's wife's uncle, a court reporter named Stanley Fraser, volunteered to do so by interviewing participants in the trial. This raised the issue of bias. Consequently, over the next decade, Chessman would teach himself law on San Quentin's Death Row and submit to the court hundreds of corrections to this fabricated trial transcript. He raised issue after issue after issue, submitting petitions with numerous allegations. On several occasions, Chessman came within hours of execution but was granted yet another stay. His execution was postponed eight times, while 94 other prisoners went to the gas chamber. In 1957, the issue of the court transcript was finally heard in the U.S. Supreme Court. By this time Chessman had a team of attorneys working for him, paid for by the profits from several books. Once again he lost. After a final series of stays of execution, Caryl Chessman died in San Quentin's gas chamber on May 3, 1960.

Chessman was not an easy man to like. Louis Nelson, the prison's captain on Death Row from 1951 to 1953 (subsequently associate warden of custody, then warden), remembers him as "the most arrogant and supercilious bastard in the world, and probably one of the brightest. . . . He was also insidious and mean."[1] Most would agree, though some commentators probe for a deeper understanding. One who managed to get close to him was Bernice Freeman, a reporter for the *San Francisco Chronicle*:

I felt that his biggest problem was his absolute lack of faith in anything. He told me once that his mother was deeply religious and that, as a child, he himself had a strong belief in God. But his mother broke her back in an automobile accident when he was nine years old, and she had been in a wheel chair ever since. After the accident, he repeatedly asked her why God had let her become a cripple. The only answer she ever gave him was that this had been "God's will" and they must accept it. Her son didn't agree. He told me he lost his faith in God when, despite his prayers, his mother never got better.[2]

Chessman had also suffered a period of severe childhood illness. At age ten he was stricken with encephalitis. Citing medical and psychological reports on the effects of this disease, Byron Eshelman, the prison's Protestant chaplain, argued that parts of the prisoner's brain could have been damaged at that time, affecting Chessman's "personality balance." The implication was that, because his criminality had a medical or psychological cause, Chessman deserved rehabilitative treatment rather than death. "Unfortunately," Eshelman lamented, "the law is not geared to use all the knowledge of psychiatry."[3] For many of the prison's staff it was difficult to find sympathy for Chessman. Herman Spector, for example, did not get along with Chessman, though the senior librarian regularly visited him on his weekly deliveries of books from the library to the Row. Chessman wanted special library privileges, which Spector refused to grant, his widow recalls, causing the prisoner to threaten both court action and bodily harm to the librarian.

Among the convicts it was often a different story. As a jailhouse lawyer Chessman was without equal, and he remains a legend on Death Row to this day. Byron Eshelman noted that "he practically ran a full-time, non-paying law office. He not only flooded the courts with his own writs, but helped others to prepare theirs even though this was against the rules of the institution. He had a collection of law books, and a typewriter that clicked steadily."[4] "That Chessman's wonderful," another Death Row prisoner remarked, "he's always doing somethin'—makin' legal papers for himself and helpin' the other guys who don't have no money for lawyers. You know, he's really not allowed to do that, but he does it anyhow."[5] Chessman got into prison fights and could be savvy and manipulative, but he also had a genius for teaching, and he helped dozens of inmates read and write, producing his own textbook on mimeographed sheets, which he used with illiterate prisoners. At one time he taught English, typing, short-hand, and bookkeeping at the prison school. Chessman's reading had made him conversant in literature, history, and philosophy, and he was a student of mathematics and logic as well as a brilliant debater. Nothing pleased him more than when he could flaunt his keepers' authority, and the prisoners cheered him on and aided him as he secretly wrote, hid, and smuggled out two best-selling books after a writing ban on the Row in 1954.

Whether they liked him personally or not—he could be petty, self-serving, and arrogant—over the years Caryl Chessman managed to impress enough prison staff with his erudition, writing skills, and frequent displays of charity toward others (Chessman gave money to the children of a needy family and once offered one eye to save the eyesight of Bernice Freeman's daughter) that many began to question whether the death penalty was a contradiction of the rehabilitative process. Was the prison's treatment strategy actually working? Had Caryl Chessman, the supposed Red Light Bandit, transformed himself from a psychopathic kidnapper-rapist into a productive member of society? Or was society being manipulated into postponing his execution by the continuing machinations of a sociopath bent on making a mockery of the law?

When Chessman arrived on the Row in 1948, access to reading was limited and writing was difficult. The prison library circulated a mimeographed list of books from which Death Row inmates could make requests. No effort was made to supply bibliotherapeutic reading, inspirational reading, or reading lists tailored to inmates' individual needs. Herman Spector did not bother to attempt the reform of those about to die. Censorship criteria were generally the same for those on the Row as for the mainline population. Access to law books at the library was extremely limited. Inmates could receive mail-order books from an approved list of publishers, providing they had money in their account. Typewriters were not allowed. Books were delivered once a week by Herman Spector, who spent little additional time on the Row. Row inmates also had access to occasional cell-study courses through the Education Department and to correspondence courses. They could read the *Look* and *Life* magazines brought by Byron Eshelman, listen to the institutional radio station KSQ on their cell earphones, or watch the television in the corridor.

On Chessman's arrival, however, things began to change. His attempt to serve as his own lawyer had failed, and he had no money for an attorney, but he was not about to give up his fight for life. This prisoner was ready to continue representing himself in postconviction appeals. He immediately set about educating himself in the law and writing legal writs, stretching the legal resources of the library and the patience of the prison administration. By degrees the prison's prohibition against law books was stretched to accommodate Chessman. The inmate began to put together his own collection of law books. He started a lending library of his own on the Row. Byron Eshelman records that "Chessman devised a cord system from strips of an old sheet. It was much like a washline in front of a tenement house. The men could clip newspapers and magazines to it, and pass them from cell to cell."[6] After Chessman's legal work won him his first stay of execution in 1952 (and partly perhaps to dissuade him from further writ-writing, which was customarily regarded as an obstruction of justice), Warden Harley O. Teets approached him: "When Warden Teets came to see me, he told me I ought to try to get some meaning out of all this—to try to find out just what in hell I was doing, and why. I asked him, 'What do you mean?' and he said, 'You're smart enough to figure it out for yourself.' Then he walked away."[7]

Former warden Louis Nelson recalls that "Dr. Norman Fenton, who was Chief of Treatment for the Department, decided that letting him write a book would have great therapeutic value."[8] According to Freeman, "He told the warden that Chessman was the only unusually intelligent, completely criminal psychopath he had ever examined. He added that if Chessman could be persuaded to write, his work might be beneficial to criminal psychologists everywhere." Freeman, too, encouraged Chessman:

I felt rather strongly that Chessman needed an interest besides studying law and preparing writs, activities which were filling his every waking moment. If he could involve himself in something else, I thought, he might become less tense. "Why don't you write something else besides legal papers," I suggested. "Like a book." "What kind of book?" he asked. "You ought to write your life story," I said.[9]

Several weeks afterward, according to Freeman, Chessman announced he was writing a trilogy. Eshelman recalls the inmate telling him, "It's about time somebody took a look at a psychopath through his own eyes—to see the world and the situation that confronts him as he sees it."[10] Louis Nelson says that "as a result he had been given a special cell up on Death Row with a typewriter and a small typewriter desk, and was allowed to stay in there from 8:00 A.M. till 10:00 P.M. every day."[11] Chessman wrote and studied in a cell thereafter called the "legal cell" and slept in cell 2455.

It was in this legal cell that the prisoner would produce his autobiography, *Cell 2455 Death Row* (1954). Once the book was complete, Herman Spector read the manuscript, disliked it immediately, and recommended against approving it for submission outside. But the manuscript went also to Dr. Norman Fenton and Warden Teets, and eventually all the way to the top, to the desk of Director of Corrections Richard McGee, who approved it. Chessman submitted it to a New York literary agent, and it was quickly accepted for publication. Not all San Quentin staff felt comfortable with the decision to let Chessman publish. "*Cell 2455* had a nauseating effect on me," wrote the prison's Jewish chaplain Julius A. Leibert: "I am positive that if the prison reviewer's estimate of it had been properly respected, the book never would have been cleared for publication. I had pity for its author, as I do for everyone on death row—but I cannot say that I saw any merit in Chessman's opus or one redeeming feature in his person."[12]

Originally scheduled to appear on July 26, 1954, *Cell 2455 Death Row* was rushed through publication to come out before Chessman's scheduled execution date, which was now May 14. Caryl Chessman sat in his Death Row cell on April 20 proudly reading the first copy of his first published work. At last his story would reach the American public. It was the tale of a sensitive white boy of devout Christian parents, who had gone bad in response to sickness, misfortune, and family poverty; who had spent his teenage years alternately in the pursuit of delinquent thrills and bitterly idled by reform school; who had finally fallen into a life of small-time armed robbery, knocking off whorehouses and bookmaking joints, but who was *not*, emphatically, the Red Light Bandit.

Cell 2455 Death Row was an instant success. New York book critics, Chessman was told, were excited over the power and genius of his writing. As Norman Fenton had wished, the work was seen as providing insights into the psychopathic criminal personality type. The *San Francisco Examiner* ran the book in four Sunday installments. The *San Francisco Chronicle* called it "an unrestrained autobiography with overtones of psychopathic fantasy and ego." That newspaper's reviewer recounted the book's story of Chessman's childhood encephalitis, then remarked that "an outstanding textbook on clinical psychiatry by Ebaugh states that post-encephalitic psychopaths almost invariably wind up in prison." This positive reception in the press presented an immediate problem to San Quentin administrators, who apparently had not anticipated public praise for the book. "One might question the propriety," the *Chronicle* reviewer went on, "of executing a man whose course was seemingly inescapable."[13] Negley K. Teeters, a criminologist at Philadelphia's Temple University, also suggested that the condemned man should be spared "on the grounds that society knows so little about the criminal psychopath that he should be used for scientific purposes to find out how and why a man becomes such a menace to society." The *New York Herald Tribune* congratulated the author for giving "a great deal of insight into a criminal's mind." The *New York Times* agreed, finding the book full of "sparkling contributions in the field of criminological thought." *Kirkus* observed that "sociologists and criminologists may well find it a human document of real significance."[14]

By July Chessman's book was a best-seller, Chessman had another stay, until July 30, and California prison authorities began nervously wondering just what all these many thousands of readers could be seeing in the book and the inmate. San Quentin had never suspected that the book would launch a movement to snatch their prisoner from the gas chamber. Chessman had been quick to reassure the state he had not published seeking to pressure the courts to review his case: "Above all things, let's not get confused. Let's not have any ideas coming from me that I am seeking out the Governor or the courts because of all this hoopla. I'm sure I'll get careful consideration.

Let's let it go at that." [15] But somehow that reassurance did not seem convincing. A former Death Row inmate remembers this story from the Row:

I knew people when I first got up there . . . who knew him personally and spent many years with him on Death Row. He never once admitted to any of them that he was in fact guilty and he was just trying to beat this. He never once admitted his guilt. So if you are maintaining innocence, it would be advantageous to put out a few books saying, "Yeah, I'm a robber and a thief and a dog, but I'm not this." In effect, he had to admit some criminality. He'd been in the joint two or three times for robbery. He had a history of robberies. It would have been futile on his part to say, "I'm not a robber." Nobody'd believe that shit. I don't really know whether he was guilty or not. But he did what was necessary by partially admitting. [16]

Part of Chessman's argument in *Cell 2455 Death Row* had been that his years on the Row had rehabilitated him and prepared him to make a uniquely useful contribution to society:

I think that I am now worth more to society alive than dead. The long years lived in this crucible called Death Row have carried me beyond bitterness, beyond hate, beyond savage animal violence. Death Row has compelled me to study as I have never studied before, to accept disciplines I never would have accepted otherwise and to gain a penetrating insight into all phases of this problem of crime that I am determined to translate into worthwhile contributions toward ultimate solution of that problem. This book is a beginning contribution; I would like to believe that it also signals the beginning for me of a journey back from outer darkness. [17]

Chessman announced that he had finished a magazine story, which was already in the hands of his New York agent, and had nearly completed a novelette. He obviously intended to write more, much more, and to live to a ripe old age. He had just gotten a $6,500 advance from Columbia Pictures on the sale of movie rights for his first book, and this was in addition to royalties. What was he doing with his newfound wealth? "I'm making bequests to eight or ten people who have been good to me," he told the press. Chessman changed his will and set up a $20,000 trust fund for three unidentified children in one family and the two children of his late father's house-keeper, Frances Couturier. Prefacing every remark with "If I have to go Friday," or "If I'm still here in another week," Chessman announced he had another autobiographical book in the works and could finish it in as few as three months. Perhaps of most alarm to the authorities, the prisoner had spent the first $1,000 he got from his publisher hiring a professional attorney, Berwyn Rice. San Quentin's worst fears had come to pass.

"My mail became heavy every time I wrote a story about Chessman," the *Chronicle*'s Bernice Freeman remarked:

With one exception, all the letters I got were heavily in his favour. . . . An Italian count once asked me to tell Chessman he had a villa in Rome where Chessman would always be welcome, either on a temporary or permanent basis. . . . A beautiful Parisian woman offered Chessman a home on the Riviera and asked me to show him her picture, which she enclosed. . . . Many women wrote, wanting me to give them my personal evaluation of the man. Some said they were interested in marriage, others that they were simply curious.[18]

The flood of support included some members of San Quentin's staff. In early May, Dr. William F. Graves, a senior medical officer at the prison, resigned in protest against Chessman's impending execution. He wired the governor: "It is my firm opinion the man is mentally ill . . . I am further convinced he is not the red-light bandit."[19]

San Quentin's response was swift and harsh. In mid-August, Director of Corrections Richard A. McGee ordered all manuscripts produced by condemned prisoners confiscated until after their execution. The department had decided it wasn't so smart to allow the condemned a public voice. Barbara Graham, on Death Row for a murder-robbery, was also asking to submit some articles and short stories for publication. She was denied permission by McGee.

Chessman was called to the warden's office. "It has been decided," Warden Teets told him, "that no more of your writings of any kind can be cleared for publication." "I nodded," Chessman wrote. "I was thinking of the manuscript of [*Trial by Ordeal*, the second book of his planned trilogy]. . . . Cranks and crackpots had demanded the state gag and shackle me, snatch away my literary earnings, lock me out of court, disbar my attorneys, disenfranchise my friends, and accord me a slow and painful death." "'As I understand it, Warden,'" Chessman recorded later, "'you're not telling me that I can't write. You're simply saying that what I do write can't be cleared for publication for the present. Is that correct?' The Warden nodded his head. 'Yes, that's correct.'"[20]

Chessman tried to evade the new rule by selling the manuscript and publication rights to *Trial by Ordeal* for one dollar to his newest attorney, Rosalie Asher, intending for her to publish it. But Warden Teets impounded the manuscript and placed it in his safe. Deputy

Attorney General Clarence Linn supported Warden Teets's action, telling the press that the "book belonged to the State and the State should even get the royalties, if any." Linn reminded reporters that Chessman was legally dead: "That book is prison property. Chessman made it in prison and it is just as though it were a sack he had made in the jute mill. Anything written by a prisoner is the property of the prison."[21] A Death Row inmate recalls: "They felt it was unfair for a talented writer to go up there and be able to write and have it result in a monetary gain with which he could combat an appeal, whereas [another inmate] comes up there illiterate and six months later he's executed."[22]

Rosalie Asher filed suit in Marin County Superior Court to recover the manuscript and hired prominent San Francisco lawyer Melvin Belli to represent her. A long trial seemed unavoidable. In mid-November 1954, Chessman teased the press with the news that *Trial by Ordeal* was "70% completed and might be ready in forty-five days." He described it as an argument against the "retributive justice" of capital punishment and the human story of the men on Death Row.[23] Chessman apparently had a carbon copy of the manuscript, which he intended to finish and find a way to publish. Louis Nelson recalls:

He appealed to me first. He promised that if I'd let him write the book he wouldn't smuggle it out. I said, "To hell with you!" Nothing to be gained by that. "If you're going to smuggle it out, smuggle it out. . . . I'll trust my officers, I won't barter with you. I'll trust my personnel."[24]

Before Asher's case went to court, Chessman's literary agent in New York, Joseph Longstreth, got a copy of *Trial by Ordeal* in the mail. Chessman wouldn't say how he got it out of the prison, though Eshelman reports that Chessman later confided to him that it "'may have gone out of Death Row in some trash' and then passed through the hands of several convicts before it reached the outside."[25] Louis Nelson has a different opinion: "I know how [it got out]. It was carried out by a member of our staff."[26] San Quentin's prison grapevine hummed with the rumor that one of the institution's doctors had taken the manuscript out.[27]

The California Department of Corrections quickly brought a suit to recover the manuscript from Prentice-Hall and a second suit to claim the book's royalties in case the first suit failed. A federal judge dismissed both suits. By July 1955, *Trial by Ordeal* was in the bookstores. San Quentin's response was predictable: "Soon as that book was smuggled out," says Louis Nelson, "soon as they announced the publication, the Warden says, 'Knock that guy's privileges down! Take his typewriter and desk away from him, his special cell. Lock him up the same as you do everybody else on Death Row. If he's gonna get fame, let him get it alone. We're not gonna cooperate with him.' So we did. We took his cell away from him."[28]

Once more, a favorable public response to Caryl Chessman's second book added strength to the movement to spare his life. With increasing frequency, reviewers noted how the convict author seemed to have changed since his first book. "Caryl Chessman has matured as a writer and a human being," wrote the *New York Herald Tribune*: "The cynical, bragging criminal who wrote *Cell 2455 Death Row* has mellowed into a philosophical, more understanding man, displaying a sympathy and tolerance completely missing in his first book."[29] The *San Francisco Chronicle* called the work "a clear and incisive attack on capital punishment," which, rather than showing disrespect, displayed the condemned man's "high regard for the law now. A more meaningful tribute to the law would be hard to find."[30] "Guilt or innocence aside," Chessman had written, "Death Row is doubtless the best thing that ever could have happened to me. . . . Luckily for me, Death Row . . . subjected me to a psychological shock therapy that got results."[31]

On October 3, 1955, Louis Nelson, by now associate warden of custody, directed a massive shakedown of Death Row. The raid turned up a handful of manuscripts: a nearly completed novel, eventually published as *The Kid Was a Killer*, and a satire of Hollywood called "Nov smoz Kapop" by Caryl Chessman; "Born to Serve" by Bart Caritativo; and an untitled manuscript by Robert O. Pierce. The three convicts were ordered to appear before a disciplinary committee to determine whether they intended to publish the manuscripts. If so, the prisoners could be rebuked or sent to isolation for one month.

Meanwhile, in the wider prison, a similar crackdown was taking place:

The Supervisor of Education, who wanted to be a warden, decided to clean his house of writers and caused the goon squad to shake down the Education building and take anything that looked like it was becoming a book. They raised a netfull—sonnets, sagas, a clutch of the dirty stories we wrote and rented out for a pack a night, and two novels under contract to be published. It was a twenty-four hour shitstorm.[32]

Chessman immediately instructed attorney George Davis to petition Marin County Superior Court for a writ of prohibition to restrain prison authorities from trying the three Death Row convicts under these charges. In the petition Davis would argue that inmates did have constitutional rights, and therefore the "rule prohibiting the writing of material for publication is a violation of the constitutional rights of petitioners to freely speak, write and publish" and as such was cruel and unusual punishment.[33]

Davis and Marin County District Attorney William O. Weissich appeared before Judge Jordan L. Martinelli to argue the matter. Davis contended that any punishment would be an unconstitutional invasion of free speech; Weissich countered that the men were civilly dead and therefore had no constitutional rights. After several hours of legal maneuvering, Judge Martinelli forbade San Quentin from punishing the three prisoners.

Next, Chessman moved to get his manuscripts back from the warden's safe. He petitioned Judge Martinelli for a writ of habeas corpus to force the prison to return the materials. But the judge rejected his plea on the grounds that he was civilly dead and therefore could not legally try to recover property. The court apparently did not want to take a firm stand on the issue of civil rights for prisoners. At the same time, in mid-October, there was a development in Chessman's larger case. In response to his claim that the transcript of his trial had been fraudulently prepared, the U.S. Supreme Court granted his petition for a writ of certiorari. This raised the prospect of a new trial.

Chessman feared that San Quentin's writing ban would interfere with his efforts to prepare his legal case for a retrial, which was scheduled to begin in San Francisco Federal Court in January 1956. The prison's tightened security made it impossible for the convict and his attorneys to pass legal documents back and forth in the Death Row visiting room without having guards read them first. Davis and Chessman regarded this as a very real threat to their ability to prepare a case. Davis took the matter up with federal judge Louis E. Goodman, who ordered the prison to permit Chessman and his lawyers to pass documents without having officers peruse them.

As if to taunt the prison authorities, on December 21, 1956, George Davis emerged from a conference with his Death Row client and told the press, "I got THE document signed by Chessman." When a reporter asked if "THE document" was one of Chessman's unpublished works, the attorney smiled brightly and repeated, "All I will say is that I got THE document."[34] Warden Teets assured the press that the document was merely an affidavit and the inmate had been thoroughly searched before entering the visiting room.

Then George Davis came up with a new approach. He struck on the idea of combining both of Chessman's causes in one. Because Chessman's resources were almost exhausted by past attorney fees, he offered to take as payment in lieu of a fee his client's agreement to write a book. How was this to be done with the writing ban in effect? Davis instructed Chessman to approach the court with the argument that he had no way of meeting his legal expenses except through the sale of "the products of his mind." Consequently, denying him possession of the right to sell *The Kid Was a Killer* and other unpublished manuscripts would "deprive him of the effective aid of counsel." Chessman also would ask the court for permission to write his attorney's biography in payment for legal services. Alternatively, Davis told the court, Chessman could be declared a pauper and the government assessed for the costs of the new trial. Chessman later wrote:

To show I had assets, if only the Department of Corrections were ordered to release them, George had required Warden Teets to produce [in federal court] the yet unpublished manuscript of my seized novel, *The Kid Was a Killer*. As though he feared someone might put the snatch on it and run, the warden had the tightly wrapped manuscript convoyed into court by two hefty prison lieutenants. No one was given even a peek at it. . . . Back the manuscript was rushed to San Quentin's safe.[35]

Judge Goodman responded that he did not have the authority to interfere with "security regulations" at the prison; he therefore declined to force prison authorities to return the manuscripts. Disappointment turned to despair when the court also upheld the accuracy of Chessman's original trial transcript.

But one last ray of hope for getting the manuscripts back would be provided by the Internal Revenue Service, which, at the end of January 1956, slapped a $3,825 lien on Chessman. Warden Teets informed the tax office that although the author's recent literary work had brought in $26,000, after attorney fees all that remained in Chessman's prison account was $17.01. For a while the agency considered seizing the prisoner's unpublished manuscripts, selling them for publication, and confiscating the profits. As it turned out, however, the release of *Cell 2455 Death Row* as a paperback provided enough income to pay the inmate's tax bill. *The Kid Was a Killer* stayed in Warden Teets's safe. It was to appear in published form only days before Chessman's execution.

Chessman's legal study cell had been taken from him. It was soon to be occupied by a newly arrived Death Row inmate, even though there were ten empty cells on the Row at the time. San Quentin's tightened security seemed to have dashed Chessman's hopes of ever publishing again, though the control over reading and writing was subject to frequent lapses. On one routine cell search, Chessman was found with a contraband copy of the published *Trial by Ordeal* in his cell. Prison authorities were outraged. How had this dangerous book found its way onto Death Row? Chessman had requested it, he said simply, and his publisher had sent it through the mail. Somehow it had eluded the prison's mail room censors.

Just how serious breaches in San Quentin's security could be was demonstrated a year later, when in mid-February 1957, in another surprise shakedown of the Row, a search of a tall stack of papers in one corner of Chessman's cell turned up a completed manuscript of yet another book, *The Face of Justice*. Further search revealed carbon copies of three letters as well: one to the prisoner's literary agent, Joseph Longstreth, assigning all the rights to the new book to attorneys Asher and Davis; a second to Governor Goodwin J. Knight, attacking capital punishment; and the last to Director of Corrections Richard A. McGee, boasting how Chessman had violated San Quentin's rule against writing by completing another book. An urgent telegram was sent to Longstreth, asking if he had received a copy of the manuscript. He replied that he had not.

Chessman was then immediately taken before a prison disciplinary committee and sentenced to 28 days in Solitary Cell 2489. Here he was allowed as personal property only the clothes he had on his back. His new home consisted of a mattress on a concrete slab and a metal combination toilet and sink. His typewriter and all the papers and books in Cell 2455 were impounded, including 51 cubic feet of legal documents and his income tax files.

The administration hoped that this new book manuscript had been discovered before it could be smuggled out. But the originals of the three letters were missing; apparently they had reached the outside. Prison security was redoubled and a massive search of the entire prison ensued.

Five days later a most curious document arrived at Marin County Superior Court. Scrawled on a long piece of toilet paper, it was a petition for a writ of habeas corpus from, of all places, Caryl Chessman's isolation cell. "Here petitioner has been held incommunicado," the prisoner began.

He has been repeatedly refused to send a telegram to either one of his attorneys of record. . . . The respondent warden's agents refuse flatly to give petitioner even a sheet of paper and a stub of a pencil with which to contact this court or any court of competent jurisdiction and seek habeas corpus or any other type of relief.

Chessman declared that the warden had no right to treat him in this way. He was afraid, he went on, that the prison would destroy his legal papers. Warden Teets, he said, was doing this to pressure him into having his book manuscript returned to the prison before it could be published. The warden was acting "in the manner of the head of the secret police in a police state when he has done and is doing everything in his power to coerce and intimidate petitioner into returning a manuscript of a book titled *The Face of Justice*." Chessman demanded that the warden "return [his papers] and respect petitioner's constitutional rights." "Can this be happening," he wrote,

in mid-20th century America, under a penal system reportedly most progressive and enlightened in the nation? . . .

Petitioner must write this petition without being seen by patroling guards. He must write it with a tiny stub of a pencil on this industrial toilet tissue. If seen, the pencil will be confiscated, as "contraband" by definition, and petitioner will be subjected to even more rugged punishment, perhaps physical violence.

And to get this petition to the court he must have it smuggled out. He is forced, thus, to defy the respondent Warden H. Teets' orders to his agents to defy the constitution in order to protect his constitutional rights. That is a tragic commentary on California justice. And it is with this very subject that petitioner's new book and the letters deal. The book and the letters show, supported by documentary and other evidence, the dangers inherent when "gas chamber justice" and an Orwellian Big Brother type of system is permitted to find root penologically and socially in our democracy.[36]

Louis Nelson, then associate warden of custody, denies any memory of this event: "If he had a petition, regardless of whether it was written on corn husks or toilet paper or legal paper, it would have gone out forthwith. If the subject was legal it would have gone out to the courts."[37] But in 1957 Nelson had been interviewed by the press concerning the toilet paper petition. He had said at that time that he assumed an employee had smuggled the petition out, and that the prison wanted to know who: "We have a full scale investigation under way. We hope to find out."[38] Chessman's isolation cell was a simple, barred cell, open at the front and lacking the solid iron door of the harsher "quiet cell," and he might have slipped the petition to a sympathetic staff member. Only about twelve San Quentin staff had access to the inmate in his isolation cell. These staff members came under careful scrutiny.

Chessman himself was hauled before another disciplinary committee on February 21 to answer questions about how he got the petition out. He was given another twenty days in isolation, to run concurrently with the term he was already serving. To the press, who met him as he exited the disciplinary hearing room, the inmate boasted, "I assure you they won't find out how I did it." [39]

In March Rosalie Asher filed a formal complaint with Marin County Superior Court on behalf of Chessman, seeking to restrain San Quentin prison from destroying the inmate's legal papers. [40] But Warden Teets refused once again to hand over the papers and twelve legal books which Chessman claimed he needed to prepare for his Supreme Court hearing. Finally, on April 10, the warden reluctantly returned some of the documents, on advice from the state attorney general's office. [41]

But by this time, to the horror of the authorities, a copy of *The Face of Justice* had turned up in New York. Sometime during the first week in March 1957, a small boy hand delivered a plain unmarked paper bundle to Chessman's agent, Joseph Longstreth. It contained a 500-page opus, each page signed and stamped with the author's fingerprint. "From the text," said Longstreth, "it is clear that probably no manuscript in the history of authorship has been written under more excruciating conditions." [42] Over the next months, Caryl Chessman would reveal just how he had managed his feat of prison authorship. "From eight to ten every evening," wrote Byron Eshelman,

he would pace his cell outlining in his mind what he would write that night. Throughout the night, sitting up on his bunk, with his writing board on his knees, he wrote his manuscript in longhand. Officers on guard could see him, but this was his usual procedure in preparing his legal documents. He would write until four A.M., then spend the next two hours copying what he had written into shorthand—another skill he had mastered in prison. His shorthand notes were cleverly interlarded with longhand legal phraseology. He would then flush the longhand notes down the toilet and lie down for his afternoon rest. [43]

Chessman's *Face of Justice* tells how he produced the final manuscript from this shorthand version:

Finally I hit on the idea of using carbon paper. I had had boxes of it in my cell for years. I used it, as everyone knew, in my legal work. . . . Experimenting,

I found that by using a heavy face and backing sheet, which could be destroyed immediately, and by not striking the keys too hard, no readable impression was left on the face of the carbon. To be detected, one of the right sheets of the carbon paper (among which were scattered numerous harmless sheets) had to be selected and . . . held up to the light in just the right way. The person doing this had to avoid being misled by other deliberately more readable matter on the sheet, especially at the top, center and bottom. . . . In such a hazardous way, this book had been authored. Now, in record time, it had to be typed on regular paper. To reduce the manuscript's . . . bulk . . . I single-spaced each sheet, using . . . onion skin. Every page bore my signature on the bottom, and on the back of each sheet I put the inked fingerprints of my right hand. . . . Not only was I under almost constant surveillance, but the guards watching me were watched by other guards. My cell was searched uncounted times.[44]

Several other inmates on Death Row helped the project along. "They read the manuscript from beginning to end," the convict wrote.[45] Chessman's defiance of the writing ban is still pointed to with collective pride on the Row. A former Death Row prisoner recalls: "It was slick. You lay it on carbons, you can't see nothin'. But if you hold it up to the light you can read it. That I know, because that was one of the little stories left over on the Row when I got up there."[46]

Chessman told Bernice Freeman that after the manuscript was completed, he had used a complicated scheme to get it out:

He completed . . . [an] original and one copy . . . and gave the original to another man in Death Row, whom Chessman identified as Convict No. 1. Chessman kept the copy in his cell, where it was easy to hide among his huge pile of legal books and papers.

Somehow, Convict No. 1 got the manuscript out of Death Row and into the hands of Convict No. 2. This man hid it either in the main yard or one of the workshops, where it remained for several weeks. He finally had a chance to give it to Convict No. 3, who had a job that brought him into daily contact with trucks going outside the prison. But before No. 3 could dispose of the book, his job was changed, and he had to pass it to another inmate. This man divided the manuscript into three sections for easier handling. This was all Chessman would tell me. Either he really didn't know or wouldn't say what No. 4 did next. Chessman "thought" that the book might have gone out in sections, "possibly in trash trucks." Once outside the walls, it could be left for a parolee to pick up and mail to Joe Longstreth, Chessman's agent.

When the warden ordered Death Row searched in March, Chessman's copy, written in pencil, was found, neatly piled up in a corner of his cell. Chessman told me he wanted it to be found there. He figured that this would throw authorities off the track, for they wouldn't dream he had written out two separate copies.[47]

California assistant attorney general Clarence Linn made a special trip east to urge Joseph Longstreth to relinquish the manuscript. The literary agent refused. Attorney General Edmund G. Brown, an opponent of capital punishment, declined to take legal action, declaring, "I cannot conceive of any legal basis for acting to halt publication, and even if there were a basis I would not be interested."[48] By September 1957, Prentice-Hall had *The Face of Justice* on bookstore shelves.

The critics were somewhat disappointed. They disapproved of a strange, new Chessman who emerged in the book, "boasting and threatening, hurling invective and innuendo at the officials who have closed in on him."[49] Some predicted that the book would reduce the ranks of those supporting the prisoner's campaign to live: "It is more cynical, brash, argumentative and defiant than the earlier books and will probably lose the author a portion of his warmly sympathetic reading audience and provide further fuel for those who would destroy him as a symbol of evil."[50]

At San Quentin prison, meanwhile, the daytime shift of Death Row officers, a sergeant and two guards, had been moved to a different assignment.[51] Throughout the prison, guards were under orders to maintain "visual observation" of visitors and prisoners during interviews. The attorney general's office was planning a sweeping investigation. Richard McGee declared his determination to find the smuggler of Chessman's latest book manuscript: "We feel somebody has certainly committed a misdemeanor and quite probably a felony by conspiring to do this thing."[52] In April, all staff with access to the Row were requested to take lie detector tests on the smuggling issue. This included nine guards, four chaplains, eight doctors, and the captain of the guards, as well as the warden and his deputies. Several took the tests. Two chaplains, however, hotly refused, expressing indignation that the prison would question the honesty of men of the cloth. Finally, the lie detector tests were dropped, but by that time, the investigation had begun to take a different direction. Governor Goodwin J. Knight had asked Marin County district attorney William O. Weissich to prosecute the smuggling case. After the lie detector tests and the questioning of all officers, the smuggler still remained a secret so a grand jury probe was begun. Weissich presented evidence before the grand jury that resulted in an indictment against Chessman's attorneys, literary agent, and publisher for conspiracy to remove *The Face of Justice* from San Quentin. Attorneys Davis and Asher were subpoenaed to testify before the grand jury. They declined to answer numerous questions, claiming the attorney-client privilege. On appeal, the California District Court of Appeal concluded that the manuscript had not been the property of the state of California and that there was no evidence of conspiracy. The indictment was dropped.

In June 1957, responding to another petition from Chessman, the U.S. Supreme Court found that he had been denied due process in the preparation of the trial transcript. His case was remanded to the lower courts for further proceedings.

Through Chessman's willpower and self-determination and under his direction a smooth-running and efficient law office continued to hum on the Row. To appeal to the Supreme Court he had to produce numerous copies of legal briefs: twenty copies for the state supreme court, five for San Quentin prison, a copy for California's attorney general, and copies for each of his lawyers, as well as copies for the Court itself. To produce the required number of legal documents for even a lower court, a typed copy had to be made, then a stencil. Stenciled pages were collated and stapled collectively by Death Row convicts going round and round the ping-pong table in the Row's corridor. A brief could be produced at a cost of only a few hundred dollars if the prisoners did the work themselves. For the U.S. Supreme Court, however, the briefs had to be printed, not stenciled, and could cost as much as $1,500, in addition to the cost of attorney fees.[53] Chessman's Death Row law office served him well. His numerous appeals over the years had resulted in more than 2,000 changes in his original court transcript and six stays of execution by 1957.

The prisoner's luck would soon begin to run out, however, when, in 1959, after rancorous debate on the issue of capital punishment, the California Senate retained the state's death penalty. Then, in December, the U.S. Supreme Court turned down Chessman's latest plea. Still he continued to receive public support. *Cell 2455 Death Row* had sold a half million copies and been translated into eighteen foreign languages. The critics had been wrong about *The Face of Justice*. Rather than diminishing after the book's publication, Chessman's popularity had skyrocketed. The convict had achieved international celebrity. And the rapidly rising tide of a movement to spare his life had made it considerably more difficult for San Quentin prison authorities to keep him from writing. Chessman was openly rewriting his novel, *The Kid Was a Killer*, and had contacted several publishers concerning its publication.

Caryl Chessman's soaring popularity cannot be explained merely by the content of his books. Today *Cell 2455 Death Row, Trial by Ordeal,* and *The Kid Was a Killer* seem unremarkable works. *The Face of Justice* still makes a good, though unspectacular, argument against state execution. Several forces combined to produce this convict's fame. Chessman received international renown in part because many European and South American nations had recently rescinded their own death penalty laws in the period just after World War II and were anxious to see the United States follow in their path. The right of a political state to execute was coming under severe criticism worldwide at this time, owing to the horrible abuses of the Third Reich in Germany. Chessman's race at least partially explained the huge support he got from his own countrymen. In a nation that had traditionally executed many more prisoners of color than whites guilty of comparable crimes, Chessman was a white man convicted of a crime other than murder. But the supremely rational convict voice of Chessman's writing, especially in *The Face of Justice,* might provide the best clue to this condemned man's reputation as a hero among Americans because this character quality—reason, the morally refining product of self-education—had great appeal to his countrymen. Chessman's life should be spared because he was a changed man, they argued, by evidence of his rational eloquence. It wasn't that he was not guilty of his crime, his public insisted; rather, the erudition, reason, and humane tone of his writing redeemed him. In an odd way, the public's embrace of Chessman makes him seem remarkably like the accused in the Middle Ages, who could avoid hanging by demonstrating that they could read. The gargantuan drive to rescue Chessman can be fully explained only as reflecting the cultural residue of the old idea that writing somehow magically equals rehabilitation, that the ability to write well is a sign of goodness because it requires what Benjamin Rush in the eighteenth century would have termed highly ordered "sensibilities," which a criminal by definition cannot have. In other words, in the treatment prison, possessing a certain kind of knowledge could trump criminal guilt. This premise, implicit in the rehabilitation rhetoric of the treatment-era prison, was about to be picked up by leftist radicals in the prison movement, with fatal results.

Viewed in another context, the facts of Chessman's criminal case seem to have had little relation to his wide public acclaim. The popularity of Caryl Chessman's books and the movement for the commutation of his sentence may have had as much to do with models of masculinity and the siren call of male criminals that were emerging in late 1950's popular American culture as they did with anything in his own person. In writing his books, Chessman may even have been consciously playing to these themes in the American cultural underground.

A decade earlier the hard-boiled detective heroes of Dashiell Hammett and Raymond Chandler had given California a new view of itself. Novels like *The Maltese Falcon* or *The Big Sleep* and the films produced from them presented their audiences with violent male heroes acting against the backdrop of a moral wasteland in the sprawling California cityscape. Sam Spade and Philip Marlowe were outlaw detectives of the big California city, never afraid to break the law themselves. They were strong, violent men responding aggressively to life in perverse circumstances, eager to use naked force when they had to, and perfectly willing to go outside the law. These characters owed much to the sheriffs of Hollywood gunfighter westerns, basically good men, but nonetheless men whose destiny was to kill and who could be fulfilled only by committing that deadly act. As Peter Biskind and Barbara Ehrenreich have observed, against this violent male model, Hollywood in the 1950's attempted to counterpose an alternative model which elevated tame male domesticity to a social ideal.[54] Television serials like "Leave It to Beaver," "Father Knows Best," "Ozzie and Harriet," and "My Three Sons" offered their viewers a docile but in the end unappealing and unpassionate male role alternative to Sam Spade. Offered these opposites and not much in between, as the 1960's approached American audiences more and more began to prefer the more violent male. America liked its men to come out shooting, like the Rifleman or Gary Cooper in *High Noon* or Sean Connery or Clint Eastwood, men who could translate mayhem into male power—men who weren't afraid to be proud outlaws. American culture in the 1960's was to enshrine this male role. America's first truly delinquent culture heroes in the 1950's, James Dean and Marlon Brando, consequently had to be tough, resilient, violent, and outside the law even while they appeared sensitive, loving, and easily hurt. It is not simple coincidence that Caryl Chessman's books were achieving best-seller status at the same time James Dean's misunderstood "bad boy" of *East of Eden* and Brando's outlaw biker in *The Wild One* were breaking box office records. In 1954, when Chessman's *Cell 2455 Death Row* appeared in print, countless thousands of viewers were adoring Marlon Brando for the terrible, purifying beating he received in *On the Waterfront*. That same year his role as Johnny in *The Wild One* ("Hey, Johnny, what're you rebelling against?" "Whatta ya got?")

almost single-handedly launched outlaw biker culture in California by giving the newly formed Hell's Angels club mass media recognition. Three years later, when *The Face of Justice* appeared, James Dean's fame was cresting as well. His *Giant* became the second biggest grossing film to date, behind only *Gone With the Wind*.

As major fissures slowly opened up in American culture during the 1950's, the lawbreaking of male convicts enhanced by mass media images of the lawless hero would come to have an unprecedented allure for growing groups of disaffected Californians. While the aggressive violence of the outlaw already provided gender definition for California males, the idea of lawbreaking itself soon came to hold attractions for those who identified with outlaws as cultural or political outsiders. Nowhere is this clearer than in the case of the Beats of San Francisco's 1950's North Beach, especially the audiences of Allen Ginsberg, Jack Kerouac, and Neal Cassady, all of whom were drawn to petty lawbreaking and fascinated by gratuitous crime. Caryl Chessman's celebrity came at the same time readers were coming to love Dean Moriarty, the charming, speed-rapping, shortchange artist-hero of *On the Road*, "whose 'criminality,'" Kerouac wrote, "was not something that sulked and sneered; it was a wild yea-saying overburst of American joy." [55]

Caryl Chessman was as much a creature of the American imagination as he was a real person. This may explain why his fame extended so far beyond those who actually had read his books and why he captured the public's heart at the very time it was calling into question the relation of law and the American male. The story of celebrity outlaw Caryl Chessman seemed necessary to the American imagination. In some sense Chessman was playing a character role, following a cultural script not entirely his own. It may be, too, that in a perverse way his death was required by the script. Robert Warshow writes that gangster stories are Horatio Alger plots nightmarishly inverted, where the hero rises to the pinnacle of criminal success but must then be tragically shot down in a hail of gunfire by the police. The genre demands death by gunfire. If this is so, then perhaps like the celluloid gangster, Caryl Chessman's literary fame and tremendous popular support were no more than caricatures of real American success. Like the gangster, Chessman had to follow the cultural script of an outlaw hero, alone and aggressively antisocial. He had to be allowed to rise almost to triumph, but, finally, true to the script, he must die. [56]

Chessman's fifteenth appeal to the U.S. Supreme Court for a writ of habeas corpus was turned down on February 17, 1960. His execution date was set for February 19. On the eighteenth, major newspapers worldwide called for mercy. The *London Daily Mail* devoted its main editorial to a plea to Governor Brown to save Chessman. Similar opinions appeared in Brussels' *La Metropole*, Madrid's *Arriba*, and Vatican City's *L'Osservatore Romano*. In Norway and Sweden the press reported that 143,000 signatures had been gathered on mercy petitions. The same day, the California Supreme Court voted against clemency, four to three, and the governor announced that he was powerless to spare the condemned man. The governor was handed a petition with 1,300 signatures from University of California, Berkeley, calling for clemency. Tens of thousands of letters were received in his mail room in support of Chessman. Governor Brown was said to be in great distress. The San Francisco chapter of the National Lawyers Guild had also appealed, citing in addition to due process and other legal issues "the evidence of Chessman's rehabilitation."[57] In San Francisco, 100 banner-carrying students marched past the state building. At Union Square three speakers denounced the execution plans: Richard Drinnon, an assistant professor of history at the University of California, Berkeley; David Armor, president of UC Berkeley's Associated Students; and Flanagan Ross, an American Friends Service Committee spokesman. The *San Francisco Chronicle* ran a huge front-page photo of Chessman's hands writing a last denial that he was the Red Light Bandit. He was scheduled to die the next morning.

A group of students announced plans to march the eighteen miles from San Francisco to San Quentin across the Golden Gate Bridge and hold a night vigil there through the execution hour. At the prison, Caryl Chessman held a last press conference in Associate Warden Louis Nelson's office. "I have said I am innocent," he told reporters. "I will say it again. I will say it in hell if there is such a place." Chessman made one last pitch for his life: if he was spared, he said, "I will spend my time at my typewriter, writing, trying to live constructively, not destructively with society." He gave firm handshakes all round the room and said good-bye. Late that night he dictated a final statement from his cell, predicting that his due process victories in the U.S. Supreme Court would help those accused of crimes in the future and expressing hope that his writing and "the intense controversy over the sort of person I was and am has led . . . people to inquire about what sort of a person comes to Death Row and why. I certainly hope this experience I have gone through never has to be suffered by anyone else in the history of this country."[58]

In the middle of the night, less than ten hours from Chessman's date with death, the governor announced another stay of execution. Governor Brown had been asked by the administration of President Dwight D. Eisenhower to issue a stay of sixty days. This would be the condemned man's eighth reprieve. The president, about to embark on a Latin American tour, had been informed of the Uruguayan government's fear of violent demonstrations if Chessman were executed. Mexican congresswoman Macrina Rabadan had also telegraphed Eisenhower that Latin American women would wear mourning during his visit. In London, six of the nine morning newspapers gave more space to the Chessman execution than they did to the impending birth of a child to Queen Elizabeth II at Buckingham Palace. Chessman's next death date was May 2.

Meanwhile, hundreds of motorists and about fifty campers had assembled at San Quentin's east gate. With news of the stay, the crowd disbanded, but the controversy did not go away. Over the next few days, while effigies of Governor Brown were hanged in Modesto, Long Beach, and West Los Angeles, the state senate's Judiciary Committee promised a full probe into the question of whether Chessman had received justice. A movie titled *Justice and Carl Chessman*, including comments by law enforcement officials, Chessman's trial jurors, and a mother of one of the Red Light Bandit's victims, opened in 43 California theaters, and its producers announced plans for the film to appear at 14,000 more movie houses across the nation and in Europe. Producer Terrence Cooney said he hoped the film was an objective portrayal of Chessman's case, though he admitted he was personally opposed to capital punishment. "Which is greater?" the film asked. "The wrong for which a convicted man dies, or the wrong society does against him?"[59] At the same time, 100,000 copies of a new song called the "Chessman Ballad," recorded by Ronnie Hawkins for Roulette Records, flooded the record stores:

> Killin' laws were made by man,
> Not according to God's plan . . .
> Let his soul be judged on judgement day.[60]

The nation's press ran major articles on Chessman throughout the spring of 1960. In an editorial called "Must Chessman Die?" the *New Republic* argued that the issue was not capital punishment itself but whether Chessman had received a fair trial. The magazine appealed for patience, contending that it was Chessman, not the law, that had been abused through twelve years of legal maneuvering. It concluded that killing the prisoner now would be unjustifiable. The *Nation*, too, questioned whether the convict had been granted due process and urged readers to send telegrams to the California Supreme Court to press for clemency.[61] By April, even Brigitte Bardot had joined the spare Chessman movement, by means of an open letter to President Eisenhower published in a Paris newspaper.

Inside the prison, Chessman chose to concentrate his last efforts to live on convincing prison staff that he was rehabilitated and could be useful to society if spared. On April 17, when a prison psychiatrist asked the condemned man to "prepare a note setting out whether I thought I had matured," Chessman replied in writing that he most certainly had. He characterized himself as socially aware and rational and wrote that as a result of his long years at San Quentin he had experienced a "burning out . . . of [his] sociopathic reaction or reflex." He said of his past life of crime:

I can't change my past, Doctor I can't erase it, I can't forget it. But I can realize I was a damned fool, and admit it. My responsibility—legally adjudicated punishment and the question of guilt or innocence of my present crimes aside—does not end there, as I see it. I feel a need more fully to grasp the nature of what we can call the psychodynamics of my particular brand of folly. . . . In sum, I damn well don't want to engage in any more irrational conduct.

Chessman then informed the psychiatrist that he was through writing autobiography and said he planned now to write "a biography of the late Jesse W. Carter, Associate Justice of the California Supreme Court, a jurist who taught me to respect the law."[62]

In Sausalito, the newly formed Marin Chessman Committee lighted a twenty-foot-high propane "life flame" while singing "God Bless America" and announced plans to carry the torch to the San Quentin gate. But by the end of April, all legal and legislative efforts had failed and the California Supreme Court had not reversed its vote against clemency. Governor Brown declared once more that he was powerless to act.

Chessman was said to be in deep depression. "I am prepared to die," he told a reporter. Yet on Saturday, April 29, the chief editor of Prentice-Hall, who had visited Chessman at San Quentin, told the press, "Believe it or not, he wanted to discuss his writing plans for the future."[63] *The Kid Was a Killer* was due to be released by

Gold Medal Books to coincide with the condemned man's Monday death date.

On Sunday, May 1, Marlon Brando, Shirley MacLaine, Richard Drinnon, and Eugene Burdick, author of *The Ugly American*, met with the governor in his office. A petition signed by 384 University of California faculty arrived by auto caravan. Pleas continued to pour in to the governor, and pickets milled around his Sacramento mansion. The approaching execution had been widely advertised on KPFA, Pacifica Radio. Hundreds gathered at San Quentin's east gate, wearing black armbands and bearing signs that read "Psycho Therapy—Not Cyanide," "The Law Is Not Holy," and "Each Man's Death Diminishes Me—Donne." A dummy was hung in effigy from the U.S. Route 101 overpass near the prison. In New York, protesters marched on Fifth Avenue. The California Supreme Court was set to convene at 8 A.M. to hear one last motion by Chessman's attorneys. The gas chamber would be ready at 10.

Twelve years and eight execution stays after Chessman's conviction, a worldwide movement to rescue him was cresting in a huge wave. Belgium's Queen Mother telephoned Governor Brown urging clemency. In Brazil, 2,500,000 citizens had signed mercy petitions. A Brazilian had offered a million dollars to help Chessman wage his fight. A Greek princess made a personal appeal to the governor.[64] Why were so many people so concerned about this one condemned rapist-kidnapper? Protestant chaplain Byron Eshelman would later attribute it to "the almost incredible clarity with which [Chessman] came to understand himself, and others who were troubled." At issue was Chessman's maturation in prison—his rehabilitation. And perhaps more than this inmate himself was at stake in the execution. It was the belief in rehabilitation itself that was the threatened article of faith. Eshelman himself was a strong believer in Chessman's reform:

I am absolutely certain that when Caryl Chessman stepped calmly into the San Quentin gas chamber, he was not the psychopath who had come to Death Row twelve years earlier. . . . I watched Chessman change during his years on the Row. I saw him grow and mature, and learn to channel the explosive forces within him into power for social good. . . . Even Chessman's IQ appeared to change on Death Row. The first time he came to San Quentin, Chessman scored 127 on the Wechsler-Bellevue testing scale. Six weeks before his death, he scored 130 on the same intelligence test.[65]

But Louis Nelson insists Chessman was merely manipulating the public:

He worked on people's sympathies. . . . I do know that Caryl Chessman was guilty of the crime for which he had been committed. In my capacity as Associate Warden I received a call one day in 1960 from . . . Director Richard McGee. . . . He said, "I want you to do something for me. . . . I want you to get ahold of Chessman. . . . I want you to tell him this. That you have received word from somebody who you cannot name. . . . Tell him that if he will withdraw his legal matters and stop getting his name in the newspaper every day, that a commutation will be forthcoming. . . . So I had Caryl Chessman brought down and told the officer to leave the room, my office.

Nelson told the prisoner what he had been instructed to say.

[Chessman] rolled his unlit cigarette around in his mouth, mulled it over, and said, "Mr. Nelson, I can't do that." I said, "Do you mind telling me why?" He said, "I have been traveling under this facade of innocence for so many years that to now admit my guilt would be to destroy all those people who have believed in me all of these years." He was satisfied that to pull away the petitions that said he was innocent . . . would be a tacit admission of guilt. . . . "Traveled under a facade of innocence." Those were his exact words. They were burned on my memory.[66]

The night of May 1, Caryl Chessman was moved from Cell 2455 on the Row, taken downstairs by elevator to the North Block's first floor, and locked in the holding cell a few steps away from the gas chamber waiting for his 10 A.M. date with death. George Davis sat up with him.

Outside the prison about 700 people huddled in a crowd just beyond a roadblock at the prison's access road. Some held lighted candles. A public address system had been hooked up to a sound truck. Marlon Brando, two professors, a retired prison guard, and an ex-con spoke. Many staged a sit-down in the road, blocking press cars. Prison guards "began to kick several of the seated demonstrators" or remove them bodily.[67]

In the morning, George Davis left the prison early for the California Supreme Court in San Francisco where his last-minute motion for a stay was to be heard. The court convened at 9 A.M. By 9:20 the court had rejected Davis's petition.

Reporters from all over the world crowded into and around San Quentin prison. Special telephone lines had been installed near the administration building to accommodate the press. Inside, in the observation room adjoining the gas chamber, there was room for only 60 witnesses. Associate Warden Louis Nelson sat in this room, near a direct telephone line to the governor's office, just in case a stay came through. At 9:50, Nelson informed the condemned man of the court's rejection. Chessman was then moved into the gas chamber, seated in one of its two chairs, and secured with ten straps. The inmate looked calmly out through the glass at several of the spectators he knew personally and said, "It's all right," or "I'm all right." At 9:59, according to attorney Davis, the California Supreme Court judge hearing Chessman's motion for a stay said to him, "I'll grant the stay of execution." Over the next few minutes, two attempts were made to call the prison. When the call finally went through, the justice turned to Davis and said: "It's too late. The warden says the pellets were just dropped." [68]

Caryl Chessman breathed in the cyanide gas, slumped forward in the chair, and was dead. Louis Nelson denies that a last-minute call was received at the prison:

Nobody, but nobody, placed a telephone call. Had they done so, the operator was always under instructions that should a call come in . . . they were to break in the line and notify us that somebody was on the line. With deference to federal judges, no call came through. Nor was received. [69]

On hearing news of the execution, the crowd at the prison's east gate grew silent. Members of the press ran to the phones. In Uruguay, picketers surrounded the U.S. Embassy shouting "Yankee Murderers!" Portuguese novelist Joaquin Paco Darcos explained the public reaction: "The man executed today is a very different man from the one who committed the crimes." [70]

To many, Chessman's death definitively exposed the sham of prison rehabilitation. He had done everything his treatment experts had asked for and more. And still they would not let him go, or even acknowledge his transformation. If Chessman's case did not count as successful convict reform, why would anyone ever again bother? For the crowd outside the prison, for those in the Bay Area who were part of the movement to spare Chessman's life, Chessman's execution day was a rite of passage. "The long march went on, slowly," wrote Michael Rossman, a member of the crowd,

and just as slowly the feeling grew that we were marching not for Chessman alone, nor even against capital punishment, but for something much more important, something transcending politics and laws. A student who had marched from the city said, "I keep feeling that what we're doing is helping each one of us more than it can possibly help Chessman." No one disagreed. [71]

Others in the Bay Area, too, remember the 1960 vigil at Chessman's execution as a "personal witness," a conversion to radical activism.

One of the early organizers of the California Prisoners' Union, John Irwin, described the change in the crowd at the Chessman execution as "the feeling that each person must demonstrate by some personal act of protest or defiance that he or she will not accept injustice."[72]

"We walked to the car in silence," wrote Rossman, "drove home in silence. By the time we reached Berkeley the first papers were already on the newsstands, their headlines three inches tall."[73] Bay Area prison activism had begun.

It was Caryl Chessman who first broke up the control mechanisms of writing and reading at San Quentin. And it was he who first turned the attention of Bay Area political activists toward the prison. Chessman had taught the world much. To his prison keepers, his example had shown how much trouble educating inmates could cause them; prison administrations after him would initially make it much harder for inmates to read and write. But to the inmates themselves Caryl Chessman had given a precious gift. This Death Row prisoner provided a model of how a convict could gain power through writing and education and then use it to seek his freedom. Finally, for the wider California society, Chessman cleared the way for outlaws to claim cultural hero status and likewise for free citizens outside the prison to see themselves as outlaws. Because of Caryl Chessman large numbers of Californians would soon come to envy the outsider's position the prisoner occupied. In its most extreme form in the 1960's and 1970's, as biker H. R. Kaye has noted, this would show up in outlaw biker culture:

The more Rivera told me about his gang and motorcycle outlaws in general, the more I came to idolize their way of life. They were outlaws like Jesse James and Pretty Boy Floyd. They were wild and reckless and they made their own laws. . . . It wasn't true that crime didn't pay. In fact, the way I saw it, a life of crime and social defiance was the only dignified way of life left open to the true individual. Rivera owned a big Harley, resplendent with custom tank, chrome galore, ape-hangers, the whole works. He was so cool all the chicks in the neighborhood wanted him. . . . And why not? He was a hero. A man on his own feet with a snarl on his face and nothing but contempt for the world at large. In short, a true outlaw.[74]

But the siren call of the California outlaw reached far beyond marginalized fringe or deviant groups. A love of the outlaw soon extended deep into the hearts even of California's middle-class sons and daughters. By the mid-1960's, the San Francisco rock group Jefferson Airplane would be telling a whole generation, "We are all outlaws in the eyes of Amerika," and Ken Kesey, fleeing to Mexico on drug charges, would proclaim, "If society wants me to be an outlaw . . . then I'll be an outlaw, and a damned good one. That's something people need. People at all times need outlaws."[75] This reverence for the outlaw was to be Caryl Chessman's biggest contribution to the California Left.

4

Taking the Yard, Freeing the Mind: The Black Muslims

Ironically, the first result of Caryl Chessman's legacy to his fellow San Quentin writers would be a rigid prohibition against all forms of creative writing on Death Row and a general tightening of restrictions on writing for the mainline prison population which lasted for the better part of the 1960's. What most infuriated prison authorities about Chessman was the way he had turned the treatment model back on itself and used the rhetoric of rehabilitation to manipulate the public into attempting to use the courts to force San Quentin prison to release him. And he had done this with words, using the same arguments about behavior modification through reading that his bibliotherapist keepers endorsed for convict reform. Chessman had turned the tables on San Quentin's intellectual pharmacists—almost.

In the decade of the 1960's both San Quentin's inmates and its treatment staff would lose what little faith remained in the notion of rehabilitation, as many convict writers moved from arguing, as Chessman had, that they should be released or their sentences be commuted because they had been rehabilitated, to the angry assertion that they did not need to be rehabilitated because they were not "bad" or "sick." It was the justice system, they argued, and American society, that needed rehabilitation; prisoners were its victims. San Quentin writers soon had rejected wholesale the prison's reading and writing controls and seem to have unanimously concluded that the treatment strategy of manipulating convicts' reading and writing, purportedly intended to lead them to self-understanding through self-examination and mental regret, actually masked the real function of the prison, which was to repress social chaos in an underclass forced into crime by desperate circumstances. Many San Quentin writers would soon unleash an aggressive wave of legal writ-writing accompanied by massive strikes and escalating racial-political violence.

As late as 1967, Death Row prisoners were punished if caught trying to write their life stories.[1] At the same time, the tremendous popularity Caryl Chessman's books had achieved offered encouragement to other San Quentin authors who wanted their stories told. Many who would not previously have cared to began secretly writing. In addition to his autobiographical works, Chessman had provided a precedent with his steady stream of petitions. His private war with San Quentin over access to law books, typewriters, pens, light, and the courts had engendered a tradition of jailhouse law and inflamed others with a passion for legal study and writ-writing. His smuggling techniques became legendary, instructing others in alternative publishing strategies if legal means failed.

Prison authorities were unsure how to respond. Consequently, their policies were at cross-purposes. On one hand, traditional corrections wisdom taught that when prison rebellion threatened, restrictions should be tightened. So the prison clamped down on prisoners' association and communication, mail privileges, and access to law books and tightened censorship. On the other hand, treatment-era rehabilitation rhetoric told prison staff to do just the opposite, to loosen restrictions, to encourage the free flow of ideas in reading, writing, and association among prisoners and to put more faith in the reformative effect of counseling and education. San Quentin managed to proceed on both of these opposite paths at once for the entire decade of the 1960's, contradicting itself at every turn. Controls on writing and reading were alternately lax and strict, as guards and administration tightened up and treatment staff loosened further. On one point, however, there was no contradiction. San Quentin's prisoners' written lives were categorically not their own. At issue was whether their writing should come under even more rigid control, their attempts to free themselves through their writs more firmly proscribed, or whether the treatment-era rehabilitative prison should more thoroughly examine and record the mental products of its wards in an attempt at better behavior modification. Case files generated in the prison's myriad counseling groups, psychiatric reports, Adult Authority, medical, library, disciplinary, and educational reports continued turning prisoners' lives into documents for future use. This system became the flashpoint for the convicts' struggle as California's prisoners moved to seize back the terms of their own definition.

No prisoners had better learned Caryl Chessman's lesson or were more ready to change the California prisons than San Quentin's Black Muslim convicts. Across the country, the Nation of Islam had been recruiting prisoners as members ever since Elijah Muhammad, the sect's chief lieutenant, had been convicted and imprisoned briefly for his draft resistance during World War II. When the defeat of the Third Reich brought universal condemnation of Germany's crimes against its ethnic minorities, black Americans after the war turned their attention to sweeping their own home clean of Jim Crow laws and reforming its racist institutions. In the antiracist wave of civil rights actions that resulted in the 1950's, the Black Muslims became the movement's in-prison political arm. By 1960 Black Muslim membership was estimated at 65,000 to 100,000 nationwide, a good portion inside prisons.[2] Meanwhile, employment opportunities in California's wartime heavy industries had drawn a large migration of blacks to the state, where they had previously made up only 2 percent of the population. By 1944, 65,000 blacks lived in San Francisco. In 1946 the black population of Los Angeles reached 200,000. The racial composition of California's prisons immediately underwent dramatic changes as well. The percentage of blacks in California's prisons quickly ballooned far out of proportion to their numbers in the population, from 19.9 percent in 1951, when blacks constituted 4.4 percent of the California populace, to 23.1 percent in 1960, to 29.8 percent in 1970, when blacks still were just 7 percent of the state's population, and then to 35.4 percent in 1980, when black population leveled off at 7.5 percent.[3] At San Quentin the proportion of black prisoners rose from 20.7 percent of the prison population in 1951 to 36.6 percent by 1980.[4]

These numbers cannot be explained simply by the claim that black Californians were more crime prone than others in this period. It is true that in the decades from the 1950's to the 1980's proportionately more black American males than other groups had been socialized in violent environments and that, as a result, in some areas the homicide rate for nonwhite males rose almost 300 percent from 1958 to 1974, a period when white male homicides increased by 25 percent.[5] By 1975 the homicide rate for black males nationwide was ten times that for white males.[6] But the disproportionate number of black males sent to California prisons during this period in all crime categories, including homicide, was also caused by racial inequities in the dispensation of justice in the state. At every stage in the justice system—arrest, pretrial hearing, conviction, sentencing, classification hearing during imprisonment, and parole hearing—California's blacks and other minorities faced a legal system controlled by whites. Many writers have noted that American criminal justice historically has codified and perpetuated the wrongs of the culture at large. A disproportionately high number of blacks have been arrested over the past four decades.[7] This is at least partly explained by the much more aggressive police presence in black neighborhoods than in white. In 1971, when California blacks were 7 percent of the state's population, they made up 48 percent of the persons killed by police.[8] Nationwide, the pattern has been similar. The 1970 census showed that blacks were 11 percent of America's population, but they represented a full 26 percent of all recorded arrests.[9] A similar process occurred in courtrooms. Research shows that low-income defendants have been more likely to go to prison if convicted than high-income defendants convicted of comparable crimes, in part because of inferior plea-bargaining by court-appointed attorneys.[10] Studies also indicate that black and other minority defendants have been twice as likely as white defendants to have public defenders.[11] The end result in the courtroom in the years 1950 to 1980 was that black male defendants were sentenced to prison at almost twice the rate of white male defendants.[12] Writers have found a racial bias as well in decisions to grant parole in this period.[13] In the decades following the great influx of blacks into California during World War II, the state's criminal justice system functioned to institutionalize the race and class inequities in the California culture at large. More aggressive police arrests in black neighborhoods, inequities for poor defendants in pretrial negotiations, higher imprisonment rates for blacks than for whites convicted of comparable crimes, and the greater reluctance of the Adult Authority to grant parole to black prisoners than to white put proportionately more California blacks than other races behind bars and kept them there longer between 1950 and 1980. In response, no other group of prisoners has shown more rage at the persecuting machinery of the state than California's black convicts. This may in part explain the tremendously aggressive attempts of California black convicts to seize and dominate the state's prison yards, where, once imprisoned, blacks found themselves relegated to the very bottom of the convict caste system and forbidden by rigid segregation from the choicer prison jobs. The passion of one early 1950's California black convict—Bob Wells—was to become legendary among the state's black prisoners.

Wesley Robert Wells, who joined with Caryl Chessman in staging the critical sit-down protest on San Quentin's Death Row in October 1950, was described by his former attorney Charles Garry as "the first

Black Panther." Garry, a noted Bay Area white civil rights attorney who had been radicalized by his participation in the 1934 San Francisco dockworkers' strike and who would become attorney for the Black Panthers in the 1960's, first encountered Wells just after World War II when the convict was at Folsom prison. According to Garry, Bob Wells was a proud black man who insisted on his rights and "wouldn't take shit from no one." He was a difficult, super-tough, street-fighting convict. Wells had first been sent to prison for receiving stolen goods, a high misdemeanor. But he got into numerous fights on the yard and finally killed another inmate. For this crime he was sentenced to serve ten years to life for manslaughter. According to Garry, because of Wells's stubborn resistance to authority he was singled out for especially brutal retaliation:

He was at Folsom, in the hottest time of the day. The warden there, a man by the name of Larkin, had buried him in the ground up to his neck in this hot sun. And then he would kick him with his boots. And if he fell unconscious they'd pour water over his head. And when he came conscious again he would still beat him. That's the kind of treatment he was getting.

Wells fought back, but the prison authorities seemed to have it out for him. According to Garry, "Anybody who took a fall out of Bob Wells would get special considerations." Finally, one day, during a hearing before a disciplinary committee, he erupted in anger and threw a cuspidor at a guard in a hallway outside the hearing room, hitting him in the head. Because Wells was already serving a life sentence, he could be tried for this new assault under Penal Code 4500, which called for a mandatory death penalty "in the event that a life-termer assaults a guard or another inmate with malice aforethought." Garry recalls his early days on the Wells case as he tried to keep this prisoner from the gas chamber:

I worked two days a week trying to make a living. The other five days I did whatever was necessary for Bob Wells. I traveled all over the country, and I amassed over 150,000 signatures demanding his unconditional pardon. And eventually the governor granted a pardon, but it only reduced his sentence to life without possibility of parole. We refused to accept that, publicly. . . . Many years later, he was let out.[14]

Garry's involvement in the Bob Wells case and the public interest he aroused in the cause, questioning whether the gas chamber was the proper way to discipline admittedly incorrigible prisoners like Wells, established the first feeble links between the black California prison population and the primarily white New Left that was emerging in the Bay Area. This alliance was to become crucial in later years. Garry himself would go on to provide legal defense for Black Panthers Huey Newton, Bobby Seale, and Eldridge Cleaver, among others.

At the time of the Wells case, convicts in the California prisons were far from the point of mounting any organized, unified challenge to their keepers. By the 1960's they would be. The earliest charge by a group of black convicts would strike at the heart of San Quentin's rehabilitative technology, in its departments of education and religion and its library. That it took this form should come as no surprise. Caryl Chessman had shown California prisoners that the way to power was through words, and he had single-handedly overcome the prison's rigid crackdown on his writing. Similarly, during the Cold War years of the 1950's American blacks in the civil rights movement outside the prisons had grown accustomed to having to fight for their basic rights of speech and assembly. In the 1950's fifteen states passed "antisubversion laws," which resulted in South Carolina declaring the National Association for the Advancement of Colored People (NAACP) a "subversive organization" and in Louisiana ordering the NAACP to halt all public meetings. Michigan made "writing or speaking subversive words" punishable by life in prison. Tennessee in 1951 called for the execution of anyone espousing Marxist ideas. Agitators for black civil rights, some of them avowed leftists such as Paul Robeson and W. E. B. Du Bois, suffered wide public censure. These skirmishes were waged in libraries and bookstores as often as in the courts. When the 82-year-old Du Bois was faced with a totally implausible indictment as an enemy agent in 1951 for his antiwar work, his writings on black sociology and history were purged from thousands of libraries and universities nationwide, even though no evidence was produced in the case, and the charges were finally dropped.[15] In the same spirit of persecution, the *Negro Digest* was widely banned as was the NAACP's publication *Crisis*. Little wonder, then, that blacks were among the first of San Quentin's convicts to pick up where Caryl Chessman had left off and mount a challenge to the prison's control of words and ideas.

Harlan Washington, a former San Quentin Black Muslim convict, explains how black convicts went about redefining themselves on the prison yard:

It's like antithesis. If you're in a society that teach you that God is white, then you come and teach that same individual that God is black. If you're in a society that teaches you that the good guys wear white hats and the bad guys wear black hats, a good lie's a white lie, a bad lie's a black lie, angel food cake is white, devil's food cake is chocolate, the white ball shoots off all the balls and the black 8-ball is shot off last, you move the white piece in chess first, black lie, blacklist, blackmail, Black Death, black market, all those negative connotations on black, so you have to go with the antithetical thing. Blacker the berry, sweeter the juice. In the beginning was darkness and then there came light. You develop a picture in a darkroom. All thoughts come from the darkness of the mind. In genetics, black is dominant, white is recessive. Antithesis.[16]

The black prisoner occupied a special place in Nation of Islam doctrine, and the teachings of Elijah Muhammad held a strong attraction for San Quentin's blacks. To Muhammad, wrote Malcolm X, "the black prisoner symbolized white society's crime of keeping black men oppressed and deprived and ignorant, and unable to get decent jobs, turning them into criminals."[17] Elijah Muhammad personally answered letters from inmates and sometimes even sent them small amounts of money. Muslim creed first emerged in the California prisons in the early 1950's as a militant defense strategy for blacks in an increasingly confrontational racial atmosphere. Recruits were trained in the martial arts and encouraged to use violence when necessary to defend individual and group religious rights. Washington recalls his first encounters with Islam:

I went to Pine Grove Camp [California Youth Authority] when I was eighteen. . . . That had to be '52, '53, thereabout. . . . And there was a big very black, dark-complected individual that called himself Abdullah. And he was a quiet individual and kind of stayed to himself. He never got loud, never showed any signs of emotions and whenever he would say somethin' it was always somethin' that would provoke thought. That was my first contact with someone of Islamic thought. And subsequently *my* Muslim name is Abdullah right now. Subsequently, I'm a big black bald-headed guy named Abdullah now. . . . Then I ran into another guy I knew. . . . He was at Preston School of Industry [California Youth Authority]. . . . And when I got out [he] was in the Nation of Islam, you know, standin' on the corners sellin papers, in '54, thereabout. But I still wasn't ready. . . .
Then one day I was down by the unemployment office, and I saw about five or six large lumberjack-type whites had this individual surrounded and they was takin' him to task about his belief about "We're white devils." And he would say, "Yeah," and he wouldn't back up on it. . . . I was impressed with his fearlessness. . . . Another time I was hangin' around on the corner of 85th and East 14th. . . . And this guy came down to sell some papers. . . . And one guy says, "Oh, man! Muhammad's pimpin' you! His mama got a pig farm." . . . He took his bow tie and stuck it in his pocket. Took his coat and folded it. Sat it on the car. . . . And the guy—this was a big, buffed

guy—he put up his hands like he was gonna box and the next thing you know he had kicked him upside the head, knocked him smooth out. Put his coat back on. Put his bow tie back on. And said, "Man, when he come to, tell him I didn't wanna do that. But Muhammad hasn't done anything to him. And don't mention pigs and Muslims in the same breath." And he got in his car and drove off. And I said, "Wow, that was hip." So that impressed me. . . .

One day I was shooting drugs—crystals, crank, amphetamines. I was over at my friend's house, and I had the needle in my arm, and I hadn't even injected, and I looked over and saw this book, *Message to the Black Man*, by Elijah Muhammad. When I saw this book, I pulled the outfit I had in my arm and sat it down and I said, "I'd like to read that." I read that book . . . and I went over to the temple . . . and I joined.[18]

As was true for this prisoner, conversion to the Nation of Islam often promised a solution for personal problems like drug addiction as well as an aggressive political practice. The Nation of Islam spread quickly throughout California prisons in the early 1960's. Eldridge Cleaver, a member of the San Quentin Muslim temple at the time, recalled that the Black Muslims soon reached a high level of organization at the prison:

Soledad, San Quentin, and Folsom were the prisons with the highest concentration of adherents to Islam. . . . Muslims in each prison had organized themselves into a Mosque, with a hierarchy patterned rigidly after the structure of the Mosques in the outside world. Each prison had its inmate minister, captain, and Fruit of Islam [the Muslim defense force]. . . . During the exercise periods, it was not a rare sight to see several Muslims walking around the yard, each with a potential convert to whom he would be explaining the *Message to the Black Man* as taught by Elijah Muhammad.[19]

Eventually, the aggressive proselytizing of San Quentin's Muslim mosque was to bring it into open confrontation with prison authorities, an ironic outcome because, at base, Islam was a spiritual discipline, not a political movement. The Black Muslim convicts' willingness to use violence for self-defense was moderated by the equally strong tenet of Islam that called for submission to civil authority. In fact, some California prison administrators believe this tenet might have kept San Quentin's Muslim prisoners apolitical had the prison not outlawed their meetings and adopted a policy of transferring or segregating Muslim recruits.[20] A white former San Quentin corrections officer remembers:

At that time our biggest problem with the Muslims was illegal meetings. They weren't a recognized religion within the prison system such as they are now. And of course any meetings where they would group together in an actual religious meeting you'd break up. We didn't let 'em group up over two or three in a group. They'd get 30 or 40 in a group. And so we would try to break 'em up. If they didn't want to break up, then we'd lock 'em all up. . . . Course, they had a lot of racial confrontations openly with the whites. . . . They were very Commie-oriented.[21]

To this guard's thinking, the prison's Muslims were less a legitimate religious sect than a subversive challenge to authority on the yard. Eventually, they would become both as the prison came down with an iron heel.

In March 1960 segregated dining ended at San Quentin, which was then 23 percent black.[22] Life at the prison was changing. The prison population was growing fast, changing demographically, and getting harder to control. Fights among inmates were on the rise. In August of the same year the prison's Adjustment Center (AC) was opened. Touted as a humane alternative to the dungeon of the past, where San Quentin's troublemakers had been warehoused, the AC promised to be the ultimate rehabilitative tool. In this special building, which had its own exercise yard, dining room, school, and work programs and cells for 101 men, incorrigible prisoners were to be assigned for three months to receive intensive daily psychiatric assistance and group therapy.[23] Five inmates were placed in the AC on its opening day. By March 1961 there were 85. Many AC cells were occupied by militant Black Muslims. According to Eldridge Cleaver:

In those days if you walked into any prison in the State of California and visited the unit set aside for solitary confinement, there was absolutely no doubt that you'd find ten or fifteen Black Muslims who were being "disciplined" for staunchly confronting prison officials with implacable demands that Muslims be allowed to practice their religion with the same freedom and privileges as the Catholics, Jews, and Protestants.[24]

As Muslim unity grew, the increasing power of black convicts on the yard threatened to reverse patterns of race domination in the inmate subculture; racial polarization intensified, and racially motivated disturbances increased. Numerous confrontations occurred during the forced breakup of Muslim meetings. In 1961 one inmate was killed and four wounded when guards moved in to break up a gathering.[25] Aside from sporadic clashes, however, the Black Muslims at San Quentin remained largely peaceful when they were transferred or segregated in the AC for their religious beliefs. In 1963, though, an incident in the Adjustment Center brought a rapid escalation of Muslim protest.

On February 25, 23 prisoners were on the AC yard. With them were two unarmed officers, one white, one black. Twenty feet overhead stood an armed gunrail officer. Suddenly fighting broke out on the yard below. White and black convicts split into two warring groups. Two more armed guards were called to the gunrail. Whistles blew, warning shots were fired, and the fighting subsided. Guards moved in to break it up. Then, according to prison sources, two black prisoners who had not previously been involved broke away from the guards, ran across the yard, and began punching and kicking white prisoners. Shots rang out, killing one of these men, Booker T. (X) Johnson, Muslim minister of the San Quentin mosque. James (X) Smith threw himself over the dead man and refused to surrender the body to authorities. For this, James X was later put in a "quiet cell" of the AC.[26]

At eight o'clock the next morning a group of 60 Muslims in the mainline gathered quietly outside the yard office, refusing to go to work. Associate Warden Nelson listened as they read a list, demanding the arrest of the gunrail officer who had killed Booker T. X, a conference with the Marin County district attorney, permission to forward a petition to President John F. Kennedy, a place to worship, and segregation of the Muslim prisoners from the rest of the prison population. Nelson hotly refused these demands, consenting only to let the Muslims speak to the district attorney. Labeling the gathering a "state of insurrection," he ordered the convicts back to work. Fifty-nine refused and were taken to isolation cells. Later the district attorney informed them that their grievances were out of his jurisdiction and he would not prosecute the gunrail officer for the death of their minister on the AC yard. The prison had ruled the death accidental, claiming that the shots had been intended as a warning. Booker T. X, the prison decided, had jumped or was pushed into the line of fire.[27] To San Quentin's Muslim prisoners this was a patent lie. The death of Booker T. X was a political assassination by a white racist administration bent on eliminating challenges to the race politics of the prison.

Realizing that further appeals to prison authorities would prove fruitless, San Quentin's Muslims turned to writ-writing to press their demand for recognition as a legitimate prison religion. Initially, this new strategy, too, seemed futile. In March 1963, federal district judge Stanley A. Weigel denied a writ brought by San Quentin and Folsom Muslims demanding freedom to practice their religion.[28] The level of outrage intensified. On August 4, 40 San Quentin Muslims gathered on the yard shouting protests against religious persecution. Ten were ordered into isolation in the AC by a disciplinary committee.[29] That same month, without legal help, the San Quentin Muslim mosque brought a $39 million lawsuit against the prison, complaining that its rigid rules denied them an approved place of worship and "qualified ministerial guidance," rights enjoyed by all other religious groups at the prison. Earlier in the year the California Supreme Court had ruled that the prison policy restricting the Muslims was justified because their creed stressed racial discrimination.[30] After long years of almost continual writ-filing, in 1970, federal judge Alfonso J. Zirpoli ruled that the Muslims were a legal religion in the California prisons. He also ordered San Quentin to allow members of the Nation of Islam to receive the Muslim newspaper *Muhammad Speaks*, to hire paid Muslim ministers, and to acquire copies of *The Holy Qu'ran* for the prison library.[31]

Possibly of even greater importance than these reforms, in the process of legal maneuvering accompanied by protests and yard demonstrations, San Quentin's Black Muslims in the early to mid-1960's had built the first popular radical convict political union in the California prisons. Although in numbers Muslim convicts never constituted more than a small minority of San Quentin's population, by 1967 the sect's membership at the prison had greatly increased and its political influence in the inmate subculture far exceeded its size. The Nation of Islam had unified the prison's black inmates, demonstrating that by acting in concert they could exert considerable pressure to change power relations within the prison.

A central battle in the Muslim struggle at the prison had been waged in the Education Building. The death of Booker T. X brought Eldridge Cleaver into the leadership of San Quentin's Muslim temple:

After the death of Brother Booker T. X, . . . who . . . had been my cell partner . . . , my leadership had been publicly endorsed by Elijah Muhammad's West Coast representative, Minister John Shabazz of Muhammad's Los Angeles Mosque. This was done because of the explosive conditions in San Quentin at the time. Muslim officials wanted to avert any Muslim-initiated violence. . . . I was instructed to impose iron discipline upon the San Quentin Mosque.[32]

Under Cleaver, San Quentin's Black Muslims moved to take control of their prison education and reading program. In 1966 Cleaver, a newly discovered rising star among radicals, wrote to his editor at

Ramparts of the Muslim struggle against reading and writing control in the San Quentin Education Department: "I am the historian of the [African Culture] class and do some lecturing. It helps me with my writing. When I got here this time, the Muslims controlled the class. There has been a struggle for control of the class."[33]

This cautious rise of convict resistance within San Quentin's education program was the result in part of the outgrown ideology of treatment. Increasingly in the early 1960's, outside experts were being invited to participate in convict reform programs at the prison, bringing inmates into daily contact with psychologists, sociologists, educators, university students, religious counselors, and community groups, many of whom were extremely sympathetic to the plight of the prisoners. New ideas flowed into the prison from the free world of the Bay Area, which was increasingly shaken by powerful winds of dissent. In visits from the Bay Area public the importation of banned reading material from the outside grew until it ultimately reached unstoppable proportions. This "free flow of ideas" from the streets, the unavoidable outcome of faith in increased community contact for inmates in an era of failed community moral consensus, sounded the first palpable death knell for rehabilitation inside the prison. First, the uncontrollable flood of illegal books undermined any last efforts of staff to modify behavior by controlling reading diet and writing production. Second, it hardened guard staff and administration in their resolve to oppose rehabilitative programs in general and convinced them to restore the prison regime to one of simple punitive custody. For radical prisoners, however, the flood of contraband reading was a welcome ideological tidal wave.

Some former Education Department staff characterize the San Quentin environment of the mid-1960's as relatively open and free when it came to reading privileges. Even in the Adjustment Center, where reading and writing were more strictly controlled than on the mainline, inmates used "fishlines," strings thrown across a tier into an opposite cell and then "reeled in," to pass reading materials.

San Quentin had contracted with the Marin County superintendent of schools in 1959 to have the county operate the prison's academic education department.[34] The academic education program used four instructors in the late 1950's and expanded to fifteen day and approximately twenty evening teachers by the late 1960's. San Quentin's school became widely renowned as a model prison education system. Roughly half of the prison's inmates were involved in the academic program at one time or another during their incarceration, attending day or evening classes at skill levels ranging from basic literacy training to elementary, secondary, and junior college–level courses taught by instructors from the College of Marin, the local community college. By 1970 the associate of arts degree was being awarded in seven fields. Advanced courses were available by correspondence from the University of California, Berkeley.

Despite the comprehensive scope of San Quentin's education program, it operated within rather strict guidelines. Instructors in the Education Department were expected to devote time to group counseling as well as to instruction. Classroom teachers submitted reading lists to the school principal, who turned the lists over to the associate warden for care and treatment for approval. Certain books were not permitted as course reading.[35] Course outlines were also to be filed in the office of the education administrator so the prison "would have an exact record of what they were supposed to be doing in there."[36] Like so many of the prison's treatment programs, the education system at San Quentin in the 1960's put the prisoner in an awkward position with the Adult Authority, which could show an uncommon interest in what he was thinking and reading and how that reflected his resistance or rehabilitation. William Malin, who taught at San Quentin from 1955 to 1969, recalls that teachers were urged to supply telling information for the cumulative inmate file:

We had to write a report on each student at the end of each semester, and they kept insisting that the kind of information they wanted is what we should put on this report. As the inmates referred to it, it was "finking" information. They wanted us to explain whether this guy was dependable, whether he was cooperative with the authorities or antiauthority and this kind of stuff. . . . They didn't ask what opinions he had expressed in themes, but that was implied. . . . We said, "No, this is not our job. Our job is teaching. I'm gonna tell you what kind of a student this man is, I'm gonna tell you how hard he worked, what kind of grades he got. I'll even show you his exam papers. But that is all."

This San Quentin instructor and many others like him resisted the prison administration's efforts to transform them into custody staff. Because the prison's academic classroom teachers were hired by Marin County, and strictly speaking were not prison employees, in the later 1960's many guards became suspicious that teachers were coming inside for the express purpose of trying to start trouble in the inmate population. As a consequence, classrooms were closely monitored.

According to former San Quentin education administrator Keith Hay-ball, "Supervisors visited classes on a regular, unannounced basis." Listening devices were never installed in classrooms, though it was widely rumored among instructors and inmates that they had been and that, in the Religion Department, the Catholic chapel confessional was "bugged." In fact, placing such a monitoring device in the chapel had been proposed, Keith Hayball remarks, but apparently was never done.

In 1963–64 the San Quentin Education Department began to offer a series of ethnic studies courses with titles such as "Minorities in the American Culture" and "Afro-American Culture." These courses immediately attracted large enrollments, a good portion of them Black Muslims. At the time, students in the Education Department were predominantly black, with lower enrollments of white and Hispanic students. With the advent of an ethnic studies program, which invited American Indians, Hindus, and blacks in to lecture, "comments came from line staff," William Malin recalls, and "this started creating comments and resistance within the administration." These programs gave San Quentin's Black Muslims hope for change. The Muslims, and Eldridge Cleaver in particular, moved swiftly to control the curriculum and choose guest speakers for the classes. As William Malin, designer of the prison's Afro-American studies course, remembers,

I had to confront [the Muslims] several times because I got a black studies course started there. They wanted to take over. It was going to be a Muslim studies course. Eldridge came down to me a couple times to talk about some of the stuff. They didn't like a couple of the men I brought in to teach. It was hard for a honkie like me to stand up and try to teach blacks about blackness. I never tried. I would lead discussions, I would assign readings, and we would discuss points of view.

San Quentin's classrooms were now under fire from both the guard staff and the Black Muslims. The Muslims' move to seize the prison's education agenda sometimes extended beyond the ethnic studies program. One former instructor recalls that, in his own struggle with Cleaver for control of an English classroom, "he and I fought for six weeks over who was going to teach the class."[37]

By the end of the decade the schism between teachers and guards at the prison had deepened and relations were acrimonious. Line officers accused some teachers of importing and distributing contraband reading material that advocated racial and political violence.

A number of former instructors later freely admitted to bringing in banned books, magazines, and newspapers but claimed it was done openly and the literature was not inflammatory. A handful of instructors, however, were clearly hostile to the prison. One former teacher, who prefers to remain anonymous, was regularly supplied by prisoners and some prison staff with "information" on the prison which he delivered to the press outside. This information included documents and blueprints of the prison's sewer tunnels.

San Quentin's officers overreacted at times to maintain prison security at the expense of academic freedom. Robert Minton, a young instructor from the College of Marin in the late 1960's who taught night classes at the prison, recalls that guards even searched his beard when he entered the prison. He was certain that his classroom was "bugged."[38] Guards and prison administrators openly repudiated the doctrines of rehabilitation and tightened controls on reading and writing when and where they could. At the same time, teachers and other treatment staff opened the prison to the radicalism brewing outside. San Quentin's policy on education became a mass of contradictions. While the warden's office and line staff were increasingly strict in their efforts to censor and control, treatment staff thoroughly subverted their efforts. And the teaching staff met a pitched battle with the Black Muslims for control of the curriculum. Bibliotherapy was at an end at San Quentin.

In Herman Spector's library, too, inmates' writing began to show signs of defiance. In 1963, when the aging librarian published ". . . Nor Iron Bars a Cage" in the *California Librarian*, a collection of prisoners' writings produced in the library following book discussions, the pieces indicated that some convicts were rejecting the penitent role the program was meant to impose in favor of a new self-definition. Spector intended ". . . Nor Iron Bars a Cage" to demonstrate the merits of bibliotherapy. Addressing the assigned topic "What My Library Means to Me," the selections were self-consciously composed, highly proper in diction and wary in tone, presumably because of the likelihood that the Adult Authority would read them. Convict D. J. Mack wrote of "becom[ing] a more cultivated member of the human race through a judicious selection of literature." Inmate John Russell Crooker said, "Through the . . . mercy of men and the help of psychiatric practitioners, I eventually was given a new lease on life and an opportunity for rehabilitation. With my interest in psychiatry thus stirred, I turned . . . to the library." This prisoner claimed he had found the library "a willing partner to those in search of an effective rehabilitation program." [39] But other prisoners had little praise for the bibliotherapy program. Instead, their words barely concealed a subversive motive for reading. Black convict B. L. Garrett, for example, at first hesitated to admit why he read: "Most of my reading is centered in history, political economy, philosophy, psychology, sociology, and trade unionism. I feel that it would be unwise to deal with the question of why I read, from a philosophical point of view." Despite this fear, he went on cautiously:

I think that it may help to explain that I do a great deal of reading because . . . by acquiring an understanding of the interconnections between the patterns of my life and the course of world history, and of my relationship to society, I am able to gauge, more accurately, the meaning of my own experiences in terms of the kind of person I am becoming. . . .

In one of my latest readings, *Africa, the Roots of Revolt*, I traveled, vicariously, amongst my own ancestors and gained a vivid . . . understanding of what is actually happening in the economic, social and political spheres of that ancient land. . . .

Other books have deepened my knowledge of the class structure of the society in which I live, the relationships of classes to each other, and the dominant values of society in general. These books included: *White Collar* and *Power Elite*, both by the late C. Wright Mills.

This prisoner had been inspired by readings on Third World revolutions and had begun a class analysis of American society. Exactly what he meant by the "person I am becoming" is well hidden, but the passage does not suggest a penitent, "reformed" ex-convict, the intended product of the treatment-era prison. [40]

Another young black convict in Herman Spector's bibliotherapy group, who was equally circumspect and similarly high-toned but tantalizingly suggestive in his written response, was San Quentin Black Muslim minister Leroy Eldridge Cleaver. Cleaver boldly titled his paean to Herman Spector's library "A Prison Cell Can't Contain Us," then left the rest to innuendo:

Whether we incline to the opinion that the individual is a "free agent" who paints himself into a corner, or a "victim," with "society" wielding the paint brush, the salient fact is that, as inmates, we emphatically are in corners. The point is to find our way out.

We do not want to suggest that one can read one's way out of prison, although the point, doubtless, could be argued. . . .

The man in the corner, unless he has hardened his heart and locked his mind, is seeking something new. . . .

If, awakening to ourselves, we can grasp the truth of the universality of humanity and learn to value no man less nor more than another, we will cease to sell or allow ourselves to be sold short, having grown so large that a painted corner, a prison cell, can't contain us.[41]

Looking back on Cleaver's career, it may seem that the "new ideas" this convict was searching for in his attempt to "read his way out of prison," the "awakening" he was seeking, were veiled references to his emerging notion of class revolution and the role ideology production was to play in it. Four years later, Eldridge Cleaver would smuggle out and publish a book with a different, angrier tone, his bestselling *Soul on Ice*. On leaving prison in 1966 he would launch himself headlong into the role of urban revolutionary, "movement" hero, Peace and Freedom party (PFP) presidential candidate, and Oakland editor of the *Black Panther* newspaper.

Accompanying this pattern of Black Muslim protest and subversion of prison education were signs early in the 1960's of a wider discontent among inmates. In October 1963, when roughly a third of Folsom prison's 2,321 convicts struck in opposition to the indeterminate sentence, pressing for higher pay in prison industries jobs, 50 San Quentin prisoners launched a sympathy strike. When a picket line appeared before the gate leading to San Quentin's prison industries shops, some 4,000 convicts refused to cross it, effectively shutting down production in the prison's textile mill and furniture shops. Authorities immediately sent workers back to their cells, while guards interviewed prisoners, trying to find out who had started the strike. But the strike's leaders had disappeared into the crowd. By the following day nearly 75 percent of San Quentin's work force was reported back on the job, though prison officials conceded that during the night inmates in the high-security B Section had burned their mattresses, thrown lighted newspapers into the corridor, and banged on cell bars, yelling and screaming.[42]

The response of San Quentin's administration and guard staff to the increasing inmate protests was, first, to identify leaders and isolate or transfer them to other prisons, and then to tighten restrictions on association and communication among prisoners, mail privileges, censorship, and access to law books. This was often a brutal process. By the following spring, tensions were still running high. In April 1964, Warden Nelson identified Hispanic convict Michael Renteria as "a troublemaker" and put him in solitary "because he was agitating other inmates to engage in a strike." Renteria later alleged in a writ of habeas corpus filed in Marin County Superior Court that officers pounded his head against the cell bars, threatened to slit his throat, ground his handcuffed wrists beneath their boot heels, and forced him into the darkened gas chamber briefly before taking him to solitary. The warden dismissed the allegations, saying the convict had a history of "magnifying grievances."[43]

But crackdowns by prison authorities could do little to stop the rising tide of inmate discontent. Following Caryl Chessman's example, huge numbers of prisoners sought relief from the courts. The number of habeas corpus petitions written by California state prisoners skyrocketed from 814 in 1957 to 4,845 in 1965.[44] At San Quentin alone in 1965 petitions were being filed at a rate of nearly 300 per month.[45] By 1966 the flood of writs had so clogged the courts that they could barely function. San Quentin authorities did not know how to respond to this explosion of Chessman-like inmate activism. California prisoners were emboldened in their protests by the weakening, during the treatment era, of the ideology of punishment. Even now, when guard staff cracked down, treatment staff loosened up. Nowhere is the equivocal use of punishment more evident than in the prison's response to the massive inmate writ-writing campaign of the 1960's.

In an effort to handle the huge volume of inmates' court petitions, the San Quentin administration was forced by its own conflicting policies to appear to be trying to speed up the writ-filing process. The prison established a small office on the second floor of the counseling center where three inmate typists transcribed writ-writers' words onto standard forms adopted by the courts. Notary services were provided, and copies of writs were run off on duplicating machines. According to prison officials, this close supervision was not intended to exert control over or to censor the petitioners. As Warden Lawrence E. Wilson told the press in 1966, "We do not impede the preparation of legal documents, nor do we alter or edit them."[46] Despite the disclaimer, however, the prison was quietly moving to silence the writ-writers. That same year the California Department of Corrections issued a directive to state prison libraries that severely restricted inmates' access to law books. The rule listed only twelve acceptable law books and ordered that all others "are to be removed and destroyed." Conspicuously absent from the approved list was Title 28 of the U.S. Code, which contained all the laws pertaining to habeas corpus in federal courts. The rule also prohibited inmates from owning their own law books or possessing copies of court decisions.* The new rule caused an uproar among San Quentin inmates, who immediately asked the federal court in San Francisco for an injunction against the prison system on the grounds that the rule would deprive them of due process of law.[47] But it would be a year before federal judge George B. Harris issued a restraining order prohibiting confiscation of personally owned law books.[48] For years afterward San Quentin's law collection remained seriously deficient.† Additional obstacles for writ-writers were Director's Rule D-2602, which forbade inmates from assisting or receiving assistance from other prisoners in the preparation of legal documents, and Director's Rule D-2601, which declared access to library law books a privilege "which may be withdrawn upon misuse."[49] Perhaps an even more powerful discouragement was the indeterminate sentencing law, which had generated fear among inmates that writ-writing would displease the Adult Authority and reduce their chances for parole. As one prisoner described the paradoxical position in which writ-writers found themselves: "If the prisoner does not write writs, he may never get out; if he does write writs, he may never receive parole."[50]

San Quentin's move to heighten restrictions on writ-writers at the same time its Education Department staff was doing just the opposite, relinquishing controls on reading and writing, offered more proof of a collapse of the prison's rehabilitative ideal. The result would be the demise of the treatment ethos. As if it feared a mob of Caryl Chessmans, the prison administration began retreating from the idea of rehabilitation and moved to quell unrest by tightening communication and other controls. Unofficially, perhaps also in Chessman's memory, its treatment staff subverted the effort.

The prison successfully defeated the writ-writing campaign. As many as 90 percent of the writs produced during this time were frivolous. Only 1 percent or fewer petitions were successful in the courts. Lacking a legal education or access to up-to-date case law, prisoners

---

*"Smashing Blow at Prison Lawyers," *San Francisco Chronicle*, Oct. 24, 1966. The items approved were the California Penal Code, the Welfare and Institutions Code, the Health and Safety Code, the California constitution, the Vehicle Code, a law dictionary, Witkin's *California Criminal Procedure*, the *California Weekly Law Digest*, the U.S. Constitution, California Rules of the Court, Rules of the U.S. Court of Appeals, and Rules of the U.S. Supreme Court.

†In 1968, according to inmate Charles Larsen, the San Quentin library had the "California Appellate Reports and the California Supreme Court Reports only to 1955; California Jurisprudence, McKinney's California Digest, and Corpus Juris had not been replaced by their respective second series; Shepards Citations terminated at 1954; and there were no United States Supreme Court Reports." See Larsen, p. 354.

had a difficult time knowing when or how to file legitimate petitions. But some of the writs found their mark. As San Quentin prisoner Charles Larsen points out, one writ-writer managed to sabotage the payroll of the entire Adult Authority and precipitate a constitutional crisis when he

noticed that Article X of the California Constitution of 1872 expressly provided that the Board of Prison Directors was to receive no salary for its services. He also found that . . . the dut[y] of the Board of Prison Directors . . .
to fix prison terms and to grant paroles . . . was [subsequently] transferred to
the Adult Authority. . . . The writer reasoned that the statute authorizing
salaries for members of the AA was in violation of Article X of the California
Constitution. . . . [Before the AA members could again be paid,] a proposition
[had] to be added to the state ballot to remove what was termed "obsolete
constitutional provisions," among them this one.[51]

The flood of protest writs was so great by 1967 that librarian Herman Spector complained that 90 percent of his seating space was being taken up by inmates doing legal work, and little bibliotherapy or group book discussion was possible. Spector had eight inmate help-ers by this time, one of whom worked exclusively on legal services. In an article for the *California Law Review*, the librarian wrote that al-though he encouraged those with legitimate complaints to present their cases for review, he felt that "some men intentionally flood the prison administration and courts with spurious claims."[52] Spector de-fended the prison's new restrictions on the library's law collections and the prohibition against private ownership of law books.

San Quentin's crackdown extended to creative writing as well. Herman Spector began actively discouraging the rapidly multiplying number of manuscript submissions to outside publishers. In 1967 prison authorities announced that the institution would start taking an agent's fee for handling manuscripts submitted to the outside. In the event of a sale, 25 percent of any profit was to be charged the convict "to defray handling costs," an action intended to decrease convict writers' chances of doing what Caryl Chessman had done, using book profits to pay for professional attorneys. Herman Spector was to serve as literary agent. In an interview with the press, the librarian stated what he deemed was "unmarketable," and therefore censored, convict writing:

plagiarized, libelous, lewd or pornographic material; criticism of any government official, the judiciary or a law enforcement agency; glorification of crime
or delinquent conduct; how-to-do-it crime stories; material offensive to any

race, nationality, religious faith, political party or other citizens group; reference to oneself as a convict.[53]

In addition to the formerly banned topics, San Quentin convicts were now forbidden to write about the prison environment, to criticize American society, or even to refer to themselves as prisoners. Prison writers were being cut off from their readership outside, which Chessman had proved was intensely interested in prison issues and willing to pay to hear from inmates.

Custody staff saw to it, as well, that a whole range of more traditional forms of communication control at the prison made it difficult for convicts to reach out to the free world. Until 1968, San Quentin inmates were strictly limited in their mail privileges to ten "authorized correspondents," and incoming inmates were required to sign a power of attorney form giving the prison permission to open all mail. A former guard recalls that "the mail used to be censored night shifts, incoming and outgoing mail, by officers that worked the cell block from 12 midnight. Along with their other duties they'd censor mail."[54] A San Quentin convict elaborates:

Any letter that is written is either dropped in an "outgoing" box that's in every unit or placed on the cell bars if it's written after your last access out of the cells. . . . From the mailbox they were read by a first-watch cop [on the 12 to 8 shift]. If it was just general, routine stuff it was sealed and put in the outgoing stack. If there was some question . . . [it was taken to] the mail room staff. They have a sergeant and two or three personnel working there. They read incoming and outgoing mail.[55]

San Quentin officials in the 1950's and 1960's regularly denied to the public and the press that inmates' mail was being censored in this fashion, especially letters to attorneys and government officials. In 1961, however, a guard admitted to reporters that "all those letters are censored, even those to attorneys, and any complaints about food or conditions or parole reports are deleted."[56] Incoming and outgoing letters were regularly returned to the sender stamped "Refused by the Censor."

Prisoners in the 1960's could maintain limited contact with the free world by listening to two local radio stations, which were monitored by prison authorities, then piped to their cell headsets. Television, too, was available evenings and weekends in the East Block and North Block, the honor and semihonor blocks.[57] With some exceptions, newspapers and magazines were freely available for purchase at the prison canteen, provided the convict had money. *The San Quen-*

tin News, the official inmate newspaper, was severely handicapped as a source of news about events either inside or outside the prison because it was tightly controlled by the warden's office and could not be "used to attack any law, rule, or policy to which inmates may object [or] take an editorial position on matters pending before the legislature."[58] The occasional visit of a family member, however, could help keep a prisoner abreast of events on the streets.

Communication control at San Quentin in the 1960's was alternately tight and loose and full of contradictions. At times and in some ways it could be very restrictive, serving to isolate prison writers so thoroughly from the outside world that their secret writings, sometimes fanatically radical, took on an air of dangerous political fantasy. At other times, restrictions became so loose that they were almost nonexistent. It would soon become obvious that rigid communication control could no longer easily be maintained at the prison. By the early 1970's, convicts were permitted to purchase televisions for their cells and make telephone calls out on banks of newly installed phones, which created the potential for an uncontrollable, free exchange of ideas between the public and those inside. Attempts to cut mainline convicts off from the outside became much more difficult. A U.S. Department of Health, Education and Welfare report on prison censorship noted in 1974 that "in the 1960's a California institution carefully deleted news of the Watts riots from daily newspapers until it was realized that the same coverage came in by way of T.V. each evening."[59] In 1973 the California Library Association predicted the demise of all prison censorship:

Penologically . . . the institution, through no fault of its own, is losing its authority, or its right, to control what an inmate does, with whom an inmate may talk and what an inmate may express to the outside. The question of censorship of outgoing mail becomes somewhat academic, for example, when one observes that almost all of the institutions now have public telephones which inmates may use to make outgoing collect long distance calls. Thus, there is no longer any control over what an inmate tells a person on the outside nor to whom he tells it.[60]

Censoring and controlling prisoners had indeed become much more difficult in the electronic age, though the Library Association was certainly overstating the physical difficulties. Inmates could still be thrown into isolation cells without free communication or assembly privileges, and the entire inmate population could be locked down, their televisions disconnected, and their outside contacts cut off.

Aerial view of San Quentin Prison. (*Marin Independent Journal*)

Prior to San Quentin's "treatment" era, inmates could be subject to a wide range of physical tortures, including solitary confinement in total darkness on bread and water or gruel in the dungeon cells shown here. Warden Clinton Duffy abolished the dungeon in 1940 and converted the cells into storage space. In 1960 the prison's new Adjustment Center reinstated the tradition of the dungeon by resuming many of its functions. (Marin County Historical Society)

In the 1940's San Quentin adopted the tenets of behavior modification. The prison library, a crucial center of inmate therapy run by the zealous bibliotherapist Herman Spector from 1947 to 1968, sought to bring the magical rehabilitative power of books to the cure of criminal deviancy. Here an inmate's mental hygiene could be closely scrutinized. In this advertisement in a library journal, Spector outlined the broad range of therapies he offered his prison readers.

Caryl Chessman, the King of Death Row, 1959. Charged with being Los Angeles's Red Light Bandit, Chessman was convicted of 17 counts of robbery, sex perversion, and attempted rape. He was sentenced to die in San Quentin's gas chamber. (Photo © Joe Munroe)

Chessman was the first inmate to subvert San Quentin's bibliotherapy strategies to his own purpose. In his years on Death Row he taught himself law, setting up an office in a cell next to his own. Chessman successfully obtained eight stays of execution while 94 other prisoners went to the gas chamber. With the profits from three best-selling books that convinced the public he had rehabilitated himself, he was able to hire a team of attorneys. (Photo © Joe Munroe)

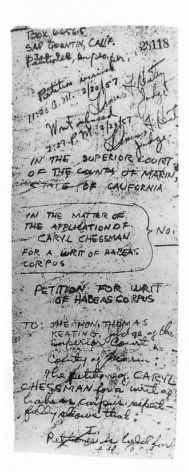

San Quentin belatedly tried to prevent Chessman from writing. In February 1957, after a search of his cell, the prison impounded his typewriter, books, and papers, including his legal notes and the manuscript of his third book. With only the clothes on his back, he was sent to a bare solitary cell for 28 days. Still, Chessman managed to smuggle out this writ of habeas corpus scrawled on toilet paper. In March a contraband copy of the book manuscript was hand delivered to Chessman's New York publisher. It quickly appeared as *The Face of Justice*. (Marin County Clerk's Office)

Chessman's writings resulted in a worldwide movement to rescue him from the gas chamber. Here Governor Edmund G. Brown contemplates a mound of save-Chessman mail. (Photo © Joe Munroe)

A lone picketer stalks the capitol. In May 1960, 12 years after his conviction, a fifteenth appeal to the U.S. Supreme Court was turned down and Caryl Chessman was executed. (Photo © Joe Munroe)

Minister of San Quentin's Muslim mosque from 1963 to 1966 and a participant in Herman Spector's bibliotherapy programs, Leroy Eldridge Cleaver launched the move toward inmate control of the San Quentin Education Department curriculum. Cleaver smuggled out the manuscript of the angry, bestselling *Soul On Ice*, whose publication drew thousands of readers to the cult of the outlaw and raised the author to the status of urban revolutionary, movement hero, Peace and Freedom party presidential candidate, and minister of information of the Black Panther Party. This photo was taken in 1968. (Photo © Ruth-Marion Baruch)

After the imprisonment of Black Panther leader Huey P. Newton (*left*) on a manslaughter conviction stemming from a 1967 shootout with Oakland police, Bay Area radicals began to apply the term "political prisoner" freely to all California inmates and to celebrate the imprisoned as cult heroes. *Below*, Panthers appear in force on the steps of the Alameda County Courthouse on July 16, 1968, for the opening day of Huey Newton's trial. Five thousand demonstrators surrounded the courthouse, filling the air with cries of "Free Huey!" (Newton photo © Ruth-Marion Baruch; Panthers photo by Ron Riesterer, *Oakland Tribune*)

Despite the fact that drug offenders and anti–Vietnam War
pacifists and other political prisoners formed only a small
fraction of California's prison
population, the white Bay Area
counterculture of the late 1960's
insisted on seeing itself in the
prisoners rather than allowing
the convicts their own identity.
In a November 1967 *Berkeley Barb*
political cartoon, prisoners are
cast as political dissidents. (© 1975
Ron Cobb. All Rights Reserved. *The Cobb
Book*.)

Ultimately, Bay Area radicals mistook all California prisoners for political captives of the state, calling for their unconditional release. In a typical demonstration in August 1970, protestors marched at the San Francisco Civic Center
and Hall of Justice in a rally for the Soledad Brothers and Los Siete de la Raza,
who had been accused of killing a San Francisco policeman in May 1969. (Photo
by Yohannes Besserat, *Berkeley Barb*, Aug. 21–27, 1970)

Bay Area radicals clamored for their own outlaw status, quickly losing sight of who the real California prisoners were. "We are outlaws!" proclaimed this manifesto of the Berkeley radical group Up Against the Wall Motherfuckers. (*Berkeley Barb*, Oct. 11–18, 1968)

What the Library Association was succinctly pointing out was that the prison had lost the moral authority to do so. As it entered the 1970's the California prison, still officially committed to the treatment rhetoric, had lost the moral authority with the California public to maintain strict control over inmates' communication.

Largely unsuspected by either the public or the Library Association, however, was that the slow process of repudiating this treatment ideology had been under way for quite some time. Actually, prison authorities favored a return to Draconian control. Officials and guard staff were fed up with permissiveness and yearned for the days of pure punitive custody; treatment staff had become jaded in their reformative zeal, disappointed by years of having their efforts both frustrated by the prison administration and spurned by the inmates; and the convicts had concluded that teachers, counselors, priests, and librarians were custody staff just as surely as the gunrail officer was.

Herman Spector retired suddenly in 1967 after a heart attack. He had become an anachronism at the prison, having outlived the system's faith in bibliotherapy. Even he had stopped believing. The previous year a young man had been hired to help him in the library. Fred Persily remembers the librarian in his last days as "a rule-crazy, ornery sucker. Everybody hated Spector." The books in the library were being stolen at record rates. The aging librarian responded with iron discipline. He strictly limited inmates to only one library visit per week, and he orchestrated prisonwide searches for stolen library books. He posted rules requiring that prisoners have their shirts buttoned at all times while in the library, even in the hottest weather. And he moved a "special collection" of books into a locked back room of the library. "He let several special cons back there," Persily recalls, presumably hoping to reach a few last souls through books in this inner sanctum, but at the end of his career the librarian "felt there were very few worth saving."[61] Terry Cuddy, a San Quentin prisoner from 1964 to 1966 and again from 1968 to 1969, portrays Spector as an embittered apostate:

Herman Spector was an anal-retentive, miserly, mean-spirited old man. He made every effort to prevent people from using that library. It was a fucking shame. All the time I was at San Quentin I only had one "beef" [disciplinary report]. And that was for too many library books. Guys would steal books from the library rather than just check 'em out. They'd just stick 'em under their coats and walk out. Then when they got through with 'em in their cells, they'd just throw 'em off the tier. And then the guys who were assigned to sweep up the first tier would pick up the library books. And at the end of the tier was a set of bars—it was like a branch library. You saw something there, you picked it up and read it. . . . [Spector] sent officers to my cell specifically to search for books. And they found ten books. And they only allowed five. He called me in and asked me what I was doing with 'em. I said I was readin' 'em! Because, Jesus Christ, that's how I did my time. And I was kissin' his ass because if he beefed me—and he did beef me and I got kicked out of the honor unit.[62]

After Herman Spector's retirement in 1967 the library program changed dramatically. At base, the changes were not so much caused by the departure of the bibliotherapist as by the gradual shift away from treatment throughout the California prisons. Still, custody staff saw the library as a particular source of trouble at the institution. Treatment-era bibliotherapy and the free reading and writing policies accompanying it had produced an ungovernable monster in the opinion of the prison administration. In replacing Spector the prison saw a chance to retreat one step back from treatment and to regain control of the library. Soon James McHenry, a correctional officer without library training (he began but did not complete a correspondence course in librarianship from the University of Utah), was installed as chief librarian, becoming the only nonlibrarian operating a prison library in the California state prison system. McHenry had left the ministry after thirteen years to become a guard at San Quentin and had served two years at various guard assignments before being assigned to the library. Officer McHenry remarks that "a lot of administrators . . . considered the library a problem. . . . Things were going on there."[63] At least part of the issue was the uncontrollable nature of the library room. As former sergeant William Hankins observes, "With all the books on the shelves, you got natural places to stash stuff for somebody else to pick up." Placing a guard in the librarian's job would put inmate library users on notice not to break prison rules there. But correctional officer McHenry did far more than beef up security in the library. By 1968 the Reader's Advisory Service had been discontinued. The new librarian also refused to read and censor inmates' writing, a job taken over by the associate warden for care and treatment. Great Books discussions continued under another staff person, but for the most part bibliotherapy in San Quentin's library had come to an end. Instead, after Spector's various reading and writing programs had been swept aside, James McHenry limited his time to helping inmates use the library's mandated law collection of twelve volumes. By 1972, after numerous court decisions and new legislation regarding law materials forced the prison greatly to expand its law collection, he would be put in charge of the legal section only. Another librarian, Patricia Caldwell, would be hired to oversee the library's 35,000-volume nonlaw collection. At that time the two collections were split and moved to three separate Quonset huts on the upper yard, during which process many books were lost or destroyed. Herman Spector's library today holds a vastly reduced number of volumes.

Although he transformed the library and terminated its bibliotherapy work, and under his direction and that of Caldwell the library was mysteriously stripped of many of its books, McHenry did not see his job as simply cracking down on convicts' reading. Quite the opposite actually happened. Responding to the inmate population's ever-increasing demands for law-related reading and advice, James McHenry would eventually become the first California prison librarian to invite outside attorneys in to give law seminars for the inmates. The warden's office was not pleased:

I wasn't looked upon too well for that [by prison administrators] because they said, "Why do you want to help them?" I said, "They're entitled to the law. They are harpin' about due process and about legal systems. I want to show them that we are allowing them everything that they're entitled to. Not that I would agree with it. But it's the law. Let's abide by it."

On January 12–16, 1967, a massive prison disturbance brought the simmering situation in the institution to a boil. The Black Muslim challenge to reverse race domination on the yard moved angrily from San Quentin's classrooms and its library out into the open. When a white guard challenged the right of black inmate kitchen worker Melvyn Ayers to have a cup of milk and put his fingers into the cup on Ayers's tray, the convict protested loudly and was sent to isolation. Customarily, convicts were permitted milk only when it was issued to all the prisoners or for medical reasons. This guard's behavior was interpreted by black inmates as an act of racial prejudice. The next day resentment of the guard was so intense among the rest of the convict kitchen crew that the prison dismissed twelve more kitchen workers (nine black and three white) from their jobs. On January 14, 31 "Chow Hall" employees walked out in protest and were quickly locked up. Another day passed. Then a group of black prisoners, led by the militant Muslims, called a strike of black workers for the following day, Monday, over the kitchen incident. The plan was to demand better jobs and job training for black inmates while protesting this particular incident.

Monday morning, January 16, the San Quentin yard was blan-
keted in icy, thick fog. Most inmates stayed in their cells. Approximately 1,200 black prisoners refused to report for work. Hidden from
the gunrail in the fog, militant black strikers warned off those few
who dared try to enter the gateway to prison industries. Three black
inmates were attacked and beaten up. Also concealed by the fog on
the lower yard that morning was the body of white inmate William E.
Walker, who had been beaten and knifed to death.

By Wednesday the strike was subsiding, but news of the stabbing
death had polarized the inmate population on racial lines. Inexpli-
cably, no prisonwide lockdown was declared, although lockdowns
were customary after strikes. After lunch, as 3,000 inmates waited in
the upper yard to return to work, racial groups slowly formed. Striking blacks were joined on the north end of the yard by other black
prisoners fearing retaliation for the death of a white man. Curses and
racial epithets began to fly from one group to another.

Whites clustered in loose, unorganized groups opposite the blacks,
against the south mess hall. Hispanic inmates collected in the west
end of the yard. Prisoners everywhere began tearing pipes off the
yard wall and breaking up benches, picnic tables, and a small guard
shack for weapons. Knives and kitchen trays were passed to white
inmates through the smashed windows of the mess hall.

The three armies, approximately 1,400 whites, 1,000 blacks, and
an unknown number of Hispanics, stood glaring at each other 50
yards apart. Then, when the back-to-work whistle blew, several
groups of whites joined the Hispanics on the west wall. The blacks
moved en masse to the east wall. A three-hour standoff followed.

According to Warden Lawrence Wilson, San Quentin guards then
threw a "wall of fire" down between the two groups with bird shot,
submachine-gun fire, rifle bullets, and tear gas: "We fired a lot of
rounds of ammunition describing the limits for people."[64] Slugs
pounded into the pavement and into the mess hall walls above prisoners' heads. A huge cloud of smoke engulfed the yard. Protected by
smoke from the gunrail, the prisoners saw their chance. Fighting
broke out at various places. Eight convicts were hit by bullets and had
to be hospitalized. Five more suffered head wounds from other weapons. One inmate had a heart attack.

Captain of the guard Calvin McEndree then decided to try to
move the white prisoners to the football field of the lower yard. The
black group was marched to the East Block, then more shots were

fired as the white and Hispanic prisoners ran a gauntlet toward the lower yard. After dark, as the winter temperatures dipped into the forties, these prisoners broke apart the bleachers and built bonfires to keep warm. Late in the night the prisoners were stripped naked, searched, and then led to their cells in small groups. At 4:05 A.M. the yard was declared secure.

But things did not quiet down. That evening blacks in the East Block set small fires and flung buckets and other objects off the cell tiers. Fires were reported in the South Block as well. The next day, January 17, the prisoners emerged onto the yard better armed and ready for combat. An estimated 300 blacks faced 500 whites and Hispanics. A race riot seemed inevitable until a barrage of gunfire separated the groups once again. Prisoners were ordered to disrobe and be strip-searched. This shakedown turned up 1,500 pounds of weapons. Eventually San Quentin's entire prison population was locked in its cells.

Several days later, Associate Warden James Park gave the press the administration's version of the event. The Black Muslims and the prison's Nazis had been behind the disturbance. The Muslims, Park said, had recently been performing close-order military drills on the yard. In response, San Quentin's Nazis were turning out German iron crosses and probably weapons in the machine shop. The *San Francisco Chronicle* quoted an interview with one of the prison's Nazis. "Although authorities have banned Adolf Hitler's autobiography *Mein Kampf* from the San Quentin library," the inmate said, "the book has found its way into many of the Nazis' prison cells. They also have literature about George Lincoln Rockwell and have made many secret attempts to contact the Rockwell forces."[65] In a letter to San Quentin teacher Robert Minton, one of the prison's black inmates agreed that the Black Muslims and white neo-Nazi gangs had provided fuel for the disturbance:

About fifteen years ago the Blacks began to come together as a result of the teachings of Elijah Muhammed, the leader of the Lost-Found Nation of Islam in the United States. The emergence of Malcolm X gave the Blacks a leader and they began to rally to that call. His teachings of Black Supremacy fell upon fertile soil in the minds of the semi-literate Blacks who had known nothing but deprivation and degradation in America and gave their starving egos long awaited nourishment. This new breed of Blacks caused consternation to the white bullies who had for years controlled the prisons. No longer did Blacks skulk about in fear. The Black Militant had arrived in the California prison system. Each step was noted by the whites, each concession won from prison administrators was a victory over the whites who saw their stature begin to diminish. No longer could a group of whites attack a black without fear of retaliation. The token integration of the prisons met with resistance and the resistance began to organize. Norman Lincoln Rockwell [sic] gave the white malcontents a leader. The Bluebirds [a neo-Nazi gang] appeared on the scene. Mein Kampf and The Rise and Fall of the Third Reich became sought after. Racial skirmishes became the order of the day and led to the confrontation between the Bluebirds and the Muslims at San Quentin around 1965. Other confrontations had taken place, especially at Soledad and D.V.I. [Deuel Vocational Institute]. After this major confrontation at San Quentin, the activists, who comprise probably 20% of the population were transferred to other institutions, Adjustment Centers and Segregation Units. It required about two years for many of these malcontents to wend their way back to San Quentin. There they joined the swelling army of newcomers from D.V.I. and Soledad as well as the rejects from the other prisons in this obselete warehouse for the rejected rejects. Rejected by society, rejected by the more "civilized" prisons and prisoners, and rejected by San Quentin, they fell upon one another in the "Riot of 67." This situation was terminated by a truce which boded little good for the future. Any assault by a white on a black was to be followed by reprisal. Any white would do for a victim. The converse was also true, and thus were the seeds of endless bloodshed sown.[66]

The "Riot of '67" set the pattern of racial-political violence in the prison for a decade. No longer would a black inmate like Bob Wells be abandoned by other black convicts to be persecuted in isolation. San Quentin's Black Muslims especially were ready to rush to the aid of their brothers, against other inmates or the prison authorities themselves. What followed was a long period of brutal race retaliation on the yard. But the responses of prisoners and staff to the 1967 disturbance soon highlighted other issues than racial ones.

First, the incident confirmed the suspicions of many prisoners that the real goal of San Quentin's treatment staff, including its counselors, educators, and librarians was to perfect the custody of inmates rather than to help them. During the riot some treatment staff "took up rifles, billy clubs, and other weapons to help put down the prisoners."[67] Keith Hayball, education administrator, casts light on this point: "During the time of an emergency, everyone in that prison is under the direct control of the warden and his field commander. And [sometimes] that requires—and I've done this myself—cell searches, strip searches or anything in the world." During the riot, prison authorities demanded that treatment staff act in custody roles, and at least some teachers, counselors, and librarians complied. The reaction of inmates was predictable. A University of California anthropology student who was interviewing inmates during that period noted that one prisoner commented, "We thought so before, but now there's no question about what side the counselors are on. They're just bulls too."[68] The 1967 incident eradicated any trust inmates still had in rehabilitation programs. This feeling was not unique to San Quentin. Across the nation prisoners were criticizing the treatment-era prison. A report to the National Commission on the Causes and Prevention of Violence observed that, nationwide, "of the more than 121,000 people employed in corrections in 1965, only 24,000, or 20% of the staff, had had any connection with rehabilitation."[69] The report noted that the ratio of inmates to prison psychiatrists was 1 to 1,140, to psychologists 1 to 803, to counselors 1 to 758. There were 295 prisoners for every prison social worker and 104 for every academic prison teacher. These were impossibly large caseloads for any treatment strategy to be successful. Consequently, the sincerity of the very motives of the treatment-era prison was being openly called into question by inmates everywhere. At San Quentin, many prisoners felt they had divined sinister intentions behind the treatment machinations of prison staff. This would soon lead to a proliferation of secret inmate study groups intended finally and definitively to subvert San Quentin's official education system.

What is more, the disturbance set inmate leaders of Chicano, white, and black groups to thinking of grievances that transcended race issues. Eventually, this process would elicit plans for unified protests. John Irwin, former Soledad inmate, sociologist, and early board member of the Prisoners' Union, who was conducting a discussion group at San Quentin at the time, discusses this point:

Soon as I got back in and met with my group I got their version of what happened. These were mostly whites, a couple of Chicanos, and one black. As the weeks went on they started redefining it, saying, "No, it wasn't race. The administration turned it into race." They were becoming more politically conscious, and they started reviewing history a little bit. So then a couple guys in the group started going around and helping organize for a strike. . . . They started getting interested in pulling off a strike for the next year.[70]

In the mid-1960's at San Quentin the treatment era ended in riots and Draconian prison crackdowns subverted by permissiveness on the part of treatment staff. By the end of the decade the prison's feted Adjustment Center, that quiet oasis where it was promised the most difficult prisoners would get intensive psychiatric counseling, had been transformed from a symbol of reform-age progress into a cruel new dungeon filled with radical Muslims and other political "troublemakers." In this prison-within-a-prison inmates received far fewer treatment programs, not more. The AC came to represent the failure of treatment, not its glorious future. Prisoners kept there were the discarded refuse of the inmate population, the growing heap of convicts that could not be "saved." Such was the final harvest of rehabilitation.

The treatment philosophy was doomed from the outset. It was inevitable that by reading and writing San Quentin's prisoners would learn their own history, including the tradition of race and class domination in American culture. And it was futile to deny them their rage over this knowledge. Convicts ultimately demanded reform, both on the yard and on the streets outside. San Quentin did not try to fulfill that demand. No prison could rectify the wrongs of the society which had produced it. Instead, it turned on its prisoners and crushed some of the best inmate products of the treatment era. Outside the prison, meanwhile, a growing New Left in the Bay Area was about to assail the institution as an emblem of a failed society. Connections between prisoners and this outside Left would create a volatile situation.

5

Eldridge Cleaver and the Celebration of Crime

I n 1967–68 San Quentin would be a prison besieged from within and without. Just outside, San Francisco and Berkeley had become counterculture meccas of the nation. The Haight "hippie" district (the term "hippie" was coined by San Francisco's *Ramparts* magazine in 1967) was at its zenith, and across the bay in Berkeley an angry antiwar coalition of students and cultural radicals eagerly engaged in massive street demonstrations. Swelling their ranks, the "'67 Summer of Love" had drawn counterculture enthusiasts from every state. Against this backdrop the recently paroled Eldridge Cleaver would emerge as a best-selling author and angry culture critic, writing for sympathetic New Left radicals as well as the wider mass audience for prison books already established by Caryl Chessman. With others, this former Black Muslim minister would succeed in bringing much of that public into loud protests at San Quentin's gate. In large part because of the charismatic leadership of Eldridge Cleaver, sizable portions of the California Left began to see prison issues as central in their fight against the state. A smaller group on the Left became obsessed with the prison's place in the struggle.

San Quentin was at the very heart of the maelstrom. Several of its convict writers won an avid readership in the Bay Area. The two groups, readers outside and convict writers inside, began to feed off each other. The product was a tremendous coming together of convict energy and public support. Inside, California inmates began to organize to seek long-needed reforms in the prisons. In 1967–68 the *Outlaw*, San Quentin's underground inmate newspaper, worked to organize inmates around common grievances, calling repeatedly for racial unity among prisoners and acting as the primary catalyst for two massive inmate strikes. Convict writing of this period increasingly applied class analysis to the prison and to California criminal justice and society. But there was also a downside to this activity. Outside the prison, some in the largely white middle-class Left found in San Quentin convict writings a street-tough new image of the male revolutionary. The defiant convict hero provided a new male gender model for the revolution, giving male violence a positive political value. In the end, this was to have fatal consequences when it linked the emerging prisoner rights movement with the most infantile and romantic elements of the New Left. These three processes proceeded at once: inmates organized to press for real, needed reforms; class analysis was applied to California prisons and society; and the Left used prison writing to fantasize a dangerously violent convict role model for revolutionary males. At the center of the relationship of the convict and the California Left was a literary trope, a transformed figure of the outlaw shared by convict writers and the Left and passed back and forth between them in such diverse cultural products as the work of prison writers, the popular image in the Bay Area of the Hell's Angels, the theater of the Haight-Ashbury, and the lyrics of California 1960's rock music. Notably absent in the new breed of convict writing was the penitent, confessional tone of traditional prison literature, or even Chessman's theme of "outlaw-gone-good." A revision of the notion of the male outlaw featured prominently in the works of Eldridge Cleaver, as he raised the call for full-scale American revolution and fed the Left a supermasculine psychosexual politics.

Rather than using the rhetoric of convict rehabilitation against itself as Caryl Chessman had, Eldridge Cleaver took the next step. As a Black Muslim he had rejected the treatment model's ideology of pathological and behavioral disorder as the cause of his crime. Instead, Cleaver opened new political vistas for convicts by replacing this rehabilitative ideology with one of "collective oppression."[1] For San Quentin writers, Cleaver's best-selling *Soul on Ice* and his many articles in the *Black Panther* newspaper and *Ramparts* marked the emergence of a genre of prison writing unabashedly celebratory of crime, bringing popular calls for the immediate release of all prisoners. Drawing on Marxist elements in the last speeches of Malcolm X, Cleaver popularized class analysis among California convict writers. Among black San Quentin prisoners Cleaver would promote a new image of the inmate as "lumpen," his adopted term for the underclass, including prisoners, who, he predicted, would initiate a people's revolution in the United States.

Eldridge Cleaver first encountered the California penal system at age twelve, when in 1947 he was arrested for burglary and vandalism in Los Angeles. Between 1949 and 1953 he spent time at both the California Youth Authority's Nelles School for Boys and the Preston School of Industry. In 1954 Cleaver was convicted for possession of a large quantity of marijuana and sent to Soledad state prison for two and a half years. In 1957, after eleven months of freedom, he was charged with assault to commit rape and assault to commit murder, was convicted, and was sent to San Quentin in 1958. Harlan Washington, a Black Muslim and San Quentin inmate of the 1950's, has an early recollection of the prisoner:

I knew Leroy Eldridge Cleaver in the California Youth Authority. We did some time at Whittier together. . . . He was a Muslim minister at Folsom, he was a Muslim at San Quentin, and him and Huey and Bobby Seale [Huey Newton and Bobby Seale, founders of the Black Panther party] and all of them individuals used to come to Temple No. 26 [a Black Muslim temple in Oakland] before they formed the Panther organization. I used to be standin' right in front of 'em when they sat in the front rows and stuff and listen to what Minister Henry Majied would teach. And what they were doin' was their ten-point program was virtually the same program of the Muslims at that time.[2]

At San Quentin Cleaver wrote about Muslim philosophy for the prison newspaper and secretly mimeographed articles on the Nation of Islam on machines in the prison hospital. He notes that to do this he had to overcome the prison's censorship rules:

One strategy for Elijah was to take out paid advertisements in the Los Angeles Herald Dispatch, setting forth his principles and editorializing on the oppressive white devil. His column was clipped and passed along to me, and I would cut the stencil for a newsletter widely circulated behind bars. While the column was banned inside, it never failed to circulate a day after it appeared in the Herald.[3]

Cleaver took over the leadership of the radical faction of the prison's Muslims after the death of Booker T. X, but beginning in 1963 he and many other San Quentin blacks left the Nation of Islam. That year an incident in Los Angeles highlighted a growing dissatisfaction among inmates of the faith. Black Muslim prisoners had long wondered at the reluctance of their temple officials outside the prisons to provide them with legal assistance. Forced to act without attorneys, at times humiliated by having no other choice than to accept help from the predominantly white American Civil Liberties Union, Muslim prisoners had nonetheless been bringing constitutional cases to establish their religious rights. This seemed like a heavy burden to bear alone. When a police raid on Los Angeles Mosque No. 27 left one Muslim dead and others wounded, several members of the sect were charged with assault on a police officer. The Muslim defendants lost their case, and four were sent to state prison, where they were greeted as heroes by black inmates. But as Cleaver later noted, this incident "became something of a scandal when the officials of the Nation outside failed to come to their heroes' aid with any legal support." Cleaver wrote, "What black inmates now look to with rising hopes is the cry for Black Power."[4]

At San Quentin, at Folsom, where he was transferred in 1963 for being an agitator, and again at Soledad, from which he was paroled in 1966, Cleaver helped to organize classes in Afro-American history and culture. As a Muslim minister he fought with Herman Spector for special library privileges and struggled for the power to control curriculum and choose guest speakers. But as the 1960's progressed, the teachings San Quentin black prisoners wanted were less and less Muslim, except for the late speeches of Malcolm X. By 1967 a popularly smuggled San Quentin text was George Breitman's *Last Year of Malcolm X: The Evolution of a Revolutionary*. The Breitman book argued that crucial last events had been unavoidably left out of Alex Haley's *Autobiography of Malcolm X*, specifically the ideological conclusions the slain Muslim radical was purportedly coming to on the very eve of his assassination. According to Breitman, after Malcolm X's trips to Mecca and places of colonial revolution throughout Asia and Africa, despite his talk of brotherhood and religious tolerance, Malcolm X was discarding religious language for a much more militant tone. In a March 1964 speech Malcolm X had told his audience, "There can be no revolution without bloodshed, and it is nonsense to describe the civil rights movement in America as a revolution."[5] That same month at a press conference he had refused to rule out the possibility of accepting communist support. Breitman traced the slow evolution of what he saw as the fallen leader's emerging socialist radicalism, from his Harlem days during World War II when he first encountered canvassers for the Communist party's *Daily Worker*, to his time as a Detroit autoworker during the McCarthy-era repression, to his eventual custom of buying the *Militant*, the paper of the Socialist Workers party, outside temple meetings. In his last year, after his conversion at Mecca, at a time when some of his followers disparaged him for his apparent moderation, Breitman had seen quite a different leader emerging. "On both of his trips," Breitman pointed out, "Malcolm X spent most of his time not in Mecca and among Muslim religious leaders but in the newly-independent African countries and among people with whom he could discuss politics."[6] The Malcolm X portrayed by Breitman was an emerging socialist revolutionary, only coincidentally a religious leader. By May 1965, after Malcolm X's second African trip, when he addressed the Militant Labor Forum he seemed to call for all-out socialist revolution:

It's impossible for a chicken to produce a duck egg. . . . The system in this country cannot produce freedom for an Afro-American. It is impossible for this system, this economic system, this political system, this social system, this system, period. It's impossible for this system, as it stands, to produce freedom right now for the black man in this country. . . . And if ever a chicken did produce a duck egg, I'm quite sure you would say it was certainly a revolutionary chicken!

The Malcolm X of the Breitman book went far beyond seeing racism as a flaw in the hearts of the American people. It was endemic to the nation's economic system, a necessary feature of capitalism. The whole structure had to go:

It's impossible for a white person to believe in capitalism and not believe in racism. You can't have capitalism without racism. And if you find one and you happen to get that person into a conversation and they have a philosophy that makes you sure they don't have this racism in their outlook, usually they're socialists or their political philosophy is socialism.[7]

Breitman's Malcolm X was a very different leader than the one portrayed in the final pages of Alex Haley's best-selling *Autobiography of Malcolm X*. Whether his portrait was more or less accurate than Haley's, for San Quentin readers the effect of the Breitman book was like a lightning strike. No longer would Muslims or other groups of radical black San Quentin inmates petition for collective civil rights within the prison or the American system. There was nothing to be gained by trying to fit in. The very structure of the society would have to be razed and rebuilt along socialist lines.

The San Quentin writer who followed this line of thought most closely was Eldridge Cleaver. Cleaver had begun in the early 1960's to write furiously from his cell at San Quentin. Former Warden Louis Nelson took a dim view of the convict's ideas:

I have read a lot of Cleaver's material. I had stacks of it that high [six inches] on my desk at one time. He was a prolific writer. Christ, he turned out that stuff by the ream. At that time the Black Muslims were writing and all this writing I had [of Cleaver's] was racist as hell, talking about the white honkies and death to the white man and that sort of thing. . . . A lot of it was this typical convict jargon about the oppressed and the—I consider it garbage, the words of a diseased mind.[8]

But the young convict writer was about to find a much more receptive audience than his prison warden. Around 1965 Cleaver happened to come across the address of white liberal attorney Beverly Axelrod, and after receiving a letter from the inmate she agreed to represent him. Almost immediately Axelrod began smuggling contraband books and magazines in to her client,* and Cleaver passed pieces of his early writing to her in stacks of legal papers, using the strategy made safe by Caryl Chessman's legal actions regarding attorney-client privilege:

On one of her earliest visits, Cleaver gave Mrs. Axelrod what appeared to be a thick legal brief . . . ; it was, in fact, a partial collection of his essays. The . . . attorney brought the writing to the San Francisco office of *Ramparts*, whose publisher and editors were as impressed as she was. Mrs. Axelrod began to campaign for Cleaver's release, and publisher Edward Keating guaranteed a job on the magazine. . . . David Welsh, then news editor of *Ramparts*, began to work with Cleaver's material while Eldridge was still in prison; his first article, an essay on James Baldwin, was published in June 1966.[9]

In February 1966, Paul Jacobs of *Ramparts* interviewed Cleaver at Soledad prison, where he had been transferred. He inquired where the magazine should send the writer's fee for articles he was submitting and, on the subject of prison censorship, advised the inmate to "leave in [the] dirty words." Jacobs assured Cleaver (erroneously) that it was "OK to damn prison authorities—Soledad and elsewhere." Cleaver complained that at San Quentin, the "screws broke the typewriter, and stole typewriter ribbon and carbon paper from my cell."[10] His connections with *Ramparts* probably eventually helped him get his parole in December 1966. Former *Ramparts* editor Robert Scheer explains:

Cleaver obtained parole only after his lawyer, Beverly Axelrod, smuggled some of his writings out of jail and their publication in *Ramparts* resulted in the support of "prominent" persons. Cleaver was offered a contract for a book by McGraw-Hill, and he was offered a job at *Ramparts*—in those days sufficiently close to its origins as a lay-Catholic literary quarterly to provide respectable cover.[11]

*Working papers of Paul Jacobs of the *Ramparts* editorial staff record statements by Cleaver at Folsom about being put in the "hole for five days for having contraband smuggled by Beverly Axelrod." The contraband consisted of books and copies of *Ramparts* and *Evergreen*. See Jacobs.

The prisoner was at work on a book that was to attract major attention.

Soul on Ice appeared in 1968 under the McGraw-Hill label, though excerpts had been printed earlier in *Ramparts*. The book's introduction, written by Maxwell Geismar, introduced Cleaver as "one of the distinctive new literary voices to be heard" and claimed a place for the text in the lineage of Richard Wright's *Native Son* and the *Autobiography of Malcolm X*, noting its similarity to the works of Frantz Fanon. "From my prison cell," wrote Cleaver, "I have watched America slowly coming awake. . . . I have watched the sit-ins, the freedom raids, the Mississippi Blood Summers, demonstrations all over the country, the FSM [Free Speech] movement, the teach-ins, and the mounting protest over Lyndon Strangelove's foreign policy. . . . I'd just love to be in Berkeley right now, to roll in that mud, frolic in that sty of funky revolution." Cleaver explained that his reading in prison had "concentrat[ed] . . . in the field of economics." He had read Karl Marx and the history of socialism (probably in smuggled works), including "Bakunin and Nechayev's *Catechism of the Revolutionist*—the principles of which, along with some of Machiavelli's advice, I sought to incorporate into my own behavior. I took the *Catechism* for my bible . . . [and] began consciously incorporating . . . tactics of ruthlessness in my dealings with everyone with whom I came into contact. And I began to look at white America through these new eyes." Cleaver then turned toward the task of politicizing the crime for which he had most recently been convicted, rape: "I considered myself to be mentally free—I was an outlaw. . . . I became a rapist. . . . Rape was an insurrectionary act." Cleaver wrote that during his second term in prison he had slowly come to regret the "bloody, hateful, bitter, and malignant nature" of this act: "The price of hating other human beings is loving oneself less." [12] To this point in the book, despite Cleaver's radical credentials, *Soul on Ice* was a text in the 300-year-old penitent criminal confession genre. But Cleaver had much more in mind than a confession. He intended to create an angry new notion of revolutionary manhood. He thus set about politicizing black masculinity.

In chapters titled "Allegory of the Black Eunuchs" and "The Primeval Mitosis" Cleaver sought to uncover what he saw as a linkage between sex, violence, and cultural transformation. What was wrong with America, he contended, was that the nation was a "civilization alienated from its biology." He saw himself as one who could help

Americans "[reclaim] their bodies again after generations of alienated and disembodied existence." The culture, he mythologized, had suffered a psychosexual split into two antagonistic classes—"the Supermasculine Menial . . . the least alienated from the biological chain . . . although their minds . . . are in a general state of underdevelopment," and the "Omnipotent Administrator [who] is markedly effeminate and delicate by reason of his explicit repudiation and abdication of his body in preference for his mind." In Cleaver's view, the appearance of the hula hoop, the twist, and the music of the Beatles and Elvis Presley (who had "inject[ed] Negritude by the ton into the whites") were clear signs that biological/racial fissures were about to be closed up. "As if a signal had been given, as if the Mind had shouted to the Body, 'I'm ready!,'" America was being transformed. For Cleaver, the 1954 *Brown* v. *Board of Education* decision, intended to bring black and white together in the public schools, "was meant to graft the nation's Mind back onto its Body." And Cleaver was ready to take the lead in this biological march toward a new American destiny. Like the narrator of his "Allegory of the Black Eunuchs," Eldridge Cleaver envisioned sex as the best method of uncovering the path back to a biologically ordained natural political order. The trick was to avoid betraying one's sexuality: "I felt powerful, and I knew that I would make it if I never betrayed the law of my rod." As a harbinger of how this sexual power might come to be employed in the coming revolution, Cleaver's Eunuch offered the following omen: "The day is here when I will march into the Mississippi legislature with a blazing machine gun in my hands and a pocketful of grenades." [13] *Soul on Ice* whipped tough cultural observations in with a froth of sexual lore, and the result was a violence-steeped Maileresque black sexual-political myth, always careful to invoke Ginsberg and Burroughs and Kerouac, achingly self-conscious that its mass-press readership would be predominantly white.

And it was. It would be hard to imagine an audience more receptive to Cleaver's brand of sexual-political mythology than the counterculture communities of San Francisco and Berkeley in the mid-to-late 1960's. While Cleaver sat in his cell composing chapters of *Soul on Ice* to be smuggled out to his *Ramparts* editors, cultural radicals were spinning new worlds in the Haight-Ashbury, in Sausalito, in Berkeley, and in communes emerging in the surrounding countryside—at Big Sur, at Morningstar near Sebastopol in Sonoma County, at Holiday Lodge in Ben Lomond. New attitudes toward sex and toward law, violence, and crime would make the Bay Area fertile ground for the preachments of Eldridge Cleaver.

The "hippies" spoke of the need to sweep away old, failed forms and institutions. As Wilhelm Reich had taught the counterculture in his popular 1961 reissue of *The Function of the Orgasm*, society was at most an impediment to the expression of the "life force." Herbert Marcuse's writings, too, were accustoming the counterculture to the notion of psychosexual and cultural repression in America, the distortion and damage to natural humankind necessitated by the dominant class's need to enforce a denial of instinctual gratification in the masses in order to impose its will. As Marcuse pointed out in *One Dimensional Man*, "administration is the purest form of repression." Reich and Marcuse had prepared the way for Cleaver. To a reader already familiar with the notion that sexual-cultural repression was at the root of America's problems, Cleaver's psychosexual male politics made perfect sense. To reform the culture, first total spontaneity had to be achieved. In the process a more natural human social order would be revealed, which could then be seized upon to replace the artificial politics responsible for the Vietnam War and the racist social order of the American past. The outcome would be nothing less than the accelerated evolution of humankind, as seers such as Timothy Leary prophesied ("Let's Mutate, Baby!"), and the establishment of a perfect human community.

Work toward the reinvention of human society was already well under way, and a rethinking of the law and outlaws became part of the process. New attitudes toward lawbreaking and the new cultural role of the outlaw became the ideological seam joining the New Left to San Quentin. In the Haight by 1965 Ken Kesey's Merry Pranksters had introduced their strategy of assaulting the public's sense of reality with "existential practical jokes"[14] in the form of puzzling or unexpected situations, and in Prankster street theater unpredictability had been elevated to the status of first principle. At the Diggers' Free Frame of Reference, too, the Haight was invited to experiment in the invention of new possibilities. The Free Frame, a Digger garage with a huge picture frame which participants walked through into a twenty-four-hour happening, was "an experimental social environment where people were encouraged to ignore all law and custom."[15] Drugs quickly came to play an important role in the Haight's social experiment, both as a tool by which normative reality could be dismantled and because in using them the experimenter had to break the law. California's October 6, 1965, LSD law only contributed to the skyrocketing demand for this drug. Lawbreaking by drug use quickly became a form of moral witness against "straight" culture and a ritual of solidarity within the radical Left "community."

The Haight transformed itself into a mammoth theater of spontaneity. Stores like the Psych Shop installed theater seats in store windows looking out on the drama of the street. A shop called Wild Colors made all the public actors when its "Pope of the New Catholic Church," originally a store clerk perched high atop a ladder to spot shoplifters, took to selling one-penny indulgences: "You Are Forgiven." Meanwhile, the Open Theater on College Avenue across the bay in Berkeley began to stage productions it called "Revelations," consisting of images projected on nude bodies accompanied by multiple soundtracks. The Haight and Berkeley were busy turning themselves into a long-running experiment in spontaneous dramaturgy. A frequent theme running through the Haight's and Berkeley's many acts was the often-expressed need for the community universally to reject straight society's laws. Many times the drama had explicit sexual/religious affront as its goal or an antilaw theme. On Christmas 1966, Diggers, winos, drag queens, and twenty belly dancers converged on San Francisco's Glide Memorial Church for a "Christmas Happening" to create a "general atmosphere of blasphemy and desecration, dramatizing the macabre comedy of life. . . . Around two A.M. a distraught vestryman came running into the church offices with the news that someone was performing cunnilingus on the altar." [16] While Billy Murcott and Emmett Grogan of the Diggers were assailing the streets with anarchist broadsides under the pseudonym "George Metevsky," a reference to the infamous Mad Bomber of 1950's New York, the San Francisco Mime Troupe, which shared rental space with the Students for a Democratic Society (SDS), launched productions of antilaw works like *Search and Seizure*. *Search and Seizure* was a play set in a police station where three drug offenders were being victimized by their arresting police officers. Of the three, a naive pothead, a methedrine dealer, and an acidhead, only the LSD freak could successfully counter the power of the police because he was so stoned he didn't acknowledge either his own criminality or their authority. At best, law for Bay Area counterculture radicals was an unnecessary cultural accoutrement. In 1967, on Alan Watts's houseboat in Sausalito, Gary Snyder would divine before an audience of Diggers and *San Francisco Oracle* staff writers that a hundred years hence, when New York had died and the "new wilderness society" had emerged, "there

would be no need for laws because people wouldn't *want* to do evil." [17]
For many, however, the counterculture's rejection of the law went far
beyond seeing it as simply an unnecessary form of state administration. Breaking the law came to be seen by some as self-actualizing,
ennobling behavior, and violent acts as ritualized fulfillments of human nature.

The emerging concept of politically creative lawbreaking was one
the Left shared with and passed back and forth to convict Eldridge
Cleaver, to whom even rape at one time had been a political act. But
many more-moderate convict voices than Cleaver's inside the walls
now also began regularly refusing to follow penitent, confessional
traditions. Instead, some issued angry statements that, because the
underclass was forced to commit crimes to live, imprisonment itself
was a political crime and the criminal a political prisoner. The crime
of the outlaw, by this logic, became a revolutionary challenge to the
state. Outlaws were revolutionaries. What had started almost two decades earlier as an idea implicit in prison treatment rhetoric—that
knowledge equals rehabilitation—had, to readers of convict literature
in the Left, metamorphosed into a dangerous literary hyperbole. Convicts, especially those who possessed the literacy skills to articulate
the plight of the prisoner in the New Left's language of class analysis,
could erase their crimes altogether by redefining them as political acts.
Ideas such as this appearing in the convict writing smuggled out of
San Quentin in sheaves of attorneys' papers quickly became the shared
literary interface between prisoners and the Left, further improvising
on the trope of the outlaw and making room for criminal male violence in the ideology of the New Left. These strains mingled with the
models of aggressive masculinity already present in American culture
since the Chessman years, evidenced most clearly in violent male film
heroes of the 1950's and 1960's. Cleaver's writing, especially, pushed
the process of male gender definition further along toward equating
machismo mayhem with male power. After Eldridge Cleaver, the ideal
revolutionary male, for women as well as men, would be supremely,
sexually vengeant and free of the laws of society.

Nowhere can the seductive forms ritualized lawbreaking took in
segments of the Left be better seen than in the 1960's California youth
culture's protracted flirtation with the concept of the motorcycle outlaw, which came to a climax with the elevation of the Hell's Angels to
celebrity status. Delinquent biker subculture had gained notoriety
years before, after the 1947 Hollister Independence Day Hell's Angels
"riot," which the media had exploited for ten years, most notably in

Stanley Kramer's 1954 film *The Wild One*, starring Marlon Brando and Lee Marvin. The image of the California outlaw biker achieved wider popular currency over the next decade, feeding off an appealing myth of the freedom of the open road inspired partly by Jack Kerouac's *On the Road* (1955). As writer Yves Lavigne has pointed out, the Angels created "life on barren stretches of road at the continent's end. They wrap their legs around hulking, throbbing Harley-Davidsons, Indians [a type of motorcycle] and chase freedom in the sea-blown wind."[18] To complete the glamour, Frank Sadilek, the leader of the San Francisco's Angels club from 1955 to 1962, even sent to Hollywood for the blue-and-yellow-striped shirt worn by Lee Marvin in *The Wild One*, and finally this media-manufactured official U.S. nightmare, the Hell's Angels club, bearing as its "colors" the grinning, winged deathshead, was eagerly adopted as the official police force of psychedelia in the Haight and as the quintessential cultural rebels in Berkeley's intellectual-hip circles. The Angels became regulars at Ken Kesey's wild La Honda ranch parties. The bikers were first invited formally out to the ranch and greeted on the roadside by a sign that read, "The Merry Pranksters Welcome the Hell's Angels." There they were treated to LSD and rubbed elbows with the elite of the Beat era. Later, Ginsberg would compose poems to their wildness that frequently appeared in the *Berkeley Barb*, dubbing them "angelic barbarians." From then on, the romantic image of the outlaw biker held a special place in the Bay Area counterculture. The Angels were the outlaw literary trope come to life. While town councils all over the state were drafting anti-biker legislation and California's attorney general, Thomas C. Lynch, in 1965 fanned the Angels issue into an hysteria, San Francisco's Jefferson Airplane was preparing to put their spirit into song: "We are all outlaws in the eyes of Amerika." The Wild One had come home in the politics of the counterculture.

The Hell's Angels provided another valuable service for the Left. Especially after reading *Soul on Ice*, white middle-class leftists had felt the seductive power of male vengeance as an ideal that remained just out of reach. To middle-class whites, male aggression seemed the special property of the working class, and especially of the black male. After all, American culture saw white middle-class males as the quiet, passive sons of the overly domesticated Ward and June Cleaver of the popular 1950's television show, *Leave it to Beaver*. But the Angels helped many white men in the Left come one step closer to real "manhood." The Angels, most of whom were white, hardly resembled Ozzie Nelson. Tom Wolfe noted in his *Electric Kool Aid Acid Test* that the Left's attraction to the Hell's Angels was not confined to the hippies of the Haight:

The news spread around intellectual-hip circles in the San Francisco–Berkeley area like a legend. . . . [The Pranksters] had broken through the worst hangup that intellectuals know—the real-life hangup. Intellectuals were always hung up with the feeling that they weren't coming to grips with real life. Real life belonged to all those funky spades and prize fighters and bull-fighters and dock workers and grape pickers and wetbacks. Nostalgia de la boue. Well, the Hell's Angels were real life. It didn't get any realer than that.[19]

And Hunter Thompson observed, in *Hell's Angels: A Strange and Terrible Saga*, that "the Angels' aggressive, anti-social stance—their alienation, as it were—had a tremendous appeal for the more aesthetic Berkeley temperament. . . . The Angels didn't masturbate, they raped. They didn't come on with theories and songs and quotations, but with noise and muscle and sheer balls."[20]

The Hell's Angels were taken to the very heart of the movement, even while they were being sent to San Quentin in increasing numbers and forming neo-Nazi racist gangs there.* For a time in 1965–66 Berkeley radicals in the antiwar effort thought the outlaw bikers would join their demonstrations, putting real grit into the street actions of Jerry Rubin's Vietnam Day Committee. When Angels leader Sonny Barger finally came out in support of the war and made an offer to President Lyndon Johnson to loose his outlaws on North Vietnam as a "crack troup of trained gorillas,"[21] only pleas for brotherly love from Ginsberg, Kesey, Neal Cassady, and the Merry Pranksters prevented the bikers from mauling, much less joining, the peace demonstrators. Offers by the Hell's Angels to aid the state in its fight against the Left eventually extended much farther. Oakland police sergeant Ted Hilliard testified in 1972 that the Hell's Angels bought weapons and explosives on the black market for the Oakland police in the late 1960's and that Barger offered "to deliver the bagged body of a leftist for every Angel released from jail."[22] But the counterculture continued to love the brawling satyrs. One Angel, Gut Turk, was drafted as the model for Mr. Zig-Zag, the trademark of Zig-Zag cigarette papers, universal choice of marijuana smokers. Another, Chocolate George, flipped over his Harley handlebars to his death, and the

---

*Irwin, *Prisons in Turmoil*, p. 75. The Hell's Angels' adoption of the Nazi swastika tattoo has been attributed by some members to its usefulness simply to elicit shock and does not always reflect true belief in neo-Nazism.

Berkeley Barb ran a sketch of the biker in a saintly pose, his devil's tail twisted up into a halo over a broken brow. Chocolate George was feted with a day-long funeral celebration at Golden Gate Park, widely attended by Haight residents, as well as outlaw biker clubs from as far away as Los Angeles. Sonny Barger read a eulogy, a passage from *The Next Hundred Years*, telling how "the outlaw of a fat society, the rugged individualist, becomes the hero of later times. Alexander the Great, Caesar, Napoleon."[23]

The Hell's Angels became major actors in the street theater of the Haight. On December 16, 1966, a file of Angels on their chopped hogs led the "Death of Money and Rebirth of the Haight" parade, as Mime Troup members silently passed out

pennywhistles, automobile rearview mirrors, flowers, lollipops, incense, candles, bags of grass (lawn clippings) and signs reading "Now!" . . .

Three hooded figures carried a silver dollar sign on a stick. A black-clad modern Diogenes carrying a kerosene lamp preceded a black-draped coffin borne by six pallbearers wearing Egyptianesque animal masks. . . .

In the lead [were Hell's Angel] "Hairy Henry" Kot with a big "Now!" sign on his handlebars and Phyllis Willner, a prominent Digger woman, wearing a cape made from a bedsheet and carrying a sign reading "Now!" standing in his buddy seat.

When police arrested several of the Angels in the parade, the marchers turned the parade around, redirecting it toward the police precinct where the arrested bikers had been taken: "At the police station they found scores of patrolmen standing in front of the building. A chant went up: 'We want George! We want Hairy Henry!' . . . When bail was announced, the Diggers quickly collected donations in the black-draped Death of Money coffin."[24]

Hunter Thompson's *Hell's Angels: A Strange and Terrible Saga* quickly became a cult classic, helping to bring the bikers to the counterculture. Thompson's book did more than tell the story of the Angels bike club in a straightforward journalistic mode; it was the tale of a straight journalist drawn into the society of outlaws. In a central passage, Thompson wrote of an aging middle-class car dealer who "broke down under the strain of respectability and answered the call of his genes." The man finally sold all, dropped out, and took to living in a half-mad, drunkenly happy delirium in the motorcycle trade. The message was clear for counterculture readers: outlaw bikers offered a release from the restraints of civilization and a return to the essential primitive. Thompson's book improvised on and passed along the outlaw literary trope, a hyperbolic figure that for its New Left readers collapsed literature into politics, joining counterculture leftists with the Hell's Angels.

In 1967 Hollywood produced *Hell's Angels on Wheels* starring the real-life Angel leader Sonny Barger alongside Jack Nicholson, and the biker outlaw continued to have strong appeal for the counterculture at least as late as 1969, when Steppenwolf recorded the soundtrack to the top-grossing biker film *Easy Rider*:

> Get your motor running
> Head out on the highway.
> Looking for adventure
> And whatever comes your way. . . .
> Like a true nature's child
> We were born, born to be wild
> Gonna fly so high, never gonna die.
> Born to be wild
> Born to be wild.

The most extreme element of the Bay Area counterculture embraced even the violence of the Angels. Although many in the Left remained openly opposed to violence, and much countercultural rhetoric was directed against it, it always lay just under the surface. Bay Area counterculture papers printed photos of revolutionary hippies striking dramatic poses with powerful weapons. In 1969 the *Berkeley Tribe* ran a cover photo of a hippie man armed with a rifle and girded with bandoliers. Beside him stood his woman, child on one hip, submachine gun on the other. Above was the headline: "Join the New Action Army." [25] Other issues printed diagrams of weapons with instructions for their use and photos of bomb factories. A September 29, 1967, issue of the Haight's *Free City Newsletter* published instructions on how to build a firebomb. And a Digger pamphlet distributed during organizing for demonstrations at the San Quentin execution of inmate Aaron Mitchell in April 1967 revealed a new, hard cynicism: "Bring Raw Meat!" Historian Laurence Leamer has noted that this cynical drift toward the violent was typical of many underground papers in the United States at the end of the 1960's, suggesting that for their predominantly white middle-class readership the attraction to weapons had a strongly psychosexual appeal:

The papers printed pictures and diagrams of rifles, pistols and other weapons. In this there is a conscious attempt to break out of bourgeois youth culture and forge ties with the lower classes, but ironically, the pictures and diagrams are telling evidence that such underground papers are as middle class as ever. Guns are very much a part of lower-middle-class and working-class American culture. A boy grows up with them. He respects them. He knows how to use them. And if he reads a radical paper, he certainly finds pictures or diagrams of guns superfluous or downright foolish. It is only these scions of the middle class, schooled in a tradition that considers guns illicit and somehow almost sensual, who need such elementary instruction.[26]

What the white middle-class Left was seeking in these weapons was an escape to a more empowering vision of manhood. Such leftists looked to convicts, to writers like Eldridge Cleaver, to bring them finally to the act.

Even among the passive, violence was celebrated in the counter-culture as a needed cultural cathartic. Though sociologist Lewis Ya-blonsky's conclusions on hippiedom in *The Hippie Trip* (1968) were skewed by his having observed the phenomenon long after its more innocent first impulse had degenerated (hippies of the Haight were *not* the anomic, delinquent deviants he portrayed them), the inclination to violence and crime *was* there. For most, it remained merely rhetoric—violence was a behavior to be celebrated in others as part of primitive nature. The 1969 Altamont Raceway Festival tragedy, in which the Hell's Angels, hired as security police by the Rolling Stones for $500 in beer, beat to death a concertgoer and injured scores of others, provided a grim postscript to the radical community's flirtation with outlaw subculture. "I was standing two feet away," wrote Greil Marcus, editor of *Rolling Stone*. "People reacted by saying, 'Wow, violence, far-out.' Nobody did anything. Hundreds of kids raised their hands in the peace sign."[27] In a rare moment of introspection, the *Berkeley Tribe* said of the Altamont debacle: "Until Saturday, evil was value-free, something to dig for its own sake. A lot of people who thought they were children of chaos dropped out of their sugar coated camp trips Saturday to see the core of their religion at work."[28]

In 1968–69 violence could be celebrated by some in the Left for its own sake. The Berkeley Commune asked in an open letter, "Is it time to admit that Hate as well as Love redeems the world? There is no outside without inside, no revolution without blood."[29] At the SDS National Office in 1968, internal education secretary Fred Gordon congratulated a Bay Area group, the Up Against the Wall Motherfuckers, for providing an example of "a new life style, a Reichian mind-body unity that expresses its alienation spontaneously and organically through violence."[30]

These were Cleaver's most avid Bay Area readers, the arm of the

Left that celebrated violence for its own sake in the move toward a perfected sexual-political utopia. Cleaver stepped out of prison into the Haight: "I embraced it, wallowed in it. . . . The Haight was at the end of the rainbow of the broken spectrum of the American mind. If you made it to the Haight, you would be saved, born again, delivered from the doom that was enveloping the land."[31]

As *Soul on Ice* slowly found its way back into Soledad, Folsom, and San Quentin prisons, anxiously anticipated and then secretly smuggled in, a very different audience awaited it. Cleaver commanded great respect inside the walls among the more radical black inmates. But unlike the hip Bay Area counterculture audience outside, a good many black inmate readers of *Soul on Ice* found themselves mystified, not inspired, by Cleaver's sexual mythologizing in this book and very nervous of his treatment of rape. A black former Soledad inmate recalls:

I was the second person to read it in Soledad. . . . I got the book from ———, who was one of the Soledad Seven.* He kept tellin' me, "It's comin'! It's comin'!" He passed it on to me. There was such talk about the book! And I said, "I wanna get my hands on it." But once I did, I had some problems with it, particularly when he gets down to the part dealin' with his crimes and such. The parts about rape. I had some problems with that.[32]

Johnny Spain, Black Panther leader, friend to George Jackson, and San Quentin Six defendant, agrees:

The first time I read *Soul on Ice*, [in] '69–70, the prisons were becoming more political. I was at Soledad Central. It was one of the books that if you were a prisoner that had political consciousness you had to read. And I thought it was one of the most disgusting books I had ever read . . . I didn't particularly care about the constant implication that women had a place. . . . I didn't appreciate that.[33]

A black San Quentin inmate who first read the book at Deuel Vocational Institution in 1972 makes much the same observation:

Nothing that [Cleaver] does should have surprised people after reading *Soul on Ice*. . . . His attitude toward sex crimes, the whole orientation of his thinking, and sex the central component in that. It's almost Freudian the way sex plays a prominent role. . . . There's no way of getting around it. There's some very disturbing things about the man and his thinking.[34]

*In the 1970 Soledad Seven case, sometimes known as the Second Soledad case, seven black inmates were charged in the slaying of a guard attacked in a yard shack in Soledad Central. All seven inmates accused in the death were participants in a radical black study group. Charges were eventually dropped.

These inmates' recollections of Cleaver's *Soul on Ice* have almost certainly been colored by the twenty years that have passed since the prisoners first read the book. Unfortunately, no contemporary data are available. But the former convicts' comments underscore at least one critical point about prisoner readers and Cleaver. Under the convict code, sex offenders like Cleaver, especially those who had committed sexual molestations, had been traditionally viewed with disrespect by inmates in California prisons, and often their lives were in danger. Thus the prominent place Cleaver gave male sexuality in his politics might have made other prisoners nervous. An additional compelling reason for San Quentin inmates' mild disappointment in *Soul on Ice*, however, may simply have been its assimilationist tone. Why was Cleaver cozying up to the white hippie radicals in Berkeley? San Quentin prisoners, many of them former Muslims, had grown accustomed to reading a different Eldridge Cleaver in contraband articles sneaked in from the *Black Panther*, where the proud outlaw literary trope was bursting into angry print. That Cleaver had a much more militant, black separatist tone than the author of this new book.

The *Black Panther* had begun publishing in San Francisco in April 1967. Its editorial staff included Huey Newton, Bobby Seale, and Eldridge and Kathleen Cleaver. The early Panther group had set about organizing community programs, including children's breakfast services, voter registration drives, legal aid services, schools, and community political education classes. And it engaged in nonviolent confrontations with arresting police officers, often monitoring police frequencies and speeding to the scene of an arrest to read basic legal rights to those in custody. But the rhetoric in the *Black Panther* often called for a different political practice. From the outset, the paper repeatedly advised Bay Area blacks to arm themselves. At first, this was said to be necessary for self-defense. In the June 26, 1967, issue Newton argued that "only with the power of the gun can the black masses halt the terror and brutality perpetrated against them by the armed racist power structure."

But the Panthers' motive for brandishing personal weapons quickly evolved away from self-defense. After their first confrontation with Oakland police in the autumn of 1966, the Panthers openly carried weapons on the street. As long as they remained careful not to point their guns at anyone, this practice was not strictly illegal under California law. On May 2, 1967, however, the California legislature convened to act on the Mulford bill, dubbed the "Panther Bill," designed to ban the carrying of loaded weapons in incorporated areas.

Twenty armed Panthers drove to Sacramento and entered the assembly's corridors, carrying their weapons, ostensibly searching for the observation gallery. Pursuing them was a mob of reporters and a television crew. Huey Newton read a statement denouncing the gun bill and called once again for all blacks to arm themselves against the state. All were arrested, including parolee Eldridge Cleaver, who it turned out later had been careful to be carrying only a camera and to have secured permission from *Ramparts* to cover the story as a reporter.[35] Cleaver's parole status was thus safe. All the Panthers involved were eventually released, but thereafter the group became indelibly fixed in the public eye as a band of armed insurrectionists. Among black San Quentin prisoners, looking outside for a corollary to their own revolutionary image of themselves as outlaws, Panther stock shot up dramatically.

Just under a year later, in March 1968, Newton issued "Executive Mandate No. 3," a general order to all Black Panther members to acquire guns. Articles quickly followed with instructions for making small hand grenades and firebombs. As 1968 progressed, self-defense seemed to be diminishing as the reason for Panthers to acquire weapons, and Newton, Seale, and Cleaver (who by September 14, 1968, was listed in the *Black Panther* as minister of information for the party) called more and more openly for acts of urban terrorism. In "The Correct Handling of a Revolution," Newton advocated "guerrilla warfare methods." "Small groups of three and four," termed "vanguard groups," were to begin "to show the people how to go about a revolution": "When the masses hear that a gestapo policeman has been executed while sipping coffee at a counter, and the revolutionary executioners fled without being traced, the masses will see the validity of this type of approach to resistance."[36] As early as July 1967, the *Black Panther* seemed to advocate the slaying of police and armed assaults on prisons:

Army 45—"Army 45 will stop all jive"
Carbine—"Carbine will stop a war machine"
12-gauge magnum shotguns with 18 inch barrel—"Buckshots will down the cops"
357 magnum pistol—"357 will win us heaven"
P38—"P38 will open prison gates"
M16—"And if you don't believe in lead, you are already dead."[37]

As the 1970's approached, the Panther paper's calls for urban terrorism became more and more strident. Field Marshal D.C. (Don

Cox) ordered vanguard groups of four to six persons to be organized nationwide. The tabloid printed lists of books on arms, guerrilla tactics, and explosives, including addresses of firms from which they could be purchased.

On the streets, the Panthers' activity never approached the militancy of their political rhetoric. Nonetheless, their image as urban terrorists, largely a literary figure of the organization's newspaper, was widely accepted by San Quentin readers. This was what the inmates expected Eldridge Cleaver to be and were disappointed to find little trace of in *Soul on Ice*. Wasn't it Cleaver, after all, who had written in a *Ramparts* review of Fanon's *Wretched of the Earth* that this book, which he referred to as the new black militant's bible, "teaches colonial subjects that it is perfectly normal for them to want to rise up and cut off the heads of the slavemasters, that it is perfectly normal for them to want to achieve their manhood, and that they must oppose the oppressor in order to experience themselves as men"?[38] Cleaver would continue to represent the violently vengeant black male for California prisoners long after his flight from the country in October 1968. Nate Harrington, a young black inmate at Deuel Vocational Institution in 1972, remembers:

Eldridge Cleaver was well-regarded among what were considered even then as ultra-leftists. His writings on "lumpen ideology" still had profound influence. . . . Eldridge was trying to promote the "lumpen proletariat" of Marx's writing to a class unto itself, the "lumpen," and he had this theory that because of technological and scientific and industrial advances in the United States a whole group of people had become what he called "lumpenized." They were too large to be considered a section of the working class, as viewed in the traditional, orthodox Marxist analysis. They became a class unto themselves, which fit in perfectly with George's [Jackson] observation that "the lumpens will initiate the revolution and the workers will carry it on." But in Cleaver's analysis at the time, the "lumpen" *was* the revolution. And a lot of interesting approaches developed out of that. It tended to give rise to a more terroristic style of political practice.[39]

Cleaver's readers inside San Quentin were by now thoroughly familiar with his brand of Marxism and his angry *Black Panther* articles. But *Soul on Ice* presented a different picture and thus it disappointed prison readers. Among the white middle-class Left, however, Cleaver was a success. Soon that Left would raise him and the Oakland Black Panthers to celebrity status.

Until 1966 the *Berkeley Barb* covered developments in the Haight in depth and focused on cultural rather than political radicalism, filling its pages with copy on the Sexual Freedom League's nude beach parties, the role free sex would play in the coming utopia, and the beginnings of the psychedelic revolution. Little coverage was given to issues of the black community and none at all to the subject of prisons. But in November the tone of the newspaper changed dramatically. First, organizers of a Berkeley Black Power conference, Jerry Rubin in particular, came under a hail of criticism for not including local blacks on their planning committee, and the Berkeley white community began seriously examining its own racism. At the November Black Power conference, guest speaker Stokely Carmichael (who had coined the term "Black Power") upbraided his predominantly white Berkeley audience at the Greek Theater for "fail[ing] miserably to develop a movement for equality in the white communities." [40]

Responding to these changing politics, by February 1967, the *Barb* had made the Black Panthers, organized the previous October, a main news staple. The paper first discovered the group in its February 17 issue, as the Panthers were making plans to commemorate the second anniversary of the slaying of Malcolm X. A week later, when the Panthers convened their noontime rally, drawing a crowd of 300 at Berkeley High School, the *Barb* officially embraced them into the company of the white Left: "Armed Panthers Here: Black Power Joins Left." Huey Newton appeared at the rally wearing a pistol in a shoulder holster, and Cleaver declared, "One day it will be Molotov Cocktails; Next, hand grenades and bullets. If we can't have our freedom, then white America will die." [41] The *Barb* was impressed with the group's aggressiveness. Still, on April 14, when Cleaver accompanied a massive peace mobilization demonstration through the streets of San Francisco to Kezar Stadium and appeared with Coretta Scott King to address the 62,000 people assembled there, the paper called his words a "predictable speech . . . on the war and white racist America." [42] By May, however, the paper was strongly supportive of everything the Black Panthers said or did. Beginning with their armed visit to the capitol on May 2, Panther stories began to appear in every issue of the *Barb,* accompanied by ads for Breitman's *Last Year of Malcolm X.*

Another text that began to be heavily advertised in the *Barb* at about the same time was *Quotations from Mao Tse Tung,* a book that was to add considerably to the growing literature of the political outlaw as prisoner. Huey Newton and Bobby Seale claimed to have been the original importers of the Red Book to Berkeley radicals and to have turned its marketability to their own advantage. While sitting in a car in Oakland in the fall of 1966, they had seen ads for the book in a newspaper:

We went over to the China Book Store in San Francisco and we bought up two batches of the Red Books, thirty in a package, and got back over there and we sold them motherfuckers at Cal campus some Red Books. We sold them Red Books inside of an hour. That shocked us. At a dollar apiece. So we took all that money and we went back to the bookstore and bought all the Red Books. Paying thirty cents for them. We told them, "We are the Black Panther Party," and could an organization get a discount, and the next thing I know, we had enough money to buy two shotguns.[43]

Seale and Newton made $170 selling the books at the entrance to Berkeley's campus and started buying guns to patrol Oakland.

One more theme was developing in the *Barb* alongside that of the Panthers in late 1967, one that would finally couple the figure of the left-wing violent outlaw to the need for change in California's prisons. Ronald Reagan's election to governor in 1966 had resulted in markedly stepped-up police repression of Berkeley campus antiwar demonstrations and of street culture in the Haight. This activity produced increased arrests and state prison sentences for white counterculture activists. Throughout 1967 the *Barb* noted in passing the escalating number of antiwar protesters going to the county jail, and in September 1967, it particularly protested the sentence of UC philosophy student Lenny Glaser, busted for marijuana possession and serving one to ten years in state prison. But not until Huey Newton's November 1967 arrest in an Oakland shootout with police, which ended in the death of an officer, did the *Barb* widen its critique of the state justice system to include the cases of the nonstudent nonwhite. The *Barb* hastily concluded in its November 3–9 issue that the incident had been a clear case of police provocation. The next week it labeled Newton, by that time in custody at San Quentin's hospital recovering from a stomach wound incurred in the incident, a political prisoner. At the end of December it published a photo of Huey handcuffed to an emergency room gurney guarded by a white Oakland policeman. This same photo would be picked up by the newly formed Peace and Freedom party for a campaign brochure.

The Panthers' increasingly aggressive confrontational stand in 1967–68 toward the Oakland police was in large part a response to police harassment, though the *Barb* could not have known it at the time. Court documents filed in cases involving the Panthers in the 1970's would reveal that the Federal Bureau of Investigation's counterintelligence program, COINTELPRO, had begun focusing on the Black Panther party in 1967 and that the Panthers were on a Nixon administration White House Enemies List.[44] J. Edgar Hoover called the Black Panther party "the greatest threat to the internal security of the country."[45] And U.S. attorney general John Mitchell stated in 1969 that the Justice Department would "wipe out the Black Panther Party by the end of 1969."[46] It is difficult to gauge to what extent these pronouncements at the federal level translated into police activity at the municipal level, but it is safe to assume that, with the tacit support of the Justice Department and the White House, Oakland police were not reluctant to engage the Panthers. Intensified anti-Panther police activity had another result as well. Huey Newton would record later that the intense governmental opposition he felt in 1967–68 seemed to him to confirm the Black Panther party's raison d'être, and it may have brought his own Panther members to commit more violent political acts.[47]

The *Berkeley Barb* finished the year 1967 with more articles on the treatment of pacifists jailed or in prison. But 1968 would bring prison news of a different sort. Inside San Quentin, events were taking place that would bring the radical Bay Area community squarely into prison activism. The growing literature on the political outlaw that had first joined prisoners to the Bay Area counterculture was about to become real-life street politics. Unfortunately, this would undermine a prisoner unionization movement just beginning to build behind the walls.

After San Quentin's massive January 1967 yard "race riot," the *Outlaw*, an inmate-written underground newspaper, originally a crudely stenciled gripe sheet for convicts, had begun to suggest that the prison administration was trying to stir up race violence to divert the convict population from unified protest. The *Outlaw* first appeared in the months immediately following the yard incident. Calling itself "the voice of the mainline," the paper consisted at first of one to four pages of handwritten or typed copy, poorly reproduced and full of erratic spelling and grammatical errors. Because access to mimeograph machines was controlled, stolen stencils were often hand rubbed with ink. Dismissing race as the root of the January riot, an early issue called for race unity to press for goals convicts held in common:

1. Parole violators to be guaranteed a hearing in court with counsel, and the right to call and cross-examine witnesses.

2. Reduction of prison terms for narcotics offenders without prior convictions. [Drug offenders were being sentenced to ten to fifteen years to life.]
3. More favorable consideration by the Adult Authority for first offenders when their minimum time had been served.
4. Removal of all ex–law-enforcement officers from the AA.[48]

Ted Davidson, a UC Berkeley anthropology student doing interviews at the prison, remembers the first days of the *Outlaw*:

Darryl Graham, who was the editor . . . had a life top [life sentence without possibility of parole] and had already served ten years for armed robbery and then ten years for . . . second degree murder, and wasn't about to get out. . . . He bought the *Outlaw* from somebody else who had it, and it was just a little game that the other person was playing. . . . Initially, [Darryl wanted the newspaper] just to give the staff a bad time. But later he realized it was a force, and he really did want to try and see if they could bring about some legitimate changes. . . . Darryl had two kinds of articles. One was a serious kind of article, which were extremely embarrassing to staff. And others were just to keep the troops happy, like what guard was having homosexual relations with who . . . which were all just farce and fantasy.[49]

Ernie Bradford, San Quentin administrator of vocational education, disagrees about the paper's usefulness:

I thought the son of a bitch was nothin' but a piece of vicious shit. They accused people of doin' things . . . totally fictitious. But it comes out in the rag paper and puts some guy on the defensive. . . . In my case, I was a machine shop instructor, I was racist, I let the whites make knives to kill the blacks. . . . That can damn well get you killed. It was just crap.[50]

Joe Morse, a white San Quentin inmate, also saw little worth in the paper: "It had about the same credibility as the *National Enquirer*."[51] Warden Louis Nelson called the *Outlaw* "a scurrilous, poison-pen type of thing."[52] Despite these questions about the underground newspaper's accuracy and intent, the *Outlaw* slowly gained in respect and readership. In late 1967, the paper presented a list of grievances and called for a general strike in early winter 1968. The *Outlaw* was hobbled by poor circulation. It was hard for inmates to get, but this actually increased the demand for it and magnified its power. According to one source, after an issue was printed on a prison mimeograph machine, the machine was seized and put under lock and key. Eventually, the paper's copy was written inside the prison and smuggled out to sympathizers, who had it mimeographed and mailed back into the prison. Inmate clerks picked it off from the mail room and transported it to prison buildings in a laundry bag. Bundles of the paper were then dropped at key cells in each cell block during timed intervals in the guards' rounds. In this way the *Outlaw* was distributed to San Quentin prisoners.[53]

The *Outlaw* called for a strike on February 15, 1968, naming the proposed action a "Convict Unity Holiday" and adding to the previous demands a call for increased wages for prison industries jobs and around-the-clock physician service to prevent "unlawful deaths" allegedly at the hands of prison staff. Ted Davidson offered to smuggle this February 15 strike issue out to the public press:

> I went to my friend Darryl once Convict Unity Holiday had been proposed. . . . I said, "What if this got public?" and of course Darryl got ecstatic. . . . I said, "OK, let me see what I can do." And so I went to the *San Francisco Chronicle*, the *Examiner*, the *Oakland Tribune*. None of them would touch it with a ten-foot pole. This was six weeks ahead of time. . . . So finally I went to the *Berkeley Barb*.[54]

Since its embrace of the Black Panthers, the *Berkeley Barb* had become the primary vehicle in the Bay Area for the developing literature of the romantic political outlaw. With a circulation approaching 90,000, a staff of dozens of writers, and an army of up to 500 street sellers, it was a natural now for stories on the prisons. The *Barb* ran front-page articles on the upcoming strike, advertising the prisoners' grievances. The paper was eager to construct ideological bonds between its readership and the San Quentin convicts. It did so by suggesting that, because Huey Newton was a political prisoner (as were the student antiwar pacifists featured in its articles, who were serving time in local jails, and the cultural radicals arrested on drug charges), all those imprisoned at San Quentin must be political prisoners. They were "political" both in the sense that their crimes had had at least subconscious political motives and in the sense that, if released, the inmates would surely become movement radicals. For its issue announcing the San Quentin strike, the *Barb* borrowed from Eugene V. Debs:

> While there is a lower class I am in it,
> While there is a criminal element I am of it,
> While there is a soul in prison, I am not free.[55]

The strike issue that followed reproduced a print of Christ crucified beside the Penitent Thief.[56] The *Barb* brought the public's attention to the strike and even found its way into the prison:

They [issues of the *Barb*] were showing up all over the place. People, guards themselves, were fascinated. . . . I have a feeling maybe the teachers . . . the teachers certainly in the high school and a lot of people were probably bringing in multiple copies. You got thrown in the hole 29 days, no questions asked, if you had a copy of the *Barb* anywhere on your person.[57]

On February 15, 20 percent of the inmate population struck. The *Barb* had drawn a large crowd to the prison's gates, where in the afternoon two bands, the Grateful Dead and the Phoenix, and several members from Country Joe and the Fish set up at the east gate and blasted rock music over the walls to the prisoners.

The Grateful Dead . . . brought a flatbed truck and brought their own equipment, their amps and generating equipment. They pulled their flatbed truck out there on the little peninsula [that juts out into San Francisco Bay before the prison], and they got up on that. It was publicized on one of the rock stations as well as in the *Berkeley Barb*. . . . There weren't many [prisoners] who could see, but they could all hear and they knew they had the support.[58]

The group of about 400 to 500 strike supporters scribbled chalk paintings before the prison gate, played drums and tambourines, and launched colored balloons up over the prison's walls. The following day, 75 percent of the prison shut down. The nonviolent strike lasted a week, accompanied by daily noontime demonstrations at the east gate by the Peace and Freedom party.[59] Nine convicts associated with the *Outlaw* were later transferred to maximum security at Folsom.

Every issue of the *Barb* now contained prison news and letters from San Quentin convicts calling for more action. Prison coverage was accompanied by photos of Stokely Carmichael wearing a "Free Huey" button and ominous pronouncements from Cleaver and Seale that "if Huey is executed" for cop-killing, "the sky is the limit." The *Barb* now referred somewhat cavalierly to "the frameup of Huey Newton on a murder charge."[60]

When the demands of the San Quentin convicts were not met, the *Outlaw* published another issue urging a strike. Again the paper was smuggled out to the *Berkeley Barb* and outside support was organized. The *Outlaw* urged San Quentin's inmates to put aside racial squabbles and unite:

Some of us cons don't seem to know what side we're on. We're obsessed with near-sighted disputes based on race, ideology, group identity and so on. We expend our energies despising and distrusting each other. All of this is helping the CDC. We permit them to keep us at each others throats. A handful of us are calling for UNITY. . . . We call for 4,000 united convicts. Wake up!!! put your prejudices, biases, and class distinctions aside for the purposes of our fight with the CDC. . . . We are going to have our UNITY DAY in AUGUST. . . . Our outside support will be backing us all the way. . . . UNITY, BLACK, BROWN, WHITE, UNITY!!![61]

Word arrived at the *Barb* from writers of the *Outlaw* that the San Quentin inmates "are willing to strike again if they know they have effective support outside." Already the Peace and Freedom party had begun to formulate a platform proposal on basic prison reform for presentation to the new political party's convention in March. Still revealing little depth in its prison reportage, however, in an article on the tyrannical caprice of the Adult Authority and the indeterminate sentence, the *Barb* cited only the cases of young whites sentenced for marijuana possession.[62]

In contrast, the Peace and Freedom party would soon be drawn more deeply to the heart of the matter. When Bobby Seale was arrested in an early March 1968 night raid on his home by Oakland police, the PFP instantly denounced the action and came out strongly backing the Black Panthers. In mid-March the predominantly white Peace and Freedom party, which had functioned up to this time primarily as the political arm of the sexual freedom movement, announced it was forming a coalition with the Black Panthers. There was intense, rancorous debate within the party at its founding convention in Richmond, however, over the issue of whether to endorse the Panthers' entire ten-point platform, which included the objective of "freedom for all black people held in jail." This demand had been adapted by the Panthers from one of the ten points of the Black Muslims: "We want freedom for all believers in Islam in prison or in houses of correction." Mario Savio argued against adopting the ten points on the grounds that it was unwise to commit the party to "burn down half the city of Oakland" to free Huey. Following enthusiastic applause for speeches by Eldridge Cleaver and Bob Avakian, however, in which Newton's captors were called a "lynch mob," the Panthers' ten points were adopted and the party endorsed a strong "Free Huey" stand. Only a handful of delegates voted against the position.[63]

The Adult Authority began to watch Eldridge Cleaver closely. He had received warnings from his parole officer. Even though he was out of prison, the Corrections Department still sought to control his speech and writing. Because a parolee could be returned at once to prison for any reason whatsoever, the prison authorities presented a real threat. Cleaver comments:

Members of the parole authority . . . saw excerpts of my [April 1967 Kezar Stadium] speech on TV and launched their campaign to have my parole revoked. . . . They advised me to cool it . . . in the interest of not antagonizing those in Sacramento who did not like my politics. From then on, I was under constant pressure through them to keep my mouth shut and my pen still on any subject that might arouse a negative reaction in certain circles in Sacramento.[64]

Cleaver had decided "not to accept these warnings. . . and to write what was on my mind." After his May 2, 1967, arrest at the capitol, the parolee had been put on notice: "I was to keep my name out of the news for the next six months; specifically, my face was not to appear on any TV screen. . . . I was not to make any more speeches. . . . And I was not to write anything critical of the California Department of Corrections or any California politician."[65] Cleaver was clearly in danger of being returned to prison on a parole violation. The near-universal acclaim in the mass media that had greeted his newly released *Soul on Ice* may have made it seem impolitic to violate him as the summer of 1968 approached. The state waited for an opportunity.

It was not long in coming. On April 6, 1968, tensions in Oakland reached a fever pitch after the assassination of Martin Luther King in Memphis. Police beefed up their patrols of the Oakland ghetto. That night, Cleaver's car was stopped by officers on a dark Oakland street. After a dramatic gun-battle standoff from the basement of an Oakland house where Cleaver and his passenger, seventeen-year-old Panther Bobby Hutton, had taken refuge after an initial skirmish, Hutton was shot and killed while apparently trying to surrender to police, and Cleaver emerged from the scorched building naked, with his hands up. The Black Panther minister of information was sent to the Vacaville Medical Facility, charged with possession of a weapon, assault, and associating with persons of bad reputation. Charles Garry, chief counsel for the Panther party, marks this incident as the beginning of the Black Panthers' sad descent toward political gangsterism:

After the shootout when Martin Luther King was assassinated, [the Black Panthers] had over a quarter million dollars in weapons. [Huey Newton] never understood that the power that they had didn't require guns, although I tried to suggest that the radical movement, the left-wing movement, the white radicals, would follow them to hell and that they didn't need guns. I tried to point out what we were able to accomplish in the 1930's where we tied this town [up in the] San Francisco General Strike of 1934. I said, "You guys have the strength in numbers. Huey is probably the greatest political strategist of the Marxist movement. Quite a few of the labor leaders that I know here want to support you. You don't need a fuckin' gun." I got no response from him.[66]

But by this time these guns and the vengeant male public image of the Panthers they conveyed were so seductively essential to the white Left's ideology of the outlaw that they were impossible to relinquish.

"To the Bastille!" was the rallying cry the *Barb* mounted in angry response to what it saw as another police outrage against the Panthers. New ultimatums were issued demanding the immediate release of Newton, Cleaver, and Seale—or else. The Peace and Freedom party marched en masse to the Alameda County Courthouse in Oakland, surrounded it, and filled the air with cries of "Free Huey." The *Barb* ran a photo of prisoners at the courthouse flashing the peace sign.[67]

The public outcry at Cleaver's arrest was resounding. Coverage of the event appeared in most national newspapers. An Eldridge Cleaver Defense Fund was quickly organized and petitions for Cleaver's release appeared in the *Village Voice* and in letters to the editor in the *New York Times* and the *New York Review*, signed by James Baldwin, Leroi Jones, Norman Mailer, and Susan Sontag, among others.[68] McGraw-Hill Book Company expressed fear that Cleaver's arrest was meant to silence his voice as a cultural critic, and Bertrand Russell called for "independent observers to be stationed in the black ghettos of California" to detect further "political persecution of the Black Panther Party."[69] Locally, reporters scrambled to interview Cleaver. Most requests were denied, and the inmate was prohibited the use of a typewriter or access to reading matter, television, or mail. A handful of news reporters eventually got in to see him. The *San Francisco Express Times* stated on May 2 that Cleaver was in a wheelchair in solitary, buckshot having been removed from his legs. On May 14, Cleaver announced from his prison cell to the *San Francisco Chronicle* that he would seek the PFP presidential nomination in July. Paul Jacobs, the influential white radical and 1968 Peace and Freedom party candidate for the U.S. Senate, proclaimed that the convict's "seeking the presidential nomination while in jail is in the tradition of Eugene V. Debs, who also ran for the Presidency from prison. And like Debs, Cleaver raises the basic questions about freedom in America which must be answered."[70] Of course, Cleaver was no Eugene Debs. This endorsement must be taken as a measure of how closely the vengeant outlaw had been embraced as a politicized gender model for white males on the Left. After nine and a half weeks at Vacaville, Cleaver was ordered released on a habeas corpus petition by California Superior Court judge Raymond Sherwin, who was convinced that he had been arrested for his speeches rather than his acts. Judge Sherwin commented that "not only was there absence of cause for the cancellation of his parole, it was the product of a type of pressure unbecoming, to say the least, to the law enforcement of this state."[71] The basic issue was communication control of state prisoners. With Ronald Reagan in the governor's mansion, the California Department of Corrections seemed to be seeking a return to the iron-fisted censorship of the distant past, even of the words of the state's parolees.

The *Berkeley Barb* soon announced that it had received word from San Quentin of another Convict Unity Holiday, scheduled for August 2. The paper appealed for public support of the prisoners and warned that "if the state government does not respond to the peaceful demonstration, the militant cons are reported ready to launch 'guerilla' assaults within San Quentin, including the use of gasoline and other flammables."[72] As Huey Newton's trial date neared, scheduled for the third week in July, the *Barb* wrote of little else but prisons, declaring that "America [had] placed itself on trial."[73]

San Quentin authorities were doing their best to shut down the *Outlaw*. One day before the February 15, 1968, Convict Unity Holiday strike, Ted Davidson had been caught smuggling the paper out and barred from the prison:

I was set up on the last day, the day before Convict Unity Holiday. That's the day I got kicked out. The guy [an inmate] who worked in the pharmacy said, "Hey, I got the latest edition of the *Outlaw*." . . . I slipped it inside my pants and went on. . . . And as I walked out the count gate the captain came down the stairs [into the yard] and said, "Ted, the warden would like to see you." I got over to the warden's office and gradually people gathered—the warden, the captain, two associate wardens, two lieutenants, a couple officers, and two members of the goon squad. Then they proceeded to accuse me of having a copy of the *Outlaw* in my possession and I really didn't know what to say. And they proceeded to say, "We believe you were the leak to the *Berkeley Barb*. . . . I heard something about going to the District Attorney, and maybe we should advise him of his legal rights. And with that I pulled out the copy of the *Outlaw* and said, "Here, you can have it." But that didn't satisfy them. They took my wallet and took out everything and photocopied things that I had in it. They had me take off my shoes to see if there were secret compartments in the heels. And they had me stripped to my shorts, arms outstretched. I was frightened to death.[74]

Davidson was not the only outsider close to organizing attempts for the Unity Day strike. Sociologist John Irwin, who was conducting an inmate discussion group at the time, had also heard rumors of the strike. Irwin, however, was cautious not to break any prison rules: "We weren't discussing it in the study group," he remarks, though some members of the group were "furiously running around trying to get support, turning out *Outlaws*, [and] having Ted take them out."[75] Herman Spector's assistant in the library, Fred Persily, was also close to inmates planning the upcoming strike. Persily had been participating throughout the summer in the Inmate Society Seminar, an evening discussion group with an attendance of 50 to 100 prisoners:

We talked about what are the problems of San Quentin. Are the problems of San Quentin the blacks versus the whites, the Indians versus the Mexicans, or are the problems of San Quentin something else? . . . They had an Inmate Advisory Committee. We talked about looking at its constitution and seeing whether that's a way to effectively affect the way San Quentin runs so it meets the needs of the prisoners. We talked about the newspaper and how you needed a newspaper that really reflects the needs of the prisoners. . . . All those things that we talked about as needs occurred. I never was involved. I think inmates were trying to protect me. I think they kept me away from that kind of stuff. When I was ever asked to do anything that was against the rules, I always said, "Well, do you think I'm more valuable to you being thrown out or do you think I'm providing a value?"[76]

On August 2 the inmates struck again, demanding an end to the indeterminate sentence and the awesome discretionary powers of the Adult Authority. Outside, two rock bands and a mariachi group entertained demonstrators who had arrived by carpool caravan from a noon rally at UC Berkeley's Sproul Plaza. At the east gate, a citizens' group calling itself the Committee for the Rights of the Imprisoned held a press conference. The newly formed group was chaired by Ted Davidson. John Irwin, who had by this time also been barred from the prison, was present, as were Paul Jacobs and Kathleen Cleaver. Eldridge Cleaver was absent. He was awaiting formal parole violation hearings and attending a PFP Cleaver for President caucus, which "plan[ned] to introduce a resolution supporting the inmates' demands."[77] The Peace and Freedom party national convention was slated for Ann Arbor, Michigan, in mid-August. Kathleen Cleaver, representing her husband at the San Quentin press conference, called for the release of "every black prisoner from every prison, local and state and federal."[78]

The force of the two unity strikes of 1968 hit San Quentin hard, and prison administrators made plans to thwart future trouble. In a working paper of the Department of Corrections, San Quentin associate warden James Park warned that the prison was becoming "the first institution to feel the impact of a new type of insurrection involving a coalition of prisoners and individuals from the surrounding communities." He noted the prison's proximity to

the campuses of San Francisco State College and the University of California at Berkeley, the Oakland Induction Center, the Haight-Ashbury District, the Telegraph Avenue Communes, four major ghetto areas, and thirty or more enclaves of the disillusioned, the drop-out, the dissident or the revolutionary. . . . San Quentin provided a testing site for a new type of prison revolt planned and executed by a mixed group of prisoners, former prisoners, academic penologists and adherents of various New Left philosophies. . . . They demonstrated, perhaps for the first time in American penal history, that outsiders could conspire with prisoners to cripple the normal operations of a prison. The age-old dissatisfactions of the convict were transformed into a well-planned and sophisticated attack on state laws and policies, the operations of the paroling agency, the limitations on legal rights of parolees, the indeterminate sentence, and other issues far removed from the usual minor food grievances.[79]

At San Quentin's east gate on August 2, Ted Davidson had motioned to reporters, pointing toward the prison yard: "You see that?" he said. "That's a miniature totalitarian state in there!"[80] The prisoners' movement had begun.

It was true that San Quentin was a totalitarian state, as all prisons are, a rigid two-class society of the rulers and the ruled. But Davidson's statement marked a growing tendency in the Bay Area counterculture to treat the prison as a microcosm of the nation. Was the shock of discovering San Quentin to be a totalitarian state proof that America itself was one? This was the conclusion many in the counterculture would come to as the radical prison critique widened to regard the American prison a subset of a larger problem in the culture. The first casualty of this move was the infant convict union movement inside.

A week after the August Unity Day strike at San Quentin, writers of the *Outlaw* got a message out to the *Barb* urging their Bay Area supporters to "do it in Sacramento instead of at Q. Going to Q is not going to do any good."[81] The convicts' focus was still firmly on getting their concrete demands met. To accomplish that, what they felt was needed was not street theater at the prison but prison reform legislation at the capitol. But the prisoners' plea fell on deaf ears. The counterculture had a prison agenda of its own.

More and more, Bay Area radicals insisted on taking to the streets on the prison issue rather than going to the legislature. And more and more, the counterculture saw itself in the prisoners rather than letting the convicts have their own identity. Even though antiwar pacifists (who usually went to federal prison if convicted of draft evasion), political prisoners, and culture radicals formed only the smallest fraction of California's prison population in 1968, radicals clamored after their own outlaw status and quickly lost sight of who the real prisoners were: "Any person active against the war or against the draft," wrote the *Barb*, "any person active in the minority liberation struggle, any person with long hair or a beard or beads or sandals could swiftly become a con." [82]

At the Peace and Freedom party's national convention at Ann Arbor in mid-August 1968, Eldridge Cleaver dismayed radicals nationwide by choosing Yippie leader Jerry Rubin as his presidential running mate. Though the two were easily nominated, many had hoped Cleaver would ally himself with a more sober candidate, possibly former SDS president Carl Oglesby. But they should not have been surprised. Though he shared the Marxist outlook of more traditional radicals, Cleaver had played to the desires of the white cultural radicals, the street people and commune dwellers whose lives constituted less a political movement than a cultural revolution with political implications, and to whom Cleaver's odd mix of sex, violence, and politics made perfect sense. It was these white fans of his *Soul on Ice*, busy experimenting with all manner of transformations in cultural behavior, to whom Cleaver's glorification of common crime, read as a metaphor, could seem to be viable revolutionary politics. And it was they, predominantly white and middle class, who most eagerly grasped at his fanatic politicization of masculinity in their search for a more potent gender model for the revolutionary male. In the person of the outlaw, what had originated for these fans as a literary trope in a San Quentin convict text had become street politics.

As Huey Newton was being convicted back home in Oakland on a reduced charge of manslaughter, Cleaver and Rubin were busy whipping the outlaw theme into street theater of national proportions, preparing the movement to shun the polls on election day and instead "vote in the streets." The *Barb* ran a full-page "Yippie Panther Pact," in which Cleaver, Rubin, Abbie Hoffman, and Stewart Albert called on the public to come into the streets on November 5 and dubbed 1968 the "Year of the Pig."[83] Because Cleaver was not yet 35 years old and therefore not eligible to run for president, only Rubin's name would appear on the ballot. The PFP proposed a mock inauguration day gala following the election, to coincide with the official ceremony in Washington, D.C. There "Pigasus the Ugly" was to take "the curse of office." On election day 1968, Jerry Rubin and Cleaver appeared on the steps of UC Berkeley's Sproul Hall, Rubin wrapped in a Vietcong flag, and the two burned money and passed out Yippie buttons.

Two weeks before the election, the *Barb* had run a full-page collage print featuring a western gunslinger and proclaiming:

We are outlaws! The cities are the new frontier. Politics is how we live. There is no longer any distinction between theory and action. A new manifesto: There are no limits to our lawlessness. We defy law and order with our bricks bottles garbage long hair filth obscenity drugs games guns bikes fire fun & fucking—the future of our struggle is the future of crime in the streets. We are all criminals in the blind eyes of pig America—In order to survive we steal cheat lie forge deal hide & kill—the future belongs to the free spirit of the outlaw and we take the outlaw's oath: All property is target. All lawmen are enemy! From now on, Total Disregard for the man's homes jobs polls streets stores churches daughters sons pets media culture games goals laws & orders WE ARE THE FORCES OF CHAOS AND ANARCHY We are everything they say we are and we are proud of it—We are obscene lawless hideous dangerous dirty violent & young.

BAMN—By Any Means Necessary
Up Against the Wall Motherfuckers[84]

More than any other prisoner, it had been Eldridge Cleaver who had drawn major sectors of the counterculture into the movement against California's prisons. Owing largely to this single charismatic convict, California became unique in the nation in the degree to which the prison movement came to dominate radical politics. In the Bay Area, for a large percentage of leftists, prison themes at the end of the 1960's gained prominence for a short time, even eclipsing the importance of protests late in the decade against the Vietnam War and the broader issue of race, or even the lure of the counterculture themes of sex and drugs. And more than any other prison book, it was *Soul on Ice* that had confused these cultural radicals into thinking convicts, all convicts, were their soulmates and could be their leaders. For some extremists, the cons had become nature spirits, self-actualized, noble, violent, sexual primitives. Even some moderates on the Left idealized prisoners. Just a few years after Cleaver, radical prisoner-rights attorney Fay Stender would repeat the naïveté of many in the movement when she proclaimed: "I certainly feel that, person for person, prisoners are better human beings than you would find in any random group of people. They are more loving. They have more creative human potential."[85]

By December 1968, after Cleaver had fled the country, having failed to appear at a formal parole revocation hearing, John Sinclair, minister of information for Ann Arbor's White Panthers, would give the cultural outlaw theme its final form. Sinclair ordered a "total assault on the culture by any means necessary" and adopted the Black Panthers' ten-point program for his own. For the white counterculture, however, Point 8, the party's position on prisoners, would now read: "Free all prisoners everywhere—they are our brothers."[86]

6

CRIME FETISHISM IN THE RADICAL LEFT

The year 1968 brought a deepening crisis of police terror against the Black Panthers, a swing toward increasingly violent urban guerrilla terrorism in response, and a concomitant romantic fetishization of crime in the radical left.* At the same time an almost total breakdown in the mechanisms of reading and writing control occurred at San Quentin when efforts of custody staff and prison administration to shore up censorship came under angry fire in several successful court challenges to the prison's censorship rules and the passage of Penal Code section 2600, the "Convict Bill of Rights." More free to read and write than ever before, large groups of convicts in San Quentin launched a concerted move to replace the prison's education and library systems with secret, underground ones of their own. Two distinct prison movements began to take shape inside the walls, each supported by separate but overlapping large groups from the Bay Area community urging them on and supplying them with reading material. One provided the germ of a moderate, reformist effort at prison unionization. The other produced both a San Quentin chapter of the Black Panther party and an ultra-leftist prison gang, the Black Guerrilla Family (BGF). Secret political education for inmates became a deadly serious business for both groups. The object was, first, control of the yard, dominance in the convict subculture, and power against guard staff and the warden's office. But one group of inmates began to push strenuously for legislated prison reforms as well. In sharp contrast, the opposing faction of prisoners looked far

*Jimmy Carr, an ex-convict Black Panther and close friend of George Jackson, refers to the "false consciousness" of California convicts "constantly reinforced . . . by the attitude of the Left, with its own romantic fetishization of crime." See Carr, p. 201.

beyond San Quentin's walls, seeing its struggle as part of a national, even an international, revolutionary movement. This group called for nothing less than the immediate release of all prisoners and the destruction of the American state. Outside the walls, an uncritical acclaim for all prisoners by the Bay Area Left reinforced and obscured what was sometimes pure prison gangsterism. When revolutionary politics hid the crimes of petty thugs, Bay Area prison activists and organizations were sadly misused at times by prisoner opportunists posing as revolutionaries.

For thirteen months after the convict unity strike of August 1968, a small group of San Quentin inmates set about gathering prisoners' grievances. At the height of the August strike Warden Nelson granted permission to certain prisoners to collect complaints from the four major cell blocks. The process continued after the strike, until 4,500 letters and lists of complaints had been culled. Word of this activity reached state legislators on the Assembly Committee on Criminal Procedure, and a date was set for the committee to visit the prison on February 18, 1969. It was to be the first of many such prison visits, historic events in that they brought a temporary end (until the 1980's) to the California legislature's traditional reluctance to interfere in prison affairs. Work began on the inmate-produced Convict Grievance Report to be presented to the committee. Convict Larry Harsha, a participant in John Irwin's inmate study group, did most of the writing. According to Irwin,

Every so often he was given a little airtime on the prison radio and he would ask for inmate grievances. In our group we would look over the grievances. He would bring me the real interesting ones. They put that stuff together into the perspectives that we were developing in that group, the criticism that we were developing in that group. Out of our group came a criticism of the prison system, and one of the manifestations of it is that convict report.[1]

A former San Quentin convict elaborates:

I took responsibility for producing the report. We handed every con a sheaf of blank paper with a single grievance printed at the top of each page, with requests that they write down their ideas, arguments, possible solutions, etc. . . . One guy, well versed in formal law education, got up the summary and the introduction . . . and another guy came up with the Red Rooster's argumentative logic. . . . Ole Rooster, one of our best analytical minds and alleged phantom mover of the *Outlaw*, was gaffled up of a sudden and bussed out—not before he'd gotten his beautiful layout of info on the indeterminate sentencing law off to Cleaver's attorneys, though. Yet another con, at the last minute, donated the use of segments of John Irwin's unpublished studies.[2]

The 78-page Convict Grievance Report was typed onto ditto masters and hand-delivered to Warden Nelson for approval before being run off. Three days before the scheduled meeting, the warden returned the masters with his disapproval. The prisoners were forbidden to submit their report.

The inmates decided to go ahead anyway. An original and four handmade copies of the report were produced secretly, just in time for the February 18 meeting. These documents were smuggled into the meeting room, where Assemblymen Craig Biddle, John Vasconcellos, and Alan Sieroty were in attendance. A San Quentin convict recalls: "Warden Nelson's five or six feet from where I'm standing. I pull the disguise from my report . . . I move to hand it to Biddle, who's chairing the meeting. He grabs it."[3] At the core of the report were the following complaints:

1. Objection to Adult Authority Resolution #171, primarily the refixing of the term of imprisonment at a length greater than originally fixed;
2. Objection to the method of effecting parole violations;
3. Objection to the long terms served by parole violators;
4. Objection to the Adult Authority speculating about the degree of criminal involvement greater than the facts warrant;
5. Objection to the inordinate amount of time served by first-termers in certain offense categories;
6. Objection to apparent lack of consideration given to time served in the deliberations that pertain to the determination of the term of imprisonment;
7. Objection to allowing criminal acts of recent offenders to aggravate the standards used in fixing the term of imprisonment of inmates who have already served time for similar offenses.[4]

Perhaps most crucial of all the demands, Item 12 called for the creation of an Office of Ombudsman for prisoners and free access to the press for the chairman of the inmate council. This was intended to open the way to a full-scale prison unionization effort at San Quentin.

The prisoners' struggle to have these demands heard had gained tremendous power in 1968, when the California legislature amended the state's penal code on the issue of the civil death of prisoners.[5] As amended, the statute greatly expanded the reading, writing, and correspondence privileges of prisoners as well as granting other rights. In some ways the statute simply codified in law reading and writing liberties the inmates had already secured by so thoroughly undermining the prison's ability to censor. But the legal acknowledgment of the communication rights of inmates gave a mighty boost to the growing convict movement inside. After 1968, according to the new law, San Quentin inmates were guaranteed the right to receive any printed matter "accepted for distribution by the United States Post Office," except materials openly inciting violence or murder or grossly obscene publications.

Alan Sieroty authored the legislation to amend section 2600 of the penal code. Sieroty, who had served on the board of directors of California's American Civil Liberties Union since 1958, had been present as a member of the Assembly Committee on Criminal Procedure the day it convened at San Quentin to receive the Convict Grievance Report. He had responded with enthusiasm when members of the American Friends Service Committee Coleman Blease, Jan Marinesen, and Joel and Emma Gunterman reminded the lawmaker of the case of Caryl Chessman and urged him to introduce legislation expanding the intellectual rights of prisoners. Sieroty was angered that the prisons continued to feel "they had the right to control all intellectual activity": "People lose their liberty. We understood that. But they should be able to think and read and write and do those things that are not a threat to anybody but are part of our basic rights."[6] After a long battle with the Department of Corrections, which opposed the bill from the beginning, Penal Code 2600 underwent the revisions necessary to reassure the prison system that granting reading and writing privileges to inmates would not compromise institutional security. Director of corrections Raymond Procunier then advised Governor Reagan to sign the bill, and the Convict Bill of Rights became law. In addition to granting relative freedom of access to reading materials, Penal Code 2600 gave prisoners the right to inherit real and personal property, to correspond confidentially with members of the bar and holders of public office, and to own written material that they produced while imprisoned.[7]

One immediate and dramatic result of the new law was that confidential letters from inmates alleging abuses in the prisons poured into the offices of California attorneys and lawmakers. Rowan Klein, administrative assistant to Assemblyman Alan Sieroty, notes how this galvanized the legal community:

We had no idea what was going on [in the prisons]. For the first time prisoners could send confidential letters to somebody in power and they wouldn't get in any trouble for it. . . . I remember, before 2600, going in and looking at copies of prisoners' files and there would be Xerox copies of these long letters they were writing to friends or to some public official. This intimidated these people from using the mails to tell people what was going on. . . . [Penal

Code 2600] was the single most important thing that happened to open up the prisons. It forced the prison system to open up to the public. . . . We received hundreds and hundreds of letters.[8]

Radical Bay Area attorneys began to show intense interest in prisoner postconviction law. The number of court cases involving postconviction prisoners' rights swelled the court docket, adding to the already great volume of habeas corpus petitions being brought by convict writ-writers and jailhouse lawyers. Many of the cases were themselves protests against the few remaining restrictions on inmates' reading and writing. Five cases that followed quickly upon passage of Penal Code 2600 deserve special note. *Gilmore* v. *Lynch* (1971) would find that limiting the prison's law library to twelve approved texts was a denial of reasonable access to the courts.[9] *Van Geldern* v. *Eli* (1971) determined that inmate authors could no longer be required to relinquish 25 percent of their profits to inmate welfare funds.[10] Most important, *Harrell* v. *McKinney* (1970) found that inmates could not be denied a particular piece of reading simply on the grounds that it did not promote rehabilitation or that it tended to incite misdemeanors or felonies, as long as it did not pose a threat to prison discipline. Echoing the fading language of the treatment era, the court in *Harrell* found that

free access to all printed materials which are accepted for distribution by the United States Post Office . . . is more in accord with legitimate prison objectives than limited access. . . . Even persons who have committed anti-social acts warranting their imprisonment may derive greater rehabilitative benefits from the relatively free access to the thoughts of all mankind as reflected in the published word than they would derive from a strictly controlled intellectual diet.[11]

The combined effect of Penal Code 2600 and the court cases it spawned forced San Quentin, at least officially, to cease using its index of disapproved periodicals as the guide to deciding which incoming literature to confiscate. These decisions were soon followed by *Jordan* v. *Grady* (1972), which upheld the right of confidential correspondence between prisoners and public officials or attorneys, and *Jordan on Habeas Corpus* (1974), which allowed this correspondence to include enclosures such as court documents.[12] The law was changing rapidly, fired sometimes by legislators' and judges' lingering faith in the rehabilitation theory that by now was archaic in the prison itself. San Quentin prisoners had for the first time gained broad intellectual rights as a matter of law.

Censorship continued at San Quentin prison, but it became more sporadic and was illegal. Erik Olin Wright, a student chaplain at San Quentin in 1970–71, believes that confidential correspondence with attorneys was allowed for only about a year.[13] Rowan Klein contends that this part of the law was complied with after *Harrell* in 1970. But radical attorney Fay Stender complained throughout the early 1970's that "regulations concerning mail, the right of lawyers to discover documents, the use of tape recorders, and the receipt of reading materials were changed frequently, with no warning."[14] Referring to his imprisonment at San Quentin and at Chino state prison, Huey Newton complained, "The authorities assume that the prisoners who associate with me are highly political. Then they find out which books these men are reading; they confiscate the books and remove all copies of those books from the library."[15] As late as the mid-1970's, the superintendent of the California Men's Colony at San Luis Obispo confided to political scientist Ronald Berkman that

although mail censorship was supposedly confined to select items for select prisoners, he knew that censorship was a widespread practice among the correction staff. This was a means, according to the superintendent, for correction officers to register their dissatisfaction with administrative policy and attempt to influence a restoration of censorship. For if "illegal" communications between prisoners and outside was uncovered, even though the means were illegal, the correctional staff believed that the administration would have to "see the light."[16]

At San Quentin after Penal Code 2600 a fluoroscope was used in the mail room to detect hard objects in attorney-client mail such as hacksaw blades or weapons parts. Staff who wish to remain anonymous have admitted as well that attorney mail to and from inmate George Jackson was frequently opened in 1970–71 without Warden Nelson's or Director Procunier's knowledge or consent. Despite these numerous examples of continuing censorship, the general trend was toward a broadening of communication freedoms, in part because of the changing law, in part because treatment staff freely transported banned reading and writing materials in and out of the prison, and in part because of the subversive efforts of the inmates themselves.

Some San Quentin custody staff responded to the laws by begrudgingly granting prisoners their new rights. In 1968 officer-librarian James McHenry, who previous to Penal Code 2600 had had the authority to refuse to allow inmates to order books through the mail, rewrote the prison's book order procedure so that inmates could file a grievance against any employee who denied their book orders. This opened the floodgates to a tremendous variety of mail-ordered books, many of them intensely political. Former San Quentin librarian James McHenry explains that he felt forced to do this by the courts: "It got to the point that I was kind of opposed to what was going through. But as long as it was legal, well, fine. The way the system worked was if there was any question on material it could be denied initially, but they had the right to appeal to a higher-up and let them decide if it was acceptable or not."[17] These "higher-up" decisions fell to Assistant Warden James Park:

> I was the chief censor. I was in charge of the mail room. [Political literature] was coming to the pets of the activist lawyers. It would arrive in the mail room and if there was not already an approval, the mail sergeant would bring it to me. They came to me, and I made the judgment. The political books I knew we could not ban. And I knew that most prisoners aren't going to wade through anything like that, because there's nothing more tedious than Marxist writing. But the stuff on locksmithing, bomb making, or *The Anarchist's Handbook* we'd never let in.[18]

By 1971, according to press reports of the time, Cleaver's *Soul on Ice* and Jackson's *Soledad Brother* could be bought at San Quentin's canteen,[19] though some inmates from the mid-1970's report the Jackson book was soon declared contraband once again. A visiting House subcommittee found that *The Autobiography of Malcolm X*, H. Rap Brown's *Die Nigger Die*, Hunter Thompson's *Hell's Angels*, Jackson's *Soledad Brother*, Richard Wright's *Native Son*, and Cleaver's *Soul on Ice* were among the titles most frequently requested by Bay Area prisoners.[20] Literature such as the *Black Panther* newspaper that openly called for specific acts of terrorism remained contraband. Richard Nelson, former lieutenant in charge of lockup units (the AC and B Section) remains bitter about the *Black Panther*: "Generally we would read it and it would advocate violent overthrow, or death to correctional officers. In fact, they would name some of us by name."[21]

Court-enforced loosening of censorship controls was accompanied by aggressive efforts on the part of some convicts to subvert the prison's Education Department by setting up convict-operated alternative education systems. Book-lending and political study networks blossomed underground at San Quentin, joined by inmates who took their education too seriously to leave it to the prison's treatment modelers. In some cases, the result horrified prison staff. Administration and correctional officers fought hard to root out the subversion. Even informal educational groups or "convict self-improvement groups," which the prison administration formally endorsed, such as the black Self Advancement Through Education (SATE), the Indian Cultural Group, and El Mexicano Preparado Listo Educado y Organizado (EMPLEO), became suspect as paramilitary revolutionary organizations within prison walls. In May 1971, Warden Louis Nelson went to the press with allegations that members of these groups were marching in close-order drill on the yard and posting sentries outside meetings with armbands reading "People's Security Guard." Guest speakers at meetings, said Nelson, were being escorted to the stage by bodyguards, who stood behind them at parade rest while the convict audience leaped to attention with clenched-fist salutes. Nelson objected to members' shouts of "Viva la Revolution" and "Power to the People."[22] EMPLEO and SATE had been formed in 1967, when treatment staff had still been able to convince the warden's office that letting prisoners meet to discuss their social concerns and allowing them to bring in outside speakers would enhance their regeneration. Similar organizations had soon sprung up at prisons all across the state, most notable among them the Black Culture Association at Vacaville Medical Facility. But by 1971 the administration was dead set against these groups. In a March 1971 memo to his assistant wardens at San Quentin, Nelson sounded a note of alarm and threatened a crackdown:

We are reading in the public press, and hearing via television and radio, that the best breeding and/or recruiting ground for neo-revolutionaries is in the prison system. . . . I am witnessing the deterioration of our ethnic organizations, which were once dedicated to the educational improvement of our men inside San Quentin, to para-military organizations with revolutionary overtones. . . . I do not believe that as the administrator of this institution it is proper for me to utilize State facilities or State monies for the purpose of providing facilities or time for the propagation of revolutionary acts or material. In fact, I believe it to be the exact opposite of my duty. . . . I intend to draw the line at revolutionary education.[23]

Nelson warned the inmate self-improvement groups to cease their political activity at once and return to their original purpose of encouraging individual moral growth. His words were little heeded, however. SATE went on teaching its members martial arts in the classrooms. And EMPLEO hung posters of Che Guevara and Fidel Castro on the walls of its meeting room in the Education Building.[24]

Though the public political displays of self-improvement groups evoked mild expressions of discontent among some inmates, Warden Nelson's attack on these officially approved groups was misplaced. The real problem was elsewhere. Underground inmate groups and gangs at San Quentin had for some years vigorously competed for political dominance within the prison and for control of the sub-rosa economy. Now they, too, began to operate covert political education departments. Most notable among these groups were the Black Guerrilla Family, La Nuestra Familia (NF), La "Eme" or the Mexican Mafia, the Polar Bear party, the Black Panther party, and the Aryan Brotherhood.

The Black Guerrilla Family was a Marxist-Leninist prison gang organized after George Jackson's death in 1971 by former members of his Black Family, breakaway followers of Eldridge Cleaver (by now calling themselves the Black Liberation Army), and San Quentin's Black Panthers. A Black Panther chapter had been formed secretly in the prison in the late 1960's when numbers of Panthers were arriving from the streets. Thirty-nine San Quentin prisoners publicly proclaimed themselves members in 1971.[25] After Huey Newton was released from prison in 1970, he had purged the extreme, terrorist left wing of the party, including Geronimo Pratt and Eldridge Cleaver, so as to take the party into the more moderate territory of electoral politics. Inside, in San Quentin's AC, George Jackson allied with Newton and was named Black Panther field marshal. After Jackson's death, Panthers and Black Family unhappy with this new moderate path formed the BGF. Soon both the BGF and the San Quentin chapter of Black Panthers were operating extensive, secret Marxist political education groups, which included instruction in basic literacy skills and production of rudimentary textbooks, along with discussion of revolutionary theory and practical tips on bomb making and gang war. In classes of the BGF many of the heretofore "unteachable" California prison illiterates for the first time acquired a will to read and write, cutting their teeth on readers simplified from *The Communist Manifesto*. A former San Quentin BGF member explains:

A whole kind of . . . revolutionary culture sprang up. There were political education classes. . . . We had printed materials, basically simplified, as much as we could: Marxist-Leninist teachings. Whether it was historical materialism or dialectical materialism or the theory of surplus value, it was all designed to make sense to a person who may have had only an elementary or junior high school education. . . . So a lot of political education classes were nothing more than our basic attempts to teach each other how to read and write, and doin' it in a context of basically introducing people to Marxist-

Leninist thought and to revolutionary ideas. . . . We saw in our efforts to teach people to read and write an opportunity to recruit, to raise consciousness, to start people thinking. . . . And it worked. It was certainly worth the effort.

This BGF educator remarks that the prison's loosened censorship restrictions by the early 1970's had made it easy to get readings for political education classes:

There were only a few books that you couldn't get. *Prison Letters* by George Jackson, *The Anarchist Cookbook*, *The War of the Flea* we could get. Che Guevara's *The Way of Guerilla Warfare* you could have. Debray's *Revolution in the Revolution*. Just about everything we could get to read except the how-to books. How to make Molotovs and timing devices or pipe bombs and that kind of stuff.[26]

A black San Quentin prisoner testifies to the effectiveness of the BGF's covert education:

We had PE classes. That stood for Political Education. I learned to read from the BGF. . . . We swallowed up Malcolm. We swallowed up George. We swallowed up Huey. We read some Eldridge, Mao Zedong, Ho Chi Minh. Those were the type of books. . . . We started with simple things like Ho Chi Minh. And if you didn't know a word you ask your homeboy, your comrade, and say, "Hey, man! What is this word, what does it mean?" And it was rewarding to have a homeboy who started out after you come and ask you and be blessed and privileged enough to teach him.[27]

Left-wing political books were loaned around free of charge by the covert schools and became the primary reading matter of many convicts who could not afford to pay the customary rental fee of one pack of cigarettes for other types of books from private convict lending libraries. This brought many to revolutionary politics. Some prisoners began to spend long hours studying classic Marxist works, poring over them for revolutionary theory and for tips on organizing. A Soledad North inmate in 1970, the convict librarian of the institution's Black Cultural Group, describes the situation at that prison:

I organized the political discussion group and I organized also the criticism-self-criticism groups. . . . I tended to focus more on Lenin than I did on anybody else. Lenin seemed to be more easier to read than Marx. I had ahold to his polemics, the whole thing. . . . It had to of been at least 30 books, 40 books. . . . I randomly went through and read the sections that I wanted to read, especially where they had the International. . . . We used Mao in Soledad in our criticism-self-criticism. That came directly out of the collected works of Mao. And those three volumes [in which] he talked about organizational methods, in terms of how within an organization to keep the balance. . . . Mao simplified it for me. . . . Mao broke it down for me, then I could get back to Lenin.

Suddenly, as this same inmate observes, status on the yard came to be determined as much by literacy in radical political readings as by gang affiliation. For some prisoners Marxist theorists and guerrilla revolutionaries became the heroes whispered about on the yard:

I smuggled the Red Book [*The Quotations of Mao Tse Tung*] in. When I got the Red Book I think there might have been two or three circling around. It was about '69. I remember that having the Red Book was almost like riding around in a Rolls Royce. You were the political theorist of the day if you had the Red Book. I mean, "He who is not afraid of death by a thousand cuts dares unhorse the emperor!" My thing with that book was it fit into any situation that I felt myself in. If I had some contradiction about something that I couldn't work out, like some event took place on the streets that had some political overtones, or whatever, then I could always refer back to the Red Book to draw some analysis from that given situation that would set my mind more at ease. I respected Mao so much. These people became bigger than life, Engels, Marx, and all them. . . . Other people were getting stuff, too, and it was kind of like an exchange thing. If someone knew I had *The War of the Flea*, there might be a three- or four-month waiting list. So guys would come up and say, "Well, hey, I've got such and such. So if I can get *The War of the Flea* now I'll pass this to you now." That went on a lot because everybody was finding ways to get stuff in.[28]

Revolutionary books were the first some convicts had been interested in reading. Even before the days of the BGF, at Soledad Central Johnny Spain had been supplied with books, including *The Communist Manifesto*, by George Jackson. When he became head of San Quentin's Black Panther chapter, Spain used a simplified version of the *Manifesto* with his own students.

I read *The Communist Manifesto* without knowing that it was *The Communist Manifesto*. It was typed up and all of the reference to *Communist Manifesto* was removed. And it was put in a contemporary sense. . . . That's the way I first read it. I didn't even know it was *The Communist Manifesto*. In fact, a few years later when I read *The Communist Manifesto* in a book, I thought, "I've read this before!" I was halfway through the book before I realized. In fact, that's the way whenever I wanted someone to read that, that's the way I would tell them about *The Communist Manifesto*, but without saying, "Well, I'm paraphrasing from *The Communist Manifesto*."[29]

Through the combined efforts of political study educators such as these, San Quentin, home to 5,000 convicts in the 1970's, began graduating considerable numbers of dedicated Marxist revolutionaries onto Bay Area streets.

By far the most elaborate covert educational system at San Quentin in the late 1960's to early 1970's was that of La Nuestra Familia. The NF was a Chicano prison gang created in 1967–68 to offer protection to Mexican-American inmates being pressured by another gang, the Mexican Mafia, and after that to capture a share of the prison's drug, prostitution, and other convict profits. Largely nonpolitical except as it sought to dominate the inmate subculture, the NF organizational structure and to some extent its educational bureaucracy served as a model for other, more overtly political gangs. This was especially true of the BGF, which allied itself with the NF in gang warfare against the Mexican Mafia and the Aryan Brotherhood.[30]

The comprehensiveness and complexity of the NF educational system suggest how developed secret education became at San Quentin. La Nuestra Familia had a formal educational department and even published "educational guidelines" for its various chapters in different San Quentin cell blocks. Meticulously hand-copied guidelines eventually were smuggled throughout the entire California prison system, guaranteeing "that each soldado [the lowest-ranking NF member] is categorized correctly according to their schooling needs."[31] Teachers were screened by the NF educational department, drilled thoroughly in NF concepts, "procedures," and constitution. Then they were expected to teach classes to NF members on the cell tiers. Three levels of classes were offered simultaneously on each tier. Beginning classes "for those in need of special skills" stressed reading and writing and discipline. But like the treatment-era teachers they replaced, NF instructors desired far more than mere instruction in skills for their students. They, too, sought to build a particular kind of character: that of the loyal warrior. With this goal in mind, beginning NF classes included "behavior, attitude, personality, personal hygiene, personal appearance, awareness, consideration for his fellow carnales, completing assignments and following orders." Beginning classes also taught the NF constitution, concepts, enemy identification and interrogation tactics, recruiting procedures, law, and guerrilla tactics. Intermediate-level instruction added to the above a "psychological approach to dealing with faults and strengthening weak points." It also required training in enunciation, leadership, investigation techniques, using the law for NF benefit, more guerrilla tactics, and memorizing 80 enemy names a week. The advanced class was designed to prepare new leadership for the future of the organization. Teachers were expected to meet with students at least one-half hour on the cell tiers and one-half hour on the yard each day. After making written assignments and collecting and evaluating student writing on assigned topics, NF teachers submitted written progress reports every other week on each "soldado."

The high level of organization the NF's educational department reached can be taken as a measure of how thoroughly by the early 1970's San Quentin's official Education Department and library had been subverted and replaced with alternative schools. Records confiscated by guards in cell searches in the mid-1970's indicate that by that time the BGF had adopted a similar, though somewhat less elaborate, education structure.[32] This was a far cry from the tight San Quentin reading and writing control and bibliotherapy of the past. Inmates had not entirely stopped participating in the prison's own school system; most still took advantage of whatever parts of it they thought they could use. But there were readily available alternatives. The convicts had learned all too well from treatment staff the power of reading and writing control. Many inmates now received their worldview as well as their basic literacy skills from educational bureaucracies operated by groups such as La Nuestra Familia and the Black Guerrilla Family.

The actual hard-core membership of any of these groups was quite small. The BGF and Black Panthers at San Quentin were estimated in the early 1970's to have only about 50 members each. The Polar Bear party, a Marxist guerrilla group of white inmates with loose connections to the radical Left Venceremos group outside, could boast only fifteen members. And even the larger Aryan Brotherhood, an arch-right-wing neo-Nazi white inmate organization, had only between 300 and 500 members statewide in 1976. The Mexican Mafia and NF had approximately that number of hard-core members as well. In a prison the size of San Quentin these groups formed a numerical minority. Nevertheless, because the prison political system was dominated by gangs and because of the gangs' paramilitary nature and their tight organization, which included a death oath for members, the influence of gangs could far surpass their numbers. Many times, too, faced with a need for protection from a hostile guard or gang member, a nongang convict often had little alternative than to join or ally with an opposing gang to ensure his own survival. In addition, many San Quentin inmates participated in gang education programs without actually joining, often out of sympathy with the gang's political goals. For these prisoners, secret study at San Quentin became an essential tool of survival.

Outside San Quentin, meanwhile, two forces were rapidly transforming the Left. Across the nation, black activists in groups such as the Student Nonviolent Coordinating Committee and the Congress of Racial Equality (CORE), many of whom had openly renounced the civil rights model of protest, drifted toward militant separatism. Integrationists modeled after Martin Luther King had been pushed aside as massive race rioting across the United States from 1964 to 1968 marked the transition to enraged calls for "Black Power!" In California, rioting in the Watts and Compton districts of Los Angeles in 1965 left 34 dead and $40 million in property damage. Sporadic disturbances scarred other California urban centers to a lesser degree. Angry new voices in the struggle were calling for stepped-up violence against the state. At CORE's 1968 national convention, Robert Carson, a young leader from Brooklyn, set his sights on a new direction for the organization, proclaiming, "I believe that capitalism has to be destroyed if black people are to be free."[33] Black radicals looking to their cultural roots found African socialist writers who readily agreed. In the wave of imported reading materials from Africa that followed, authors such as Julius Nyerere taught eager black American revolutionaries that, whereas capitalism was the root of race hate, "socialism and racialism are incompatible."[34] The task at hand seemed more and more clear. The American state had to be destroyed. Popular black American writers such as Nikki Giovanni soon were calling for revolutionary killing, recalling Eldridge Cleaver's myth of black manhood denied, then achieved at last in violent acts:

> Nigger
> Can you Kill
> Can you Kill
> Can a nigger kill
> Can a nigger kill a honkie . . .
> Can you splatter their brains in the street
> Can you kill them . . .
> Learn to kill niggers
> Learn to be Black men.[35]

To today's reader Giovanni's poem may seem indiscriminate in its praise of criminal terror, but by the beginning of the 1970's any crime, including homicide, regardless of motive, might become justified as a revolutionary act.

For some white revolutionaries a parallel transformation was under way. By the spring of 1970, when U.S. troop withdrawals from Vietnam were suggesting that the war was finally drawing to an end despite the incursions into Cambodia, the white Left had begun to search about for domestic issues to reinvigorate the flagging movement. Many white radicals saw the black American GI as the second victim in a genocidal war. By the tens of thousands, America's young black men had been shipped overseas to the jungle, fighting in numbers far out of proportion to their strength in the American population, and American casualties in Vietnam were more than 20 percent black.[36] A segment of white radicals in the Bay Area expected these black GIs to become urban guerrillas on their return, joining the white Left and newly released revolutionary convicts in a mammoth push toward Marxist revolution. Bay Area press reports from Vietnam seemed to confirm this impression. A June 1970 survey of 833 black and white GIs in the field published in the *San Francisco Chronicle* showed that nearly 50 percent of the returning blacks acknowledged that "they would use weapons" in the struggle for their rights back home. Thirteen percent said they would "if forced to." "Only 37.8% of the Blacks agreed that weapons have no place in the struggle for their rights in the U.S."[37]

As the war wound down, campuses across the country were losing interest in antiwar actions. Wartime inflation was making jobs scarce, and alarmed students were deserting movement life-styles for slots in professional and business schools. Faced with mass desertions, the white Left had to find a way to galvanize its followers into renewed radical activity. But the war years and police repression at home had taken their toll ideologically. By 1970 some radicals in the Bay Area had adopted such a reductionist Marxist model of American society that the left wing threatened to cut itself off from its remaining support on college campuses. Left extremists now insisted on representing American society as a rigid two-class capitalist system governed by a ruling clique. Not surprisingly, considering that one influential source for this oversimplification was *Soul on Ice*, the picture resembled Eldridge Cleaver's two-class myth of the omnipotent but feminized administrators versus the supermasculine menials more than it reflected real American culture. The real America was much more complicated and, for some, the movement model of America ended up being a caricature of the real state. Thus some of the most extreme segments of the Bay Area Left were in a curious position at the war's end. Casting about for somewhere, anywhere, in the real world of America that would fit its rigid two-class model, a portion of the Bay Area Left at last struck upon the California prison. Obsessed with the neatness of the idea that the two-class prison, comprising rulers and ruled, was a model of a two-class state, some would make bringing down California's prison walls their single postwar rallying cry. The bloody chapter of Bay Area history that resulted would show just how obsessed these members of the far Left had become with this notion and just how thoroughly moral consensus had broken down in the region on the subject of crime. Deep ideological rifts had grown between the Left and the rest of the region on this issue as leftists, being fed a steady stream of revolutionary convict writing from the prisons, totally confused with reality what had started out as a convict writers' trope on the outlaw and had then undergone a long literary evolution. Some formed convict personality cults and participated in prisoners' escape attempts. Others proved easy prey for ex-convict opportunists posing as revolutionaries. These mistakes were major political blunders.

Just behind the scenes was the continuing struggle in the Left for revolutionary education, for control of the power of the word, on the streets as well as in the prisons. To the state, strict communication control of prisoners and paroled ex-convicts remained a crucial part of dampening the growing threat of widespread popular revolt. In the ongoing conflict, the role of one convict writer in particular continued to loom very large. Eldridge Cleaver, whose attorneys and wife, Kathleen, had aided the San Quentin convicts in their efforts to publicize the Convict Grievance Report in the winter of 1969, had fled to Canada, then to Cuba, and later to Algiers by the time the report was presented. Earlier, in California, where his skyrocketing popularity after *Soul on Ice* had made him a statewide sensation and his biting public speaking style helped get him selected as a presidential candidate, Cleaver had openly courted a dramatic confrontation with the governor's office.

In September 1968 Governor Ronald Reagan and the regents of the University of California moved to restrict the freedom of faculty to set curriculum and hire instructors at the chaotic Berkeley campus and to establish more controls over the mushrooming number of experimental courses. Berkeley's student body had just asked Cleaver to give a series of ten lectures in a course titled "Social Analysis 139X." The governor was outraged and demanded that the ex-convict be thrown bodily off the campus. But when the regents refused to grant credit for Cleaver's course, the UC faculty and students were adamant and the class went forward as planned. In a speech at Stanford on October 1, Cleaver made clear what he thought of the state's right to limit a parolee's speech: "I know that my parole officer has his representatives here. And for him, for Reagan, it's the same thing—baby, fuck you, because I'm going to say what I want to say. You can revoke my parole." On October 26, he underscored the point to the governor once again: "Who in the fuck do you think you are, telling me that I can't talk, telling the students and faculty members at UC Berkeley that they cannot have me deliver ten lectures? I'm going to do it whether you like it or not. In fact, my desire now is to deliver *twenty* lectures."[38] The course went ahead as planned.

Huey Newton was then under heavy guard at San Quentin. The Black Panther leader got messages out to Cleaver that he wanted a "red light finale," an all-out confrontation "with the Panther forces attacking and breaking into San Quentin." Cleaver explains that the Panthers' plans to assault the prisons went much further:

Some of the leadership wanted a private plane assault on all the prisons of California, with our people landing within the walls and freeing everyone inside. Thousands of Panther-oriented prisoners would be released, and our grand strategy for guerrilla warfare against Washington could commence. . . . By now a steady flow of military equipment and pilfered supplies was showing up in our armory. Military depots and national guard armories leaked like sieves. Some armaments were sold to us; others were gifts for the Movement.[39]

The Panthers' willingness, even eagerness, to advance their struggle to the level of armed anti-state terrorism was driving a wedge between themselves and the more moderate factions of the Peace and Freedom party. In July, David McReynolds, New York's PFP candidate for the Senate, had written an angry note to Cleaver complaining that the New York Panthers had threatened to use guns against him if he did not withdraw in favor of a black candidate: "My aversion to guns has been pretty well confirmed when I find them used or their use threatened not in terms of self-defense against cops but in terms of resolving political differences between groups, radical groups at that."[40] Despite this and other left-wing critiques of the Panthers, their popularity, especially Cleaver's, among the Left continued to soar. *Soul on Ice* had sold 40,000 copies overnight, and interviews with the parolee were appearing in major periodicals. Cleaver was lecturing at Harvard and on televison talk shows; the charismatic ex-convict's reputation made prisoners fashionable even among the staid middle classes. By winter a national constituency much broader than the radical Left seemed attuned to prison issues. In November the *Saturday Evening Post* called Eldridge Cleaver "this Black Panther, this Tom Paine of the New Left." [41]

Cleaver continued his campaign to make convicts the centerpiece of the movement. In an October *Playboy* interview he repeated one of his common themes, by now very familiar to the Bay Area Left, that crime was justified in an unjust world: "What we have in this country is a system organized against black people in such a way that many are forced to rebel and turn to forms of behavior that are called criminal in order to get the things they need to survive." [42] To see all convicts, whatever their crimes or motives, as political prisoners, street crime had to be redefined. This notion was to appear again and again in the prison movement until in 1971 Fleeta Drumgo, one of the "Soledad Brothers," took it to its limit, regularly speaking of "so-called crime." [43] This literary sleight of hand worked. A growing contingent of the Bay Area public was lionizing convicts as political heroes behind bars.

In November, just a few days before his scheduled parole revocation hearing, Cleaver called for all prison walls to be brought down. He implied that the inmates would make good Panther converts:

The only attitude I can have towards the prison system . . . is tear those walls down and let those people out of there. . . . One person acting alone could in fact be engaged in a civil war against an oppressive system. That's how I look upon those cats in those penitentiaries. I don't care what they're in for—robbery, burglary, rape, murder, kidnap, anything. . . . The system is evil. It is criminal; it is murderous. . . . Let them out. Turn them over to the Black Panther Party. Give them to us. [44]

On November 22, he qualified these remarks:

When I speak up for convicts, I don't say that every convict is going to come out here and join the Peace and Freedom Party. I'm not saying that. Or that he would be nice to people out here. I'm not saying that. Yet I call for the freedom of even those who are so alienated from society that they hate everybody. Cats who tattoo on their chest, "Born to Hate," "Born to Lose." [45]

Cleaver conceded that all San Quentin's convicts might not sign up for the revolution when their walls came tumbling down. Few in the Left seemed to be listening to Cleaver's fine distinctions on this point, however. For the most part, the Bay Area counterculture continued to insist that prisoners inside were potential, if not actual, movement radicals eager to join the revolution.

Cleaver was due to surrender to prison authorities on November 27, 1968. When he failed to present himself, a federal fugitive warrant was issued for his arrest. A milling crowd of supporters clustered outside Cleaver's house on Pine Street in San Francisco seeking to shield him from federal agents. But the prisoner had already slipped away. At a farewell party for him held by students of Class 139X, with Cleaver in absentia, Kathleen Cleaver compared the California prison system to the Nazi concentration camps. In the previous weeks an estimated 100 students had occupied UC Berkeley's Moses Hall, which housed the administrative offices of the School of Letters and Sciences, protesting the state's mistreatment of Eldridge Cleaver. Just as the protesters announced their demand to rename the occupied building "Cleaver Hall," the structure was rushed and taken back by police. Many across the nation were outraged at Cleaver's forced exile. In March 1969, when Reuters' Havana correspondent reported that the fugitive was in Cuba, even the *Saturday Review* put out a call for amnesty for him.[46] To many in the Bay Area Left, supporting Eldridge Cleaver had become as much a personal as a political cause. Cleaver was threatened with imprisonment without a new trial and for a mere parole violation—for possession of a weapon, assault, and associating with persons of bad character stemming from the April 6, 1968, shootout with the Oakland police. This fact seemed to make coming out in his support a ready form of personal witness against American injustice and a rite of solidarity with the movement. But for more than a few, committing crimes in the name of this movement and in the memory of Eldridge Cleaver was about to become the ultimate, irrevocable act of solidarity.

By the early 1970's, partially owing to Cleaver's case, convicts who were released from California prisons frequently enjoyed instant hero status in radical organizations and often quickly assumed leadership positions. The hero worship of prisoners was most pronounced, understandably, in the cases of imprisoned Black Panther members. Betsy Carr, a movement radical who worked in the San Francisco Black Panther office in 1970 and later became the wife of ex-convict Jimmy Carr, recalls her own experience: "I got off on myths. I was completely fascinated with the Panther elite—the glamor, the bizarreness. It was my Hollywood. I'd never discussed anything with any of them, just watched in total awe."[47] Charles Garry, Black Panther attorney, blames many of the Left's subsequent difficulties on the convict star system that this hero worship generated: "The white Left who followed the prison system . . . completely got mesmerized on looking upon the inmates as their heroes, and a lot of horrible mistakes were made. "[48]

Convict cultism had tragic and politically disastrous consequences as some in the Left pushed their romantic glorification of crime to ridiculous extremes. When Berkeley policeman Ronald Tsukamoto was shot to death in 1969, the *Berkeley Tribe* voiced approval of the act.[49] Also in 1969, in a show of support for prisoners, the radical Weathermen organization bombed a California Department of Corrections office in San Francisco.[50] These acts did not go uncriticized in the Left, but many silently sympathized with them. The most extreme in the Left went much further. In October 1972, a group of Bay Area radicals engineered a prison escape for inmate Ronald Beaty at Chino's California Institution for Men. By composing articles for underground prison newspapers about what Che or Fidel Castro would have done in various situations, Beaty, known to his fellow prisoners as a small-time heroin hustler, had misled the Bay Area radical white leftist Venceremos organization into thinking he was a loyal movement radical. When a car transporting Beaty to court was stopped not far from the prison by two vehicles carrying members of the Venceremos group, a gunfight erupted and a guard was killed. The breakout ended in a fiasco. After his indictment on new charges, Beaty quickly forgot the revolution. At his trial the convict made statements implicating the entire leadership of the local Venceremos organization in the escape plot. Venceremos never recovered from the blow dealt by this mistake when the inmate's motives turned out to be more opportunistic than politically radical.[51] And this was not the only case in which convict cultism made the Left vulnerable to prisoner opportunists pretending radical credentials. In 1971 a similarly uncritical spirit of praise for convicts permitted former San Quentin prisoner "Popeye" Jackson to wrest leadership control of the fledgling California Prisoners' Union and then use this position as a front for drug selling and prostitution until he was ousted by other union officers.[52]

The most notorious case of convict cultism gone awry was the post-prison career of onetime Black Panther leader Huey P. Newton. Newton returned to the streets in 1970 after an imprisonment of three years on a manslaughter conviction in the shootout death of Oakland police officer John Frey. In his absence, the Panther organization had grown into a multimillion-dollar operation dedicated to perpetuating his myth. Nobody could have lived up to the image this organization generated of him as "Supreme Servant of the People." Newton's violent temper and his cocaine habit guaranteed that he would not. Soon after his release, the Panther and a handful of his closest followers attempted to enter and control Oakland's drug, extortion, and prostitution rackets, vowing to use the profits to "serve the people." Instead a corrupt form of revolutionary gangsterism evolved when Newton's people extracted protection money from liquor store owners and took over houses of prostitution.[53] Loyal Panthers, nostalgic for the old days of the party's school and community health programs, fled the Bay Area fearing for their lives. Newton himself spent time in Cuba and Mexico between 1974 and 1977, then returned to face charges that he had killed a prostitute and pistol-whipped his tailor. In 1987 Huey Newton was reimprisoned for a year on a gun possession charge. The revolution came to a sad end for the "Supreme Servant" when he was gunned down in a midnight Oakland ghetto drug deal in August 1989. It would be hard to imagine a more disappointing epilogue for a revolutionary's life. Even taking into account the hundreds of undercover actions the FBI's COINTELPRO launched to destroy the Panthers, in the end Newton probably did more than anyone else to bring his own organization and reputation to ruin.[54] The Huey P. Newton of the Black Panthers' heyday, brilliant Marxist theorist and people's gun-toting hero, had probably always been more cult myth than reality. In any event, only the myth survived his imprisonment into the 1970's. Shamefully, by that time even his Marxism had become a pretense for gang crime. Black Panther leader Johnny Spain, inmate at San Quentin during Newton's incarceration there, casts light on the issue of convict opportunism:

A lot of people, their heart was not into it. One of the guys who really helped me understand a lot of concepts that I spent years studying got out and within two, three months he was selling drugs. . . . That was devastating for me because I couldn't believe that this guy could ever do anything wrong. I expected much more than he could possibly give. At the time I respected his intelligence . . . and yet his heart was really not into changing anything on a socioeconomic level or a political level, it was out to get what he could get out of life and that was the extent of his involvement. As it turns out, [this type of opportunism] was pretty widespread. And I was a lot closer than other people were. I'm sure people on the outside couldn't see, people on the outside who were involved with the Left. They're seeing people inside who they really think because of economic factors are political prisoners. And

they're supporting these people because they believe there's a political just-
ness in it. That feeling, that understanding, and that political perspective
wasn't shared by most people inside. I certainly became a lot more conscious
of that because I was slapped in the face with it when I became one of the
leaders of the Black Panther party.[55]

Convict opportunists certainly took their toll on the Bay Area prison
movement Left. This is not to say, however, that every revolutionary
prisoner inside the walls was cynically leading the movement. On the
contrary, the destructiveness of opportunists became more a measure
of the blind romanticism of the Left after Cleaver and its ignorance of
the world of the prison than a gauge of real currents inside the walls.
Despite the opportunists, at San Quentin and elsewhere a deep-
flowing tide of sincere convict hope clung stubbornly to its faith in
people's revolution.

Secret political study in the California prisons had only accelerated
its deadly pace after Eldridge Cleaver's exodus in 1968, and the struggle would go on for control of the word. Nobody understood the importance of the fight for words better than this resister of Herman
Spector's bibliotherapy programs. On the college campuses as well as
in San Quentin prison, supporters of Cleaver eagerly awaited word
from their fugitive hero from abroad in the late 1960's. When his communiqués finally began to arrive, they laid the foundation for the next
decade of skirmishes in the prison and outside to seize and direct
education programs.

For San Quentin prisoners, Cleaver's departure had been doubly
hard to take. Had they been betrayed? Why had Cleaver deserted
them? Was he less a revolutionary than they had been led to believe?
A 1968 open letter from a black San Quentin inmate to his fellow
prisoners searched for answers:

Since the forced departure of Brother Eldridge Cleaver, there has been an
inordinate amount of clamoring, vociferating and downright niggeristic emo-
tionalism directed at the course Brother Eldridge reluctantly took: "Man, I
told you that dude was jiving; he is in the wind like most of the brothers do
when Whitey do his thing." . . . Brother Cleaver's departure can be and must
be interpreted as a temporary expedient withdrawal and not a flight in the
heat of battle.[56]

But Cleaver's voice did not remain absent for long. In a communication from Algiers in June 1969, sold on area streets as a 25-cent pamphlet under the title *Revolution and Education*, Cleaver underscored
once more for his followers the crucial importance of seizing control

of the culture's systems of education, the lesson he had learned best from his San Quentin treatment modelers:

We understand that those who control the mind can control the body. . . . It's necessary for them to control the learning process in order to brainwash people, in order to camouflage the true nature of society. . . . The education that is given is designed to perpetuate a system of exploitation. Historically, the struggle in the educational arena, in terms of black people, has been waged from, on the one hand the slavemaster not even wanting black people to learn how to read and write, to black people, on the other hand, learning how to read and write, and then the struggle transposed itself over into what black people were allowed to read and write, until today black people have reached a point where they want to control totally what they read and write. . . . We have realized the necessity of taking control over our education.[57]

The job of seizing the culture's education mechanisms had already been accomplished at San Quentin prison by this time. Now the prisoners, having fully formed their own educational networks, were about to move to flaunt their keepers by bringing their political study openly, confrontationally onto the yard, beginning the transition toward violent political actions. The "Soledad Incident" provided the final push into the open.

7

The Construction of George Jackson

By 1970 many in the Bay Area Left, most visibly the besieged Black Panthers and a campus vanguard of Marxist-Leninist parties, Maoist study groups, political communes, and prisoner defense committees, looked to the California prisons for their revolutionary leaders. Huey Newton, Bobby Seale, and others of the original Panther leadership were imprisoned or had been killed in police raids, and Cleaver was living in forced exile. More prisoners were sought for leadership slots in the coming struggle. The prisons appeared more and more to the Bay Area radicals as giant camps for political prisoners in a growing countercultural uprising, martyrs to an unparalleled campaign of political repression conducted by a capitalist ruling clique against the oppressed classes. The prison was regarded as a microcosm of the larger American society, and inmates subjected to long years inside were assumed to have developed special insights into the essential nature of capitalism. They had received the ultimate political education. Predominantly white middle-class Bay Area radicals who had been first introduced to the crude two-class American sexual mythology of Cleaver's *Soul on Ice* had thoroughly assimilated a two-class view of the state. Some had gone on to read deeply in Marxism-Leninism. But for most, for the street culture that absorbed its politics largely from handbills and the rhetoric of rallies and demonstration speeches, class analysis remained primitive. For these people the rigid totalitarian two-class society of Cleaver's prison presented a ready emblem of the American state which had to be swept away. Opposing factions had developed in the Bay Area prison movement Left, however, which by this time had taken on a multiplicity of voices and was deeply conflicted. Some in the movement, including the diverse group of liberal supporters of the legislation that had produced Penal Code 2600, would limit their prison activism to reformist efforts at improving prison conditions and extending civil rights to the imprisoned. Inside, a growing group of moderate reformist prisoners now massed to form the United Prisoners Union. But the force of events was to undermine these efforts toward moderate reform as prison movement radicals set themselves fully to the task of bringing the prison walls tumbling down and enlisting the prisoners as revolutionaries.

Convicts at San Quentin and elsewhere were eager to be given a new role to play in the culture and became easy converts to the revolution. It was true that regardless of their crimes they were in some sense political prisoners, as the radicals were quick to point out to them. Few who were not poor were in prison. The balance of justice was heavily weighted against the underclass. Consequently, numbers of San Quentin's "convict class" had become avid disciples of the Left and students of Marxism-Leninism, ready consumers of the radical literature that poured into the prison after Penal Code 2600 in 1968 and earnest pupils in the covert educational programs of the Black Guerrilla Family, the Black Panthers, La Nuestra Familia, SATE, EMPLEO, or the Indian Cultural Group. Even the hundreds of more conservative convicts who rejected Marxism and revolutionary ideology adopted limited aspects of class analysis. And they, too, yearned for a new cultural role for the prisoner as they came together in 1970 in a systemwide convict unionization movement.

The years 1970 to 1971 were to bring a bloody climax to the prison struggle in San Quentin and the Bay Area. The Soledad Incident in January 1970 ignited an already explosive situation in San Quentin and Soledad prisons. This would be followed by rapid escalations in radical prison movement organizing outside the walls and increased political and gang-style warfare within. Thousands in the Left were drawn to the cause of freeing the Soledad Brothers, including Hollywood stars and California congressmen as well as Communist Party of America member and UCLA lecturer Angela Davis. A series of inmate and guard killings at San Quentin would inexorably lead to the bloody Marin County Courthouse shootout of August 1970.

As events began to move at a faster and faster pace, some inmates tragically misapprehended the political circumstances outside the prison and concluded that a shooting war was actually under way in Bay Area streets. Nowhere was this more true than in the case of George Jackson, the most notorious of the Soledad Brothers. In this inmate the heroic cultural role of the defiant male outlaw reached its tragic zenith. The result of the conjunction of both of these forces was an escalation of convict revolutionary violence unwarranted by outside conditions. This was a fatal overestimation of the strength of the Bay Area Left by California's prisoners, especially those at San Quentin, as well as a culminating end product of 1960's America's imprisoning male gender discourse. But it was not the only tragedy of distorted judgment. The inmates' misreading of the Left was complemented by the Left's own poor understanding of prisoners. Both misreadings—of prison culture by the Bay Area Left and of the level of struggle outside by San Quentin prisoners—accelerated a move toward bloody confrontation.

Bay Area radicals were very clear about what kind of revolutionary prisoner-leader they were looking for in 1970. Ho Chi Minh's phrase had been circulating for years: "When the prison gates fly open, the real dragons will emerge." At the war's end radicals assumed that what was true for Ho's Vietnam also held in the United States: political captives constituted the majority of inmates, and they would be the best foot soldiers for American revolution. As Angela Davis reminded the Left in 1971, Marx himself had claimed a place in the revolution for criminals, writing that they were as capable of "the most heroic deeds and the most exalted sacrifices, as of the basest banditry and the dirtiest corruption."[1]

The prison revolutionary leader the Left sought would have to be one who proudly celebrated his crimes, as Cleaver had, who supplied the white middle class with a defiant model of masculinity urging them to revolutionary acts, and who reaffirmed the model of a simple two-class American state. But even more important, this prisoner revolutionary would have to be one who could show the Left how to build a socialist revolution now that popular support on the campuses seemed to be declining. Two books that appeared in 1970 contributed to the construction of the sought-after prisoner-leader. These were George Jackson's *Soledad Brother: The Prison Letters of George Jackson* and Min S. Yee's *Melancholy History of Soledad Prison: In Which a Utopian Scheme Turns Bedlam*. Jackson's posthumous *Blood in My Eye* (1972) would then provide both a postscript for the period and a script for the future of the revolution.

As both books pointed out, George Jackson easily met the first requirement of revolutionary leadership. In *Soledad Brother*, Jackson rejected outright the notion of individual or collective violence as crime. It was simply an antithesis to the capitalist state's thesis. "For

Jackson," Min Yee instructed his readers, "criminality in America . . . is a 'very small knot of men and women' who are protecting their constitutional right to own and control the resources, the labor and the minds of the people who live on this continent and, by a logical capitalist/imperialistic extension, the world."[2] Yee compared the prisoner Jackson to Nat Turner, who, according to the author, had declared at the scaffold, "I simply don't feel guilty. I have ventured my life for the deliverance of my kind." Similarly, Jackson had told Yee, "I'm supposed to be a criminal. I'm supposed to have a criminal mentality. Why, I was robbing people when I was twelve, with a great big ol' gun. But always, always, my whole slant in plundering things was in solidarity with other blacks against the white world."[3] This was exactly the redefinition of street crime as political insurrection that many in the Left sought from their prison leaders in 1970. George Jackson soon proved that he met the other criteria for leadership as well.

Inside San Quentin, yard politics were becoming increasingly dominated by revolutionary black inmates. As political scientist Ronald Berkman has noted, the formal abolition of segregation in the California prisons in the early 1960's had created a power vacuum in the prison social structure. The result had been chaos. Black inmates attempting to assume new power in that structure still had to overcome "differential policies for white and black prisoners; discipline, job classification, and parole favoritism toward white inmates; [and] higher incidence of official violence against black prisoners."[4] A group of California senators visiting the state's prisons in July 1970 confirmed one result of these policies: "We found few blacks in the more desirable trade training areas, namely, the maintenance shop, print shop, hospital, dentistry."[5] Faced with lingering racial inequities in the prison and denied the political means to remedy them because participation in strikes, demonstrations, or other large political actions was grounds for disciplinary action, revolutionary black convicts, the ideological products of secret political study groups, were by 1970 more and more often resorting to secret, retaliatory gang-style slayings aimed at changing the way power was distributed in the prison. The major actor in this movement toward gang-style politics was George Jackson.

George Lester Jackson, prison number A-63837, had lived to age fourteen in the Chicago ghetto where he first participated in teenage gang activity. By 1957, when his family moved to the Watts area of

Los Angeles, he was a six-foot-tall, 200-pound teenager accustomed to trouble with the law. Jackson's first brush with the California police followed his theft of a motorbike, after which he moved quickly on to robbery and burglary. Once while being booked on a breaking and entering charge, young Jackson knocked down a juvenile officer and kicked a woman. The youth was detained briefly and released. After another burglary of a store at age fifteen, he spent eight months at a California Youth Authority camp. He escaped from that camp and fled to Illinois, where he was involved in a knifing and was subsequently captured and returned to California in chains. In 1958 he escaped once more and was again recaptured and returned to the Youth Authority, from which he was paroled after sixteen months. In February 1961, nineteen-year-old George Jackson pleaded guilty to second-degree armed robbery as an accessory in a $70 gas station holdup in Bakersfield and was sentenced to one year to life as an adult under the Indeterminate Sentence Law. George Jackson's reception questionnaire read:

My name is: George Lester Jackson, Direct descendant of Lester and Georgia Jackson. One member of the human race.

I would make enemies if: I conducted myself in an antisocial manner.

I would get better if: I had a proper education.

I like to make love: When it rains.

A husband has a right to: Some freedom.

I am scared when: [blank]

Goals: To be a successful writer, and to take a normal place in society.

Philosophy: I am of stoic nature. I believe in live and let live. I try to be easy to get along with and I try to get along with others. I don't make friends easily but I accept others as they are.[6]

Jackson's accomplice, who confessed to having played the lead role in the Bakersfield gas station robbery, would be released from prison after two and a half years. Jackson's sentence as an accessory, in contrast, was to bring him major prison time. Over the next ten years of his imprisonment, George Jackson joined in prison gang activity and assaults on guards, receiving disciplinary action 47 times. The result was numerous extensions of his sentence. A psychiatric report written at Soledad in 1961 concluded that

Jackson is an egocentric individual who states that he is satisfied with himself and sees no need for any change within himself. He rationalized at great length that his antisocial behavior was justified and that it is his intention to continue with his antisocial acts "until he accumulates a sufficiently large sum of money that would satisfy him."[7]

At this early date in his imprisonment, the young convict made no claims to political motives for his crimes. Luis Talamantez, a Chicano ex-convict and friend of George Jackson, casts light on the prisoner's earliest years:

George grew up in the prison system, and before George became politically aware, George belonged to a black prison gang, the Capone Gang. Mostly members from Los Angeles. I knew the guys that he ran with. George wasn't all that big of a heavyweight in that group. He was still a follower, just like I was. I knew George back from Tracy [Deuel Vocational Institution], [and] Soledad Central. He was a young kid who grew up in the system. They all ran together in the Pack, out on the mainline doin' their prison culture number, rippin' off, getting somebody's canteen [stealing or strong-arming for another convict's canteen draw], doin' that whole string of stuff like we all was. George Jackson had a very bad reputation with the administration as being a black thug, pressuring other prisoners and stuff. You could say San Quentin made gangsters out of all of us.[8]

In 1965 Jackson was charged with stabbing a Chicano prisoner in a dispute over $10 and being caught with "escape tools." The next year he met San Quentin's prison boxing champion, W. L. Nolen. Jackson was working in the prison hospital as an orderly. When Nolen was stabbed in a gang fight, he came to Jackson for help, and Jackson secretly sewed up the wounds. Afterward they became good friends and, it is said, formed one of the earliest of the prison's clandestine study groups, using the works of Marx and Fanon to politicize San Quentin's black Capone gang (also know as the Pack).[9] In the great "yard riot" of January 1967, Jackson was seen emerging from a fight with strikebreakers wielding a length of pipe. In February and April he was charged with attacks on Mexican convicts on the tier. And in June 1967, it was alleged that he had refused an order and then assaulted an officer. Soon all hope of parole had disappeared for the prisoner Jackson. Then, for some reason, George Jackson slowly began to undergo a change.

In late 1967, George Jackson's fellow prisoners began to notice a difference in him. Luis Talamantez recalls:

In the middle of 1967 or '68 somehow or other George Jackson started becoming political, started taking political positions for his actions. I don't think it was before that because in 1966 George and me were up in the old gym at

San Quentin lifting weights. And he was still pretty much into people that owed him. He was a collector. He collected debts at discounts. Somebody would give him a debt and he would go collect it. Or something would happen. He would buy debts. A lot of people did that. I did that for a long time. You muscle somebody to pay their bills.

Eventually, Jackson moved away from pure prison gangsterism and found political motives for his behavior. As he would later write,

I met Marx, Lenin, Trotsky, Engels, and Mao . . . and they redeemed me. For the first time in four years, I studied nothing but economics and military ideas. I met the black guerrillas, George "Big Jake" Lewis, and James Carr, W. L. Nolen, Bill Christmas, Tony Gibson, and many others. We attempted to transform the black criminal mentality into a black revolutionary mentality.[10]

Some who knew him then now call into question the sincerity of those political motives. "Marxism is my hustle," Jackson once told his New York editor, in a teasing comment.[11] Did that mean the convict was using Marxism to hustle converts into the revolution? Or could it mean that he was cynically using it to manipulate inmates and the public to his own opportunistic goals? Why did George Jackson become a political radical? "Years and years ago," writer Jo Durden-Smith quotes him as having told a visitor in 1970,

I was angry. I was in prison and I looked around for something that would really bother these cats. Well, I couldn't find anything that bothered them more than a philosophy. I gave everyone a chance. I gave Adam Smith as much attention as I gave Karl Marx. But Smith's whole point was to justify the bourgeoisie and because that was his aim, his conclusions were strained. The things I read in Marx made more sense.[12]

Here again the prisoner seems to combine selfish with altruistic motives. Most among the prison's custody staff and administration continued to view Jackson's newly adopted politics as pure manipulation. Associate Warden James Park's opinion is representative: "Jackson was a hoodlum. He was a sociopath, a very personable hoodlum. He didn't give a shit about the revolution."[13]

Whether the inmate was sincere or self-serving in his motives, or perhaps both at once, George Jackson's newfound political ideology soon began to influence the prisoners around him. Luis Talamantez, tier tender in San Quentin's B Section, recalls the convict's political organizing in the late 1960's:

George Jackson was in B Section with me in 1968 before going to Soledad around Christmas. He'd been in the B Section with me for about six months

on the tier above mine. I'd climb the railings to get up on that floor to hustle.
He would be tellin' me about Che Guevara. Every time I went by his cell he'd
say, "Come here! Come here!" He'd be quoting me stuff out of his book,
standing at the bars to his cell in his black wool jacket. He'd want to lay some
of this education on me, this revolutionary rhetoric on me. . . . But, hey man,
I was like, "You got anything to eat?" you know, "or a sex book? I'm hungry,
man, I gotta hustle something. I ain't got time for that stuff, history lessons,
revolutionary stuff." . . . In B Section he told me about Che Guevara. He told
me about a lot of people. Fidel Castro. And I said, "Fidel Castro! That guy's a
communist and he killed Kennedy! Fuck that dude!" He said, "No, man! He's
a good dude, man, he's fighting Uncle Sam." And I said, "He is?" because
anybody fighting Gabacheria, white America, man, you can get me on your
side. And that influenced me right away. . . . George loved Chairman Mao,
and I said, "Hey man, fuck that dude. He's a chink, man. He don't got anything to do with me." But, see, George liked other nationalities. He believed
in Black Pride and all that stuff, [but] George was an internationalist. He
identified with Che Guevara, Ho Chi Minh, Cesar Chavez. I remember the
Vietnam War was going on and I said something about "We're winning,
huh?" He said, "No, man, the yellow brothers are winning." I said, "The Viet
Cong?" He said, "Yeah, the U.S. is over there trying to kill the yellow brothers. They didn't do nothing to us." I said, "You're right." George was already
having an influence on me.

According to Talamantez, Jackson's influence was felt among white
convicts, though to a much more limited extent:

I remember there was a couple of white guys that lived by me. They had
swastikas on their walls. That was not cool after a while, I realized. Pretty
soon I seen that these white guys had tookin' them down. We all felt our
enemy was the warden and the goon squad who was Nazis and to keep that
focused. It was like, "You know what, man, you oughta get a red star for
your cell. But this other stuff, this Nazi shit, don't go." That's the Man's
bag. . . . The white guys mostly identified with the system. This is their flag,
their society. They believed in that American shit. This was why George was
not accepted by the majority of white guys in the joint.

When Jackson was transferred to Soledad prison in December
1968, he was already busy formulating what he thought should be the
role of prisoners in the approaching revolution. In *Blood in My Eye* he
would write:

Prisoners must be reached and made to understand that they are victims of
social injustice. This is my task working from within (while I'm here, my
persuasion is that the war goes on no matter where one may find himself
on bourgeois-dominated soil). The sheer numbers of the prisoner class and
the terms of their existence make them a mighty reservoir of revolutionary
potential. . . . Only the prison movement has shown any promise of cutting

across the ideological, racial and cultural barricades that have blocked the natural coalition of left-wing forces at all times in the past. So this movement must be used to provide an example for the partisans engaged at other levels of struggle.[14]

The radical political transformation of George Jackson left many wondering what had happened to him. In some ways he hadn't changed. He could still be a ruthless and manipulative convict, but his motives now seemed paradoxical. A white convict takes up this point:

I hated him. He was the meanest mother I ever saw, inside or out. And you want to know why he was what dumbass people on the street call a prison leader? 'Cause everyone was shit-scared of him. . . . I mean, he was into everything when I was inside. Dope, booze, peddling ass—you name it. Strong-arm. Hit man. He was making his way in the joint. And that revolutionary stuff he was peddling? Crap. . . . Yeah, he was all smiles for the lawyers and the kids that trooped in to see him. But what did they know? They didn't know nothing. They didn't see him inside the joint, the way we did. They'd got their fuckin' star, and what did they care about all the little guys he walked over. They had their revolutionary meat to beat. Shit.[15]

John Irwin, an early board member of the United Prisoners Union, makes much the same point:

One of our guys knew George Jackson. George Jackson was not very well liked. We hated his guts. Not for his politicality. . . . He was a mean, rotten son of a bitch. He was a bully. He did a lot of things which were in the right direction, but he also was an unscrupulous bully. . . . [When] he came to the hero stage, to us it was just a peculiar twist of events because he really was in many ways the epitome of a self-serving, aggressive asshole. He wrote some powerful stuff, that's true, and you had to agree with it. But that wasn't the kind of guy that we knew.[16]

These comments exhibit a marked differential perception of Jackson along race lines. Whites who knew him more frequently portray Jackson as self-serving than do blacks. But as both groups admit, George Jackson never cast off the ways of a tough convict. In a critical sense, as Durden-Smith points out, the prison world was the only one that Jackson ever knew. Most of what he knew of the outside world of America he had read of in books or had learned in visits. This was to become of fatal consequence for him. George Jackson's political influence in the prison depended on his prisonized toughness just as much as his gang life had. In some ways they were the same practice. Luis Talamantez notes that, when Jackson was making the transition from gang activity to political activity, a lot of people thought George had gotten soft, [but] George survived because a lot of prisoners listened to him because he was a proven warrior. I could tell you that myself from personal experience. George was living a lot of the time off his past gangster reputation. Not only could he get down on you physically if he wanted to, but he was somebody the warden didn't like. They were fucking him over. So it isn't cool for me or you to fuck with this dude. They [the prison administration] hated George because George fought the guards and beat them. George would fight the guards physically. He wasn't afraid. George challenged them, and they just couldn't stand it to see a black guy challenging them.

George Jackson was transferred from San Quentin to Soledad in December 1968. At Soledad, he stepped up his radical political proselytizing, combining politics with demonstrations of his prowess in martial arts. Johnny Spain, a young black Soledad inmate, met Jackson there in 1969:

They sent me to Soledad Central. I heard about this guy, George Jackson, that he was supposed to be a really tough guy. He never backed down from people. And I thought, "Yeah, right. George Jackson. OK, fine." . . . So I was playing basketball in the gym one day and these guys used to practice martial arts in the gym bathroom, and I went in one day to use the restroom . . . and I was watching them. So my friend comes over and he brings George, and he says, "George, this is the kid I want you to meet. This kid's all right." We talked a few minutes and he says, "You know anything about martial arts?" "Not much," I said. "I don't need that stuff. I'm good enough." And he said, "Well, let's do a little sparring. You try to hit me." And in my mind I'm saying. . . , "I wonder what could I do with him? What could I do in a fight with that guy?" And I watched him, I watched [his] movements. . . . So I squared off and I threw a few light punches out there, and he just kind of eased into them and kind of flicked them away. . . . So I said, "Let me put a little speed on it." . . . So I put a little more speed and he flicks it away just as easy. Then I got involved in it, and I'm really tryin' to hit this guy now. And I couldn't lay a hand on him. Didn't lay a hand on him.

Having first impressed the Soledad prisoners as a warrior, soon Jackson also started encouraging Spain and others to read:

He started giving me books. . . . I was getting a lot of books from a lot of people after that. He said, "You know, you ought to do some reading. I got a few books you might like." . . . I knew how to listen, I questioned, I read, I studied. And I was arrogant. He really liked that.

Jackson continued combining political ideology with martial arts:

I had got totally hooked on martial arts by then, you know, 'cause I said, "I wanna be able to do that, where a guy can't touch me. I wanna be able to do that." . . . George would give you these things to study. He would tell you the maneuvers. Then he'd tell you one day, he'd say, "C'mon, we're goin' on up in the shower and practice." And he'd walk in and wait till four people got in there and he said, "ATTACK!" And you better. If you'd been around George any amount of time you knew that if he said that, you might as well attack. You might as well do it because *he* was, he was gonna come after you. . . . That's what you went in there for, to fight, and you'd better fight.

Jackson could be both brutally aggressive and tender:

One day, I saw George's movement. . . . I saw it before it ever happened. I saw it play out. I knew what position he'd be in and I delivered a roundhouse kick to his back that was devastating. It was awesome. And this guy took the shot on the back, appeared to be crumbling from it, and before I know it, he backlashed his foot and almost tore my face off. It was a good shot to the side of the face. . . . That's the incident when I understood . . . he was pound for pound the toughest guy I ever knew. . . . And yet this guy could reach in and say, "You're very special." . . . I don't care what the circumstances were, he would listen.[17]

Although Jackson was admired for his physical courage and prowess, as Luis Talamantez explains, his successes as a radical teacher came much harder and more slowly:

A lot of guys were afraid of George. But I was never afraid of George. He was a real likable guy. He had humor. He knew how to laugh. He used to call me Macheesmo. . . . I loved George, George was a good buddy of mine. But George kind of talked above everybody sometimes. A lot of people couldn't relate to George on that level. Too political. Too abstract. Too distant for a lot of guys. He was too well-read. He knew Marxism real good. Leninism. He knew all the books. He passed around books. . . . He'd lay one of those on you and tell you to read it and tell him what you thought it meant later. . . .

I'd say, "What d'you mean by that? All right, explain that to me, break that down to me." He'd say, "Macheesmo, the whole thing, man, is the means of production." "The means of production of what?" "The whole struggle is about seizing the means of production." I used to pass the [food] trays through the cell slots [as tier tender]. "So what're you tellin' me? You're gonna seize your tray, or what!"

Jackson worked to convince Talamantez that he was a political prisoner:

I went through a couple of years trying to figure that out, of how am I a political prisoner. Well, . . . because this is a racist society and I didn't have a even chance, and I had a racist judge. I excused my actions. They became secondary. The system was corrupt. I shouldn't be in prison. The real criminals were out there. They were the people in power. . . . George sneered at . . . people who accepted guilt for their crimes. [He] said, "Look, brother, you were just trying to eat." I said, "Yeah." From that time on I started seeing myself on the opposite side of things, the underdog, not only locally but globally. George was already there.

Former San Quentin officer William Hankins contends that Jackson's efforts to radicalize inmates were not always successful even among the prison's black convicts:

We had him locked up in the AC. One black inmate he was trying to swing into the fold was a guy named ———. He had a large following of blacks himself and he was a bad convict himself. But ——— was an American. He didn't believe in all this commie stuff. . . . He was locked up in one of the first cells in the second floor of the AC and George Jackson was down in one of the end cells. And George knew ——— was in there, 'cause the word went right down they just brought ——— in. So I stood there and listened to George start talkin' to ———, 'cause he's yellin' down there, down the tier, you know, and he's, "We're gonna take over this and we're gonna take over that," you know, and "the day's comin' close now and you better come join us," you know, and talkin' all this and Christ! he went on for fifteen minutes. Finally, when he come up for air, ——— says, "You done, George?" "You talk to me," he says, "when you've taken over somethin'," he says. "The only thing you've taken over," he said, "is the cell down there." And he says, "I got one just like it here and I haven't done nothin." [laughs] So he didn't waste his time with ——— no more.[18]

Other observers, especially whites, insist that Jackson's Marxism was insincere. A *San Francisco Chronicle* reporter who interviewed the convict in San Quentin prison in the 1960's and 1970's says:

To say that George Jackson was a Marxist I'm not so sure is correct. George Jackson might have liked to hear that. I don't think George Jackson was a true Marxist. He might have quoted from Marx and he might have quoted from Lenin, but I don't think he was a practicing Marxist. . . . Jackson was a convict. He knew convicts.[19]

By 1969, George Jackson was putting together his first book of letters, *Soledad Brother: The Prison Letters of George Jackson*, which would be released to instant acclaim the following fall with a preface by Jean Genet. A letter from Fleeta Drumgo, another Soledad Central prisoner and a close friend of Jackson's at the time, provides insight into how thoroughly Jackson and others had managed to politicize Soledad's black prisoners. Drumgo also underscores Jackson's emerging internationalism:

Soledad
1-1-70
Dear Comrade ——— ,

It got very deep last night here New Years Eve. Over the years guys use to holler and act absurd at 12:00 but last night it was deep, quiet. I feel a new consciousness, difference, and solidarity was created. It's always been my understanding and feeling that consciousness comes when more of us are willing to feel it.

Comrades are strong: its deep man. Cultural nationalists and other cats that talk a bunch of shit aren't struggling for the same thing we are, they can't be, they are still wrapped up in the riot stage, hung up on identity and shit like that. They know nothing and do nothing but talk a bunch of rhetoric, we don't relate to that. We relate to the party, the weathermen, Mao, Che, Fanon, Lenin & Marx.

Like I mentioned to you comrade, the system blinds cats, destroys their mind and body if they let them. Like George said in his book [which Drumgo must have been reading in manuscript] these places are to destroy a cat, no one leaves here a good guy in the way the system thinks they are, this place builds a lot of hate, love, and revolutionary spirit into a guy. When the prison gates open the real dragons will fly out.

I guess everything is said except Power and Love to the People:

Sincerely,
Fleeta Drumgo[20]

Many more black prisoners than either Chicanos or whites were participating in secret political study groups. Substantial numbers of these black convicts were now ready to take aggressive action on the yard. Less than two weeks later, Soledad's revolution would explode into the open, and George Jackson would find himself at the center of the maelstrom.

On January 13, 1970, the day a new exercise yard was being opened for Soledad Central's AC inmates, a group of thirteen prisoners, thoroughly frisked for weapons, was released into the AC yard. Racial tensions had been running at a fever pitch. Everybody expected trouble. A single guard, O. G. Miller, was stationed above the yard with a carbine.

After a fistfight broke out, Miller fired four times, killing three black prisoners, including Jackson's close friend W. L. Nolen, and wounding one white. Inmates afterward said that no warning shot had been fired. A white convict present on the AC yard that day, Robert Wendekier, underscored the tremendous racial tensions that had built up to the incident and testified in court that Nolen had come up to him in the yard and punched him on the forehead. Wendekier later testified: "I knew he was a boxer. I knew I couldn't play his game, so I decided to street fight him. I reached down and grabbed him by the cuffs of his coveralls and started to jerk his feet up when the first shot rang out."[21] Wendekier said he then saw Nolen lying glassy-eyed on the ground. A total of four shots were fired. Two other blacks, Alvin Miller and Cleveland Edwards, also lay on the concrete yard. A black inmate in Soledad North recalls the black prisoners' response to this incident:

I remember clearly. I heard the shots, and I remember them telling us "Lock-down!" I think they kept us locked up a few hours, and then they made an announcement. They called us back out and they said that some guys earlier today had jumped on a white dude or somethin' at the Adjustment Center. . . . "These black guys jumped on this white guy and the guard fired warning shots and blah, blah, blah, and consequently we believe that one inmate is dead and some guys are critically injured." And I remember one of the guys in the group blurting somethin' out to the effect that "I heard that you killed some blacks!" So as the guy was beginning to get more pressed for answers he finally said, "Well, yeah, we know that a few blacks have been killed." And that was it then, man, I mean everybody got to throwin' chairs around and breakin' windows. And he scooted. And they run us all back to our cells and locked us down again.[22]

Following the yard deaths known as the Soledad Incident, black prisoners throughout the California prisons readied themselves to take the most extreme reprisals. George Jackson and others had already begun to preach a doctrine they termed "selective retaliatory violence" in an attempt to devise a strategy by which black inmates could band together to survive the quickly escalating number of prison gang murders. Basically, the rule was "If you kill one of ours, we'll kill one of yours." This was nothing new in the gang dynamics of the prison yard. But after the Soledad Incident, Jackson added a unique twist. The threat was now extended to corrections officers as well as other convicts, a move that redefined the guard staff as just one more gang in the political struggle for control of the yard. A Soledad inmate remembers:

There had been talk goin' around for some time that the officers were subject to the same treatment that the inmates were getting. . . . And I think there was a kind of concerted kind of thing goin' on to where one would be taken from all the institutions. It was a thing like when one gets knocked in Folsom, then one will go in Quentin, one will go in Soledad, one will go in Tehachapi, all down the line.[23]

Johnny Spain agrees that the desire to kill guards was widespread and adds: "I've had guys come up and [say], 'Look, I'm really thinkin' about killin' a guard.'" Immediately, the level of killing in the prisons increased dramatically. Nine guards and 24 inmates would be killed in 1970–71.

Three days after the Soledad Incident, just hours following a Bay Area television news report that a grand jury had ruled the AC yard deaths justifiable homicides, a young, inexperienced white Soledad officer, John Mills, was beaten and thrown to his death from the third tier of Soledad's Y wing. George Jackson, Fleeta Drumgo, and John Clutchette were immediately charged in the officer's death and became instantly renowned in the press as "the Soledad Brothers." For Drumgo and Clutchette, both serving six months to fifteen years for second-degree burglary, this was a serious charge. But for Jackson, serving one year to life, it was a capital offense under California's Penal Code 4500, which at the time declared any assault on an inmate or a noninmate by a life-termer grounds for death. George Jackson was now facing the gas chamber.

Instantly, shock waves went out through the Bay Area Left, and George Jackson, yet an unknown outside the walls, became an overnight cause célèbre. The Soledad prison administration was accused of unfairly singling out Jackson, Drumgo, and Clutchette to quell the revolution that the Left knew was brewing inside. A white Soledad AC inmate, Allan Mancino, would later state that Soledad custody staff had been seeking Jackson's death for some time. In an affidavit made public after George Jackson's death, Mancino claimed that an officer had once asked him to kill Jackson.[24] As Angela Davis put the case of the radicals to readers of the *Black Scholar* in early 1971:

A guard was killed. George, John, and Fleeta were elected by the Soledad Prison administrators to pay with their lives for the death of this guard. . . . The death of the guard was seized upon as a convenient opportunity to off them because of the enormous contributions they had made in heightening and intensifying political consciousness in California's prisons. . . . Three black activists had already been unceremoniously assassinated. Without incurring the suspicion of democratic-minded inhabitants of the outside world, it would be difficult to repeat this with grace. This time the legal machinery was set into motion. George, John, and Fleeta would be legally assassinated. Their murder would be veiled by the external trappings of a democratic trial. . . . If the fascists were correct in their calculations, the immolation of George, John, and Fleeta would act as a brake on revolutionary prison activities. Strikes would subside. Rebellions would cease. There would be few remaining inmates courageous enough to utter words of liberation when it might be at the expense of their lives. These are the dynamics of terrorism.[25]

Jackson contacted San Francisco prison movement attorney Fay Stender, who agreed to defend him and to find movement lawyers for the other Soledad Brothers. She began organizing a defense committee. But the evidence against the three was compelling. John Irwin and other prison activists were consulted on the case:

[Jackson] wrote her to come down and see him for a defense. She went down, and she decided to organize his defense and she wanted us to listen to these tapes which were of the witnesses that saw George and Clutchette and Drumgo throw the guy off the tier, and, you know, the case against them was powerful, particularly against George.[26]

The case was moved to San Francisco, and Jackson, Drumgo, and Clutchette were sent to San Quentin's Adjustment Center to await trial. Inmate Luis Talamantez, who had been moved to San Quentin's AC as the result of a gang fight, recalls his reaction to the evidence:

It was serious. It was very serious. The snitch described in every detail what he seen George do from his Soledad Y-wing cell. . . . When George showed me [the state witness's deposition], I said, "Hey, man, goddam! That's heavy." . . . From what he said he seen, it was pretty incriminating. . . . It was pretty damaging stuff, as far as an eyewitness goes. . . . George let me read it. . . . It was kind of chilling. When George showed me that snitch transcript I said, "Shit, if I got that evidence against me, man, that's an automatic conviction right there." . . . They got ID'd accurately by this snitch. Drumgo to a lesser extent. Drumgo to the extent that he only served as an assistant to the assault, whereas Clutchette was supposed to have just been the lookout.

A black convict, Thomas A. Yorke, who in 1970 had occupied a cell across the hall from the scene of the assault on the third tier of Y wing, later testified that he had seen Jackson murder officer Mills:

I saw Mr. Jackson holding the guard in an armlock. Mr. Clutchette and Mr. Drumgo were present. . . . Mr. Drumgo was punching at [Mills's] face area. . . . I saw Mr. Drumgo go down the stairwell and didn't see him again. . . . Mr. Jackson went to Mr. Clutchette's cell with Mr. Clutchette and returned. . . . Then Mr. Jackson started beating the officer in the face area. . . . Mr. Jackson knelt on the area of the guard's chest and chopped him, so to speak (a karate chop). . . . It couldn't have lasted more than two or three minutes. . . . Then Mr. Jackson got up, returned to Mr. Clutchette's cell, came back with a flashlight and started beating (the unconscious) officer in the area of the head with it. . . . Then I think Mr. Clutchette came out. . . . Both went back to his cell. . . . Then Mr. Jackson came out, lifted the guard up and slid him between the bars over the tier.[27]

The Left, Angela Davis most vocally, strenuously insisted that this witness's testimony was forced. In fact, Yorke admitted that his life had been threatened by both sides during the trial. He claimed that he had been told by officers that if he did not agree to take the stand to tell what he had seen, he would lose his protected witness status and be put back on the mainline where radical inmates might attack him. And he stated that the defense as well had identified him as a "snitch" by circulating his photo in the prison. Two other white Soledad convicts occupying cells near the scene of the incident, Thomas Worsella and Larry Thomas Eskew, gave the authorities depositions corroborating Yorke's story.[28] Yorke himself would be paroled in December 1971, a month before the trial was to begin.

The Left considered George Jackson to be supremely innocent of the charges against him. In court his posture of proud defiance was beautiful to behold. In April 1970, during a preliminary hearing of the Soledad case, George Jackson struck a court bailiff and had to be subdued in the fracas that followed. Attorney Stender confided to Jackson's New York editor, Gregory Armstrong, that she saw only "one chance in twenty of winning. A possibility of getting a reversal on appeal."[29] Armstrong later claimed that the inmate had himself admitted to the killing of officer Mills in a 1970 interview.[30]

After the Soledad Incident and the indictment of the Soledad Brothers, the formerly secret political education systems at both Soledad and San Quentin exploded into open view. Johnny Spain comments:

After George went to the hole [charged in the guard killing], the administration was in such turmoil they didn't know what to make of it. It was business as usual for them when they killed those three guys. But after that, nothing made sense. You had these people running around talking revolution. They were killing guards. . . . Before that, PE classes were pretty much hidden, but after George went to the hole I made 'em do it in the open. On the yard, in the chow hall, in the library, in the wing, anywhere people could meet.

San Quentin prisoner Nate Harrington agrees. After the Soledad Incident, PE classes throughout the California prisons were conducted en masse and even on the yard: "The classes would attract upwards of fifty people, which was almost unheard-of in the era before because those types of gatherings were considered riotous and would result at least in the noticeable leaders being locked up."[31]

The lid seemed about to blow off the California prisons. Many prisoners now began to think that a full-scale people's revolution outside the prison was engulfing the state. A Soledad North inmate in 1969 discusses this point: "I'm sittin' up in a cell in Soledad and from the limited amount of information I'm gettin' from the streets I'm thinkin' that everything is burnin' down out there. [laughs] . . . That there was an armed struggle goin' on, a people's revolution."[32] This misperception was to persist among California prisoners for the next several years. Dorsey Nunn, who entered the California system in 1971 at Tracy's Deuel Vocational Institution, observes: "From the letters I was receiving from the streets I was expecting when I got out, 'Give me a machine gun, put me in the field!' I thought there was a revolution goin' on."[33] Nate Harrington indicates that many prisoners were eager to be part of this larger revolution: "We saw what we were doing as just a small part of not just a national but an international revolutionary movement. And we very strongly identified with national liberation struggles around the world. And with the world communist movement."[34]

In July another Soledad guard was found killed in an exercise yard guard shack in the North facility. Seven black prisoners, members of a radical study group at Soledad North, were charged in the death and held for 49 days in solitary confinement. Charges were later dropped for lack of evidence. Nonetheless, the level of intensity both of radical inmate study and of administration response to it at Soledad was so high that the study groups were seen as forming the ideological center that fomented the assaults on guards.

George Jackson and the other Soledad Brothers, Fleeta Drumgo and John Clutchette, were by now sequestered deep within San Quentin's AC, where despite their isolation they managed to maintain limited covert contacts with the outside and with radical factions of the prison's mainline population and to radicalize other black and Hispanic AC inmates, drawing a tight-knit group of revolutionaries about them. Despite his isolation, maybe even to some extent aided by it, Jackson was becoming a hero of mythical proportions to black and Hispanic convicts and to countless thousands outside, part prison martyr, part priest of vengeance, part fantasy, part reality, following the publication of *Soledad Brother*.

That summer the Soledad Brothers Defense Committee mushroomed into an organization with a rudimentary bureaucracy and seven subcommittees.[35] Durden-Smith notes that defense committees also were organized and donations solicited abroad.* In California,

---

*Durden-Smith mentions a George Jackson defense committee in London in 1971.

the central committee's list of sponsors included a tremendous variety of leftists, celebrities, and other mainstream cultural spokespersons: Julian Bond, Ron Dellums, Pete Seeger, Jane Fonda, Jean Genet, Barbara McNair, Herbert Gold, Terry Southern, Jack Newfield, Noam Chomsky, Benjamin Spock, Lawrence Ferlinghetti, Ralph Gleason, Beniamino Bufano, Allen Ginsberg, Huey Newton, Robert Scheer, Tom Hayden, Mario Savio, and Angela Davis. Publicity and fund-raising subcommittees arranged press conferences and interviews with George Jackson through attorneys Fay Stender and John Thorne and produced leaflets, posters, news releases, lapel buttons, bumper stickers, and fund-raising letters. The Grateful Dead played concerts for the benefit of the Soledad Brothers, and speakers such as Jane Fonda and Angela Davis appeared on their behalf. Poetry readings, art auctions, and bake sales added to the committee's coffers.[36] The Soledad Brothers had become much more than merely a cause of the grass-roots California Left. Overnight George Jackson was a national celebrity and a very marketable commodity.

Left-wing romanticism attached to the Soledad Brothers reached the dimensions of cult worship. The Soledad Brothers were instantly recognized as figures in the by now familiar genre of outlaw literature, as improvisations on a theme from *Soul on Ice*. As such, they found a ready-made place in California culture. A *Berkeley Monitor* article in the summer of 1970 illustrates the adulation of the Left and portrays George Jackson at the start of his meteoric rise:

Each appearance of the three black inmates, accused of killing a white prison guard, proved to be a rallying point for "the people." The courtroom was filled with friends and relatives at each appearance. After each appearance, the three men were cheered as heroes as they were driven from the court-house to their maximum security cells. . . . George Jackson, the oldest and the most political of the three accused men, writes powerful, eloquent letters to friends, relatives and his lawyers (one of whom is Berkeley attorney Fay Stender). Some of his letters are reminiscent of the writings from prison of Eldridge Cleaver. Bantam Books hopes to publish a collection of Jackson's letters.[37]

John Irwin watched the hero-making process unfold:

We first walked over after Fay [Stender] opened her [1970 Prison Law Project] office and here were all these huge posters of the Soledad Brothers. And here were all these little tiny giggly radical gals in the office. All of 'em had picked one of 'em as the one that she was worshipping. That was just so fuckin' silly to us. We also saw that it leads to . . . stupid acts.[38]

Gregory Armstrong comments on the final result for George Jackson:

He became the idol of many radical groups in this country. Adoring women filled the courtroom during his appearances. Dozens of newspapermen and television reporters flocked to the prison to interview him. He elicited fanatical loyalty from friends and supporters both inside and outside prison.[39]

Part of the cultism surrounding the Soledad Brothers was pure romance for the defiant black male outlaw hero. More and more, manhood, criminality, violence, and terrorism against the state had become entangled in an imprisoning gender discourse for the left-wing American male. For both men and women of the extreme Left, manhood was increasingly being defined in acts of anti-state violence. The romance of the male outlaw had become so seductively alluring, so sexually loaded, that outlaw status seemed to be the unique property of males. California's women convicts would get scant notice as the prison movement swept along, an almost exclusively male-focused cause. With the single exception of Angela Davis, no California women prisoners would become folk heroes in the prison movement, and women's prison issues never attracted the interest men's did. In one sense, the swing toward male convict personality cults had little to do with actual prisoners. The myths of convict heroes in the early 1970's were fantasies produced largely by the continuing desperate need for new male gender roles in the white middle class.

Ignoring Angela Davis's 1971 warning in the *Black Scholar* to avoid "the tendency of building personality cults around specific individuals," the Left all across the nation quickly elevated Jackson, Drumgo, and Clutchette to star status. Lost in the process of mythification were all the other prisoners of the California prison system, their needs, and their political struggle. And as the marketing of George Jackson gained momentum, money started pouring in to the Soledad Brothers Defense Committee.

Form letters bearing the signatures of Jane Fonda, Benjamin Spock, William Kunstler, and other white liberal notables had gone out to members of the middle class, introducing Jackson as the latest incarnation of the outlaw literary figure, "a brilliant writer [who] will soon have an anthology of his letters from prison published. Support the Soledad Brothers!"[40] The *Berkeley Monitor* similarly teased its audience with the inmate's yet-unpublished literary efforts. An issue of the tabloid lauded Jackson, by now the white Left's black Everyman, with a cover photo showing an American flag turned on its side and superimposed over a sketch of street people so they appeared to be behind bars. It invited its readers to see George Jackson as the latest in the line of California literary outlaws when it repeated the words of the defense committee describing the inmate as "a brilliant writer, [who] will soon have an anthology of his letters from prison published."[41]

When Jackson's book finally came out in fall 1970, it was a bombshell best-seller. But events had already outstripped the book. And when the Soledad Brothers' case finally came to trial in the autumn of 1971, it would be almost an afterthought, for George Jackson would be dead in his grave.

The Black Panther party was a major manipulator of the George Jackson myth in the last year of his life. After the Soledad Incident, the party had sought Jackson out. According to Nate Harrington, "The Black Panther party leadership saw a vast recruitment potential in the prison, and they saw George Jackson as the most effective leader."[42] Jackson became a San Quentin Panther field marshal in 1970. As Durden-Smith notes, he "addressed his supporters through a stream of tapes and memoranda that issued from the San Quentin visiting rooms, carried out by family, friends and lawyers."[43] But another prisoner, the soon-to-be-released Huey Newton, was to make Jackson's efforts to communicate difficult. After Newton had spent 22 months behind bars, his 1968 manslaughter conviction was overturned in the summer of 1970 and a retrial ordered, on the grounds that in the original trial the judge had improperly instructed the jury. Huey was out on bail. He was greeted at Alameda County Courthouse by a crowd beside themselves with joy, chanting "Huey's Free! Huey's Free!" On taking back the reins from David Hilliard, who had controlled the party in his absence, the Panther leader found himself bound by the double constraints of the ongoing anti-Panther police war and the insistence of those in his own party calling for "action now" terrorism in response. Publicly, Newton chose a middle course. In a series of purges, he drove the more militant Eldridge Cleaver, Geronimo Pratt, and others from the party. As one more part of his effort to regain leadership, Newton took over the management of George Jackson's communiqués. Jackson's messages were processed through the Panther Central Committee by Newton himself, who valued Jackson as a figurehead but felt a need to keep him under control. Consequently, many of George Jackson's tapes and memos were never delivered.[44]

By 1971 George Jackson had become a myth almost wholly constructed by opposing Bay Area groups. In the eyes of San Quentin prison staff he seemed an almost superhuman threat, a superconvict now held personally accountable for each and every San Quentin guard death and suspected as well of being the elusive leader of the emerging Prisoners' Union. In the eyes of black revolutionary prisoners he was the promised deliverer, a shaman of revenge, the Dragon. To the Black Panthers outside he was the figurehead of a valued, but expendable, adventurist wing. And to the white middle-class Left of the Bay Area George Jackson was at once a passive, suffering black martyr of America's racist prisons and a defiant, supermasculine warrior role model for the revolution ahead.

Why was George Jackson's public image so manipulable? First, because of the convict narrative genre to which it belonged and its heavy editing, his *Soledad Brother* book was easily appropriated by different groups for different uses. Next, his increasing long-term isolation from his followers in the mainline San Quentin prison population as well as from the Bay Area public led Jackson himself to misperceive and to be misperceived.

From his cell deep in the San Quentin Adjustment Center, the prison within a prison, the inmate strained to maintain contacts with three worlds. To maintain communications with his Bay Area supporters, he sent and received "kites," smuggled letters and messages, through lawyers, visitors, and legal investigators. He organized his closest comrades on the AC tier about him. And he smuggled messages to the prison mainline population by such conveyances as the meal tray cart and sympathetic prison service personnel. But as the months passed, George Jackson's contacts became fewer and fewer. Tightened restrictions on prison visiting would limit the number of visits he could receive each week from those passing as "legal investigators," including Angela Davis, his New York editor, Gregory Armstrong, and others who were functioning as his main conduits to the outside.

But the prison's increasing restrictions had an unpredictable effect. Jackson's view of the world outside the prison became dangerously fantastical. This should not have surprised anyone. Soledad prison's chief psychiatrist, Frank Rundle, wrote in early 1971 that as isolation was increased for the convicts under his care, they had little "opportunity to apply the reality-checking logic which is imperative to the maintenance of a rational state of mind. Many inmates [in isolation cells] slipped in and out of an autistic world of fantasy as a consequence of this isolation." [45] Gregory Armstrong, who visited the inmate at San Quentin frequently in 1970–71, has commented on what may have been a similar process taking place in George Jackson: "I realize[d] with a sinking feeling that the world outside his cell [wa]s completely unreal to him." [46] George Jackson's world was closing in on him. His contacts with the outside were being cut off. All that would remain would be the lingering images of an unreal free world. Cut off from the real, Jackson succumbed to others' views of what he should be. Johnny Spain agrees:

George . . . was given only the views of people who were extremely, romantically revolutionary, fantastically revolutionary in some instances. Being constantly fed that perspective, along with his own studies, which didn't include the perspective of the outside world, you lack in perspective. And if you lack in perspective, any conclusions that you're going to draw are going to be deficient. . . . That's what happened to George. . . . He was an extremely intelligent man. Unfortunately, his intelligence wasn't nurtured by enough of the larger world to be more effective than he was.

Outside the prison, too, supporters of Jackson, lacking real, continued contact with the prisoner, fabricated various George Jackson myths of their own. When his book appeared in the fall of 1970, Jackson's appropriation by the white middle-class Left outside the prison was accelerated.

Soledad Brother was a collection of Jackson's letters to his younger brother Jonathan, to Angela Davis, to his mother and father, to his attorney Fay Stender, and to his editor and others from 1964 to 1970. The *Times Literary Supplement* called the book "revealing not so much for the contribution that it makes to the theory of revolution or to the analysis of Black Power but as the record of a human personality developing under conditions of extreme stress." [47] Other mass press reviews concurred. George Jackson's text was a personal testament to the endurance against overwhelming odds of a black man caught in the trap of racist America. This was both the strength and the weakness of the book. As Durden-Smith put it, *Soledad Brother* was read as a victim's book, and George Jackson disapproved of the product almost as soon as it appeared: "He came to realize that . . . *Soledad Brother* had traduced what he really believed in. It had painted a false picture of him; it had made of him not a man on the offensive, a fighter, but a man on the defensive, an inert victim." [48] *Soledad Brother* highlighted Jackson's personal prison struggle and political development, but it conveniently omitted any reference to his more mercenary gang involvements. It also worked in the opposite direction, erasing the prisoner's individuality to portray him as an archetypal victim of American racism. Because the book consisted of letters, readers easily privileged those sections that fit their particular myth of the inmate. In the following excerpts from a letter to Fay Stender, for example, readers in the Left could see Jackson as the archetypal black victim.

April 4, 1970

Dear Fay,

For very obvious reasons it pains me to dwell on the past. As an individual, and as the male of our order I have only the proud flesh [a medical term for the abnormal growth of flesh that sometimes forms around a healing wound] of very recent years to hold up as proof that I did not die in the sickbed in which I lay for so long. I've taken my lesson from the past and attempted to close it off.

I've drunk deeply from the cisterns of gall, swam against the current in Blood Alley, Urban Fascist Amerika, experienced the nose rub in shit, armed myself with a monumental hatred, and tried to forget and pretend. A standard black male defense mechanism.

It hasn't worked. It may just be me, but I suspect that it's part of the pitiful black condition that the really bad moments record themselves so clearly and permanently in the mind, while the brief flashes of gratification are lost immediately, nightmare overhanging darkly.

My recall is nearly perfect, time has faded nothing. I recall the very first kidnap, I've lived through the passage, died on the passage, lain in the unmarked, shallow graves of the millions who fertilized the Amerikan soil with their corpses; cotton and corn growing out of my chest, "unto the third and fourth generation," the tenth, the hundredth. My mind ranges back and forth through the uncounted generations, and I feel all that they ever felt, but double.[49]

Soledad Brother became an overnight best-seller in the fall of 1970 and, as Durden-Smith remarks, soon Jackson "became capable of assimilating every vision, every metaphor, projected onto him." The book sold well in markets as far away as London. Durden-Smith, who attended Soledad Brothers Defense Committee meetings in that city, would observe that from one meeting to the next George Jackson's myth could change as he was turned into "distorted opposites": "In one he had been made to seem a passive figure, a cause, a man without intention. And in the other he had been made to seem a wholly active figure, a god, a man without extension."[50]

Gregory Armstrong's editing of *Soledad Brother* had contributed greatly to keeping the book a personal narrative, preventing it from becoming a polemic or a practical guide to revolution, as Jackson might have preferred it to be, and as his final book, *Blood in My Eye* (1972), was to become. In his own memoir, in an entry dated May 1971, Armstrong complained that "George's recent writing is all pronouncements and polemics. Hardly a trace of his humanness is left. I guess this is what he thinks people expect of him." Armstrong had carefully deleted anything approaching the polemical from *Soledad Brother*. Feeling that the original set of letters sent to him by Fay Stender lacked "the kind of circumstantial detail you get in a novel," Armstrong had decided from the outset of his working relationship with Jackson "that the letters needed a running commentary that could be put together out of George's answers to certain questions I had prepared." To provide this commentary, the editor had visited San Quentin, conducting hours of taped interviews with the prisoner and compiling information that could serve to highlight the prisoner's personal biography in the final text. At one point in the editing of his book, Armstrong admits, inmate Jackson complained to him, "I don't want anyone cutting me up like this." "That's me," Armstrong confessed, "trying to improve you." [51]

Armstrong and Jackson worked through the spring and summer of 1970 putting the inmate's book together. During this time the editor passed officially through the prison gates posing as a legal investigator attached to attorney John Thorne, and he and the prisoner traded sheafs of the manuscript concealed in stacks of legal documents. In August, prison guards confiscated part of the manuscript. Thorne "worked out a deal" with the warden, and the papers were returned to the editor when he left the prison. Soon afterward, however, police seized Armstrong's interview tapes and scattered parts of the manuscript in a nighttime raid at the San Francisco Defense Committee's Soledad House where he was staying. The tapes were returned by court action. [52] In the end, when the finished *Soledad Brother* was on the shelves and Bay Area readers were eagerly buying it for a view of the real George Jackson, the inmate's mother, Georgia Jackson, claimed that "the book is all lies put out by white people." [53] This comment, Armstrong insisted, sprang from Mrs. Jackson's disappointment that in the book her son had expressed pride for his crimes. His mother had hoped instead for a text that would vindicate him as innocent. But the larger question remains. How much was *Soledad Brother* the product of white middle-class mass readership desires and a white editor eager to meet them?

Armstrong and Fay Stender, the first to make a selection of the inmate's letters for the book, did not bowdlerize Jackson's text as some have claimed.[54] But Armstrong did edit heavily, even writing himself into the hero-prisoner's book and thereby bringing it into conformity with a convention of the American "criminal narrative" literary genre. For three centuries editors and religious confessors had participated as silent partners in the production of the texts of American convicts, often controlling their content.[55] *Soledad Brother* proved no exception. Three letters in the volume from Jackson to Armstrong established the editor as a behind-the-scenes participant in the action of the Dragon's unfolding prison drama. The book began with a long letter to the editor intended to create a biographical context for those that followed but also presenting Armstrong's character next to the person of George Jackson. Armstrong had compelling personal reasons for writing himself into Jackson's book, as he openly admits in his 1974 memoir, *The Dragon Has Come*. The black outlaw George Jackson's supermasculinity promised solutions to the editor's lack of identity as a white middle-class male:

For most middle-class whites like myself, life is a matter of chronic discontent. The problem is that there doesn't seem to be any explanation most of the time for the way we feel. There doesn't seem to be anyone to blame. . . . I know why so many middle-class whites like myself identify with blacks. We say to ourselves that only blacks possess true authenticity. I know that loving George, caring about him, is part of my desire to be real.[56]

For Armstrong and for many of *Soledad Brother*'s white middle-class readers, both women and men, the seductive power of George Jackson's politics lay in his defiant masculine imagery. Armstrong's memoir speaks candidly of the editor's failed marriage, of what he regarded as his own tame, domestic passivity, of his middle-class male "slave mentality." He took George Jackson as a personal savior:

Everything about him is flashing and shining and glistening and his body seems to ripple like a cat's.

John [Thorne] suggests that I feel George's arm so I can sense the results of all those push-ups. I am still shy, but George offers me his tensed arm and I take it in my hand and it is like a horse's haunch. "I almost can't believe that," I say.

George, constantly in motion, like a generator emanating energy in an almost visible form, a scintillating yellowish light carving up space with every inch of his body, cutting it with gestures of his hands, pounding it with his head, rising up from his chair and almost levitating with the sheer displacement of force. It is as if he were taking the very space inside himself, absorbing, pulling in everything that surrounds him, almost visibly swelling with the intake of substance. Always alert, always wary, watchful, responding to every sound. . . . On the other hand, my body, when I sit, is limp, my hands rest wherever I put them and remain inert. As someone who leads an almost completely protected life, I have no need for my body. It is only a means of propelling my head from place to place.[57]

George Jackson's was an intensely politicized masculinity that, for Armstrong and other readers, could lend the story of his crimes, even the subject of crime itself, an erotic appeal:

I can see that George is excited by the memory of stealing. I am excited too. It is almost as if the idea of stealing were sexually stimulating. Like seeing a woman lifting her skirts. One immorality must lead the mind to another, and from there to everything that is forbidden.[58]

By including his name in the pages of Soledad Brother, Armstrong could bring his own persona closer to his romantic myth of the prisoner George Jackson. In his 1974 memoir, Armstrong wrote that during the period of his interviews with Jackson he, too, had contemplated killing a police officer.[59] The New York editor was not alone in his dreams of romantic "irrevocable acts" of revolution. There were many others in the white middle class who indulged in similar fantasies concerning Jackson. Some of these fantasies would become reality.

Durden-Smith writes of having asked an unnamed associate of George Jackson's how much of Soledad Brother, in the end, was Jackson's:

Well, not much of it was his, as far as I can tell, and he was madder than hell about it. The irony in the end, I guess, was that the book was sold all over the world, and attracted all kinds of people, thousands of them, to the defense committee. They put their money in the hat, organized meetings, and made him a hero. And yet the guy they were doing it for wasn't George. He never really existed for them. They were doing it for the guy in the book, whoever he was. Some guy who'd been cut, edited, rewritten, recomposed and bowdlerized somewhere outside the walls, to fit the image they wanted. All this and Jean Genet too. God knows what they'd have thought of each other if they'd ever met.[60]

After it was all over and the manuscript had become a best-selling book, a copy of Soledad Brother would be delivered to George Jackson in his San Quentin AC cell. It was confiscated as contraband within an hour.

On October 15, 1970, Gregory Armstrong and members of the Soledad Brothers Defense Committee held a small publication party just outside San Quentin's east gate, chanting "Free the Soledad Brothers!" and denouncing the prison's attempts to silence the inmate. *Life* and *Time* magazines were soon clamoring to do cover stories on Jackson, and the nation's underground newspapers were filled with Soledad Brother material. Mike Wallace, National Educational Television (NET), and Canadian and British television all sought interviews with George Jackson. San Quentin prison responded by limiting journalists to one visit apiece. The mass response was so overwhelming that public reactions could be extreme: in Milwaukee a woman was apprehended trying to hijack a plane in an attempt to ransom the Soledad Brothers' freedom.[61]

Meanwhile, the Soledad Brothers Defense Committee had grown to gargantuan proportions and become rich on public donations. Now the committee began to reap substantial royalties from *Soledad Brother*. A film was produced and circulated in metropolitan areas, and the case became a prime organizing vehicle in the ghetto.[62] So successful had the committee been in fund-raising and so lucrative were the royalties from Jackson's book that money quickly became a source of friction within the committee. Rumors began to circulate and accusations fly of secret accounts set up and money being creamed off into them, of volunteers pocketing substantial portions of the take, of lawyers misappropriating funds for private use, of money spent on lavish clothes. Min Yee records that

a relative of one of the Soledad Brothers walked into the Defense Committee offices one day and was dumbfounded to see a committee member sitting on the floor counting and neatly stacking thousands of dollars. To the relative, the question was who could tell if the white volunteer was counting one-two for the committee and one for her own pocketbook? How much was there? Where was it all going? the relative asked. The volunteer didn't know. She was just counting it prior to depositing it in the bank. The relative stormed out.[63]

Though none of the allegations of theft was ever substantiated, by early summer 1971 the money controversy totally incapacitated the committee. The San Francisco branch of the committee suddenly found itself locked out of its own headquarters. George's sister Penny Jackson, his mother, Georgia, George's close friend ex-convict Jimmy Carr, and a group of other Panthers had seized the committee's account books and announced that, henceforth, the Black Panthers would be running the committee.

In 1969, Bay Area underground newspapers began openly calling on white radicals to commit acts of anti-state violence. A front-page photo in the *Berkeley Tribe* featured a hippie couple, the man armed with rifle and bandolier, the woman resting a submachine gun on one hip and an infant on the other. In its quest to offer a potent model of the white guerrilla revolutionary, the *Tribe* used not a photo of real revolutionaries but a movie still from Paramount's 1968 release "IF," the story of a revolt in a British boarding school. (Courtesy of Paramount Pictures, Copyright © 1968 by Paramount Pictures. All Rights Reserved.)

"WITHIN THE NEXT 14 DAYS WE WILL ATTACK A SYMBOL OR INSTITUTION OF AMERIKAN INJUSTICE"
- WEATHERMAN, MAY 21, 1970

A fanatic minority of prison movement leftists eagerly answered the summons to violence. In May 1970, the *Tribe* honored one such revolutionary cell, the Weathermen, by printing their ominous threat. By August, the Weather Underground had claimed responsibility for bomb blasts at three state buildings, including the headquarters of the California Department of Corrections in Sacramento. (*Berkeley Tribe*, May 29–June 5, 1970)

The year 1970 saw a steep escalation in revolutionary acts inside San Quentin and in violence between guards and prisoners, as well as the first attempts by Bay Area citizens to aid in prisoner escapes. On August 7 George Jackson's 17-year-old brother, Jonathan, kidnapped the judge, the prosecutor, and three women jurors during the trial of

prisoner James D. McClain, after tossing guns to two inmates who had been called as witnesses. *Above*, the group makes its escape; from left, Jackson, inmate William Arthur Christmas, juror Joyce Rodini, McClain, Assistant District Attorney Gary Thomas, Judge Joseph Haley, and inmate Ruchell Magee. (Two other jurors not shown.) With a sawed-off shotgun taped to his head (*left*), Judge Haley was led to a van by James McClain. Before the van could leave the parking lot, police gunfire ripped into it, instantly killing Jackson, McClain, and Christmas. Judge Haley died of a shotgun blast inside the vehicle. One juror was slightly injured. (*Marin Independent Journal*)

A REVOLUTIONARY FUNERAL

WE ARE THE PEOPLE

HUEY'S EULOGY

EULOGY DELIVERED BY HUEY P. NEWTON, MINISTER OF DEFENSE, BLACK PANTHER PARTY, AT THE REVOLUTIONARY FUNERAL OF COMRADES JONATHAN JACKSON AND WILLIAM CHRISTMAS, ST. AUGUSTINES CHURCH, 27TH AND WEST STREETS, OAKLAND, CALIFORNIA, AUGUST 15TH, 1970.

While it is viewed as a tragedy and many would weep for Jonathan Jackson and William A. Christmas the Black Panther Party serves notice that it is not brothers Jonathan Jackson and William A. Christmas for whom we should weep. They have achieved freedom and we remain slaves.

If we must weep let it be for those of us who remain in bondage. The Black Panther Party will follow the example that was set forth by these courageous revolutionaries. The people refuse to submit to the slavery and bondage

(see p. 9)

Photo by Gary Freedman

The *Berkeley Barb* celebrated Jonathan Jackson, McClain, and Christmas as martyrs to the revolution (*above*). Near the approach to San Quentin's east gate, a crowd of protestors assailed the state in Jonathan's name (*below*). (*Barb* photo by Gary Freedman, *Berkeley Barb*, Aug. 21–27, 1970; protest photo, *Marin Independent Journal*)

How To ADDRESS MAIL

Excerpts from Chapter 1
Postal Manual

POD Publication 28   July 1966

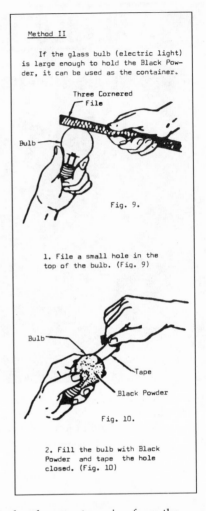

Method II

If the glass bulb (electric light) is large enough to hold the Black Powder, it can be used as the container.

Three Cornered File

Bulb

Fig. 9.

1. File a small hole in the top of the bulb. (Fig. 9)

Bulb

Tape

Black Powder

Fig. 10.

2. Fill the bulb with Black Powder and tape the hole closed. (Fig. 10)

After George Jackson's arraignment on murder charges stemming from the Soledad Incident of January 1970, the tone of literature imported to San Quentin's radical convicts from outsiders grew more inflammatory. Inmates now sometimes received detailed instructions for bomb and weapons manufacture. One pamphlet confiscated in 1970 before it reached the Black Family, a group of black revolutionaries tied loosely to Jackson, claimed on its cover to be a U.S. Postal Service brochure (*above left*). Inside, however, were 46 pages of instructions for explosive devices and detonators. Here an ordinary lightbulb filled with gunpowder or gasoline and screwed into a wall socket becomes a bomb at the flick of the lightswitch (*above right*). (Papers of William Hankins)

On August 21, 1971, in a ten-minute revolution, George Jackson and other convicts took over the prison's Adjustment Center. Three guards and two inmate tier tenders died of slit throats. Three other guards recovered from their wounds. Jackson was killed by a gunrail officer in the plaza shown above. In the aftermath, AC prisoners lie shackled, some hogtied, on the plaza lawn just outside the AC building. Beside a running stain of blood from the wounded and dead, guards and other staff can be seen entering and leaving the circular guard station called "Four Post." (Photo by Russ Reed, *Oakland Tribune*)

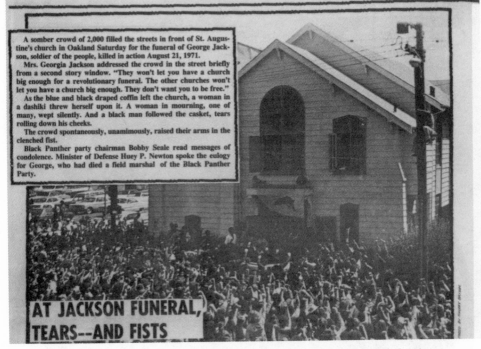

GEORGE JACKSON IS BURIED

A somber crowd of 2,000 filled the streets in front of St. Augustine's church in Oakland Saturday for the funeral of George Jackson, soldier of the people, killed in action August 21, 1971.

Mrs. Georgia Jackson addressed the crowd in the street briefly from a second story window. "They won't let you have a church big enough for a revolutionary funeral. The other churches won't let you have a church big enough. They don't want you to be free."

As the blue and black draped coffin left the church, a woman in a dashiki threw herself upon it. A woman in mourning, one of many, wept silently. And a black man followed the casket, tears rolling down his cheeks.

The crowd spontaneously, unanimously, raised their arms in the clenched fist.

Black Panther party chairman Bobby Seale read messages of condolence. Minister of Defense Huey P. Newton spoke the eulogy for George, who had died a field marshal of the Black Panther Party.

AT JACKSON FUNERAL, TEARS--AND FISTS

Above: George Jackson's death briefly galvanized the anger of the prison movement. Two thousand people attended Jackson's Oakland funeral, where loudspeakers above the church entrance played "I Wish I Knew What It Feels Like to Be Free." The mourners eulogized their fallen warrior with fists clenched in the air beside his coffin draped with the Panther flag. (Photo by Sherry Bryson, *Berkeley Barb*, Sept. 3–9, 1971)

Bottom right: Bombings and other forms of urban terrorism now regularly accompanied protests. The *Tribe* urged its readers to "war without terms." As Jackson's funeral services were taking place, bomb blasts shattered two state buildings. (Photo of George Jackson from a cropped portrait © Ruth-Marion Baruch, *Berkeley Tribe*, Aug. 27–Sept. 1, 1971)

In response to Jackson's death, prison movement supporters marched outside San Quentin (*left*) and led demonstrations and "teach-ins." (*Marin Independent Journal*)

By 1975, when Eldridge Cleaver returned to the United States in the custody of two FBI agents, the moral discourse on crime and the criminal had come to be dominated by the Right. In *Soul On Fire* (1978), Cleaver renounced his radical past and embraced the rhetoric of the eighteenth-century evangelical-Christian convict penitent. Cleaver appears here in 1983 at his West Oakland home, with his American flag and a print of Washington in prayer at Valley Forge. (Copyright © 1983 *San Francisco Examiner* / Kim Komenich)

At bottom, this struggle was as much for control of Jackson's myth as it was for his money. The San Francisco committee claimed the Jackson family wanted to destroy the committee because they did not control it. The committee accused family members of manipulating the prisoner to acquiesce with their wishes because as the summer progressed and prison restrictions were increased only they and his attorneys were allowed to visit him. But George Jackson was worried about the money too. He wrote to his editor demanding an accounting of the book's profits, arranged for royalties to be assigned to the newborn son of his brother Jonathan, and then accused the San Francisco committee of being reactionary because of its reluctance to expand the Soledad issue into a declaration of total people's revolution.[64] The fight for George Jackson's legend was on.

Outside, the Jackson myth seemed balanced precariously between the prisoner's two postures of "victim" and "revenging warrior" as the struggle for sole possession of his legend went on between factions of his supporters. Gregory Armstrong reflects on the degree to which the prisoner had become the property of others: "George's power was our power almost as a fact of ownership. If he had been outside, he would never have belonged to us in the same way, but locked away, he was ours. We possessed him and everything he was. We even felt we had the right to live through him."[65] Alone in his San Quentin AC cell, the inmate was clear about his choice between victimization and revenge. Jackson immediately set about rewriting his public self, becoming more the warrior, deleting the merely personal, and adding back into his writing stronger doses of Marxist critique of the American state and practical suggestions for urban guerrilla war.

In an August 1, 1971, *New York Times Magazine* interview, the prisoner underscored his ideological rather than his personal identity, comparing himself once more to Nat Turner and insisting of his own crimes and the crimes of others in the movement that "resistance to unjust bonds, organized injustice, can never be interpreted as crime." In the same interview, Jackson stated that he was busy revolutionizing California's convicts through education and study, even though he was almost totally cut off from San Quentin's mainline population and any proselytizing was confined to the AC cells adjoining his:

There are still some blacks here who consider themselves criminals—but not many. Believe me, my friend, with the time and incentive that these brothers have to read, study and think, you will find no class or category more aware, more embittered, desperate or dedicated to the ultimate remedy—revolution.

The most dedicated, the best of our kind—you'll find them in the Folsoms, San Quentins and Soledads.

George Jackson claimed that he was finally reaching even the white convicts: "They walked in goose-stepping and when they leave they'll be wearing the black beret." And he finished the interview with a disavowal of parts of the *Soledad Brother* book, especially those sections in which he seemed to be holding out hope for parole, claiming these remarks had been intended only to appease the Adult Authority. Jackson now preferred a much more confrontational stance: "The whole truth," he quietly told his interviewer, "is that I would hope to escape." [66]

But a sequence of events begun in 1970 inside San Quentin had built up an inexorable momentum that would finally take George Jackson's fate out of his own hands and fix his legend for all time. The trail of fateful incidents stretched back to the night of February 26, 1970, when yet another black inmate had died at the prison. Fred Billingslea was a six-foot-two, 200-pound black man regarded by prison authorities as mentally unstable. In one of the "quiet" cells on the first tier of San Quentin's maximum security B Section, Billingslea had set his mattress on fire. Guards arrived. When the inmate refused to come out, tear gas was discharged into the unventilated cell and the solid door was closed. After some time, officers entered and removed the prisoner. By morning Fred Billingslea was pronounced dead. A certificate of death would record asphyxia and a fractured larynx as the causes of his death. [67] Luis Talamantez, whose cell was on the third tier of B Section above Billingslea at the time, remembers the incident:

I happened to be in San Quentin's B Section. That's the lockup unit a little bit lower status than the Adjustment Center, and that is in the South Block. . . . I was in B Section on the third tier when it occurred. . . . As I recall, it was towards late evening. There was some smoke coming up from the first floor out of the strip cell area. . . . There was a lot of smoke. They brought in the goon squad. . . . And I'd say there was at least about ten to fifteen of them officers down there. There was quite a force of guards in there. And that smoke got real, real bad. And I don't know if he refused to come out of his cell or whatnot but there was water bein' squirted in there. Then they used that gas. . . . Plus with the fire going on it was just a total mess. . . . I remember it got so bad, burying my head under the covers . . . and wearing a rag. I couldn't even get out from under the covers to wet the rag no more because it was that bad. It was just terrible. And I think the guards went in there to get him and there was a lot of fighting going on and I don't know if he got a choke hold put on him or if the smoke got him or what, but hey, the next morning we heard he was dead.

A $1.3 million wrongful death suit would eventually be filed on behalf of Fred Billingslea's mother by the office of radical San Rafael attorney Salle S. Soladay, based on the testimony of eight witnesses to the prisoner's death, including Luis Talamantez. Before it came to trial, the suit was settled out of court for $50,000.[68] But Billingslea's death had much more immediate and far-reaching effects than this suit. Talamantez continues:

By [the following morning] all the blacks were talkin' on the tier in their cells. Everyone was being kept locked in their individual cells. These guys were incensed. . . . They were pissed off, man, they were gonna do something. . . . George wasn't there no more but George had just recently been on the fourth tier. He had just gone to Soledad from out of there. George Jackson . . . had left a heavy influence with these black guys. Everybody had a new name. "Khatari" and "Chibari" . . . and "Kaidi" and all. George Jackson had left a heavy influence in that section and these guys were gonna do something. I could tell.

In September 1970, attorney Soladay sought a federal court injunction to prevent the prison from harassing the inmate witnesses in the case. Prisoners who were providing the lawyer with information about Billingslea's death had been punished by being thrown into "strip cells" or the AC. Some had been quickly transferred to Folsom, far from Soladay's office.[69] Luis Talamantez recalls the efforts of prison staff to weaken the Billingslea suit:

I remember there was a sergeant who came in there the next day. He went cell to cell on the tier . . . and he stopped and asked, "Would you be willing to sign a paper, in regards to that incident, that you haven't seen anything, that you're not a witness?" He took me out of earshot. . . . He wanted to know what I'd seen. I said something like, "Well yeah, I didn't see shit, see, because, you know, how can you see when there was so much goddam smoke and gas." But I said, like, "Listen, you ain't gotta see to know when somebody's bein' killed and makin' a bunch of noise and chokin' and stuff down there." . . . He said, "Would you be willing to sign a paper that says you ain't seen nothing then?" "Fuck," I said, "I ain't signin' shit, man. Last time I signed somethin', man, I went to the fuckin' prison, man, they tricked me. I ain't signin' shit from now on."

The following month Judge Albert C. Wollenberg would rule that lawyers were to be allowed to inspect San Quentin's AC regularly to prevent any abuse of witnesses in the case.[70]

But many inmates at the prison were not content to wait patiently for the outcome of this suit. San Quentin's black guerrillas had their own notions of redress for Billingslea's death. Soon black inmate James D. McClain was charged in a nonfatal stabbing of a guard on the San Quentin yard. Talamantez explains:

A lot of people said that McClain was motivated solely just to prove something, you know. . . . I don't know if it was revenge or what. McClain was a real nice guy. He was in the cell just next to me for a while. I knew him personally. McClain never said, "Well, I'm doing this for that," but he was a person very conscientiously driven to get justice for black people. McClain really was. . . . There was just too much goin' on. And these guys were all fired up to set the record straight as far as blacks getting wasted. . . . They didn't want anything happening no more to blacks, period. . . . One thing fueled somethin' else and if that Billingslea thing had everybody in B Section pissed off, it eventually got out to the mainline. Word of that killing got around. Within a couple of weeks' or months' time everybody knew about it in the prison system. And by that time everything had gotten magnified and exaggerated to the extent that everybody said, "Yeah, man, I knew Billingslea, I knew that brother." There was a kind of identification with the whole thing.

Early in the morning of August 7, 1970, Ruchell Magee and another San Quentin inmate, William Christmas, were brought from the prison to the Marin County Courthouse to appear as witnesses for James McClain in a retrial of this guard assault case (the first had ended in a mistrial). The trial was to take place in the courtroom of Judge Joseph Haley. During the court proceedings, a young black spectator in the courtroom suddenly rose to his feet. George Jackson's seventeen-year-old brother Jonathan drew a sawed-off shotgun from beneath his coat. He raised it into the air. "All right, gentlemen," the young Jackson said calmly. "I'm taking over now."

Jonathan Jackson tossed several more guns that he had concealed to Magee and McClain. Christmas was released from a holding cell outside the courtroom while Jackson taped the shotgun under the chin of the judge. The four then took as their hostages Judge Haley, the prosecutor, Deputy District Attorney Gary Thomas, and three women jurors. According to one witness, on the way out of the courthouse James McClain shouted, "Free or Release the Soledad Brothers by 12:30 or they all die!"[71] Another witness would later testify that McClain's words were "Free All Political Prisoners!" The prisoners hurried their hostages outside to a van that Jackson had rented. By this time, however, news of the attempted escape had been broadcast on police frequencies. Police and San Quentin guard roadblocks were already in place around the courthouse where heavily armed officers sat waiting, well aware of San Quentin's "no hostage" policy. Moments later their gunfire ripped through the van, knocking Jonathan Jackson over the front seat and killing him instantly. McClain and Christmas died in the crossfire, too, but not before their shotgun had discharged in Judge Haley's face. Prosecutor Thomas was permanently paralyzed by gunshot wounds. Ruchell Magee was critically wounded but would survive. One of the jurors was slightly hurt; the remaining two women were miraculously unharmed. After the smoke had cleared, Haley, McClain, Jackson, and Christmas lay dead in the van outside the courthouse.[72]

George Jackson quickly denied to the press that his brother's action was an attempt to help him escape from San Quentin. He insisted there was no escape plan. He appeared inconsolable with grief: "If I'd known ahead of time, I would have stopped him. I know the guards here. I knew they'd shoot. I knew they'd kill Jonathan."[73] Other sources suggest that there may have been a plan. Editor Gregory Armstrong, who visited Jackson immediately after the shootout, later quoted the prisoner: "Did they shoot him up very bad? He didn't mean to hurt anyone. It was going to be a nonviolent action. You know I sent him in there. I sent him in there. To think after all that I've been through, he was the one to do it. I haven't shed a tear because I am so proud."[74]

Did Jackson mean that, having politically radicalized his brother in letters and visits, he felt he had created the motive for his brother's tragic act? Or did he mean that he and his brother had joined in a conspiracy to help him escape from San Quentin? Whatever the truth was, San Quentin and the state of California saw the incident as a conspiracy to help George Jackson escape. Here, as elsewhere, the motives of Jackson's editor Armstrong in seeming to confirm an escape plot might be called into question. Again, George Jackson seems an actor following a script written by others. It is true that Jonathan had visited his brother on each of the four days immediately preceding the event. Warden Louis Nelson's theory was that the prisoner had discussed the escape plans with his brother and had then passed word of the plan to James McClain four cells away.[75] A *Washington Post* reporter claimed that George Jackson admitted to a "clandestine connection" between McClain and his brother.[76] Although these circumstances imply that George Jackson was actively involved in the shootout, the testimony of one convict close to Jackson casts doubt on his conspiracy. Luis Talamantez reports:

I think that George didn't even know what was going on, wasn't in on the plan. After that happened, George didn't say anything to indicate he had had prior knowledge. George was stunned. I think he was surprised. I think George felt more than a little bit responsible because all this time now George is talkin' revolution to anybody and everybody who will listen to him. And, hey man, there are some people who really listen. They acted on it, too. . . .

I remember a conversation once. I said, wanting to cheer George up, "Hey, man, your brother really loved you. He really put it out there. You gotta give the guy respect. I'm sorry what happened to your kid brother." George was proud of the fact that his young brother put it on the line for him. But I think what George felt also was, "Well, goddam, I never told him to go do it!" He was sad that he might have spurred somebody on.

Talamantez insists that if there was a conspiracy, some of the principal actors had no knowledge of it:

Ruchell [Magee] had the funniest joke to tell. He said, "Next thing I knew they were putting a gun in my hands and saying 'Time for Revolution.' And I said, 'What is "Time for Revolution"?' [laughs] Man, I didn't know what was goin' on. Next thing I knew someone put a gun in my hand. I went for freedom." He said, "I know about that!"

The Marin County Courthouse tragedy had four immediate results. First, following Angela Davis's hasty departure from the Bay Area after the shootout, a major police search was launched to capture her as a prime suspect in the breakout attempt. Davis had recently been fired from her post as a philosophy instructor at UCLA by the UC regents at the special urging of Governor Reagan for being "a member of the Communist Party."[77] She had been very active in the Soledad Brothers Defense Committee. Angela Davis was a frequent visitor of George Jackson and a close personal friend of his young brother Jonathan and other family members. Several of the guns that Jonathan Jackson used in the Marin shootout were registered to Davis, a .38 caliber pistol, a .30 caliber carbine rifle, a .30 caliber M-1 carbine, and a 12-gauge shotgun. A nationwide dragnet followed Davis's disappearance after the shootout, and she was arrested in a New York hotel in October 1970. On national television President Richard Nixon smugly congratulated FBI director J. Edgar Hoover on her capture, prejudicing the jury in her future trial by declaring her arrest an example to "all other terrorists."[78] In court eighteen months later, after ten months in jail awaiting trial, Davis would readily admit the weapons had been hers. They had been bought for self-defense, she testified, after she had received numerous death threats following her firing from UCLA. She had intended their use, too, for the defense of the San Francisco Soledad House. All the weapons were legal. The state had no evidence that Davis knowingly furnished Jonathan Jackson with the guns or that she knew what he was going to do with them. Some witnesses placed her at the scene of the crime in the rented escape van on the day before the shootout, but this testimony was discredited under cross-examination. No other charge of complicity in the Marin County Courthouse shootout was proven against Angela Davis, and she was acquitted in June 1972, to the relief of thousands of her supporters in the United States and worldwide, who had come together in more than 200 support committees formed in coalition with the various chapters of the Soledad Brothers Defense Committee.[79] Angela Davis had become the single woman in the pantheon of prison movement heroes.

Inside San Quentin the Marin shootout spawned a plan among black revolutionary inmates to seek "one for one" revenge for the deaths of McClain and Christmas. The prison anticipated this. On August 13, 1970, Associate Warden James Park announced that two San Quentin guards involved in the courthouse episode were being transferred. Two prisoners, he said, had been caught passing a knife in the mess hall, and informants had tipped off the authorities about their plans to attack the guards.[80] The pace of assaults on guards continued to escalate. In July 1971, officer Leo G. Davis was killed in San Quentin's hospital, where he was stationed to protect convict Earl Johnson, who had testified for the prosecution in the Soledad Seven case.[81] Inmates Larry Justice and Earl Gibson later received life sentences for their role in Davis's death.[82] The war against the guards continued, openly supported by many leftists outside the walls. The most extreme of these held Jonathan Jackson in highest esteem for his role in the death of Judge Haley and viewed this act as a productive revolutionary deed. In speeches at rallies across the land, the Left honored Jonathan Jackson. Julian Bond and others referred to the shootout as the "revolt at San Rafael."[83] Some called the escape attempt a "slave insurrection."[84] Huey Newton added to the mood of revolutionary adulation, declaring, "I view Jonathan Jackson as a man who should have been and would have been my successor."[85]

A third major effect of the shootout was an effort by the prison to change the venue of the upcoming Soledad Brothers trial. Four days after the Marin shootout, as 30 police cars escorted Judge Haley's solemn funeral cortege to his grave site and some eighteen of San Quentin's maximum security inmates refused their meals in what was believed to be "a display of sympathy for the dead escapers," Associate Warden James Park announced that facilities for the Soledad Brothers' trial would be provided within San Quentin's walls, complete with state-of-the-art metal-detecting devices.[86]

Finally, and of most importance, the Marin shootout functioned to take George Jackson's fate entirely out of his own hands. He would live for only one more year, completely driven by the cascading force of events and personalities around him. By this time, Jackson's very existence was the tangled product of others. As he sat in his AC cell facing a likely conviction for a capital offense and found himself contemplating the gas chamber, word reached George Jackson of the triumphal praise of the Left for his young brother's suicide. Warrior revolutionaries inside now looked to him expectantly. Prison staff continued to pressure him, blaming him for assaults on guards that he had no power to stop or control. And the ongoing constrictions of his visiting rights left him more and more out of touch except with his immediate family and a tiny group of the most extreme radicals. The struggle for George Jackson's identity was at an end. All these forces now joined to determine the final form the myth would take. They guaranteed that Jackson would try to live up to his brother's brutal sacrifice. He had no choice. He would truly become the Dragon. Former lieutenant Richard Nelson remembers these words of George Jackson on the AC tier: "He'd joke and swagger and say, 'Just Wait! It's Coming! The Revolution!' We were all to be killed. He pointedly told us that. We were dead."[87]

8

PRISONER UNIONS AND THE
"IMPRISONED CLASS"

Commitment to prison reform among the mainstream California public swelled in 1970–71. Banner-waving contingents urging prison reform joined in the last of the antiwar parades, suggesting that the Left had made the transition into a new decade by using prison reform as its rallying cry. Universities sponsored prison "teach-ins." Bay Area newspapers ran exposés of conditions in California prisons and provided extensive coverage of the growing convict unrest. Attorney groups such as Fay Stender's Prison Law Project, its later splinter group the Prison Law Collective, and the National Lawyers Guild were receiving thousands of letters from prisoners complaining of conditions and alleging unfair treatment. Movement attorneys took on the grueling task of representing in court as many inmates as they could. When a full-scale prisoner unionization movement emerged in the prisons in 1970, using the rhetoric of class analysis originated by the prison system's radicals, scores of community groups turned out in support and lobbied the state government for change. But sadly, revolutionary convicts would insist on adding to the moderate reform goals of union inmates absurdly impossible demands as the spirit of the Marin County Courthouse shootout seized control of the explosively angry movement and turned reform aside for terror, as if demanding bloody confrontation. This would not have happened had radical prisoners not been misled into thinking they were center-stage leaders of an already advancing American revolution. Worsening matters further, the left-wing romance of the convict crested in dizzying fantasy. A handful of voices in the movement had at last begun to realize how destructive the cult of the convict was. But it was too late. In the public eye, the final form the tale of the prison movement assumed was told in the person of one hero convict. The stage was set for the beatification of George Jackson in the role the culture had created for him: ultimate wordsmith of the outlaw trope, the Dragon, priest of supreme male vengeance, convict god, and martyr to the racist past. A dramatic change in the radical literature imported into the prisons accompanied this last, most extreme wave of leftist convict romanticism. By late 1970 the tone of San Quentin's imported literature became noticeably more inflammatory and more practical rather than theoretical, including detailed diagrams and instructions on bomb and weapons manufacture. Unfortunately, this change, well noted by prison staff, furnished the state with just the evidence of conspiracy it had so long desired and fueled moves toward a prison crackdown and a conservative repudiation of prison reform directed from both Sacramento and Washington. The first hint of things to come was San Quentin's attempt in 1970 to conduct trials of inmates accused of committing crimes while in prison in a courtroom inside the prison walls, denying the defendants constitutionally guaranteed public trial. The just-emerging moderate reformist convict union movement would by small steps be turned aside in its infancy as more and more both the state and the extreme Left read the prison movement exclusively in the exaggerated figure of George Jackson. Tragically, that script now seemed to both far Right and Left to make his death necessary. And after the carnage, predictably, the same script would allow prison authorities to blame his death on outsiders and to go on ignoring prisoners' legitimate grievances.

In letters written in 1970–71 from her pretrial detention cell in the Marin County Jail, Angela Davis reaffirmed the Left's ultraromantic vision of its prison revolutionary leaders. She assailed any remaining in the Left who continued in the "assumption that individuals who have recourse to anti-social acts are incapable of developing the discipline and collective orientation required by revolutionary struggle." Davis accurately described how some prisoners were being transformed into revolutionaries in their cells:

A major catalyst for intensified political action in and around prisons has emerged out of the transformation of convicts, originally found guilty of criminal offenses, into exemplary political militants. Their patient educational efforts in the realm of exposing the specific oppressive structures of the penal system in their relation to the larger oppression of the social system have had a profound effect on their fellow captives.

Davis reaffirmed, as well, the Left's dangerous conflation of all crime with political crime: "Crimes are profound but suppressed social needs which express themselves in anti-social modes of action. Spontaneously produced by a capitalist organization of society, this type of crime is at once a protest against society and a desire to partake of its exploitative content."[1]

Crime was a product of capitalism. This statement and others by Davis struck one note of genuine truth: crime *is* a response to social need. But Davis went much further, encouraging the Left to view the type of crime committed by the vast majority of prisoners, property crime, as an artifact of a capitalist society. At the same time, she asked her readers to see crime both as a symptom of and a political challenge to that society. According to this view, crime, any crime, was political protest and *all* prisoners were revolutionaries, including even those inmates who did not themselves claim political motives. This accomplished, Davis and Bettina Aptheker, in the preface to *If They Come in the Morning: Voices of Resistance* (1971), could refer to "literally tens of thousands of innocent men and women" who filled jails and prisons in the United States, reinforcing the Left's conviction that the prisons were rife with political prisoners.[2] In a November 19, 1970, letter to Angela Davis, James Baldwin referred to the prisons as modern concentration camps and drew an analogy between Angela Davis and "the Jewish housewife in the boxcar headed for Dachau."[3] Although it was true that race-skewed patterns of arrest and race-skewed differentials in access to bail and lawyers had long made blacks and other minorities disproportionately represented in California's prisons, it was an unhelpful oversimplification to suggest that all or most state prisoners were innocent of their crimes. Angela Davis herself was an innocent political target of the California and national right wing, but to argue from her own case to the conclusion that the California prisons were full of innocent victims of right-wing political death squads was a gross perversion of the truth. Moreover, it was beside the point in the struggle for inmate rights, and it was certainly not what the prison movement Left in the Bay Area needed to be told in 1970–71.

But few in the movement were ready to rethink the issue of crime and the convict. Instead, unexamined romanticizing of the convict continued to crest as Mom-and-Pop grocery store robbers fell under the rubric of "political prisoner" and a handful of groups in the movement devolved into what some participants now label Leninist street gangs. George Jackson's friend, ex-prisoner Jimmy Carr, comments on his own experience:

I came charging out in 1970 expecting to find a Red Army ready for revolutionary war. What I found was a handful of red criminals with the same world view I'd had as a poolhall hustler, reinforced with heavy doses of ideology and drugs. But my disappointment at their lack of power was softened by the tremendous amount of money they had to spend on me.

At the same time, to fulfill my parole, I had to be in school in Santa Cruz. [Carr was enrolled at University of California, Santa Cruz, where he had become a teaching assistant for sociologist Herman Blake.] So being a "revolutionary" consisted mainly of tripping back and forth between there and the East Bay—target shooting and attending classes and small-time protest meetings in Santa Cruz, snorting coke and puttin' on the style in Oakland. The main difference between these people and a non-political criminal gang is that here the ideology of Leninism greatly solidifies the position of the leadership; this is, in fact, the main purpose of that ideology. Never a leader myself, I contented myself with guarding those at the top and reaping some of their material benefits for myself. . . . I had doubts, but I swallowed them down with heavier doses of white powder and red book.

By this time, George had become a Soledad Brother. I worked a little for the defense committee, more out of loyalty to my friend than from any great passion for legal work. The meetings were endless. The strategy of radicalizing the masses by "exposing" the prisons and courts was contemptible to me even then; but since I was a celebrity to them as George Jackson's friend, and my presence seemed to inspire them to maybe do something to save his life, I went to the meetings.[4]

Carr's condemnation of Bay Area prison movement organizations is overly harsh, but he makes a good point. This ex-convict came to feel his own hero status was unwarranted, and he became disillusioned with a movement that was elevating prisoners to leadership roles based simply on their convict-class identity.

At San Quentin, meanwhile, custody staff increasingly felt beleaguered by a threatening pattern of left-wing legal and legislative victories against the prison. The growing list of defeats included the state's failure to capture Eldridge Cleaver and return him to prison, the overturning of Huey Newton's 1968 manslaughter conviction, the failure to bring the Soledad Seven to trial, the successful out-of-court settlement of the Fred Billingslea wrongful death suit, the passage of Penal Code 2600, and more. All this, combined with revolutionary activity within the prison aided and encouraged by some teaching staff and activist attorneys, had caused San Quentin to feel itself under siege and its guards to fear for their lives on the job. After the Marin County Courthouse shootout, San Quentin staff dearly yearned for a court victory against the Left. Consequently, the prison look forward in grim anticipation to the trial of George Jackson and the other Soledad Brothers, eager that nothing should interfere this time with the state's well-oiled legal machinery. When the Marin County Board of Supervisors announced the week after the court-house shootout that "it is board policy and intent that all future San Quentin inmate trials be held at the prison," nobody was happier than the prison administration.[5]

The Marin County Superior Court, Judge Joseph G. Wilson pre-siding, scheduled its fall 1970 calendar session to be held inside the prison in a small, makeshift auditorium in the in-service training area. Four prisoners were to appear on the first day, August 24, 1970. Left organizations, irate at what they saw as a violation of the constitu-tional guarantee of a public trial, announced a demonstration protest at the east gate and peppered the Bay Area with handbills.[6] Carpools were set up to deliver protesters to the isolated prison from Glide Memorial Church in San Francisco, from the Peoples' Office in Berke-ley, and from the Black Panther national headquarters in Oakland. On August 24, as the four inmates to appear that day sat through an hour-long hearing to set their future trial dates, 50 spectators and 12 newsmen looked on. And at the east gate, Tom Hayden, George Jackson's sister Penny, and Black Panther Masai Hewett addressed a crowd of about 100, decrying the "move toward secret, anonymous trials."[7] Judge Wilson and the court officers arrived in two unmarked cars, followed by five sheriff's cars filled with riot-equipped deputies. Plainclothes officers at the east gate took photos of the crowd, and a dozen police and guards stationed themselves along the access road to the gate. Inside, on the San Quentin yard, there occurred just one peaceful and almost overlooked inmate protest. The court within pro-ceeded with its business.

A preamble to the set of demands San Quentin convicts presented at the inconspicuous yard strike that day protesting the in-prison court sessions had ended with the words, "HELP US HIT THEM WHERE IT HURTS, IN THEIR POCKET." This act marked the birth of prison unionism in California. That the California prison was a profit-making enterprise benefiting from enforced labor was one opinion a majority of San Quentin convicts, both radical and moder-ate, had come to share by 1970. It thus might be the basis of a strat-egy for change that all convicts could embrace. As one consequence, starting in 1970 demands of convicts involved in agitations at the prison would take on a different tone than in the past. Inmates had become aware of the vulnerability to strike of San Quentin's profits from prison industries, the complex of manufactories that produced products largely for the state, including clothing, furniture, dairy products, canned goods, and printed materials used by prisons, mental hospitals, state offices, and colleges.

The day after this inmate gathering, prisoners returned to the yard in a much more volatile mood. On August 25 at 8 A.M., an angry, racially mixed coalition of an estimated 800 San Quentin prisoners insisted on speaking with Warden Nelson to press the demands they had served him with the previous day. Written by Black Panther Warren Wells,[8] the demands were a patchwork of the goals of two distinct convict groups. The ultimatum proclaimed:

1. Free All Political Prisoners!
2. Free The Soledad Brothers!
3. Close the prison's two disciplinary cellblocks
4. Appoint a black warden
5. Appoint black and Mexican-American associate wardens
6. Hire more black and Mexican-American guards and counselors
7. Abolish the Adult Authority
8. Abolish capital punishment and grant "political asylum" for all prisoners on death row
9. Apply the provisions of the Geneva Convention to Blacks and other American "political prisoners"

> All men presently committed to condemned row awaiting state execution should immediately be granted asylum in those countries under the flag of Africa, Asia, Russia, North Korea, Cuba . . . and other points of the world where the American revolutionaries have established a free world solidarity pace.[9]

The call to abolish the Adult Authority and the disciplinary units and to integrate the prison staff was typical of the unionists' requests for reform. The remainder show the hand of San Quentin's revolutionaries. The unrealistic nature of some of these demands, to free the Soledad Brothers without trial and grant political asylum in socialist countries to large portions of the prison population, including condemned inmates, for example, shows the extent to which the more radical convict faction was misreading the level of revolutionary struggle going on outside the walls and overestimating the support it would receive. This mistake would be fatal. After an hour of talk, during which time Warden Nelson insisted he was powerless to grant the demands, tear gas was fired into the crowd of inmates from the gunrail above the yard, and in ten minutes the protesters had been driven to their cells and locked down. That night rampaging inmates in B Section segregation smashed 73 toilets, 47 washbasins, 4 beds, and 13 light fixtures and burned 3 mattresses. There were no injuries, and no effort was made to halt the destruction. The next day half of the men returned to work. Four suspected ringleaders were transferred to Folsom.[10] A day later prisoners in B Section ripped out 17 more toilets and 5 washbasins. Afterward, most returned to work and the incident was declared at an end.[11]

For the second court session at San Quentin, on September 1, 1970, about 50 protesters convened by the Soledad Brothers Defense Committee milled about at the east gate while two prisoners appeared in the prison courtroom: Luis Talamantez, who was accused in a gang stabbing, and Tommy Lee Walker, a black former gang acquaintance of George Jackson charged with two counts of assaulting a guard.[12] On September 29, pretrial motions began in the San Quentin courtroom for the Ruchell Magee escape conspiracy trial, on charges stemming from the Marin shootout. Magee protested, calling the proceedings inside the prison unconstitutional and illegal. Luis Talamantez exhibited the same spirit of protest, kicking over a chair, and had to be subdued by five guards while shouting "Screw you all!" Talamantez was subsequently manacled to his chair.[13] The first full jury trial of a prisoner at San Quentin, of inmate Leo Robles for the murder of another inmate, was scheduled to begin October 13.

But on October 1, 1970, judges for the Marin County Superior Court announced a change of plans. No trials would be held in the prison after all. They would take place once again at the Marin County Courthouse. Presiding judge Joseph G. Wilson explained the decision: "All of us have grave doubts as to whether it would be possible. There is no question that taking jurors, many of whom have not been there before, onto prison grounds, cannot fail to have some impact on their ability to be fair and objective." Judge Wilson also feared, he said, that trying cases in the prison might arouse "those disruptive elements who are only too eager to seize upon any excuse to attack our institutions."[14] San Quentin's court experiment was at an end. The prisoners would again have public trials.

The two growing and ever more distinctly separate factions of San Quentin prisoners now turned back to the struggle for primacy as agents of change on the yard. Moderates and radicals remained loosely united by the shared view that the prison was turning slave labor to profit. On one extreme, however, radical black prisoners now viewed racism as a fundamental economic strategy of capitalism, a way to maintain a cheap pool of labor and a way to keep the labor force divided.[15] According to this view, convicts formed a special stratum of the exploited working class, and black convicts were more special yet. Huey Newton had broadened this argument in 1970 into a formulation that invited whites and moderate prisoners to see themselves as the victims of exploitation of the "convict class":

> The prison is a capitalistic enterprise. It differs very little from the system where inmates are "farmed out" to growers. In those instances the growers compensate the state. Most civilized people agree that that system is abhorrent. Yet the California method is to employ the reverse system. The convicts are not farmed out, the work is farmed in. What factors remain the same? The convicts are still exploited by the state; the work still is accomplished; the state is still compensated.[16]

Eldridge Cleaver and George Jackson had long been teaching San Quentin's black prisoners to see themselves as victims of an unjust economic order that had to come down. By 1970 the lesson had been assimilated by white and other prisoners as well. John Clutchette presented the unifying notion this way: "Under the existing social order men and women are sent to prison for labor (free labor) and further economical gain (money) by the state. Where else can you get a full day's work for two to sixteen cents an hour, and these hours become an indeterminate period of years? This is slave labor in 20th century America."[17] "The prison system is a slave system," Kenneth Divans would write from San Quentin's AC and Larry West from Folsom in 1971. "Look into the California Department of Corrections industry books, and see the millions of dollars profited each year."[18] Bay Area activist-writer Jessica Mitford was already busy doing just that. In her *Kind and Usual Punishment* (1973) she would argue that, as the Department of Corrections budget for 1968 showed, the profit realized from a convict worker's labor could be worth up to 86 times his wage.* These figures were not available to San Quentin prisoners in 1970, and they have been disputed since by critics who point out that in 1989 prison industries employed only about 7,000 workers out of a prison population estimated at 80,000, so the system as a whole actually operates in the red.[19] Nonetheless, radical and moderate California inmates alike became convinced in 1970 that their work under the Correctional Industries Commission, which was supposed to

---

*According to the budget, these profits were estimated from the labors of a convict dairy worker, whose production was valued at $14,279 and who was paid $3.40 a week. The cost of housing the inmate was $2,680 for the year. See Mitford, p. 181.

"contribute to their rehabilitation, training and support,"[20] was instead contributing to a profit-making venture, and they deserved more compensation for their labor.

Though they might be counted as strike supporters by the prison's emerging moderate unionists, San Quentin's revolutionaries had long since proceeded far beyond any demand for pay equity with outside nonprison labor. They would be contented with nothing less than the total destruction of the capitalist state. This divergence of ideology among change-minded inmates at San Quentin became ever more extreme in 1970. In part, imported reading, which had always been a force driving convict ideology, was deepening the differences among inmates. After George Jackson's arraignment on the Soledad Incident charges, the tone of imported literature reaching the prison's radicals had gotten noticeably more inflammatory and more practical rather than theoretical. One pamphlet mailed in quantity to a member of the Black Family, a group of black inmate revolutionaries tied loosely to Jackson, was confiscated in the mail room in 1970 by the San Quentin Special Investigations Unit. It claimed on its outside cover to be a U.S. Postal Service brochure titled "How to Address Mail: Excerpts from Chapter One, Postal Manual, Publication 28." Inside, however, were 46 pages of detailed instructions on how to make explosive devices and detonators from simple materials. Former officer William Hankins remarks that the pamphlet was part of a large mailing: "When I picked this one up, why, there must have been 200 of 'em comin' in."[21] The pamphlet had been mailed to convict radicals throughout the California prisons. A Soledad North inmate remembers receiving one: "I got this same thing when I was in Soledad. It showed how to use a live bullet as a detonator [in an explosive device fashioned from a common light bulb], and when the light cuts on it goes off."[22] Radicals who followed the path this pamphlet laid out for them now made a fundamental and irrevocable split from their more moderate brothers. Prison staff allege that some reading material inciting radical prisoners to increased violence entered the prison in stacks of legal papers carried by radical attorneys. Former guard staff claim that much of this material was passed in to George Jackson in the AC by his legal investigators and attorneys and that it included covert messages from groups outside, messages said later to contain escape plans, and reading still considered contraband even under the relaxed guidelines of Penal Code 2600, such as that calling for overt acts of prison revolt and the killing of prison guards.

Jackson's reading and writing during his last year in San Quentin's

AC proceeded relatively unrestricted. Luis Talamantez reasons that this was possible because "he had a lot of legal protection. They couldn't mess with him. George had Fay Stender living on the warden's front steps as far as filing complaints went. She was on their case constant for George."[23] Former AC lieutenant Richard Nelson agrees that, even though the prison wanted to stop some things coming in to the prisoner, its hands were tied:

We were taking him to court off and on in those days and the judges were just adamant that we could search legal material but we couldn't read it. So it was all intermixed with his legal material. You'd have a stack of papers nine or twelve inches thick and you'd just shuffle through 'em [looking for escape tools or weapons].[24]

Jackson's mail was being read regularly by prison staff in 1970–71. And his comparative freedom to read and write was unique in the AC because control over communication in this high-security unit remained more severe than elsewhere in San Quentin, even after Penal Code 2600. Nevertheless, Jackson saw to it that contraband revolutionary reading still circulated even in the AC, sometimes apparently with the knowledge of guards. As Luis Talamantez reminds us, "George had all the books, man. He had Debray, Fanon, Du Bois. . . . George had all these books. . . . There were a lot of books goin' around. . . . I was tier tender. . . . I passed a lot of books up and down that tier." Ideologically, Jackson now maintained himself on a steady diet of Marx, Mao, Lenin, Fanon, Hegel, Trotsky, Ho Chi Minh, General Giap, Nkrumah, Fidel Castro, Che Guevara, and other revolutionary authors.

In addition to the change in imported radical literature that now included practical tips on making weapons and bombs, a reading-inspired ideological transformation was under way among the prison's revolutionaries, especially George Jackson, that would drive a wedge between them and the moderate convict reformers. Two books that figured prominently in Jackson's and other revolutionary San Quentin inmates' reading at this time were Regis Debray's *Revolution in the Revolution? Armed Struggle and Political Struggle in Latin America* and Robert Taber's *War of the Flea: A Study of Guerrilla Warfare Theory and Practice.*

Debray's book had appeared in translation by Grove Press in 1967 and had had an immediate effect on the Bay Area Left. Huey Newton's references to "vanguard groups" in his "Correct Handling of a Revolution"[25] shows a clear influence of this author. Debray was a

young French philosophy student of Louis Althusser's who had traveled throughout Latin America in the early 1960's observing the guerrilla revolutions in progress there. In 1965 he returned to Cuba, where
he conducted extensive interviews with Fidel Castro and others in the
revolution. He was arrested in Bolivia in 1967, largely because of his
growing reputation as a guerrilla strategist. For the Bay Area Left, and
most especially for George Jackson and his followers, Debray became
best known for his theory of the "foco," a notion that, despite the
long periods of party building that had preceded the great communist
revolutions of the past, guerrilla revolutions in the future could be
built largely without the support of the populace; or rather, that organizing "vanguard groups" of guerrillas should *precede* party building. The politicization of the populace would grow out of the insurrectionary activity of the vanguard. According to Debray, this was the
lesson revolutionaries the world over could learn from Fidel Castro's
Cuban experience. Debray pointed out that

in Cuba it was not the party that was the directive nucleus of the popular
army, as it had been in Vietnam according to Giap; the Rebel Army was the
leading nucleus of the party, the nucleus that created it. . . . The vanguard
party can exist in the form of the guerrilla foco itself. The guerrilla force is the
party in embryo. This is the staggering novelty introduced by the Cuban
Revolution.

How can this "heresy" be justified? What gives the guerrilla movement the
right to claim this political responsibility as its own and for itself alone? . . .
The guerrilla army is a confirmation in action of th[e] alliance [between workers and peasants]; it is the personification of it. When the guerrilla army as-
sumes the prerogatives of political leadership, it is responding to its class
content and anticipating tomorrow's dangers. It alone can guarantee that the
people's power will not be perverted after victory. If it does not assume the
functions of political leadership during the course of emancipation itself, it
will not be able to assume them when the war is over.

The people's army is its own political authority. The guerrilleros play both
roles, indivisibly.

The guerrilla force is the political vanguard "in nuce" and from its development a real party can arise. . . . That is why, at the present juncture, the
principal stress must be laid on the development of guerrilla warfare and not
on the strengthening of existing parties or the creation of new parties. . . .
That is why insurrectional activity is today the number one political activity.[26]

Debray's foco theory pleased the San Quentin prisoners in Jackson's
military wing of the Black Panthers, flattering them with the appella-
tion of "vanguard" and reassuring them that they, who represented

the lumpenproletariat at its most oppressed (in sharp contrast even to the intellectual leadership of the Black Panther party outside), would become the future seed of the revolution. In fact, if worse came to worst and they were cut off from even the support of their own party, they could conduct the revolution alone once they got back out on the streets, in small vanguard groups of four to five urban guerrillas.

In 1970 Debray's book was a hot item at San Quentin. It drew the line deeper between the prison's moderates and radicals. Debray's foco attack would be the strategy George Jackson began to expound for his next book, *Blood in My Eye*. The intense appeal of such a theory for prisoners already isolated, cut off from the people, may be obvious. At a time of dwindling student support for the Left on college campuses it is easy to see, too, how Debray's analysis could have strong appeal among other groups in the radical Left of the Bay Area. It showed both groups a way that they could still be leaders, even without popular support, even from the depths of prison cells. Party building among the masses did not have to precede the revolution. All that could come later. How tragically flawed this logic was would become apparent only later, when Jackson's and Debray's writings were put into practice in the failed extremism of the Symbionese Liberation Army foco.

The 1965 *War of the Flea* had a special appeal for prisoners as well. Its author, Robert Taber, had spent time with Fidel Castro in the Sierra Maestra in 1957.[27] *The War of the Flea* argued that, although contemporary communist struggles seemed confined to Latin America, the urban race riots in the United States in the mid-1960's were signs that revolution might break out there too at any moment. And it reminded its readers that Fidel Castro, "fighting within a population of close to 7 million, never had more than 1500 armed men with him." Here again, revolution was a struggle that could be won by a small, isolated group of warriors. In fact, Taber argued that it was far better if the rebel army remained small, "elusive and insubstantial as the wind." These were heady words for San Quentin's armies, waiting for their chance to break down the walls and capture Washington, D.C. "The guerrilla fights the war of the flea," the prison's guerrillas read, "and his military enemy suffers the dog's disadvantages: too much to defend; too small, ubiquitous, and agile an enemy to come to grips with." For Jackson and his San Quentin comrades, *The War of the Flea* became much more than a practical guide to urban guerrilla warfare in the United States. It was also a dream book couched in word figures of disappearance and escape, language that had great appeal to the imprisoned. Taber reminded the prisoners that in China "Mao had no scruples . . . about recruiting bandits; they . . . could be easily indoctrinated to fight in the popular cause." And the book recommended methods of warfare already familiar to prisoners experienced in gang fights and assaults on guards: "Battles are not prolonged. On the contrary, it is Mao who has invented the 'five-minute attack': it consists of a sudden onslaught, a brief and furious interval of fighting, and then the assault is broken off as suddenly as it began and the guerrillas rapidly retire." In answer to the question "Is the United States itself immune?" Taber's answer was a firm no: "The complexity of modern, urban, heavily industrialized societies makes them extremely vulnerable to wide-scale sabotage."[28] *The War of the Flea* called for the guerrilla to create a climate that would eventually cause the state to collapse. Conveniently, to launch a revolution following this blueprint, California prisoners would not have to wait to be paroled. They could work for the collapse of the prisons, the microcosm of the American two-class state. Prison was the one place in America in which the assumptions of Marxist analysis made perfect sense. It all fell into place. George Jackson's "one for one" strategy of attacking guards could be seen by the revolutionaries as the start of a class war that would bring the prisons down from the inside.

In spite of the ideology of the class exploitation of convicts San Quentin's different factions of prisoners held in common, the imported foco theory of Debray and Taber, coupled with the trend toward increasingly practical instruction in warfare, set the prison's revolutionary inmates off on a path that diverged sharply from that of its emerging unionists. The two factions were now on courses that subverted each other.

In October 1970, Sacramento's KXTV, Channel 10, reported that it had learned that a general strike was being called at Folsom prison for November 3. This was to be the first major action by the prison system's coalition of moderate unionists and revolutionaries. Inside Folsom organizing for a strike had been gaining momentum for some time. According to former Prisoners' Union attorney James Smith, prisoner Martin Sousa, the strike's principal organizer, "worked in the print shop at Folsom, and he printed the demands . . . and various grievances that they had, and organized a sit-down strike on the yard at Folsom."[29] Sousa had sent copies of demands out to several

Bay Area leftist groups, including the Prison Law Project and the Coordinating Council of Prisoner Organizations. John Irwin recalls: "One of our council [Coordinating Council of Prisoner Organizations], a Chicano woman whose husband [Sousa] was serving time in Folsom, he sent out to us through her a list of demands. . . . They were going to go on strike the day before election day in 1970."[30] This list, patched together by diverse groups of convicts, contained 31 grievances, roughly divisible into housekeeping, political, and labor demands. It ended with a declaration that the strikers were to be represented in negotiations by Huey Newton of the Black Panthers, attorney Charles Garry, the "Third World Legal Defense Counsel," Sal Candelaria of the Brown Berets, and an as yet unappointed representative of the emerging California Prisoners' Union. This was the first most had heard of the union. Demands 6 and 7 ordered an end to punishment by confinement in segregation for "political beliefs" and a halt to continuing attempts to confiscate political reading. Demand 25 ordered the eradication of the Adult Authority. Demand 10 called for an end to the indeterminate sentence. More controversial, Demand 16 insisted once again that

all condemned prisoners, avowed revolutionaries and prisoners of war be granted political asylum in the countries under the Free World Revolutionary Solidarity Pact, such as Algeria, Russia, Cuba, Latin America, North Korea, North Vietnam, etc., and that prisoners confined for political reasons in this country, until they can be exchanged for prisoners of war held by America, be treated in accord with the 1954 Geneva Convention; that they, their personal property be respected, and allowed in their possession, and that they not be manacled.[31]

Demand 19 ordered political asylum for "celebrated and prominent political prisoners," among them the Soledad Brothers. These last two demands became an immediate source of contention outside the walls. John Irwin explains:

There were two demands on there that we looked at and told [Martin Sousa's wife] Rosa, I think was her name, to go back in there and tell Martin to remove those two demands because they will divert all attention away from the others. . . . We told him, you know, we can't fly with this. . . . This thing is gonna make the media puke. . . . If you left these two in there these guys will just all be written off as stupid fucking Marxists who want a revolution. And so they did, they sent us back out a list of 29 demands. But Fay [Stender]'s group [the Prison Law Project] had gotten ahold of the original 31, so now there's two bodies of people who are circulating around, gonna organize the outside support for the strike, but we've got two different sets of demands.

According to Irwin, Demands 16 and 19 had been added to the list as a concession to radicals by the moderate unionists inside: "As they were forming these demands they were bringing in other prisoners. . . . In order to get their support, they had to cater to a lot of very forcefully asserted irrationality."[32] Aside from the inflammatory nature of Demands 16 and 19, perhaps the items in the list that represented the most serious challenges to the prison's system of governance were those that clearly showed the way to a prisoners' labor union. Demand 12 called openly for a labor union for prisoners, 11 insisted that private industries be allowed to engage convict labor at union scale wages on the prison grounds, 15 demanded compliance with state and federal minimum wage laws, 21 called for compliance with state working conditions standards, 22 demanded the establishment of inmate workers' insurance to compensate for work-related accidents, and 23 sought to create a unionized vocational education program. Demand 8 argued that prisoners could not be forced to work against their will.[33] The strike was slated to begin on November 3, 1970.

On November 2 all was calm at Folsom prison. A small band of 30 to 40 picketers gathered in the morning outside the gate. The next day, a contingent of Black Panthers arrived, swelling the ranks of the protesters to about 80. But it was not until November 5, 1970, that the strike picked up momentum inside. Administration sources reported about 500 men absent from work that day. Sources inside claimed much higher strike participation:

Wednesday
November 4
The situation at this time is that we have approximately 2100 people who did not work or function in any programmatic capacity today. We had approximately 152 people who did fulfill their work and vocational assignments. However, it is our feeling that within the next 24 hours we will have 100% response.[34]

Folsom's warden Walter Craven locked down all prisoners. As former Folsom guard Michael D. Brown later wrote,

Delivery of newspapers was halted. The radio system aired only selected stations. This attempt to curtail the dissemination of news proved ineffective as many inmates had their own transistor radios. There was no interruption of mail, though all correspondence was closely scrutinized. Inmates were placed on twice-a-day feeding schedules with bag lunches delivered to the cells.[35]

The union's various outside support groups had convened a press conference on the steps of the capitol building in Sacramento on the first day of the strike. John Irwin recalls that the divisions between unionists and revolutionaries inside the walls were replicated on the outside in a shaky coalition of moderate and radical supporters:

We were holding the press conference on the day the strike started. There were two groups that were supporting the strike. One was ours, the Coordinating Council. And then all the array of groups supporting Fay [Stender]. Tom Hayden was one of the speakers . . . and [so was] a member of the Black Panther party. . . . I wasn't going to speak, but they were all talking about the revolution and socialism and so on and so forth and they had forgotten the demands, so I finally took the microphone and I said, "You know, this is all great and I hope this comes about, but we got these twenty-nine demands and these are concrete, substantial things, and the prisoners are listening." . . . And I started going down the list of demands.

The Folsom strike lasted for a record time, nineteen days, aided by outside support and media coverage on local radio and television stations. On November 17, 1970, outside support groups called another press conference on the steps of the capitol. Irwin regards this day as the birth date of the United Prisoners Union (UPU):

We had another press conference . . . and it was clear that the convicts were about to give up the strike. Martin [Martin Sousa had just been granted parole] and Jim [Smith] and I were sitting there talking and one of the demands had been that the prisoners be allowed to form a union and so we said, "What do you want to do, Martin?" . . . He said, "We'll all form a union." And so I said, "OK, let's start working to form a union in there."[36]

On November 22 Warden Craven broadcast a radio speech to his Folsom prisoners, offering them the chance to return to work and explaining the consequences if they chose not to. The strike was over, but the union had just begun.[37]

Before the year was out, a small group of attorneys and ex-convicts met in Los Angeles to work out the terms of a constitution for the United Prisoners Union. The wording of the preamble to the UPU constitution reveals the unionists' inheritance from the ideology of San Quentin's radicals:

We the convicts and our people imprisoned or at large throughout the state of California are being subjected to a continuous cycle of poverty, prison, parole and more poverty; the same cycle that prisoners the world over have endured since the first man was enslaved. It is more than a game of Crime and Punishment; it is a social condition of inequality and degradation that denies us the opportunity to rise up and pursue a dignified way of life as guaranteed by the UNITED STATES CONSTITUTION. Once convicted, forever doomed has been the practice of society. We are the first to be accused and the last to be recognized. We are branded the lowest of all people: We the CONVICTED CLASS.

The right to organize for protection and survival is an inalienable right which is guaranteed to all people regardless of their social, racial, religious, economic, or political condition. Therefore, we the CONVICTED CLASS have banded together to form a cooperative Union to be hereafter called the UNITED PRISONERS UNION. We believe the creation of this Union will enable us to put an end to injustice, protect the lives and interests of our people, gain our constitutional rights and free us of our bondage.[38]

The language of the UPU constitution owed a clear debt to the thinking codified in Penal Code 2600 regarding prisoners' civil status, but the influence of class analysis on the thinking of the unionists was even clearer. The document depicted prisoners as an enslaved class and insisted on their right to organize to wage class struggle. But it stopped well short of any use of explicitly Marxist language. John Irwin takes up this point, underscoring the fact that, inside and outside the walls, the Left in 1970 was diverse and conflicted on the question of how to solve prison problems: "All the people that worked with me to form the Prisoners' Union were very consciously avoiding Marxist rhetoricisms and avoiding tactics which we thought were counterproductive."[39]

This reluctance to embrace revolutionary language quickly set the union on a collision course with other, more vocally Marxist and Maoist radical groups in the Bay Area, both inside and outside the prisons, and opened the organization to charges of being merely "liberal" or "progressive." Michael Snedeker, an attorney for the union in the early years, explains the organization's strategy: "People were mostly very pragmatic. There were very few ideologues or people who enjoyed keeping up with trends in political thinking at that time in the Prisoners' Union."[40] John Irwin points out the deep resentment of the radicals: "[Other radical groups] had the broader vision of constructing the communist world, and they had a very clear vision of what that would be like. And they would be the leaders of it. We were really reacting to what we saw as Stalinism in the movement. We were really very disgusted by it, angered by it, and tried to keep ourselves somewhat free of it."[41] Prison unionists had reason to perceive their revolutionary counterparts as a threat, for just as the moderate reformist United Prisoners Union was getting under way, the prison movement would turn to its foco period, spawning enclaves of superradical Bay Area urban guerrilla terrorists inspired by the late writings

of George Jackson. One result would be a quick drop in public support for prison activism.

Public interest in prisons continued to be strong through 1971.
Both the *San Francisco Chronicle* and the *Sacramento Bee* were printing
long series of articles exposing prison abuses and examining inmate
subculture, and in January a two-day Symposium on Prison Conditions and Political Defense was held at the University of California,
Berkeley. Marxist and Maoist ideology, too, was at its zenith among
the Bay Area Left. In the fall, Huey Newton, just back from a two-
week trip to the Peoples' Republic of China, told reporters he had
asked "Chairman Mao Zedong . . . to negotiate with Prison Warden
Nixon for the freedom of the oppressed peoples of the world." Newton, free on $500,000 bail pending his third trial, described China as
"liberated territory." He had found the Chinese life-style "beautiful"
because "the people are one and the same with the government." The
Black Panther leader quoted Chou En-lai as having expressed solidarity with the Black Panther party "and all political prisoners fighting for their freedom in San Quentin."[42]

Meanwhile, in the prison's AC that year George Jackson worked
feverishly to finish his second book. Luis Talamantez remembers his
friend at work:

Right at the end, when he was writing *Blood in My Eye*, I'd ask him, "George,
what you doin'?" He said, "I'm diggin' a grave." "Diggin' a grave?" "Diggin'
a grave, brother." He'd [put on his] earphones . . . and he'd sit crosswards
on his bed with his foot on the commode, with a folded blanket for a pillow
at his back. He always had a yellow tablet on his lap and his black jacket on
in his cell. He'd sit back there and scribble all day and smoke cigarettes and
drink cold coffee. Write, write, write. . . . George wanted to get it done. He
wanted to get the book done before anything happened because the guards
thought he was going to do something, because he was supposed to be going
to start trial. He already had one big fight happen at one of the trial hearings
before. Something was gonna come down, everybody knew it. It was important for George to get his book done. That was going to be his last testament.
He was talkin' about "diggin' a grave." He was diggin' a grave for them.
George wasn't about diggin' his own grave. . . . He wanted to stand for something, make a stand. He wasn't going to give up his life that easy. But George
felt that a lot of things were out of his control. He felt they were going to try
to kill him some kind of way. George knew that they would never allow him
to be free.

The end result of Jackson's long hours writing in his AC cell, posthu-
mously published in 1972 as *Blood in My Eye*, would be a bitter po-

lemic, a practical handbook of guerrilla war, and a vehicle that would accelerate the end of the Bay Area prison movement.

Blood in My Eye was filled with moments of dangerous military fantasy, as in an excerpt Jackson included from a letter his brother Jonathan had sent him:

It's come down on us hard now. There are twenty different breeds of pigs patrolling every street in the colony here. . . . We overestimate them, or perhaps have little sense of our own power. In the short run, and here I mean in an isolated tactical operation sitting within a particular political design, with military weapons we could easily out-gun the establishment's first line of defense. What, for example, would the city pigs do if they are confronted by a .38 snubbed revolver in the hand of a brother who's fired that .38 perhaps 10 times in his life? Then take the same situation but give the brother a flame-thrower, give him also two comrades in arms, one equipped with an M60 machine gun, the other an anti-tank rocket launcher. Pigs are punks. Give me 10 cells armed as I've just mentioned and we could start to enforce some of the demands of the people.[43]

In this and another of Jonathan's letters included in the book, the Jackson brothers' visions of revenge clearly showed the influence of Regis Debray. The strategy of launching urban guerrilla raids with small armed cells would accomplish much more than simple military objectives, the brothers argued. Such raids would force the police to retaliate, further exposing their repressiveness and bringing the public into the ranks of the revolutionaries. Jonathan Jackson believed that "by drawing violence from the beast, the vanguard party is demonstrating for the world to examine just exactly what terms their rule is predicated on." George Jackson wholeheartedly agreed with his young brother. He endorsed Debray's foco theory for use in the American city: "[The] power of the people—their greater potential violence—can be brought to fruition only if the conditions in an urban society are created by the application of the foco theory."[44] Jackson was careful to insist that the engagement of the armed cell should precede party building. The development of a revolutionary vanguard had to move through stages of long, careful preparation, he believed, but these were to be graduated stages of combat. He quoted John Gerassi in *The Coming of the New International*: "New Left revolutionaries all over the world know very well that a revolutionary life style is a warrior's life style."[45] Who were these revolutionary soldiers to be? The ideal warrior in the cause would be someone who had already been hardened in battle. Veterans of gang fights in prisons, Jackson's convict comrades, seemed made for the purpose.

From his AC cell, George Jackson prescribed the proper corrective for the enemy in the ghetto:

There are many thousands of ways to correct individuals. The best way is to send one armed expert. I don't mean to outshout him with logic, I mean correct him. Slay him, assassinate him with thuggee, by silenced pistol, shotgun, with a high-powered rifle shooting from four hundred yards away and behind a rock. Suffocation, strangulation, crucifixion, burning with flamethrower, dispatch by bomb. Auto accidents happen all day. People drown, get poleaxed, breathe noxious gases, get stabbed, get poisoned with bad water, ratsbane, germicides, hemlock, arsenic, strychnine, L.S.D. 25 concentrate, cyanide, hydrocyanic acid, vitriol. A snake could bite him, nicotine oil is deadly, an overdose of dope; there's deadly nightshade, belladonna, datura, wolfsbane, foxglove, aconite, ptomaine, botulism, and the death of a thousand cuts. But a curse won't work.[46]

Jackson envisioned that the first engagements of the armed cell shock troops using guerrilla techniques would be followed by the emergence of a wide popular struggle:

We must accept the eventuality of bringing the U.S.A. to its knees; accept the closing off of critical sections of the city with barbed wire, armored pig carriers crisscrossing the city streets, soldiers everywhere, tommy guns pointed at stomach level, smoke curling black against the daylight sky, the smell of cordite, house-to-house searches, doors being kicked down, the commonness of death. Then we must learn the forms of resistance: the booby trap, the silenced pistol and rifle, the pitting of streets to slow them down, the wrecking of heavy equipment to block their efficient movement, false walls, hidden sub-basements, tunnels (Vietnamese style), destruction of the critical elements of the facilities that support establishment order.[47]

But as Johnny Spain would point out to a Black Panther visiting him in San Quentin in 1972, Jackson's fantasizing was unreasonable in the extreme:

We talked about the . . . things that were changing for us [the Black Panthers] at that point. . . . There were a number of people that were members of the party who believed that there existed a sufficient enough infrastructure to maintain a sublevel organization that would commit itself to armed struggle. I said, . . . "The fact is there *aren't* going to be any army tanks in the street putting down some rebellion of the Left." I said, "The police force is quite sufficient. You're not going to have to get the army out here. There aren't going to be tanks in the streets. We're not going to overthrow this government this year. . . . What we've really got to do is struggle for some more immediate, more reachable things. . . . And we can through those efforts educate enough people to see what we're trying to say and to get some help.

But right now to think we're gonna run out and grab an AK-47 and go change the world," I said, "let me tell you!" [48]

Unfortunately, Jackson, who was allowed fewer and fewer contacts with the outside as 1971 progressed, and therefore had fewer means to gauge the level of struggle outside the walls, persisted in his exaggerated sense of the actual level of outside conflict and what it might become. Moreover, though he referred in *Blood in My Eye* to the Black Panther party as "the people's natural, political vanguard," [49] Jackson had grown increasingly suspicious of the party hierarchy in 1971 over the issue of the disappearing funds of his defense committee and the royalties from his first book. [50] Now he dreamed of himself or escaped convicts like him leading the revolution alone. "The outlaw and the lumpen will make the revolution," he wrote. "The people, the workers, will adopt it." [51]

Each one of the opposition's own tank shells that is fired inside the manufacturing city at the elusive guerrilla will destroy some aspect of that factory-city and undercut the ability of the establishment to produce another tank shell. It will not help the fascist cause very much at all when the armored personnel carrier or jeep patrol equipped with 30-caliber machine guns fires into a downtown shopping crowd at the elusive guerrilla who has taken refuge among them. The people just will not understand. . . .

The cities of fascist U.S.A.—built straight up and with very little real planning or pattern, the twisting side streets, gangways connecting roofs, manholes, storm drains, concrete and steel trees—will hide a guerrilla army just as effectively as any forest.

We will make use of all forms of disguise: mailman, policeman, telephone repairman, priest, nun, National Guardsman. This principle will soon have them shooting at each other or turning the innocents against them. The result—perfect disorder!

All dwellings should be either rented or expendable. They should be equipped so that when forced to leave by tunnel or other hidden exits, the place can be burned to create further confusion for the attacker and destroy evidence. Food and clothing should be purposely simple. Clothing must always be available for disguises. [52]

The Left would be far from unanimous in its praise of these words from *Blood in My Eye*, as it had been of Jackson's first book. A 1972 National Lawyers Guild position paper would caution its members against encouraging prisoners to adopt Jackson's theory and tactics:

Most revolutionary prisoners seem to relate almost exclusively to the military side of the revolutionary struggle. They see themselves as warriors. . . .

George Jackson, in his last book *Blood in My Eye*, called for urban guerilla warfare. The call for armed uprisings comes out of Jackson's analysis that we are presently living under fascism. . . . We feel obliged to say that although repression in America is growing . . . we do not believe fascism is here. . . . This does not mean that we should not do all we can to prepare ourselves and others for the eventual fight, but it does mean that premature calls for guerilla warfare are counterproductive.[53]

In a last letter to John Gerassi, Jackson wrote, "No matter what I do, they will always explain me away with the fact of my eleven years in prison and my supposed loss of contact with objective reality. So I rage on aggressive and free."[54] These sentiments were sadly true; to most observers the prisoner's isolation had come to seem his undoing. Whether the rest of the world would remember George Jackson from his final book as a brilliant revolutionary theorist or a dangerously deluded and victimized convict genius, at least one group of readers was to take his foco theory and urban guerrilla tactics very seriously. This group was the Symbionese Liberation Army (SLA). Inside San Quentin, too, George Jackson's forceful advocacy of foco strategy on the AC tier worked to pull the prison's revolutionaries further and further away from union moderates and seriously diminish the chances of maintaining an inmate coalition. Jackson at last turned the movement away from the unionists and took his place at the cause's fatal critical mass. From here on, moderates within and without the prison were eclipsed by the force of his personal revolution.

Rumors of an escape plot now swirled about San Quentin.* Later, the state would produce a letter it claimed was in the handwriting of both Jimmy Carr and Jackson, outlining preparations for an escape. The note had reportedly been found by a dry cleaner in a pair of Carr's pants. Next, Penny Jackson was barred from the prison after an apparent attempt to test the prison's metal-detection device by taping a toy gun to her toddler son's leg. Suddenly, on August 20, 1971, the prison isolated the prisoner even further. Associate Warden James Park announced a new policy under which news reporters would be allowed to interview inmates in lockup units only once every three months. This policy applied to about 180 men but was clearly directed at the Soledad Brothers and Ruchell Magee. Park cavalierly told the press the new rule was aimed at cutting down on the multiple visits of "funny people who I doubt are really reporters" asking to talk to

---

*In *The Dragon Has Come*, Jackson's editor, Gregory Armstrong, writes of Jackson's own part in these escape plot rumors.

these "celebrity inmates." [55] It was now clear that George Jackson's fate was sealed. The outside Left demanded some spectacularly heroic act from its leader. And however he did it, Jackson had to surpass even his younger brother Jonathan's fiery revolt. Revolutionaries inside, too, would be utterly disheartened unless an act of supreme vengeance was forthcoming from George Jackson very soon. And the state was moving in—Jackson could not be allowed to live to come to trial. If he won his case, it would be seen as a sign of demoralizing defeat of the prison system. Prison guards would mutiny. The system would fall apart. Yet Jackson's conviction could be even worse, possibly launching a bloody war inside and on Bay Area streets.

The details of exactly what happened on the next day, August 21, 1971, are impossible to sort out with any certainty. Multiple stories contradict one another. But at least one fact is clear. In the words of AC inmate Johnny Spain, "There was a gun introduced into the Adjustment Center on August 21." According to most versions of the legend, on the way back to the Adjustment Center from a visit, Jackson drew a gun on his escorting officer and launched the bloodiest day in San Quentin's history. First, he released his fellow AC revolutionary convicts, shouting, "The Dragon has come!" Certain AC prisoners then helped Jackson take six officers and two white convict tier tenders as hostages. Five of these men, three guards and the tier tenders, were later found dead in Jackson's cell, stabbed and with their throats slit. Three other wounded guards would recover. [56]

As a call for aid went out to Marin County law enforcement agencies and scores of heavily armed California highway patrolmen and Marin County sheriff's deputies began converging on the prison, blocking off all access roads, George Jackson made his final stand. "It's me they want," he said simply. Gun in hand, accompanied only by Johnny Spain, the Dragon bolted out through the AC lobby and into the prison "plaza." There he was killed instantly by a marksman on the yard gunrail with one shot to the middle of his back, which, according to official reports, then ricocheted off his spine or pelvis and exited the top of his skull. Johnny Spain dived into a bush outside the chapel and was spared. Librarian James McHenry witnessed the killing: "He got shot just as I came out of the library. I saw him fall." [57] McHenry and another officer were ordered to take Jackson's body to the morgue, to make a count of the bullet holes, and to take an accounting of the personal possessions in his pockets.

The state at first claimed that Jimmy Carr's attorney, a young white activist lawyer from Berkeley named Stephen Bingham, had passed

Jackson the pistol, having carried it in on his last visit, concealed in a tape recorder. Bingham, however, was later acquitted of any part in the escape attempt. It is possible that Jackson assembled a gun himself from parts smuggled piecemeal into the prison and thrown over the AC yard fence by mainline prisoners. However, there is some evidence that points to the smuggling of an already assembled gun. A message written and afterward erased, but still visible under oblique light, was reportedly found in Jackson's AC cell after the incident. "Take the bullets out of the bag," it said. "Hurry and give me the piece in the bag. Keep the bullets."[58] According to prison officials, who had to change their version of the story several times over the next weeks to resolve its contradictions, the weapon in question was a 9mm Astra M-600, almost nine inches long and weighing two and a half pounds, which Jackson quickly concealed under an Afro wig he had worn to the interview with Bingham. This scenario seems implausible in the extreme. After the visit, the prisoner supposedly rose and walked the distance back to the AC, about 50 yards, balancing the long and bulky weapon on his head. An opposing scenario alleged that San Quentin guards had received a nonfunctioning weapon with a filed-down firing pin from an outside source, either the Criminal Investigation and Identification Department of the state attorney general's office or the Criminal Conspiracy Section of the Los Angeles Police Department, which they planted on Jackson in a setup for an assassination. According to this version, the functioning 9mm Astra was placed beside Jackson's body after his death.

After Jackson's death, the Adjustment Center was retaken by heavily armed guards. Richard Nelson, lieutenant in charge of the AC, reveals how this was done and something of what it was like for the guards:

It was a Saturday. I was painting my dining room in my home, which is up on the hill here, a city block away. . . . I heard a muffled gunshot. . . . I heard a very distinct rifle crack then. Right after I heard the first rifle shot I heard a second distinctive rifle shot.

I ran in the house, jumped in my uniform, and ran down the hill. As I got close to the prison wall, the wall officer . . . told me that George Jackson was in the chapel area with a gun. I went directly to the armory and picked up a .45-caliber Thompson submachine gun and several pocketsful of 20 round clips . . . I was going out with enough firepower to kill George Jackson. That was my sole intent at that time.

I . . . came in through the [count] gate. The front and back count gate officers knew somethin' was wrong. Shots fired. Inmates loose in the AC.

Gun inside. [But] they didn't know what was goin' on. As soon as I got into the plaza I loaded the machine gun, took it off safe, and I ran toward the Catholic chapel. An officer hollered to me from the AC door and said, "Comon over here, we got hostages." I said, "What about Jackson? Is he in the chapel with a gun?" And he said something to me and I couldn't understand it, and I said, "I'm goin' in to kill him!" And he said, "He's already been shot!" And I said, "Is he dead?" And they said, "Yes." I then went to the Adjustment Center. . . .

We knew there was a lot of inmates loose on the south side, probably all the inmates from the first floor, we just didn't know yet. They were hollering at us and telling us, "We got hostages." We were hollering at them to come on out and they were hollering back and cursing us, and we were cursing back at them and hollering. They were saying, "We got hostages and we got guns and we're gonna kill all you so-and-so's." We in turn said, "You come on out or we're comin' down and gonna kill all you so-and-so's." We didn't make any progress there. They weren't moving and we weren't going down the tier just yet. We determined that we still had two officers missing. [Several officers had come out.] We had a yard officer and one of my AC officers were missing still. Somebody fired a shotgun down the tier, the first tier, and it went silent for a minute, and then they just hooted and hollered and booed. And hollered, "We're gonna kill the hostages." Unbeknownst to us, they had tied the officers up using their own belts and rags and handcuffs. And they slit their throats and were trying to pierce their jugular veins with a pencil. We fired the shotgun, and that didn't regain control for us. So we fired a rifle down the tier, one shot from a rifle. That did not get their attention or gain control. We hollered at 'em for a few more seconds, trying to convince 'em that they gotta surrender because we're comin' through. I then fired five rounds out of the machine gun, a big burst of fire, slid the gate open, couldn't see anybody. I just stood in the middle of the tier and shot right straight down the tier, waist high. Back at the back end of the AC are five or six quiet cells. Hollow core doors. The doors were swung halfway open. I shot into the first quiet cell door. Unbeknownst to me, that's where they had the two officers with their throats slit. There were inmates in that cell as well. That scattered 'em when that door started exploding when I shot machine-gun fire into it and big holes started blowin' up in that door. The inmates ran. I didn't shoot at 'em. They came out of the cells and then ducked back quickly in the next cell down or two. One of the officers was laying on the bunk, his hands handcuffed behind him with his own handcuffs and his feet tied. He was on the bunk on his back. The other officer was tied inside the cell with his back to the cell bars and tied up there. He was unable to untie himself. . . . They were able to run out then. I recognized Rubiaco [officer Urbano Rubiaco, Jr., whose throat had been slit]. . . .

We got Rubiaco and Breckenridge [officer Charles Breckenridge, who had sustained stab wounds and a penetrated trachea] toward the front of the unit. Rubiaco slipped and fell into a cell. It was right near the front. I didn't know if anybody else was in there. I fired another burst of machine-gun fire to keep 'em away from him while he had the opportunity to wiggle out and get back on his feet and come on out. Still, we didn't know where the inmates were in that tier. We got Rubiaco and Breckenridge out and got medical attention on them. I fired another burst of machine-gun fire down the tier. The inmates began to surrender. They realized their hostages were gone and we had the firepower. I wound up firing 28 or 30 rounds in that unit that day. The inmates just came out one at a time then. . . . There were four of us. We formed a team and we went down, just like you do Second World War style. Ease up along the wall, stick the machine gun into the cell, and pop a round or two in there just to get their attention if anybody's there. . . . We got down to Cell 1-AC-66, the second to the last cell, and I could see inmate blue stockings on the feet laying on the bed face up, toes up. I hollered, "Get up! Get out of there! I'm gonna come in shooting!" They did not move. I went in shooting and it was an inmate, Ronny Kane [Ronald L. Kane], that had had his throat cut by the inmates and his head was flopped back. That secured that side. The next cell we secured rather quickly. We had the inmates outside the unit on the lawn and the unit was secured.

The next day in a coarse oversimplification that revealed just how out of touch with the inmates' grievances the prison administration had preferred to remain, Associate Warden James Park would blame the incident on "the bullshit talk of dilettante revolutionaries, on people who emptily advocate murder from the safety of outside the walls. I believe that they have encouraged these men to take desperate action while they sit safely looking on."[59] San Quentin authorities had decided to blame the incident entirely on outside agitators.

Despite the prison's supreme unconcern for the real underlying causes of inmate struggle, Warden Park's remarks did strike one note of truth. George Jackson and his revolutionary comrades in the AC *had* been manipulated by outsiders. Jackson was at once a free agent and a victim of the machinations of others. He was at once isolated from outsiders and manipulated by them, out of touch with the outside world and a tragic product of it. How had this happened? Jackson was a man preeminently capable of acting on his own, apparently indifferent to the opinions of others. Yet, over the long years of his imprisonment, the circle of his contacts in the wider world outside the prison and even on the mainline had steadily narrowed, and thus his sources for information from that world had dwindled. Prison efforts to monitor, then restrict, his access to ideas via reading and writing had led him first to fight these limitations through his attorney, then to subvert them with smuggled contraband reading and communiqués sneaked in to him by a small radical circle of outsiders. The further, extreme narrowing of his approved visitors in the months and weeks preceding August 21 had finally cut him off from all but a handful of fanatic outside contacts who supplied him with information. These people had definite ideas about how they wanted Jackson to perform. So James Park was correct in a sense; in a limited way the AC revolt *had* been the product of outsiders—though to say so conveniently ignored the blame that the prison system itself shared for perpetuating the conditions that led to revolt and for engineering AC prisoners' isolation from a wider exposure to ideas and sources of information in the real world.

The manipulation of George Jackson was to continue even after his death. In spite of his efforts to rewrite himself in interviews and in *Blood in My Eye,* by the time of his death in the San Quentin plaza and the ten-minute AC revolution that preceded it, George Jackson's life had become the property of those who owned his myth. Whoever the real prisoner Jackson was on that day, whatever he and others in the AC did or did not do, and however outsiders or prison staff helped or manipulated him into behaving as he did, the facts would quickly become confused, forgotten, and ultimately mythologized in the memories of survivors. The real George Jackson quickly became unimportant anyway. For those who had appropriated his myth as their own, for the BGF and the SLA, Jackson was now the Dragon, who had passed on to them the foco tactic, key to the future struggle. For the California Correctional Officers Association and other groups on the Right, on the contrary, Jackson's memory would become a rallying cry for a conservative backlash against further prison reform.

Jackson, the tragic product of a failed legacy of prison communication control that yawned over the centuries all the way from Benjamin Rush, had given both the Left and the Right what they wanted in 1971. In a time of increasingly reductionist class analysis among many radical groups, when mere convict-class identity was a ticket to leadership of the Bay Area Left, he became a superhero, a warrior-leader. And for the white middle-class Left, Cleaver's feminized "Omnipotent Administrators," still wary of committing the irrevocable act, Jackson came to represent a psychosexual bombshell of defiant masculinity that almost, but not quite, had incited even them to revolutionary violence. The end of the Bay Area prison movement among the Left, however, was rapidly approaching.

The movement swerved dramatically to the Left briefly after George Jackson's death. For a time, even the moderate UPU outside the prisons joined radical Bay Area groups in waging a broad struggle against the American state, demanding the unconditional release of all prisoners. On November 6, 1971, a contingent of the union marched in a large anti–Vietnam War demonstration in San Francisco carrying a banner that read "OUT OF ALL PRISONS *NOW*: The UPU demands that all prisoners be free from state, federal, military and P.O.W. camps."[60] By 1972, however, the union had recovered its center and was quietly putting its major efforts into building a covert membership organization inside the prisons, working through the courts and in the legislature on issues relating to prison unionization and responding to specific problems of inmates as they arose. In 1972, as the result of a court action, the official organ of the UPU, the *Outlaw* convict newspaper, was finally officially permitted into San Quentin. Former UPU attorney James Smith explains the importance of the *Outlaw* in union building:

They found out about us from the *Outlaw*. That was our voice. We found out about them by either correspondence, phone calls, or attorney visits. And there would be incidents from time to time and they would get busted for passing a petition about the Prisoners' Union, and they would get thrown in the hole or gaffled up. And we would hear about these things.

To a large extent, and to the disappointment of some, the UPU now took on the character of a civil rights advocacy organization for prisoners. Smith comments: "One of the things I did personally was to contact legislators to get them to raise hell with the CDC. The same with the media. . . . We spent a lot of time trying to project images of our struggle and what was going on." Ultimately, the UPU did not become a labor union. The core of its work did not involve economic issues. Many UPU board members came to see the union's work on lawsuits and legislation outside as more important than organizing for work stoppages behind the walls, though the building of a supportive constituency of prisoners in the institutions remained crucial to this strategy. The list of court victories expanding prisoners' civil rights in the period of early unionization is impressive proof of the effectiveness of the early UPU and other prison movement attorneys through litigation. Because it adhered to a civil rights model, however, which some inmates had long since rejected, the more radical California prisoners came to view the UPU as a tame, self-help organization. Smith remarks: "We had our problems with the Right and we had our problems with the Left from the beginning. Our civil rights conception by definition [made us] out of it. . . . That was a band-aid analysis from their point of view. We were wrong."

Within the UPU, serious disagreement raged from the very first about whether to expand the struggle or confine union work to litigation and legislative efforts. This, combined with other issues, would finally fracture the union by 1973 into two separate organizations, the Prisoners' Union headed by Willie Holder and the United Prisoners Union led by Popeye Jackson. At issue was a controversy over the exact meaning of a union, whether that necessarily included using work stoppages and large inmate agitations as a strategy, and whether the union's battle should be widened and joined with other radical groups fighting for destruction of the state. The Prisoners' Union faction, which still survives, chose to confine itself to prison issues, even if that meant being labeled "liberal" and "reformist," and largely to renounce work stoppages as a union strategy. Former Prisoners' Union attorney Michael Snedeker explains that group's position on strikes:

[Strikes remained] an indirect threat. And the threat of a strike is probably more powerful than the strike itself. [But] strikes in a prison context have no economic muscle at all. They might be useful as an informational device, [although] if prisoners went on strike there would just be overtime for prison employees. There would be a greater flow of state funds to prisons. Most . . . officials would profit from it. There was little or no economic leverage in the hands of prisoners. . . . Prison industries are not that significant. They make products only for state industries. Most everything they make is readily available on outside markets and could be purchased and would be purchased.

The Prisoners' Union still considered strikes useful for certain purposes:

However, [strikes] are an important way of pointing something out. It can be an occasion for a press release to point out the underlying problem. And it can show some coordination, some political sophistication. I think strikes are an effective way of protesting over specific things that sympathy can be gained for, particularly if it has a specific remedy, like the firing of some incompetent person. The strike is an effective means of highlighting that, . . . a one-day strike coordinated with a press release.

Despite the Prisoners' Union's renunciation of work stoppages, San Quentin officials continued to assume that the union's sole purpose was to foment large-scale labor agitations. Associate Warden James Park recounts the prison's attitude: "We thought [the union] was dumb. Unions were for working people. The Prisoners' Union at that point existed only to agitate. It didn't exist to do anything useful in our opinion. . . . Most inmates were happy to have a job. It wasn't seen as slave labor. This was a break to get a job."[61]

The UPU faction, headed by Popeye Jackson, drew considerable numbers of members away from the Prisoners' Union when it split off in 1973, primarily taking with it the union's more radical convicts. When Popeye Jackson took up the leadership of the UPU, the prison authorities assumed that this tough black former San Quentin convict, who had been acquainted with George Jackson, had been passed the leadership directly. Until his death in 1971, San Quentin officials had erroneously suspected George Jackson of being in control of what they referred to as "the clandestine 'Convict Union' within the walls." Prison authorities blamed the union and George Jackson in particular for acts of in-prison violence, claiming that "messages from one prison to another has been intercepted which indicated that the secret organization had some control over the violence in prisons."[62] But Popeye Jackson's accession was of his own making. Former Soledad inmate and Prisoners' Union board member Jay Halford explains:

Popeye was a tough guy who had killed a couple guys in the joint. . . . He allegedly put a hatchet in a guy's head up in the gym in Quentin one time over some disagreement. But he lived off the credentials of George Jackson. . . . Because . . . he was tight with George Jackson, you know, he just felt he couldn't be wrong on anything. . . . Popeye was not a Panther. He acted like George endorsed him, which was not the case. . . . He was a hope-to-die criminal.

According to Halford and others, Popeye Jackson continued to commit crimes while on parole and even while serving as the head of security of the United Prisoners Union. Halford continues:

When he disagreed, he slapped guys around and shit. He was a real violent, tough guy. He really was frightening. I consider myself tough, too, but he was a terrifying type guy. And he had a way of scowling at you. He just had this demeanor. And he just wouldn't countenance you disagreeing with him. And he dismissed you like you were a counterrevolutionary. . . . Popeye felt like the convicted class was the vanguard of revolution. . . . Guys like Popeye believed only in the convicted class as a revolutionary force. . . . They didn't think I was lumpen enough. They were lumpen and I was a progressive dupe.[63]

To John Irwin, Popeye Jackson was a convict opportunist, plain and simple: "All of our group knew [Popeye] in prison. At the time, people who were just total unscrupulous opportunists could wheel into all kinds of positions of advantage. It was a very fluid period. If you acted a certain way you could be shoved up to leadership." When Popeye Jackson finally left the UPU in 1973, his departure would be unceremonious. Irwin notes, "We couldn't shake him, but we caught him stealing money so we booted him."[64] Jackson may have been an opportunist of the first order, but he was more than that. Regardless of what his own motives and behavior may have been, to his followers Popeye Jackson was a loyal revolutionary in the cause. A former Soledad inmate remarks that "[Popeye Jackson] impressed me to be really a warm, caring individual. I seen him at that time as somebody that I would want to aspire to have those kind of characteristics. Charisma maybe."[65]

There were ideological reasons as well behind the split between the UPU and the Prisoners' Union. As Smith explains, "The Prisoners' Union . . . was viewed as not with the revolutionary radical ideology that they oughta be by . . . the Bay Area radical chic." The UPU, in contrast, embraced the more fashionable revolutionary ideology. Inmate Nate Harrington recalls both union groups: "There was a more radical, more extreme lean by the United Prisoners Union. And the Prisoners' Union itself was more of an informational and educational affair. The United Prisoners Union was connected with other things that potentially could have become much more than just an informational and educational affair."[66] In Smith's opinion, that ideology was created for it by the extreme Left:

Radical chic types . . . always were . . . critical of us for not having radical revolutionary ideology and didn't like our program and our platform for that reason. And therefore when Popeye Jackson came along, these very individuals . . . sought to . . . place their ideological baggage on the shoulders of Popeye Jackson, which were not broad enough to carry any kind of baggage, let alone misguided ones. And so I think he was *viewed* as having an ideological purpose in the break-off by those who had other political agendas, but in fact that wasn't the case.

Some board members of the Prisoners' Union today feel that by the end of the mid-1970's their struggle for prison reforms had been subverted by elements of the more radical Bay Area Left.[67] George Jackson's revolution had stolen the movement away. Still, the process of upstaging the prison system's unionists was a slow one. Inside the California prisons unionism competed well with the revolution for several years.

Beginning in 1972, a member of San Quentin's Nation of Islam temple, convict Harlan Washington, functioned as the Prisoners' Union's main operative inside the walls. Washington remembers early union organizing:

I sat down and I composed a letter and I sent it to Mike [Prisoners' Union attorney Michael Snedeker]. At that time I imagine there was maybe 200 or 300 people at the most that were in the Prisoners' Union throughout the whole state. In this letter . . . I told him, "My name is Harlan X Washington. I'm a Muslim. We are approximately 250 to 300 strong. We have the respect and rapport of anybody in the institution." I said, "We are interested in giving you 25 members plus myself from the Nation of Islam as members in the Prisoners' Union within two weeks' time. Within a month's time we would like to give you the whole 300. Within a month and a half to two months' time we'd like to give you a thousand throughout the institution. What *we* need is for someone to come in and converse with us. . . .

At the same time I had to be able to smuggle [union] applications out to [Snedeker]. So I had to get it to the visiting room. But what we had to do first was, I went to a white that worked in the print shop. I told him what we were tryin' to do and he indicated that he would underground reduplicate these applications. After he reduplicated a thousand applications, I then took fifteen brothers out of the Nation of Islam and I gave them the sales pitch. I said, "Go to the cells in your wing, in your building, in your block, and go from cell to cell. Say, 'Hey, man . . . we're tryin' to get a thousand dudes involved with the Prisoners' Union. . . . Would you care to join? These applications will not leave my hand. . . . They will go directly to the attorney. You have our word on that. . . .'" [The response] was 100 percent favorable. This one guy claimed to be a Nazi and his head was split all the way to the side and he wore the big swastika and [German] cross. One day he walked up to me and he says, "I don't have to like you," he said, "but I can respect what you're doing." And he says, "And if you need any help from me, I'll give it to you," he says. "But I still don't like you." He brought in the ones [from the Aryan Brotherhood] that we needed.

Washington's union inductees held secret gatherings disguised as Nation of Islam meetings or meetings of the Wives and Husbands in Prison (WHIP), an organization Washington also headed:

We had [meetings] in Chow Hall. There were guards present. . . . They would come and [they] would think it was a WHIP meeting. But we'd go through the WHIP meeting and then show the latest Prison Union paper and we would deal with it in such a manner as if to say, "What are we doin' now?" . . . And so they couldn't touch it. We had 300 or 400 people [in the Chow Hall]. . . .

And we called social events. We would cut the social events in half and have roundtable talks. We would bring the leaders in from the Mexican Mafia, the ABs [Aryan Brotherhood], the Texas Syndicate, the BGF, all the gangs on the yard. We'd taken out money and bought chips and soda waters and cookies and chocolate and coffee, and we just had a big feast. And we would kick it. But we would invite Michael [Snedeker] in. . . . But [Associate Warden Glenn] Swaggerty . . . he came in from the warden's office and the first time when he got up on it he said, "These guys are organizing! These guys are in a union up under our very noses!" The next thing you know several of us was shipped out. I was shipped to Soledad.[68]

By 1973 the Prisoners' Union had a membership roll of 3,000 and the *Outlaw* was reaching 5,000 convicts in state and federal prisons across the nation.[69] By mid-decade the mailing list for the *Outlaw* had swelled to 25,000.[70] By that time, however, the union had passed its prime. Prison movement foco terrorism, inspired by George Jackson's *Blood in My Eye*, had soured the public on prison reform and the bottom had dropped out of the movement. Pro-union sentiment would persist in the California prisons till the end of the decade. The future should have been bright for the California Prisoners' Union. In a 1978 survey of inmates at San Luis Obispo Men's Colony conducted by political scientist Ronald Berkman, 91 percent of the prisoners believed they should have the right to form unions. Inmates were "almost unanimous" in the opinion that one union should represent all, both working and nonworking prisoners.[71] Attitudes were probably similar at San Quentin and throughout the California system. Instead, the union movement stalled, the public withdrew its support, and the California Department of Corrections successfully blocked unionization.

This failure may be explained in part by the resistance of the prison system to unionization. After George Jackson's death, imported literature confiscated at the prisons called plainly for the killing of more guards. This enabled the Department of Corrections to argue successfully for more funding from the state legislature to finance a crackdown and to put down all forms of inmate activism, including moderate reformism. The Cleaver Panther faction's October 1971 issue of *Right On!*, for instance, called on black guards to smuggle weapons in to black San Quentin inmates. A November 1973 number of the National Lawyers Guild newsletter *Midnight Special: Prisoners News* reproduced letters from convicts explicitly calling for the death of prison guards.[72] Impounded literature like this only added fuel to the flames when representatives of the Department of Corrections appeared in 1973 before the House Internal Security Committee to make a case against continued freedom of reading and writing in the California prisons.

But there was an even larger reason for the eclipse of the California Prisoners' Union. Early in the 1970's it became plain that the movement had simply passed the union by. To leftists the union seemed increasingly irrelevant to the cause after George Jackson's death. The far Left was intent on following in the Dragon's path and had little use for unions. The Jackson revolution would go on. In San Francisco in August 1971, behind floor-to-ceiling bullet-proof and soundproof glass walls, the Soledad Brothers' trial played itself out without the fallen leader, George Jackson. In the San Francisco headlines of fall 1971, news of the My Lai massacre court-martial case competed with that of the courtroom melees of the remaining Soledad Brothers, Fleeta Drumgo and John Clutchette. A bloody struggle erupted between several black men and police tactical squad members when the judge tried to have Clutchette's mother forcibly removed from the courtroom for causing a disturbance.[73] Courtroom spectators, mostly black, stood and gave the defendants clenched-fist salutes. Some pounded on the glass barricades. Defense attorneys charged that their clients were being beaten. Drumgo, who had appeared in court walking stiffly and covered with raised welts, cried out, "Kill me now, man, you're going to kill me anyway!" Drumgo and Clutchette would be acquitted of the charges against them. George Jackson, had he lived, might not have been so lucky. Luis Talamantez discusses this point:

I think that George might have felt that he'd get convicted, railroaded at the trial. But at no time did George ever show defeat, or show that it was the end of anything. George always had plans of action goin' on in his thinking. . . . George's attitude was that he really didn't believe in the criminal justice system or its right to try him. He wasn't honoring it with recognizing its severity because, first of all, he was someone that was illegally enslaved and he was a political prisoner and one of the guys that had been killed at Soledad by the white guard was Nolen, one of his best comrades. So it was like the law of the jungle, tit for tat, man, you know, shit, it's a whole different attitude, view of right and wrong. I got an attitude saying, well, all right, if you kill one of mine I'll kill one of yours and so far we're even. Perfectly OK. That's the way my reasoning was shaping up at the time. And George expressed the same thing. We all did. George never seen himself having done anything wrong. I didn't think he'd done anything wrong either. If he did it, he did it. I think that his action was a bold action. If he did it, man, more power to him, man, he got even. These fascists needed to be pushed back. And if it takes a violent act like that, then that's what you do.

As the trial continued into October 1971, George Jackson's legend had taken on such mythic proportions that he seemed to transcend his death. Despite the state's commonsense practice of routinely dropping criminal charges in the event of a defendant's death, Jackson's attorney John Thorne submitted a motion in the Soledad Brothers' trial to go on representing the dead revolutionary or be granted a dismissal on the grounds of innocence.[74] Jackson's memory took total possession of the prison movement. For much of the Bay Area Left the union was already an afterthought. Events now called for much more violent political practice. On the streets a 25-cent National Lawyers Guild pamphlet was advising militants to

keep your weapons hidden. . . . Large stores of weapons should be in a very safe place, like in a house that could not be linked to the movement.

Kim Il Sung says, "You should think of camouflage first of all when you build a house."[75]

The prison movement had spun away from its union-building phase. In 1972 the National Lawyers Guild reaffirmed once again the leadership of revolutionary convicts and repeated its faith that they would soon make their break to the streets to raise the level of struggle: "Prisoners are the revolutionary vanguard of our struggle. When prisoners come out, they will lead us in the streets."[76] The next year the guild would wisely begin to rethink this position. A position paper of 1973 found fault with the organization's previous role in the movement:

We *idealized* prisoners, and, consequently, our work was approached with incredible amounts of romanticism. To many of us, prisoners who enunciated revolutionary rhetoric under the most extreme form of repression from the state became not comrades, brothers and sisters struggling in common with the rest, but super revolutionaries, super dragons, and our response was very typical, very petty bourgeois; it was very romantic.

The guild also blamed itself for "failing to give prisoners an accurate picture of what is happening on the streets . . . [which] increase[d] the chances that people will, on being released, become totally depressed by not finding . . . military struggle going on. . . . This only heightens the already strong tendency to revolutionary suicidal acts."[77] The guild undoubtedly here referred to Jackson's death on the yard as well as the Marin County Courthouse shootout of the year before and Ronald Beaty's escape attempt in 1972. Few joined in this reexamination of strategies, however. The romance of the convict continued too strong. In fact, George Jackson's last book was about to leap to life. In the end it would be the plot of a convict's book, not the plan of a union, that the movement was destined to follow.

9

"Foco" Terrorism in the SLA

As the autumn of 1971 approached, the deaths of George Jackson and the guards and inmates in San Quentin that day in the AC provided a rallying cry to both the California Left and the conservative Right wing. The experience was not unique. A similar ideological fracturing was repeated in other communities all across the nation as domestic political turmoil substantially worsened. Many Americans were angry and soured on government. In early spring the war in Vietnam had appeared to be flaring back up when U.S. forces swept into Laos. In June, publication of *The Pentagon Papers* had further embittered the public, eroding what little confidence remained in American government. In the fall, prison riots began to sweep the country. In by far the largest of these, on September 9 through 13, 1971, inmates revolted at Attica Correctional Institution in New York State. Thirty-two prisoners and eleven staff lost their lives when a police and National Guard army a thousand strong put down the uprising with gas, helicopters, and heavy gunfire.[1]

The Bay Area Left was outraged. Prison demonstrations and teach-ins multiplied, as did Left literature identifying prisons once again as the focus of the people's revolt. In January 1972, a three-day Prison Action Conference was held at the University of California, Berkeley, which included workshops, films, tapes, slides, and speakers. A conference handbill urged participants to "Tear Down the Walls." Then it equivocated, saying that far-reaching prison reforms at least were necessary.[2] But Left extremists in the Bay Area took the first message to heart. Now bombings of California Department of Corrections offices and other forms of urban terrorism began to accompany protests. Responsibility for many of these acts was claimed by radicals in student and citizen groups that had split off from California's Revolutionary Union—in most instances the Weathermen and Venceremos. In more than a few cases there were direct links to San Quentin's Black Guerrilla Family and Vacaville prison's Black Culture Association, members of which would soon form the Symbionese Liberation Army.

For the Right, too, the fall of 1971 was a time of heightened organizing activity. Conservative groups seized on George Jackson's AC revolt and the Attica incident as signs of a sinister, linked underground network of communist conspirators loose in the land. The fall's prison riots provided opportunities for these groups to bargain successfully with the state for increased funding of law enforcement agencies and to launch what was to become a years-long process of dismantling "liberal" prison reforms. At San Quentin new guards were hired, new security devices installed, a host of other security measures taken, and rehabilitative programs such as education and library service for inmates greatly curtailed. Major scrutiny was given to San Quentin inmates' reading, with the intention of bringing strict communication controls back into the service of criminal correction. In 1973 the House Committee on Internal Security would show an intense interest in testimony by San Quentin staff on the importation into the prison of revolutionary literature. The committee supported in the strongest terms the prison's effort to reinstate rigid control of inmates' reading and mail censorship.

Despite these efforts to increase controls, and no doubt partly in response to them, inmates' resistance toughened within San Quentin's walls. The Black Guerrilla Family, born of the Black Family after George Jackson's death, became a dreaded force in the life of the institution, committing terrorist acts both within and without the prison. Hundreds of San Quentin's moderate reformist convicts continued in their activism as well and maintained their contacts with outside support groups. The process of prisoner unionization went on. By 1974, though, the interest of the Bay Area public in prisoners was flagging. The Vietnam War had ended. Marxist-Leninist and Maoist groups had lost almost all appeal on campuses. For most people, these groups' two-class model of the culture did not seem to fit the real world beyond the prison, and despite growing criticisms in the ranks of the Left, major segments of the movement had failed to modify the model to fit the complexity of the American state. Changing this reductionist class model might have led to the discovery of a wider variety of rallying issues in the early to mid-1970's, and it most certainly would have resulted in a more rational approach to effecting changes in the prisons. But a small group of extreme leftists in the Bay Area, renouncing the need for grass-roots support, instead chose to isolate themselves from the public even further. In a few cases their analysis led them to become participants in emerging foco groups led by paroled or escaped convict guerrilla warriors. This alliance was a clear mistake. The unreasoned extremism of one such foco, the Symbionese Liberation Army, came straight from the pages of George Jackson's *Blood in My Eye* and was to undercut in 1974 what little remained of the last public support for the prison movement. Jackson's book became a living legacy as convict writing came full circle. What had begun as the bibliotherapy component of the treatment-era California prison, a rehabilitative program designed to nurture prisoners' penitent souls, had evolved into a powerful, covert inmate writing campaign against the state, producing in some of the prison's best convict minds works of purely destructive rage. Their wide popularity among the reading public gave some inmate works the potential for engineering acts of terrorism outside the walls.

On August 21, 1971, immediately following the San Quentin Adjustment Center revolt, 26 subdued AC prisoners lay stripped nude in handcuffs and shackles on the plaza grass just across the walk from the spot where George Jackson had fallen. Then came the beatings. Three days later, two of the inmates—John Clutchette and Fleeta Drumgo, the remaining Soledad Brothers—appeared in court walking stiffly and covered with welts, their hair cut in uneven, short patches and clumps. At that time the AC 26 delivered a petition to the press: "We, the undersigned, [are] each being held incommunicado. . . . [We are] suffering from both wounds and internal injuries inflicted upon our persons by known and unknown agents of [Warden] Louis S. Nelson." The *San Francisco Chronicle* reported the inmates' claim that they were "now being threatened constantly" and were "sure that Nelson will continue the beatings and threats."[3] The conservative backlash had begun. Retaliatory beatings and assorted other mistreatments were being meted out regularly to the surviving prisoners of the AC riot. Luis Talamantez and others later indicted for murder for their involvement in the revolt would claim that AC lieutenant Richard Nelson had told them, "None of you will ever leave here alive."[4] In October, the attorney for AC inmate Hugo Pinell, one of those charged, declared that his client had been assaulted four times by San Quentin officers close to the guards who had been killed.[5] Representative Ronald Dellums (D-Berkeley) and Assembly-man Willie Brown visited the prison and reported that "the prisoners showed definite signs of some bodily injuries."[6] Fleeta Drumgo's co-counsel complained to the press that AC guards were singing, to the tune of "John Brown's Body," the lines

> George Jackson's body is rotting in the grave.
> The revolutionary soldiers are rotting in their cells.

He claimed that inmates' mail was being delayed at least a week, newspapers and magazines were again being censored, and no press interviews were allowed.[7] In addition to the stepped-up regime of physical coercion, the prison authorities were busy recapturing com-munication control. Three days after the AC bloodbath, James Park had told the press, "We're going to take a hard look at . . . publica-tions."[8] The whole prison, as well as Folsom, Soledad, and Deuel Vocational Institution, was in general lockdown. San Quentin spokes-man James O'Brien announced that a section of the south block had been set up "to control militants until we can take a look at them," conceding that prisoners put there included anyone who had strong feelings about the August 21 incident.[9] These numbered in the thou-sands. At Soledad, black inmates were said to have wept at the news of George Jackson's death. From some quarters outside the prison as well the response was similar.

Outrage against the Department of Corrections mounted. The United Prisoners Union, at a press conference at Glide Memorial Church on August 24, called the death a "setup," though it conceded it had "nothing from the inside" to confirm this charge.[10] The Munici-pal Council of East Palo Alto, a predominantly black community south of San Francisco, passed a resolution calling Jackson's death a "summary execution" and "an act of genocide."[11] Word began to come in of protests as far away as London, where about 150 young people picketed the U.S. Embassy.[12] On August 25 an unnamed radi-cal group claimed responsibility for a local fire:

Brothers and Sisters!
After learning that the San Quentin pigs had murdered our beloved comrade George Jackson, we set fire to the Bank of America on Cortland Street in San Francisco and burned out one of the bank walls. This action, limited as it was, was the first of this kind for all of us. . . . Action overcomes fear.[13]

At San Quentin's east gate on August 26, the day of the funeral for San Quentin's slain guards, an estimated 250 protesters, marching under the shotguns of officers positioned in cars blocking the access road to the prison, shouted:

> Open the gate!
> Smash the state! . . .
> Three dead pigs
> ain't enough! . . .

and

> Murderers!
> Murderers!
> The guards are
> Murderers![14]

Associate Warden James Park reveals the hatred toward the Left that these actions engendered in San Quentin staff:

It was a very dangerous situation for a lot of kids because we had, in one of the garages of the houses near the gate, a bunch of officers with shotguns ready to go out and blow them away had they assaulted the gate. We were afraid they would work and push on that gate. . . . There were a number of instances like that. . . . We had the feeling that these hippies were everywhere, and we warned the officers, "Don't look for a Black Panther to kill you. Look for some little hippie girl sitting out there with her knitting. She's the one who's gonna blow you away." And we felt that. . . .

We had crowd control things. In one case—this was some kind of demonstration in which they had invited all the radicals and the hippies and everybody to come—the Highway Patrol stationed a car down at the end of the access road and waved people on, onto the Richmond Bridge, which would cost them the toll, both ways in those days, to get back near San Quentin. . . .

After the Jackson incident we had many, many threats. . . . The officers went from nobody carrying a gun to several hundred carrying a gun. In fact, we put two file cabinets at the main gate so they could put their guns in it. It could scare you to death. You go out there and here's this pile of guns in there. They all ran and got permits or carried them without permits. It's a wonder somebody didn't get killed. We just had hundreds of armed officers, not all of them the brightest people in the world.[15]

The San Quentin administration even feared an armed invasion and made preparations to defend the prison from outsiders. Former sergeant William Hankins recalls the realization of the prison's vulnerability:

There used to be one armory tower that housed all the weapons. Now you're talkin' about people that had sophisticated weapons, they had rocket launchers, everything on the street. If a group come in there and knocked out the armory tower and moved right in, the only weapons they woulda had to contend with at the time was old .25/.35 rifles that were up on the wall. . . . They've changed their structure now.[16]

On August 28, about 125 persons marched eight blocks from Alamo Square to Duboce Park in San Francisco, protesting George Jackson's death and racism in the Department of Corrections. That same day, a crowd of 2,000 gathered at Oakland's St. Augustine Episcopal Church, their fists clenched in the air, to honor Jackson's memory. Loudspeakers above the church entrance played "I Wish I Knew What It Feels Like to Be Free," and 200 close friends and family looked on as Jackson was eulogized, his body clothed in the dress uniform of the Black Panther party, a black beret and black polished calf-leather jacket over a sky-blue turtleneck and black trousers, in a coffin draped with the Panther flag. Huey Newton and Bobby Seale spoke to the crowd, reading letters of tribute from Representative Ronald Dellums, Angela Davis, and imprisoned Black Panther David Hilliard. Listed on a funeral program as nonattending "honorary pall bearers" for the occasion were Jonathan Jackson, fellow Soledad Brothers Fleeta Drumgo and John Clutchette, and Hugo Pinell, recently indicted in the AC riot, "plus all revolutionary brothers in the prison camps across America."[17] As the funeral services were taking place, bomb blasts shattered two state buildings, a Department of Corrections psychiatric clinic in San Francisco, and the restrooms next to its Sacramento headquarters. A letter received by the *San Francisco Examiner* claiming responsibility called the bombings an "outraged response to the assassination of George Jackson." It was signed by the Weather Underground and stated: "Two small bombs do not cool our rage. We nurture that rage inside us. . . . We view our actions as simply a first expression of love and respect for George Jackson and the warriors of San Quentin."[18] The next day, Jackson's body was transported to Mount Vernon, Illinois, where he was buried next to the unmarked grave of his brother Jonathan.

The Bay Area Left was not univocal on the issue of prisons and prisoners at the time of George Jackson's death. But Left opinion on the subject had become dominated by groups like the Black Panthers and the Revolutionary Union, which by 1970 had for the most part devolved into political prisoner movements. Though many disagreed with their tactics, in 1970 the Weathermen were at the ideological center of this prison movement. A 1970 Weather faction communiqué signed by Bernadine Dohrn reminded the movement of its central article of faith: "We believe that the resistance and political leadership that is growing within the prisons demands immediate and mass support from young people. . . . Demonstrations in support of prison revolts are a major responsibility of the movement. . . . The women and men in jails are POW's held by the United States." [19]

That American prisoners were prisoners of war was by no means a minority opinion among the prison movement Left in the Bay Area in 1970. This notion was already weakening the popular appeal of the prison movement. The Harriet Tubman Prison Movement of Los Angeles, with contacts to San Quentin's inmate self-improvement group SATE, claimed in 1971 to have set up an underground railroad that could transport escaped California inmates to Mexico and Venezuela. On another front, a defense committee was established for the six San Quentin AC inmates eventually indicted in the August 21 incident: Johnny Larry Spain, Luis Talamantez, Hugo Pinell, David Johnson, Fleeta Drumgo, and Willie Tate. But the prison movement Left was beginning to come apart, attacking itself, especially those in its ranks who had begun to question its prison ideology. On April 6, 1972, one of the movement's critics, Jimmy Carr, was shot dead in San Jose. At the time some in the movement whispered that he had been skimming money from both the Soledad Brothers and the Angela Davis defense funds. Others labeled Carr a police agent and said he was involved in George Jackson's death. [20] Whatever else was true of Jimmy Carr, at the time of his death in 1972 he was a vocal critic of the Left's prison ideology and a thorn in the side of the Black Panthers. Two hired killers would eventually be convicted of his murder and sentenced to life in prison. No motive would ever be established. As his widow, Betsy Carr, wrote later:

[Jimmy] blamed our ideology for George's death, and blamed the leadership more. He even sent a few messages to the elite on how the movement had to change itself or perish. Those who didn't resent what he was saying simply didn't understand it. After a few weeks he gave up.

We'd read Nietzsche out loud. . . . One of our favorite passages was: "Shedding one's skin: the snake that cannot shed its skin perishes. So do spirits who are prevented from changing their opinions; they cease to be spirit." [21]

By 1972 the public was deserting the Left in major numbers. Organizing was not going well. In 1973 the Chino Defense Committee and members of the United Prisoners Union nonsensically labeled charges against the Venceremos members arrested at the scene of

Ronald Beaty's escape attempt a "frame-up." "They Are Innocent" declared a Chino Defense Committee demonstration flyer. "Free All Political Prisoners!"[22] This rhetoric had lost its appeal to many. In response to an increasingly uncaring public, a few remaining in the movement chose to renounce organizing, dig in, and get tough. In March 1972, after a police search of a Berkeley garage, three persons were charged with "intent to terrorize," as well as possession of a machine gun, explosives and explosives components, and a live bomb.[23] In September, three more leftists were arrested for stockpiling explosives.[24]

Some in the movement were already operating from secret underground cells. In July 1973, the *San Francisco Chronicle* received a cryptic note threatening the deaths of "many prison officials" unless the San Quentin Six defendants were immediately flown to Cuba or Algeria. The note was signed by the "August Seventh Guerilla Movement," a group unknown to police at the time but purporting to be underground followers of a secret army linked to George Jackson.[25] The 1974 *Prairie Fire* political statement of the Weather Underground again sounded the movement's sacred themes:

The courts are machines for administering the penalties of white rulers to Black victims. The prisons are living tombs. They function as a major institution of economic and political control over the Black nation—the ruling-class safety valve for the rebels, for the alienated. . . . The prison movement . . . has produced a heroic resistance and has given birth to many great leaders.[26]

Despite the erosion of public support for the prison movement, these radicals still clung tenaciously to the two-class model of the state and the notion that a revolutionary leadership would emerge from the black slave-captives held in America's prisons.

The Right, meanwhile, was riding the crest of a nationwide law-and-order campaign directed from Richard Nixon's White House. And California law-and-order conservatives were motivated, even more than conservatives elsewhere, by a perceived need to surmount the state's prison movement Left. The California Right had from the very first reacted with intense fear to the Marxist language in which the Left had chosen to couch its prison ideology. Fired by the bogeyman of communism, conservatives had generously contributed to committees funding police units to investigate California radicals. By the time of George Jackson's death, multiple local, state, and federal agencies had infiltrated the California prison movement: the FBI, army intelligence, President Nixon's private espionage organization, the Criminal Conspiracy Section (CCS) of the Los Angeles Police Department, and the Criminal Investigation and Identification Department (CII) of the California attorney general's office.[27] Even the private lives of some prison staff had come under official scrutiny. In 1970, former Soledad activist-psychiatrist Frank Rundle had been approached at his home by a "wired" Soledad inmate clerk who had been promised an early release for his cooperation in an information-gathering scheme, while a Soledad guard and a member of the state attorney general's office monitored their conversation from a car parked nearby.[28] In 1971 Attorney General John Mitchell announced to the press that the nation's Law Enforcement Assistance Administration had just been allocated $178 million for "correctional aid to the states and localities." Mitchell predicted the amount would be doubled in 1972.[29] Conservatives all across the nation were convinced of the existence of a carefully orchestrated communist conspiracy to take over the U.S. prisons. Noting a "similarity of rhetoric" in inmates' demands from prison riot to prison riot and from state to state in the fall of 1971, the House Committee on Internal Security would point out in 1973 that "the so-called Attica Manifesto of inmate demands allegedly authored by five Attica inmates and utilized during the bloody uprising at Attica in September 1971, was a rewritten version of a November 1970 document written by inmates at Folsom prison in California."[30] It was true that inmates at the two institutions had communicated. But the Internal Security Committee blamed the Folsom strike, as well as the massacres at Attica and in George Jackson's AC, entirely on the intervention of Marxist revolutionaries. Nothing could have been further from the truth. In fact, prisoners nationwide had been airing shared grievances. The Right, too, had been deflected from an understanding of the nation's real prisoners by an ideology.

At San Quentin thirteen officers resigned from the prison immediately after Jackson's death. Guards complained of threats to their lives on the way home from work. Wives reported ominous phone calls.[31] The California Correctional Officers Association (CCOA) called for sweeping changes at the prison, including the purchase of electronic alarm systems for each guard, additional gunrail coverage, and more guards to provide heightened, near-constant supervision of prisoners. The guard organization also advocated the partitioning of large cell blocks into smaller units and the installation of closed-circuit televisions in certain areas. It also irrationally proposed that the Department of Corrections find a way "to accommodate revolutionary prisoners who request renouncement of citizenship and transfer to other countries," and it announced that it was in the process of weeding "revolutionary elements and their sympathizers and other subversive elements" from the CCOA's own ranks.[32] That autumn a statewide "California Correctional System Study" ordered by Governor Ronald Reagan in 1970 recommended that the state hire 318 new guards and advised that the Adult Authority be abolished or at least that the state modify the procedures of the indeterminate sentence,[33] changes that would have made concessions to the demands of both the right- and moderate left-wing prison reformers.

But to the Right this was not nearly enough. In hearings before a congressional subcommittee investigating San Quentin in October, Moe Comacho, president of the CCOA, called for the creation of separate, maximum security prisons for revolutionary inmates and demanded stricter treatment for the remaining maximum security prisoners. This was to include "a complete search of all visitors, including attorneys; complete censorship of all mail, both incoming and outgoing; custodial supervision of all movement within the facility; a more restricted visitor list and closer control of visiting hours; and reduced privileges in general."[34] Sadly, the CCOA would get much of what it asked for.

Regaining control of inmates' mail and reading had been an acknowledged priority of San Quentin staff since early 1971. In April, Director of Corrections Raymond Procunier had rescinded the year-old rule allowing prisoners to write sealed letters to their attorneys, although sealed correspondence to legislators and judges was still permitted.[35] State attorney general Evelle Younger defended this return to mail censorship[36] and accused Bay Area radical attorneys of conducting a "revolution by mail."[37]

Fortunately, the state's courts were proceeding in the opposite direction. While the prison administration and the CCOA moved to take back the prison, the courts resisted a return to strict communication and other controls, with the result that Folsom inmate Robert Charles Jordan was able successfully to challenge the new censorship directives. In September 1972, the California Supreme Court ruled unanimously that penal officers could not read letters between prisoners and their attorneys.[38] And by the next year, 1973, a Federal Appeals Court panel in San Francisco had struck down nearly all of the new mail censorship regulations. The ruling protected even "writings . . . expressing inflammatory political, radical, religious, or other views or beliefs . . . which if circulated among other inmates in the judgment of the warden . . . tend to subvert prison order. . . . Statements critical of prison life and personnel cannot be subject to censorship by the very people who are being criticized, simply to stifle such criticism."[39]

The CCOA was incensed. As G. Norton Jameson, editor of *Grapevine*, the house organ of the American Association of Wardens and Superintendents, had put it in 1971, "It is absolutely amazing how soft our courts have become. Not only the courts but the entire public has become infiltrated with a sloppy sentimental attitude."[40] California correctional employees resented these and other court actions as "inappropriate intrusions into the operation of correctional institutions . . . [which have] shifted the balance of power within institutions away from the staff and toward the inmates."[41]

The inmates themselves strenuously resisted the crackdown from the Right. These three opposite movements by the courts, the Left, and the Right made it impossible at times to tell who was really in control of the prison. In December 1973, continuing waves of inmate violence against prison staff (which had jumped from 32 assaults systemwide in 1969 to 84 in 1973)[42] precipitated an unprecedented general lockup of all inmates at San Quentin, Folsom, and Deuel Vocational Institution. The lockup was to last until June 1974. Ironically, at the same time, an in-house prison staff Task Force to Study Violence recommended making concessions to prisoners by implementing some of the Folsom strike and union demands, including increasing, not restricting, inmates' access to reading, radio, and television. The report also recommended "mak[ing] available to every inmate full employment and training at private industry standards of production coupled with levels of pay and other means of compensation sufficient to be genuine incentives." "The possibilities of joint ventures with outside industries should be explored."[43] The report called for an education program and libraries as well as other "rehabilitative attention" to those in AC units. The report was out of touch with the times, however; there was a much stronger impulse within the Department of Corrections and the state government to move in the opposite direction, to retreat from treatment altogether and return to simple, retributive punishment. As just one measure of this sentiment, in the 1973 session of the legislature the death penalty was restored. Department of Corrections director Raymond Procunier made a sweeping tour of the prisons in 1973, announcing a tough new policy: "We've lost control. We've already lost the inmates and now we're close to losing some of the staff. From now on, we're going to go back to running these places instead of letting some of the inmates run 'em for us." [44]

After all the dust had settled at San Quentin in the early 1970's; after all the false claims that the prison was augmenting rehabilitation programs when these programs had actually long since ceased to exist; after all the false promises to expand reading privileges and programs and to offer industry-scale wages for prison jobs; and after the extremist conservative calls for sending revolutionary prisoners to Cuba or putting them in separate institutions, what would emerge at San Quentin was a nightmarish plan.

In 1970 Warden Nelson had served on the Committee on Riots and Disturbances of the American Correctional Association. Reflecting the alarm of the Right at ever-rising inmate activism in the nation's prisons and its links to the outside Left, the committee took it as its task to plan future strategies for "the handling of demonstrations, or even assaults on the correctional institution from outside the walls." The first firm decision the group came to was that convict ringleaders must be "removed and isolated from the general population before an opportunity to carry out their plans presents itself." [45] In other words, "troublemakers" were to be identified and punished *before* they had committed any offenses. Next, "every building in which inmates could barricade themselves should be studied with the thought of executing a quick emergency entrance by the use of axes, cutting torches, wrecking bars, or by any other practical means." There was no mention in the report of any room for inmates to express legitimate, peaceful grievances by demonstration or labor strike. Riots and work stoppages were to be treated identically; both were "insurrections." In the event of either, "floor plans or sketches of buildings should be instantly available to command personnel." Wardens were discouraged from negotiating, whatever the circumstances: "Inmates, in defying the authority of the government, are in the act of committing a crime. . . . It is the bargaining and the indiscreet giving of promises which should be avoided." [46] In the event of a disturbance, the prison was to be immediately locked down: "If necessary, as many inmates as possible should be locked in their cells until the situation can be evaluated and brought under control. . . . Ringleaders . . . should immediately be taken from the scene and locked into cells as far apart as possible." [47] Then, "if necessary," the prison population was to be contained—"trapped" may be the more accurate term—by "the addition of fast-closing but relatively light steel grills." The crucial importance of preserving the prisoners' case files in an insurrection was brought to the particular attention of wardens by the report, which preceded the Attica riot by less than a year. One area of the prison "not to be overlooked" in an insurrection, the report advised, was "the administrative area where the destruction of records may be an objective."[48] Here prison administrators had special reason to fear. Losing the cumulative inmate files to the convicts might be as serious as a mass escape because it would erase the convicts' written lives, threatening among other things the rhetorical purposes of the prison in American culture. At bottom what was at stake was the literary as well as the physical ownership of the lives of the prisoners. Which discourse of their crimes was to become normative? Were the convicts in American prisons to be political heroes as many in the Left now portrayed them? Or were they to remain as depicted in their "jackets," society's pathological freaks and sociopaths? Which would be America's prisoners' national story?

Despite the cruel plans of prison administrators, convict agitations continued well after Attica and the San Quentin AC revolt, into the mid-decade. In San Quentin's Adjustment Center in January 1972, 26 convicts went on a week-long hunger strike, throwing food and feces onto the cell tier. In a letter to Warden Nelson, the "San Quentin 26" complained of continuing harassment and demanded better medical care, more lenient visiting rights, and better access to "literature on brown and black culture."[49] Those involved in the August 21 incident were now allegedly finding "inedible material" in their food, including hair, matchsticks, and urine. Some claimed they were still being beaten. In June 1972, the six AC inmates since indicted as the San Quentin Six filed a $1 million civil rights suit asking an injunction to prohibit "further acts of harassment and violence."[50]

On the mainline, too, as San Quentin continued its crackdown, approximately 2,000 of the institution's inmates struck in January 1973 for privileges that supposedly had been guaranteed as a matter of law. The prison brazenly ignored both the courts and the law. In addition to housekeeping demands such as better food and hot water in the cells, the convicts again called for "an end to mail censorship," "the right to receive all publications," and "an end to all official and unofficial harassment for political, racial and sexual beliefs."[51] A spokesman for the United Prisoners Union, claiming to represent the prisoners, was denied even a meeting with Warden Nelson, who resolutely refused to negotiate.[52] The strike was quickly broken. Five hundred prisoners were locked down. Twenty-five were placed in solitary confinement for being found with pro-strike leaflets. Warden Louis Nelson came down on the strikers with an iron fist, declaring plainly, "We want to find the men who are causing the trouble."[53] Intermittent hunger strikes and inmate sit-downs would continue at the prison for another year, with no more success in redressing prisoners' grievances.[54] In the end the victory would go to the Right.

In its campaign to recapture San Quentin from its radical convicts, the prison stepped up suppression of mail and books. This was especially true in the AC, where the San Quentin Six, George Jackson's alleged conspirators on August 21, were still attempting to organize. A letter of November 9, 1972, from San Quentin Six defendant Luis Talamantez to the chief librarian, James McHenry, reveals one inmate's resentment of the return to strict censorship:

November 9, 1972
Officer McHenry:

I am writing you this communication from the prison's Adjustment Center, A/C, in response to your memo of Oct. 6th, 1972, concerning the matter of the book entitled *Coming of the New International* authored by John Gerassi. I've acted in accordance to the strict procedures recently instituted here by the fascist administration of the San Quentin prison complex in moving to secure the approval required so as to be able to receive this book, but, again—you have arbitrarily exercised your petty authority so as to block and cancel my request. . . .

Your prison policy of suppressing political materials diametrically opposed to your views is evident. It is common knowledge among the prison administration that John Gerassi was a friend of our fallen comrade George Jackson whose life was viciously taken by your psychopathic henchmen and whom your now anxious in trying to erase from the political understanding and revolutionary memory of the prisoner class by not only denying us access to *Coming of the New International* but also by not letting us obtain *Blood in My Eye* written by Comrade George Jackson. . . .

I am one of the many prisoners who are becoming aware of your morbid right wing efforts in your position as the prison librarian to keep me and other prisoners in a void of political unconsciousness by denying us certain political books, periodicals, and underground newspapers. . . .

All Power to the Prisoners!

Luis Talamantez[55]

Despite the prison's heightened precautions, radicals in the mainline population, at least, still were managing to get these books. Neither the prisoners, the staff, nor the courts were in complete control of important areas of San Quentin life at this time. While censorship controls in the AC were severe, Nate Harrington, an inmate at San Quentin's B Section in 1973–76 tells how loose they could be elsewhere in the prison:

I got just about everything. *Blood in My Eye* was banned. I hand-wrote the *entire* book. I got out [into the mainline] for a month or two and I enrolled into college extension classes and I managed to talk one of the instructors into bringing in a copy of *Blood in My Eye*. So the copy was smuggled in and I wrote it out in long hand and we had copies of the book xeroxed. We had two copies. And then later we xeroxed the handwritten portions.[56]

In the face of the conservative backlash, inmate radicalism took on uncontrollable forms. After George Jackson's death, one of the most extreme of the prison's guerrilla groups, the Black Guerrilla Family, quickly became a major gang in B Section and the mainline. The BGF's 1973 constitution defined the goals of the organization:

Who is the Family? . . . We are the brothers who, in reality are a chosen family of comrade George Jackson, instead of one "George Jackson," we are many. We are the brothers who will dish out vicious and strategic moves within the confines of the concentration camps whenever injustice is perpetrated against the BGF or its members, and all Black Brothers. . . . For the revolutionary there only exist one pleasure, one reward, one consolation, and one satisfaction—THE SUCCESS OF THE REVOLUTION AND THE LIBERATION OF ALL POLITICAL PRISONERS. . . . In the very depths of our beings not only in words but also in deeds, we have torn our selves away from the bounds which tie us to the cultivated world, with all its laws, moralities and customs, and with all its generally accepted conditions. We are the pig's implacable enemy, and if we continue to live with them it is only in order to destroy them more quicker and effectively.[57]

Beginning in 1972, the BGF would "hit" many inmates and some staff, black, white, and brown, and carry out operations outside San Quentin as well. The BGF continues to be a major California prison gang. A former San Quentin BGF member remarks that

the BGF was essentially a political gangster operation. At least that is what it had become by '73–'74. . . . From the time I got to prison until I got out of prison, I lived in constant fear that somebody in the BGF would try to kill me because I spoke out against some of the sick stuff they were doing. . . . I certainly feared for my life. And my biggest fear was not from the prison administration or the Aryan Brotherhood or any other of the Aryan groups. It was from the BGF.

Fortunately, this organization was not the only politically active group of black radical convict militants, as the same BGF member pointed out: "The BGF represented the most visible and the largest group of black political revolutionary prisoners. But it doesn't account for all the other people, and there were a lot of other people involved."[58]

This ongoing high level of inmate radical organizing, seemingly resistant even to the severest prison discipline, continued to alarm prison officials. In December 1973, San Quentin sergeant William Hankins and other officers testified in Washington, D.C., before the House Committee on Internal Security, which was particularly interested to hear about "the unrestricted flow of extremist propaganda into the prisons" that the late FBI director J. Edgar Hoover had claimed "stimulated the hardened criminal inmates into an alliance with revolutionary extremists." The committee observed that "a substantial amount of revolutionary literature was entering penal institutions and that groups were being formed in the prison under the sponsorship of subversive organizations." In addition to the testimony of San Quentin officers, the committee heard the remarks of Russell G. Oswald, commissioner of correction for the state of New York. Oswald agreed with J. Edgar Hoover: revolutionary reading materials were a major problem at his prisons, too, including Attica. San Quentin officers present at the hearings blamed the formation of a Black Panther chapter at their prison on "the influx of revolutionary literature," which had "caused many black inmates to become revolution-oriented."[59] In its conclusions, the committee's report would advise prison administrations to adopt training programs for officers that included instruction on how to identify materials that should be excluded from prisoners' reading.[60] Long lists of dangerous books and left-wing publishing houses were incorporated in this report, including, among many others, the major works of Malcolm X and Angela Davis.[61] For the Committee on Internal Security and the San Quentin officers who testified before it, San Quentin's problem with radicals was entirely an imported one. Again the San Quentin administration chose to ignore the genuine grievances of inmates as a source of prison rebellion. The problem had been caused wholly by outside agitators. Therefore, a prime solution to the prison's ongoing unrest was simply to bring back the iron gag, to retake control of the prisoners' reading and writing. The committee was in part correct in its observations. Imported radical literature and the support of radical outsiders had certainly contributed to San Quentin's revolution, though beneath this surface was a long history of unresolved, legitimate prisoner grievances that had little to do with the ideological wars of the California Right and Left that were being reproduced in San Quentin's battle of books. Despite this fact, in the California prison system a solution was already in the works. The plan was to turn the prisoners away from reading anything whatsoever.

In 1972–73 televisions were installed in administrative segregation cells at Deuel Vocational Institution. As inmate Nate Harrington recalls, the event was part of a strategy of heightened control: "I tried to refuse mine. We were told if you were in administrative segregation and you refused a television, they put you in isolation, which was about as bad as you could get—the strip cell with the padding on the door and wall, the little grill on the floor, and the darkness."[62] This move coincided with the introduction of televisions into mainline cells at San Quentin. The desired effect was achieved. Inmates' reading and writing was supplanted by television watching. Inmate Harlan Washington discusses this point: "[After they] put the idiot boxes in, the televisions and the radios, people stopped studyin' and developed a TV mentality and that killed off everybody's studying revolutionary thought, political thought."[63] San Quentin inmate Dorsey Nunn agrees: "I think the institution said, like, 'What the fuck we doin'? Let's give these motherfuckers a TV. That'll stop 'em from readin' and writin'."[64]

The brilliance of the prison's new television strategy was that, whereas communication control formerly had to be achieved through censorship and authoritarian constraint, now the prison could feign permissiveness by issuing televisions and at the same time produce the same heightened control. Introducing televisions appeared on the surface to be a concession to inmate agitators and seemed to represent a further widening of inmates' contact with the community outside the walls. But the contact was to be carefully controlled. The prison soon set about collecting a set of precensored videotapes to be piped to the cells during times of unrest. By 1979 San Quentin prison would employ a full-time video technician. The crowning feature of the new strategy was that whereas television or video watching was designed to displace its analogue, reading, the new behavior conveniently lacked any analogue for writing. Because prison staff now feared inmate writing, its total elimination was greatly desired.[65] An accompanying technology perfected the recapture of inmate communication. In 1974 a Department of Corrections policy permitting prisoners to make collect telephone calls out of the institution seemed yet another welcome breach in the prison walls to inmates aching to maintain ties with the streets.⁶⁶ The telephone calls were monitored, however. Although both televisions and telephones seemed signs of increasing permissiveness, in times of insurrection both new communication technologies could be turned to the administration's higher goal of controlling inmates' unrest by narrowing rather than expanding their communication with the outside world, thereby augmenting the prison's surveillance and communication control arsenal.

San Quentin authorities were shrewd to attempt to turn the inmates away from reading. In spite of the prison's ambitious attempts to contain the spread of radical ideology, by 1973 little could be accomplished by simply stopping the importation of literature. The damage was already done. The prison was full of secret convict libraries of radical books. And radical prisoners were ready to resist any suppression of their reading. What was more, the most extreme of San Quentin's radical inmates had by this time wholeheartedly adopted from the writings of George Jackson and Regis Debray the strategy of forming small "vanguard" units with links to the outside expressly designed to make guerrilla strikes. The most notorious of these foco units, and one that maintained continued links with San Quentin radicals, was the Symbionese Liberation Army.

The SLA had its roots in Vacaville prison's Black Culture Association (BCA), an inmate self-improvement group similar to San Quentin's SATE, designed to advance the education and cultural awareness of Vacaville's black prisoners through reading, discussion, and contacts with the Bay Area black community. Beginning in June 1972, however, the election of Vacaville inmate Donald DeFreeze to the chairmanship of the organization signaled the BCA's transformation from an educational into a political action group.

Donald DeFreeze was not a highly respected convict at Vacaville; he had never been to one of the "big houses," Folsom, Soledad, or San Quentin. But what he lacked in convict status he more than made up for in zealous energy and devotion to the revolution. DeFreeze's arrest history had been a litany of small-time auto and gun thefts. In 1965, after an explosion at his home in East Orange, New Jersey, he was arrested for possession of an unregistered rifle and a shrapnel bomb. Soon afterward he was arrested in Los Angeles for running a red light on his bicycle and was found to have two homemade bombs and a .22 pistol in his bike basket. By the mid-1960's Donald DeFreeze had established a small-scale black market business in weapons, selling to such groups as the Black Panthers and Ron Karenga's United

Slaves. In 1967 police confiscated from his home in Los Angeles approximately 200 weapons, part of property missing from a military warehouse. In 1969 he was arrested for armed robbery and assault and sent to Vacaville Medical Facility.

At Vacaville, he began to read extensively. An inmate friend, Ron Eagles, remembers that "DeFreeze spent the majority of his time in the joint reading. Every time I'd catch him, I'd catch him with a book. . . . He was always concerned about black people's position in [the] struggle, black people's position in the American society, on his particular position as a black man in relation to society, especially a black convict." [67] Soon he had renamed himself Cinque M'tume, a combination of the Swahili word for "prophet" and the number five assigned as a name in the 1830's to a Mendi chief enslaved by the Portuguese. Convict Cinque M'tume joined the Black Culture Association and read widely in Marx, Lenin, Trotsky, Fanon, Malcolm X, Nkrumah, Jackson, and Debray, meeting with the BCA on Wednesday and Friday evenings in Vacaville's library. After his election to the group's chairmanship, M'tume soon established a special committee within the organization, the Unisight Committee, which was to become the militant wing of the BCA, seed of the Symbionese Liberation Army. M'tume requisitioned typewriters, tape recorders, file cabinets, blackboards, sound equipment, and office machinery from the prison. Amanda de Normanville, a white UC Berkeley student who volunteered her time as a tutor in the BCA, provides a picture of a typical meeting of the group:

It blew my mind the first time I went up, the amount of freedom we had there. We had to go through metal detectors and sign in, but that was essentially it. And we walked through this big library and then all of these guys just started walking in in blue jeans. And you could talk with anyone, sit with anyone. . . . They played the Black National Anthem. And just as it started to play I saw a couple of brothers down front raise their right arms. And I thought, "Shit, they're going to get into trouble for that." And then as the record started playing everybody stood in a black-power salute. And I thought it was impressive. I really dug that. And they carried the flag to the front and carried it back. [68]

Another volunteer tutor was astounded at the level of revolutionary fantasy among the prison's inmates:

There were inmates in Vacaville who had mapped out the revolution from beginning to end, leaving nothing out in between. They knew what time the revolution would start in the morning and what day. They knew how to form a vanguard and how it would split up into cadres from the east and the west and the north and the south. To hear them talk you would think that they knew exactly how to do away with the system. The guards would hear this shit twenty-four hours a day, seven days a week. There were people who could quote long passages verbatim from Che and Mao and Marx and revolutionaries that I never even heard of.[69]

Several Bay Area radicals later associated with the SLA on the streets first came into contact with Cinque M'tume when they volunteered as BCA tutors. Some of them—Nancy Ling Perry, Willie Wolfe, Russ Little, Angela Atwood, Joseph Remiro, and William and Emily Harris—were residents or regulars at Peking House, a Berkeley commune.[70] In spring 1973, when M'tume was transferred to Soledad, where he was assigned a job as an automatic-boiler attendant in an unoccupied compound, he climbed a twelve-foot fence one night and walked and hitchhiked his way to freedom. He showed up on the doorstep of Peking House reportedly with the words, "Looka here, you know, I'm here. Let's start the revolution."[71] Peking House took M'tume in.

From his newfound Berkeley hideout the prisoner sent to the BCA's outside coordinator, UC Berkeley teaching assistant Colston Westbrook, for materials from his Unisight committee and began to put together a new organization. Patricia "Mizmoon" Soltysik, who worked as a janitor at the Berkeley public library, stole books, pamphlets, magazines, and documents for the group, and the SLA read law enforcement journals, studied the structure of government agencies, and learned the lives of corporate officers. Throughout the summer and fall of 1973 the SLA members discussed their ideology and strategy for the future. Several of the group made frequent visits to members of the BGF at San Quentin. William and Emily Harris visited San Quentin nine times in 1972–73 to meet with James "Doc" Holliday, head of the BGF. Robin Steiner, another early SLA member who later left the group, made fifteen visits to Holliday in the same period.[72] Other members of the SLA also made numerous trips to San Quentin. Messages passed regularly between the SLA and San Quentin's BGF, disguised in a crude code. In intercepted correspondence between the two groups, the BGF referred to the SLA as "Shirley Loraine Anderson." A portion of this mail was stopped in San Quentin's mail room.[73] An SLA document found in a burned-out house the group would leave in January 1974 named 23 inmate contacts.[74] The SLA foco maintained its contacts as well with Vacaville's Black Culture Association until November 1973.

Late that year the SLA swept into action. George Jackson had warned his readers against "right-wing traditionalist" blacks: "I'm thoroughly sick of the old Jess B. Simples. . . . That will be your main source of opposition—the black running dog."[75] On November 6, 1973, the foco gunned down with cyanide-capped bullets Oakland's superintendent of schools, Marcus Foster, a black man, and his assistant, Robert Blackburn. Foster had recently suggested using city police to patrol the halls of Oakland's crime-filled public schools. Only Blackburn survived.

The Left was almost unanimously critical of the assassination. Many now fully realized just what havoc on prison movement organizing foco terrorism could play. But it would prove impossible to stop. The only question was how many would have to die before it was crushed by the state. Throughout November from within the California prisons, communiqués sent to the *San Francisco Chronicle* by the "August Seventh Guerilla Movement" claimed that "Guerilla Command Cells" had been organized in every prison in the state "to 'execute' such prison officials who have been found guilty of extreme brutality against Political Prisoners." The group claimed responsibility for the November 27, 1973, death of officer Jerry Sanders at Deuel Vocational Institution and for the downing by gunfire of an Oakland police helicopter in October. It warned as well of a plot to assassinate Raymond Procunier: "There has been a special squad assigned to effect the public execution of this man."[76] By this time the media was giving the SLA news major coverage. Russell Little and Joseph Remiro had been surprised and arrested at an SLA "safe house" in Concord. The rest of the group had escaped. Plans were already under way in the foco to kidnap Patty Hearst.

San Quentin convicts had long yearned for the outside Left to kidnap the families of their prison guards; Jimmy Carr had once also advised targeting the children of the wealthy.[77] On February 4, 1974, the SLA broke into Patty Hearst's Berkeley apartment and took her as a "prisoner of war" over the protestations of her boyfriend, Stephen Weed. A week later a tape and an accompanying letter sent to Berkeley's radio station KPFA demanded that the Hearst family sponsor a huge food giveaway to the Bay Area poor. Each family was to be given about $70 worth of food. State authorities at the time estimated the total cost of the giveaway at $133 million. If the deal went ahead, Governor Reagan declared in his inimitably callous humor, he hoped those who took the food would die of botulism.[78] The Hearst family compromised with an offer of a food gift worth $2 million. Reverend Cecil Williams of San Francisco's Glide Memorial Church was to co-ordinate the food disbursal, with the help of the faction of the United Prisoners Union headed by Popeye Jackson, among other groups.[79] Despite the reservations of most of the outside Left about the SLA's plan, support for the group among San Quentin's inmates was run-ning extremely high. San Quentin inmate Dorsey Nunn records his own feelings at the time:

I was sympathetic with the demands of the SLA. I was! Shit, yeah! I didn't know Patty Hearst. Fuck her. When the shit started hittin' the paper, you know, when names started hittin' the paper I was familiar with the people. I had met these people here and there. I'd look at the paper and say, "Ah, shit!" . . . I can tell you when I was in prison, I along with everybody else was rootin' for the motherfuckers to get the fuckin' money. . . . Tell my momma to go down there and get a sack of that chicken, you know.

Nate Harrington adds that the SLA foco was a practical outgrowth of revolutionary ideology: "At the time, I felt good about it. It was a case study. . . . The SLA tried to apply the foco period to urban Amer-ica. And obviously it didn't work. But it was certainly an interest-ing idea, an interesting notion, and much of what they were doing I applauded."[80]

In the end, a food distribution took place, but it fell far short of the SLA's expectations. As writers Les Payne, Tim Findley, and Caro-lyn Craven recorded at the time,

Fights broke out at a distribution center in East Oakland. Frustrated by hours of waiting, potential food recipients surrounded two loaded transport trucks that finally arrived. The food was thrown from the truck. Each person was to have received one or two frozen turkeys, a box of saltine crackers, a can of tomato juice, a box of Bisquik mix; there was also some milk and fresh eggs. In the melee some people were injured by the tossed turkeys and by rocks; more than twenty people were treated in hospitals.[81]

The SLA foco, now counting Patty Hearst in its ranks, moved quickly on to Daly City, where the daughter of the scion of capitalism reportedly became Cinque M'tume's lover and an improbable student of Debray and Jackson. In a March 10, 1974, communiqué Patty Hearst proclaimed her newfound dedication to the revolution:

Everyone who hears this tape, I hope you will believe me and not think that I've been brainwashed or tortured into saying this. Please listen to me be-cause I'm speaking honestly and from the heart. . . . They have given me some newspaper reports to read about the current practices of psychosurgery and the daily use of drugs and tranquilizers in prisons throughout the country. I have also been given some journal commentaries about kinds of conditions that exist in the adjustment center at San Quentin in particular. Members of the Federation have also given me a choice of books to read. I have been reading a book by George Jackson called *Blood in My Eye*. I'm starting to understand what he means when he talks about fascism in America.

Another message from Patty, sent to radio station KSAN on April 3, 1974, enclosed a photo of the captive socialite, now rechristened "Tania," standing before the SLA flag: "I have been given the choice of, one, being released in a safe area or, two, joining the forces of the Symbionese Liberation Army and fighting for my freedom and the freedom of all oppressed people. I have chosen to stay and fight."[82] On April 15, 1974, Patty Hearst was filmed taking part in an armed robbery of San Francisco's Hibernia Bank on Noriega Street. The bank's surveillance photographs gave no indication that she was coerced. By May the group had fled south to Los Angeles, where Patty Hearst and several others were involved in a shootout at a small store. William and Emily Harris and Patty Hearst apparently then left the area and headed to the East Coast. This move would prove a stroke of luck for the three.

On May 17, 1974, police quietly surrounded a small house at 1466 East 54th Street in Los Angeles, where the remainder of the SLA had taken refuge. Then, for the Right, the bitter years of waiting for revenge on California's revolutionary Left ended in a fiery blast. First, the police poured tear gas and then 5,371 rounds of ammunition into the home. All six SLA members in the structure were killed, including Cinque M'tume, who, the police said, "shot himself through the head to avoid being taken." According to a police report, the massive assault caused "the barrel riflings of some of the [police] weapons to completely wear out and the magazine springs to become unserviceable."[83] Police terror proved more than a match for the terror of the SLA.

Inside San Quentin, radical prisoners were devastated at the news of the death of the SLA members. Former San Quentin inmate Nate Harrington recalls: "I was in San Quentin when the [SLA] house was burned up in L.A. And I was right next to Lumumba, who was . . . one of the [SLA's] alleged in-prison leaders, him and Doc Holliday. . . . He cried. He was torn apart."[84] The inmates' support for the SLA was by no means unanimous. Some radical convict leaders had sensed early the futility of the group's resort to foco terrorism. Johnny Spain comments:

I objected to the SLA right from the beginning because . . . my analysis told me that, no, there isn't going to be armed struggle in this country. . . . We don't have the infrastructure in this society, we don't have people who even understand the Black Panthers, who are far more in the news and everyday life than people like the SLA. And if *we* can't pull off some things—I mean, there were cops who were coming to our headquarters starting shootouts!—if we can't even defend ourselves in the press when we're attacked, how could we possibly go out and wage an offensive and expect to be understood? . . . I knew nothing about Marcus Foster. But this guy was black. And you're trying to unite black people. I just don't think you're gonna get a lot of people to understand. . . . You're gonna wipe him out and you're gonna give 'em a bunch of revolutionary rhetoric as to why you did it? You talk about dialectical materialism, and you talk about historical materialism and the international struggle, and people in the welfare lines and the jobless and the homeless, they look at you and say, "What! What're you talking about!"[85]

Spain gauged the public reaction accurately. Most of the Bay Area was aghast at what the SLA had done. What little remained of public support for the prison movement now soured quickly. Some movement organizations ceased to exist altogether. Rallies became noticeably ill-attended. The spirit was gone from the movement. A "George Jackson Unity Day" handbill of August 1974 sounded a fading, desperate appeal: "The momentum of the sixties and the cry to 'free all political prisoners' has died. . . . Before it is to late, before another of us who oppose fascism is lost—we must involve the masses of people in aggressive and successful plans that will transform liberation into reality."[86]

The last extremist pronouncements supporting the SLA drove the few remaining supporters away. In a rally on May 18, 1975, at Berkeley's Ho Chi Minh Park, the United Prisoners Union's Popeye Jackson had seemed to call for acts of Left terrorism similar to those of the SLA: "I wonder why when we drop bombs in buildings, particularly [California attorney general] Evelle Younger, we don't bomb him. Until we begin to adhere to these things the S.L.A. taught us we can't say that we are revolutionaries."[87] The next day, several hundred yards from San Quentin's west gate, a bomb went off in a prison building at the prison's rifle range, taking away part of the structure's roof. The letters "NWLF" were scrawled on the building. A telephone call from the New World Liberation Front to the *San Francisco Chronicle* later declared: "We have just made an attack on San Quentin prison." A message received at San Francisco's radio station KPOO claimed the raid was intended "'to demonstrate our solidarity with the convicted class' and to attack the 'power structure' by exposing 'the hypocrisy and brutality of their 'justice' system.'"[88]

Soon the Harrises and Patty Hearst would be in police custody in San Francisco, where Hearst signed herself into jail as "an urban guerilla." Almost immediately, however, affidavits with her signature would claim she had been brainwashed by the SLA into participating in the group's terrorism. Although the movement had lost its momentum, lingering pockets of support in the Bay Area, even for the SLA, still held out hope for the revolution. A handbill tacked to telephone poles in Berkeley by New Dawn on October 4, 1975, included a message from the arrested Emily Harris. She greeted her supporters and urged them on with assurances that the arrests of the SLA members would not stanch the movement: "The war that was brought home over five years ago is here to stay," she wrote. But fewer and fewer in the movement actually believed these words.

By the fall of 1975, prison movement foco guerrilla strikes had ceased in the Bay Area except for occasional gangland "hits" by the BGF outside the walls. The most tragic of these would come in 1979, when, as if to sound a definitive death knell for the movement, BGF political gangsterism claimed one of the movement's most ardent supporters. George Jackson's onetime attorney Fay Stender, who had withdrawn from the Soledad Brothers case just before the San Quentin AC bloodbath, became herself a victim. A former BGF member retells the story:

A woman knocked on the door of Fay Stender's house. When Fay answered, a man appeared with a gun [and] came into the house. I think Fay's son or daughter was there at the time. He accused her of betraying George Jackson and the revolutionary movement and shot her several times. . . . For years rumors had been going around, people would talk about killing Fay, doing this and that. Rumormongers, people who just wanted to see stuff happen, would start rumors about her stealing from the [Soledad Brothers] defense fund. . . . She didn't betray anybody. . . . She moved on.[89]

Black Panther attorney Charles Garry blamed radicals inside San Quentin for Stender's shooting: "The screwballs in prison said she didn't give the guns that George Jackson demanded."[90] Stender was not killed, but she was paralyzed. She took her own life a year later. Ironically, Fay Stender was a victim of the prison movement foco theory that had appeared originally in California inmate self-improvement organizations and covert study groups, the mutant offspring of prisoner self-education crystallized in and made finally inevitable by George Jackson's *Blood in My Eye*.

As the nation moved to the right in the mid-1970's, the Bay Area public finally and for good renounced the prison movement for having resorted to urban terrorism. San Quentin black inmate Nate Harrington reflects on the process among black convict activists that had made the terrorism possible:

Looking back on it, it was almost inevitable that the gangster elements took over. . . . Ho Chi Minh wrote, "When the prison gates fly open, the real dragons will emerge." Well, that is patently not what did happen. When he wrote that, it was in the context of a national liberation struggle where many of the people who were in prison were there as a direct result of their participation in that struggle. And it wasn't the situation we had in this country where most of the people were there for some type of anti-people activity, whatever the reasons, the justifications giving rise to that. That's what they were there for, that's what I was there for, that's what most of us were there for. And only the few were there for, right or wrong, their political work on the streets. So when the prison gates flew open, dragons emerged, but they weren't the kind envisioned by Ho Chi Minh. And they certainly weren't the kind that would promote revolution.

What George Jackson referred to as converting the black criminal mentality into a black revolutionary mentality quite simply did not work. It got stuck in the midway point where you had a fusion or synthesis of the criminal mentality and revolutionary politics, with the end result being you had political gangsterism. You didn't have a black revolutionary mentality. You had a black criminal mentality infused with some of the rudiments of political thought, revolutionary thought, which was used on a basis of convenience. It was convenient to spout rhetoric and continue committing crimes, and that's exactly what happened.[91]

For too many California convicts, criminal opportunism had overpowered revolutionary ideology. Other former prisoners add that convict disillusionment also played havoc with the movement. A former Soledad inmate explains: "They came out. They became disillusioned. . . . But when they begin to turn it around, instead of usin' it for the betterment of everybody, they used it for their own thing. I don't want to mention any names. . . . Just because I know drug dealers who were big."[92] One San Quentin convict is more bold: "Huey Newton is on drugs.* He got into big drugs. He became cor-

---

*Huey Newton was killed soon after this interview by three point-blank shots to the head in Oakland on August 22, 1989, in what was reported to be an argument over a cocaine sale.

rupted. When they started off, I don't think they actually thought it would become as big as it became. When it became as big as it became, a lot of money became involved. You know, power, if it's not handled correctly, can be worse than no power."[93]

It soon was plain that foco terrorism had so frightened the California public and so enraged California's law-and-order Right that even lingering public support for the simple civil liberties of prisoners was weakening rapidly. The worst had come to pass. The struggle for the rights of prisoners had passed out of the hands of the convicts themselves, out of the prisons entirely, to small, outside pockets of ideological extremists on both the Right and the Left. Because the language of those identified as the ideological center of the movement was stridently Marxist, it had conjured up its opposite. In the noisy scuffle that followed, the real prisoners were forgotten. While Governor Reagan called for the permanent closing of San Quentin in 1972 and the development of newer, high-tech maximum security prisons for these troublemaking convicts,[94] red-baiters in the House Committee on Internal Security were busy labeling as communist "dupes" any inmates who continued to seek even modest prison reforms. The committee could see no other possible motive for the inmates' struggle than a pernicious will "to depict Government (in this case the penal system) as inept, repressive, brutal, and inhumane, thus hopefully weakening the trust of the people in their Government and thereby weakening the Government."[95] From the early 1970's, the pervasive climate of conservative backlash stopped progressive prison legislation dead in its tracks. Governor Reagan had vetoed a 1971 bill passed by both the California Senate and Assembly that would have established a prison ombudsman.[96] That same year, crucial due process legislation failed in the legislature that would have given prisoners facing disciplinary charges the right to call witnesses and to cross-examine their accusers, the right to representation in hearings, the right to have guilt decided by the preponderance of evidence, and the right to appeal.[97]

At the prison, meanwhile, efforts continued to crush all political activity by inmates. Major repressive changes were under way at San Quentin. Educational programs were terminated. More guards were hired. Cell blocks were subdivided for closer scrutiny of inmates. And prisoners' movements were monitored more closely than ever before. When out of the cell, inmates learned to be careful to walk only on the newly painted yellow lines crisscrossing the yard and walkways.

They left these walk lines at deadly peril. And inmates' contact with outsiders was severely cut back.

The issue of inmates' contact with the free world had quickly become the flashpoint of a conservative backlash. Prison custody staff was bitterly resentful of the role treatment staff and rehabilitation programs had played in aiding the inmates' rebellion. Former San Quentin lieutenant Richard Nelson, presently the prison's associate warden of custody, explains the guard staff's point of view:

For years we invited people to help us in the prison system, for years we invited people to help us. . . . The philosophy was to provide as much opportunity and out-of-cell activity that you could possibly provide. When we began to get help from people in the community we got the people we didn't want. The revolutionaries and the folks with an unwritten message, with a hidden agenda, infiltrated under the guise of being the good benefactor of the inmate. . . . The revolutionaries came in and did it to us, did it bad to us, killed a lot of us, hurt a lot of us.[98]

To gain better control, the prison began to cut off its contacts with the Bay Area community. In the 1950's the American Prison Association had viewed an inmate's contacts with outsiders as crucial to his reformation. Now San Quentin decided to take away that contact. In 1977 the Department of Corrections terminated its educational contract with Marin County and hired its own teachers. This would make them easier to control, guaranteeing that San Quentin classrooms were no longer schools for revolution. Former San Quentin instructor William Malin notes that some custody staff wanted to eliminate education entirely at San Quentin: "The correctional officers wanted to shut [the educational program] down for a long time. . . . I think there is an inherent prejudice here. 'We run the prisons. You stay out.'"[99]

New policies brought changes to San Quentin's library as well. In 1974 the library's books had been split into two collections and legal volumes set aside in a separate law library. In 1977 an old toolroom became the new home for this legal collection. Boxes of books from the remaining nonlaw library collection were then moved by forklift to two Quonset huts in the lower yard. In the process many of the books disappeared. Former San Quentin law librarian James McHenry discusses this point: "I think there was some that wanted to get rid of 'em. . . . From about 1978 on, the library really went down."[100] San Quentin inmate Joe Morse regrets the changes in the library:

Respect for the library began to dissipate around 1973 when television became allowed inside prison. The reading decreased. Prior to that, books were hot items. . . . At one time San Quentin had a really great library for a prison. It was kept well-stocked because of more of a demand for the books. There were a lot of hardbounds. We have very few hardbounds over there now. I personally watched them dump a hell of a lot of things that would be on the verge of being classics.[101]

In 1974 the San Quentin library possessed 36,000 volumes.[102] In July 1990 its collection numbered just 8,902 books.* Three-quarters of the prison's library collection had disappeared. The attempt to tighten communication control led to the almost total destruction of the prison's library in the mid- to late 1970's. Certainly, a combination of motives lay behind the book purge. At times, as staff is quick to point out, hardback books could become weapons. And even paper had to be controlled because it could be burned or wet and then rolled up into spears. These facts only underscore the level of continuing struggle inside. One fact remains: the final result of the library's dismantling has been the veritable end of reading at the prison. For prison staff, preventing any further revolutionary convict writing was a goal of the first order. No more scripts for the revolution would spring from convict hands. More immediate even than the threat of paper spears, in the minds of San Quentin prison staff during the book purge the memory of George Jackson's *Blood in My Eye* loomed large.

Jackson's book had brought the prison to a crucial realization. The rehabilitation philosophy of the treatment era had encouraged a belief that part of the cure for criminality lay in subverting the values of convict subculture by encouraging the reading of elite literature. This notion was tragically flawed. Now, when it became obvious that San Quentin head librarian Herman Spector's eternal truths were not the truths that the imprisoned underclass held sacred, the iron gag had to be reapplied. Harsh censorship was reintroduced. And television and video watching was engineered to supplant inmate reading and writing.

Outside San Quentin, too, George Jackson's book had produced paradoxical results. As the prisoner intended, *Blood in My Eye* had brought prison movement foco terrorism to life in the Bay Area. In the end, however, rather than accomplishing Jackson's goal of moving

*According to current San Quentin chief librarian Mary Mims, telephone interview, summer 1990. This count includes both the prison's law collection and its general collection. As of July 10, 1990, San Quentin library contained 135 hardback fiction books, 2,600 nonfiction books, 2,500 paperbacks, and 3,667 law books.

the Bay Area masses to a people's revolution behind the foco prison guerrilla leadership, the book had helped to bring the prison movement Left to a premature end. Slowly the truth began to sink in. The thinking of the prison movement had come full circle with foco theory. The foco model of the outlaw as cultural hero, as savior, was the exact flip side of the treatment model of the outlaw as pathological, though curable, cultural deviant. And it was no more accurate than its opposite. Both models were flawed. This was an expensive lesson for the Left to learn.

In the end, all the special programs, the inmate self-improvement groups, the counselors and teachers from the outside were abandoned. After Jackson's book and the terrorist acts of the SLA and other foco prison movement terrorists, the prison put a quick end to all political organizing among San Quentin's inmates. Motivating the changes was the desire to dismantle the mechanisms capable of producing radical ideology in inmates. Consequently, restrictions on the importation of radical literature were vastly heightened, the library of even nonradical and "classical" books was destroyed, and the prisoners were shepherded away from written texts. Only in the area of mail correspondence had San Quentin's prisoners' communication liberties been sustained. The 1970 riot plan of the American Correctional Association was prescient when it reminded wardens to protect their records in insurrections. The writing of inmates' lives was one of the primary ways the prison had of reenacting the power relations within the culture. The manner in which prisoner's lives were recorded *mattered*.

10

THE FORCE OF IMPRISONED WORDS

The Bay Area Left was well aware of the power that lay in controlling the written lives of convicts, and it was prepared to struggle to create an altered image of the American prisoner. No one was more conscious of the power of convict words than George Jackson. Luis Talamantez recalls Jackson writing *Blood in My Eye*: "He was going to bury them with the power of the word. He believed his book was going to . . . lay everybody flat."[1] Originally, in the mid- to late 1960's the Left's dominant voices had forced Californians to acknowledge that the underclass was being victimized by the justice system. The prison movement had found for almost a decade that it could build popular support in the Bay Area on this point. But this had happened at a time when support in the legislature was hard to build and aid from Governor Ronald Reagan's office was nonexistent. At that juncture prison movement moderates had looked to the judiciary for help and had set about building a convict union. But events had spun out of control. Just as the nation's much more potent Right was becoming increasingly powerful and vindictive, directed from the offices of the likes of Ronald Reagan, Richard Nixon, and J. Edgar Hoover, radicals took the prison movement far to the left into its foco period, resorting to a terroristic political practice. The clash of radical Left and radical Right that ensued in the Bay Area ultimately was fatal for the prison movement.

In the mid-1970's the Prisoners' Union came very close to being legally recognized as the official representative of California prisoners. Then, following several crucial court losses and faced with the intransigent opposition of the California Correctional Officers Association, and its influence on the California Department of Corrections, prison unionism in northern California suddenly became a dead issue in 1976. Foco terrorism in California had alienated many, including the judiciary, which finally chose not to let the Prisoners' Union into the prisons. The prison movement stopped dead, though it need not have. At the end of the decade the California public remained as leery of the corruption of its agencies of law enforcement as it was of left-wing terrorism, as the San Quentin Six decision would show in 1976–77. Under different circumstances, absent the polarizing fanaticism of both California's far Right and far Left, the movement might have continued much further than it did.

In spite of its losses, the movement was not without important victories in its last days. The acquittal of three defendants in the San Quentin Six trial, on felony assault, conspiracy, and murder charges stemming from the August 21, 1971, AC bloodbath, would be seen as a clear victory by many. That same year, 1977, the California legislature swept aside the Indeterminate Sentence Law and the Adult Authority was abolished except as it continued to oversee the sentences of prisoners convicted of murder or kidnapping. After this, most prisoners would be informed of their release dates at the outset of their imprisonment and "programming" to please the Adult Authority would become a thing of the past. These were major reforms. Passage of California's Determinate Sentence Law and the dissolution of the Adult Authority in 1976–77 represented real liberation for prisoners. California's prisoners had long struggled to free themselves from the rehabilitative language of the treatment-era prison, which characterized them as unregenerate, and the new law finally officially repudiated the philosophical underpinnings of that prison. After 1976 prisoners were no longer inscribed as "pathological deviants" needing the help of experts to effect their cure over interminable years. Instead, they were simply people who had broken the law. Imprisonment became simple punishment once more. Although this change must be viewed as real progress, the prisons' return at the same time to rigid censorship of reading and writing showed that the only thing that prison officials had learned from George Jackson's *Blood in My Eye* was that convict writing must be even more strictly controlled than before and altogether forbidden when possible.

Divisive internal problems in the Prisoners' Union were one cause for the final failure of unionism in California. Prisoners' Union board member Jay Halford notes that since the earliest days the volatile temper of Popeye Jackson, eventual leader of the splinter-faction United Prisoners Union, had often sent the organization into a tailspin:

The day we found out George Jackson was murdered he nutted out. I was there, at Shirley Sutherland's house in Beverly Hills,* the afternoon we heard George Jackson was murdered, and he nutted out at this meeting, right there. See, the FBI was across the street, about six of 'em, monitoring us and shit. They had orders from the CDC that we were all criminals and revolutionaries, so they were out following us around. He wanted to kick their ass right there, and about three of us tackled him, including me. He said, "That's it! That's war!" He got up from the table and he started walking toward the front door, and he said, "I'm gonna fuck them niggers up out front for openers." And he said he wanted to kidnap wardens and hold 'em for ransom. I mean, he kind of nutted out, man. So we tackled him at the door. And when we were holdin' him down and he was screamin', I remember he threatened me then, you know. He says, "You fuckin' punk! I'm gonna get you for this!" . . . He didn't like me anymore.

In 1971 Jackson was caught stealing money from the union and expelled from the group. Enraged by accusations of opportunism, he broke into Prisoners' Union headquarters with a pistol. "He tried to kill me, man, in San Francisco," Halford recalls of this incident.[2] John Irwin has a similar memory: "The day we threw [Popeye Jackson] out of the office he came back an hour later with a pistol and chased us all over the building, had a gun to my head, had me up against the wall. . . . We let him rant and rave." Later, according to Irwin, the union suffered public accusations of racism for expelling a black convict leader: "We endured a lot of abuse because we threw a black man out of our organization. You know, he went around and told 'em we were racists."[3]

After its violent factional split in 1971, the Prisoners' Union followed a moderate route while Popeye Jackson's splinter United Prisoners Union allied more closely with movement radicals. Following the death of George Jackson, Popeye steered his faction in directions considered by the Prisoners' Union to be further and further from prison issues. For just one example, claiming to have known Cinque M'tume in prison, Popeye Jackson volunteered his wing of the union to help distribute provisions in the SLA's food ransom scheme. In the end, Popeye Jackson managed to make enemies of almost everyone. After his Berkeley speech in May 1975, in which he called for more SLA-style prison terrorism, a New World Liberation Front commu-

---

*Shirley Sutherland, the ex-wife of movie actor Donald Sutherland, had donated a van and provided the Prisoners' Union with patronage connections to Hollywood celebrities. She later would go to trial, accused of buying guns for the Black Panthers. Though acquitted of this charge, Sutherland was deported to her native Canada. Jay Halford, telephone interview, summer 1989.

niqué signed by Black Panther Geronimo Pratt charged him with being an agent provocateur.[4] On June 2, 1975, Popeye Jackson and a
woman, Sally Voye, were shot dead as they sat in his parked car in
San Francisco. A member of the radical underground Tribal Thumb
organization would later be tried and convicted of the murder.[5] Following Popeye's death, the United Prisoners Union splinter faction
soon passed from the scene.

The Prisoners' Union continued working secretly within the prisons to build an underground membership. Harlan Washington, transferred to Soledad for union organizing, continued his membership
drive there in 1975:

When I first got there . . . they were underground in Soledad, the Prisoners'
Union. . . . What we were doing, we were going to the library like we were
collecting books, in boxes. And then these books would go to O-Wing, the
hole, for individuals who didn't have nothing to read, which was a legitimate
thing, but while we were meeting for this, we were talking that [i.e., recruiting union members].

Soon union members called Prisoners' Union attorney Michael Snedeker to Soledad for a planning meeting. Washington recalls:

The way we did it, I applied for fifteen individuals from every major group
and organization in the joint, whites, blacks, browns, Indians. . . . I learned
that all I needed was the leaders. If you get the leaders, you get the followers. . . . So Mike came down and we had a most successful meeting. . . .
We got the whole institution with that move. We got the whole institution.[6]

In 1975 the growing union entered into a series of negotiations
with the Department of Corrections to legalize the organization inside
Soledad prison. By October, following talks with high-ranking members in the state prison administration, outside members of the Prisoners' Union submitted a formal proposal to make the union a recognized inmate body within that prison.[7] Internal Department of
Corrections memorandums sent to Director Jiro J. Enomoto from Nelson Kempsky, then deputy director for policy and planning, reveal
him characterizing the union proposal as "quite reasonable and moderate."[8] The department was ready to let the union in. By January
1976, a plan had been tentatively agreed upon. Success appeared assured. The Prisoners' Union was to have the right to represent inmates at Soledad and to organize inside, though the department reserved power to suspend the union immediately following a public
hearing. Although the union was to represent inmates in grievance
proceedings, the agreement expressly forbade material that "calls for

disruption of institutional routines, work stoppages, or other organized demonstrations."[9] Representatives from the department and
the union were to meet regularly and confer, after which the two
groups would publish and post signed memorandums of understanding. As a first small step toward real prisoner unionization, the Soledad plan seemed a solid advance. The union plan was to be announced at a January 20, 1976, meeting with prison administrators.
On the day before, however, the scheme leaked to the press. Immediately, the CCOA flew into a rage and denounced the proposal in
the strongest terms, threatening to strike and demanding that Enomoto be fired. Prisoners' Union attorney Michael Snedeker blames
the CCOA for the final ringing defeat of the Soledad plan:

It was the CCOA that eventually shot us down, with allies in the warden's
office. We were just faced with the enormous institutional inertia of these
thousands of employees who were the people with the keys. They were just
seething and resentful. . . . And they just chose us as their cause célèbre that
they were gonna die over. And they effectively blocked it.[10]

The Soledad inmates went ahead anyway. In August 1976, 32 prison-
ers submitted to the Soledad administration a charter and by-laws for
Prisoners' Union Local 1, Soledad Central.[11] The prison's superin-
tendent, George W. Sumner, immediately rejected the application.
When the decision was appealed to the top, Director Enomoto upheld
Sumner's action.[12] The union had exhausted its administrative means.

The next step was to go through the courts. A group of Soledad
prisoners petitioned for a writ of habeas corpus to permit them to
hold union meetings. The Monterey County Superior Court denied
the petition. The California Supreme Court issued an order to show
cause, then decided that "a prisoner's union is incompatible with current and lawful policies of penological confinement. Its existence
would violate institutional security. Therefore, in-prison meetings of
the inmate and non-inmate membership of such Union are properly
disallowed."[13] While this case was working its way through the California courts, in June 1977, the U.S. Supreme Court concluded in a
similar case, *Jones v. North Carolina Prisoners' Union*, that for a prison
to deny permission for a union "offended neither the first nor the
fourteenth amendments."[14] This decision sounded the final death
knell for prison unionism in California and elsewhere, according to
Michael Snedeker: "Before [*Jones v. North Carolina Prisoners' Union*]
the idea of unions was possible. No one knew whether or not it was
legal for prisoners to hold meetings. . . . Once that was laid to rest

legally, the . . . interest dried up . . . and the organizing itself within the prison gradually diminished."

A minor court victory in 1979 permitted Prisoners' Union members to continue to wear their union lapel buttons.[15] But as Harlan Washington notes, the back of the union had already been broken by that time and few dared to declare their union membership openly: "Those of us who were out in front would wear 'em. Some of us would wear four or five on our jacket at the same time. And [the guards would] look at you and plan what they was goin' to do with you. . . . Gradually you had guys that were afraid to wear 'em. They'd get 'em but they wouldn't wear 'em."[16] The same year the California Supreme Court upheld the Department of Corrections policy of forbidding mail correspondence between union members inside and paroled ex-convict union officers outside.[17] With union correspondence now effectively cut off, the Prisoners' Union was dead. Harlan Washington, by this time transferred to Vacaville prison for union organizing, concludes with some bitterness, "They allowed it to grow, and then they ripped it."[18]

The California Prisoners' Union continues to exist, though it has devolved into strictly an informational and self-help organization, a source of support for individual prisoners with grievances. It makes no effort to organize and hold meetings inside the prisons. It functions, too, as a watchdog of the legislature, the courts, and the Department of Corrections, advising inmates and their families on how to influence their elected officials on prison issues. It publishes a resource guide for prisoners. As one measure of its current moderation, the union's newspaper has changed its name from the *Outlaw* to the *California Prisoner*. Despite the final losses of the Prisoners' Union and its reduced level of militancy, its role throughout the 1970's as a powerful lobby for prisoners in the California legislature and its voice in the courts as the California prisoner's truest advocate cannot be denied. In 1976, when California's Indeterminate Sentence Law was swept aside and with it the Adult Authority, the Prisoners' Union was at least partly responsible. Now only those convicted of murder or kidnapping are subject to the vagaries of indeterminate imprisonment by the Board of Prison Terms. This has been no mean accomplishment. Doing away with the indeterminate sentence and the AA were the two most consistently demanded strike goals of prisoners involved in San Quentin agitations throughout the entire 1960's and 1970's. Just the same, it is impossible not to imagine what else the union might have accomplished for California prisoners if popular support for the prison movement had been sustained into the 1980's.

In 1976, just as the union was entering what turned out to be its days of decline, the San Quentin Six case came to trial. An important conjunction of national events was to influence the outcome of the trial, reflecting the mood of the Bay Area public in the waning days of the movement. In 1976 the U.S. Senate Select Committee on Intelligence Activities made public the stunning degree of surveillance of innocent American citizens the U.S. government had been conducting for years. For twenty years the CIA had been illegally opening private mail. A hundred thousand Western Union, ITT, and Radio Corporation of America cables to individuals had been intercepted as well by the National Security Administration (NSA), in violation of the Fourth Amendment guarantee against illegal search and seizure. The committee revealed a nightmarish pattern of domestic spying against U.S. citizens and the existence of hundreds of thousands of NSA and CIA files on individual Americans. The FBI, too, had made a regular policy of harassing dissidents. It had carried out vendettas against civil rights leaders. Martin Luther King's motel rooms had been electronically bugged and the tapes then sold to local newspapers unfriendly to his cause. The FBI's COINTEL program was revealed by the intelligence committee to have been a malicious, secret counterintelligence effort designed to "disrupt" and "neutralize" citizens' groups that J. Edgar Hoover had personally deemed national threats. Finally, the Internal Revenue Service had been regularly misused as an agent of state coercion. Citizens deemed enemies of the state were threatened with IRS investigations without evidence of tax delinquency and their confidential tax information was illegally transferred to other government agencies. When reports of the intelligence committee's findings appeared in the national press, it became clear that on the Right forces of state power more potent and vindictive than anything even the most fanatically destructive Left revolutionaries could possibly raise had been at work throughout the entire Nixon administration. The end effect was that, precisely like the treatment-era California prisoners, the entire American public now seemed victims of the state's panoptic paternalism.

This did not come entirely as a surprise to Californians. The state's Big Brother panopticism had been a minor theme in Bay Area newspapers since the early 1970's. In a winter 1971 preview of the Watergate hearings, Senator Sam Ervin, chairman of the Subcommittee on

Constitutional Rights, was reported by the local press to be collecting expert testimony from lawyers and social scientists on the government's expanding role in the surveillance of its citizens' lives. Professor Arthur R. Miller of the University of Michigan Law School, appearing before the subcommittee, warned that "Americans are scrutinized, measured, watched, counted, and interrogated by more government agencies, law enforcement officials, social scientists, and poll takers than at any time in our history." He further declared that "the information gathering and surveillance activities of the Federal government have expanded to such an extent that they are becoming a threat to several basic rights of every American—privacy, speech, assembly, association, and petition of government." [19] This testimony appeared in the *San Francisco Chronicle* that winter. The fear of Big Brother it engendered was to be further inflamed by Richard Nixon's Watergate scandal and his consequent resignation in 1974, raising doubts about the state's respect for its own laws. The findings of the Senate Intelligence Committee only compounded public anxiety. This fear would have far-reaching consequences for the prison movement in its last days. Two preoccupations of the Bay Area public, its dread of what had become left-wing foco gangsterism and its allied fear of big government lawbreaking and illegal surveillance of innocent civilians, would play major roles in producing the jury verdict in the San Quentin Six trial of 1975–76.

After three and a half years of delays, defense committees for the Six in late 1974 found left-wing prison movement support had declined so severely that raising fees for attorney and court costs had become difficult to the point that some of the defendants were forced to use public defenders. And without a critic as biting as George Jackson to call the public's attention to the political background of the case, it appeared that San Quentin AC inmates Johnny Larry Spain, Fleeta Drumgo, Willie Tate, David Johnson, Hugo Pinell, and Luis Talamantez might be convicted without arousing much public interest.

Three prison guards and two inmate tier tenders had lost their lives and three guards had been wounded in the San Quentin AC bloodbath on August 21, 1971. As a result, 46 felony counts were brought against the San Quentin Six. A seventh defendant in the case, attorney Stephen Bingham, accused of smuggling a pistol to George Jackson, had fled California and was still at large. When the trial opened on March 25, 1975, in the courtroom of Marin County Superior Court judge Henry Broderick, five of the accused appeared in court chained and shackled to their chairs. The issue of the legality of chaining defendants in court would be debated hotly in the California press throughout that spring.* There were precedents that argued for restraining defendants. Black Panther Bobby Seale had been gagged and shackled in his 1969 Chicago conspiracy trial. And, more recently, in the California murder trials of captured members of the SLA, defendants Joseph Remiro and Russell Little had been shut out of the courtroom altogether, forced to watch their fates being decided from a remote room via closed-circuit television. But both the California public and its legal community remained nervous about the use of courtroom restraints. Luis Talamantez protested the treatment he was receiving, crying out in court, "I will not sit here wearing chains!"[20] With the exception of Willie Tate, who had been paroled shortly before the trial commenced, the defendants were transported together from San Quentin to the Hall of Justice in a specially constructed bus in which each was enclosed in a separate compartment. In the courtroom they sat behind a bulletproof screen. Metal detectors and body searches assured that spectators and journalists were unarmed.

The prosecution began its case. It would prove, it argued, primarily on the testimony of surviving guards Ken McCray and Urbano Rubiaco, Jr., and surviving AC inmate Allan Mancino, that George Jackson had been smuggled a pistol in a visit by attorney Steven Bingham and that he had shot and killed one guard with it. The other dead guards had had their throats slashed by the conspiring AC prisoners, prosecutors would claim. Two inmate tier tenders were killed, the state would argue, because they refused to take part in the bloodbath.[21]

What the defense was about to declare was by far the more surprising. Marin County chief deputy public defender Frank J. Cox, attorney for David Johnson, charged that various California law enforcement agencies had joined in a conspiracy to assassinate George Jackson. Apparently conceding the existence of various inmate plans to escape, Cox countered that "there was an attempt to kill George Jackson by a pre-emptive first strike."[22] The attorney claimed he had

---

*See, for example, "The San Quentin Six Trial: Do Chains Have a Place?" *Los Angeles Times*, May 22, 1975. In the mood of a different decade, the prejudicial effect on the jury of defendants in chains would lead to a reversal of Johnny Spain's murder conviction in the case. In August 1989, the Ninth U.S. Circuit Court of Appeals ruled that Spain's shackling with 25 pounds of chains during the seventeen-month trial had caused him undue pain and humiliation and had prevented him from assisting his attorney. See "Shackled Ex-Panther Wins Appeal," *San Diego Union*, Aug. 23, 1989.

evidence from before the Soledad Incident that agents of the Los Angeles Police Department's Criminal Conspiracy Section had infiltrated California's left-wing radical groups, including the Black Panthers. Cox promised the jury testimony showing that the CCS and the California Department of Corrections had planned and carried out a political assassination of George Jackson. He compared the level of California government conspiracy in the events leading up to August 21, 1971, to the role the Nixon administration had recently been revealed to have played in the Watergate conspiracy. This analogy was to leave a lasting impression on the jury.

In the months to follow, surprise defense witness Louis Tackwood, brother-in-law of Jimmy Carr, would testify that he had been an agent of the CCS. That agency, according to Tackwood, had learned of a plot to free Jackson. Tackwood claimed he had been assigned "to assassinate George Jackson" before the inmate could make his own escape. Tackwood testified that he and two policemen had traveled to San Quentin on August 1, 1971, to deliver to a prison guard an inoperable .25 caliber revolver meant for George Jackson. Jackson, he said, was to be smuggled this gun and then shot when he had the weapon in his hands on August 23, as he went to a scheduled Soledad Brothers court appearance.[23] Responding in the press to Tackwood's assertions, Los Angeles police chief Ed Davis, Attorney General Evelle J. Younger, and a Department of Corrections spokesman called the claim of a planned assassination "absurd."[24]

Despite these and other defense claims of the existence of a statewide network of prison movement infiltrators, agents provocateurs, and police assassination squads, the Bay Area public remained remarkably cool to news of the San Quentin Six trial. At the outset of the trial, about 100 demonstrators milled around the front of the courthouse.[25] Five hundred people attended a San Quentin Six support rally in June at Berkeley's Community Theater, where Angela Davis spoke.[26] But considering the enormity of the charges the defense was making against the state of California, this was a pitiful turnout. Five years earlier, such serious allegations would have spawned street protests by thousands.

San Quentin officer Urbano Rubiaco, Jr., testified for the prosecution that he recognized Hugo Pinell as the one who had slashed his throat. Rubiaco said as well that Johnny Spain had held a gun to his head and had shoved him into a cell, where David Johnson had tied his feet.[27] The defense, for its part, alleged that Rubiaco was the one who had brought the gun that launched the incident into the

AC.[28] Much of the argument over what had happened that day in the AC centered around this gun. The Department of Corrections had changed its mind several times in the first few days following the bloodbath about exactly what weapon George Jackson had allegedly used. The weapon the department originally claimed was discovered under the prisoner's body, a 9mm Astra, was too large to have been smuggled in inside attorney Bingham's tape recorder or to have been hidden under George Jackson's wig, as the prosecution argued it had been. The department then had changed its mind, saying it was instead a .38 caliber Llama Corto that had been used. Complicating matters further, Louis Tackwood insisted that the gun he took to the prison for Jackson was a .25 caliber revolver.

By the following June, defense attorney Charles Garry had thrown up his hands at this welter of contradictory testimony. But he was sure of one thing, he said. The escape theory was "garbage." Garry claimed instead that the AC was simply "a cesspool that overflowed that day." The bloodbath was the result of "an emotional upheaval," not a conspiracy to escape.[29] The trial would drag on for another month. When it finally drew to an end in August 1976, after seventeen months, it had been California's longest criminal trial to that date and had generated 23,000 pages of trial transcript.

On August 13, 1976, after deliberating 124 days, the San Quentin Six jury brought guilty verdicts on only six of the original 46 felony charges. Johnny Spain, Hugo Pinell, and David Johnson were convicted: Johnson of one count of felony assault on a guard, Pinell of two counts of felony assault on a guard, and Spain of two counts of first degree murder and conspiracy to commit murder.* Paradoxically, this verdict seemed to confirm parts of the cases of both the prosecution and the defense. The jury convicted those defendants against whom it had heard eyewitness testimony. The rest were exonerated. The final jury finding was that there had been an inmate conspiracy to escape on August 21, 1971, a gun had been smuggled in, and Johnson, Pinell, and Spain, at least, had joined George Jackson in assaulting guards. The involvement of the other defendants, however, was in doubt. At the same time, as journalist Karen Wald pointed out after the trial had ended, the jury's decision was a measure of how deeply affected the Bay Area public had been by Watergate and related revelations of government conspiracy to bring false charges against innocent citizens.[30] That the defense attorneys for the San Quentin Six

---

*Spain's convictions were reversed in 1989.

were able to argue convincingly to a Bay Area jury that the events of August 21, 1971, were in part the result of a coordinated plan of various law enforcement agencies (especially the Criminal Conspiracy Section of the Los Angeles Police Department, the state attorney general's office, and the California Department of Corrections, but extending even to the FBI's COINTELPRO operation) to assassinate a black political prisoner and then frame six innocent San Quentin AC inmates in the death was powerful evidence of this new distrust of government. By its equivocal decision the jury seemed to be confirming and condemning *both* the existence of a San Quentin AC foco group of prisoner guerrillas *and* a government conspiracy to assassinate them. The six convictions were upheld in the state Court of Appeal in July 1980.[31] This puzzling verdict was a clear indication that by the decade's end, with prison unionism dead and the prison movement Left in disrepute, the state still had far to go to convince the California public that its prisoners posed a more serious threat to law and order than the police and courts did.

But by 1976 a sea change was already under way in the attitudes of this public, and by the early 1980's the transformation would be complete. The Left's vision of the criminal as cultural savior would by then be utterly extinct, as the state had once again taken back firm control of the terms of discourse on crime and criminals. The California prison, San Quentin perhaps more than others, played a major role in this recapture of the terms of definition of crime. How was this so? Much of San Quentin prison's history in the treatment era had been the story of a struggle for control of its inmates' self-expression. This is not a simple claim to make. Methods of controlling prisoners' reading and writing are just one part of a set of related prison practices. In some eras they are not a very important part. But at all times, in all prisons, attempts to control inmates' use of books and writing at least reenact other sets of primary power relations within the prison. In particular eras and particular prisons, the control of convicts' communication sometimes describes a primary power relation. This is likely to be especially true of prisons within communities experiencing social unrest and turmoil, where uncontrolled public communication is seen as a risk to public order. It is then that the voice of the convict reader/writer will be most strenuously controlled because these are the times when it may come to have real subversive power. Such was the case at San Quentin prison from 1950 to 1980. As social unrest in the Bay Area increased, rigid communication controls returned to San Quentin, though smuggled inmate-written texts continued for a time to have tremendous power outside the walls.

Since the dawn of the prison in America during the early federal period, the struggle over prisoners' reading and writing and the need to keep the populace from reading prison-written texts, or at least to control their form and content, has been at the very heart of the issue of how power was to be distributed, or redistributed, in the culture. That San Quentin should resemble America's earliest penitentiaries in this respect is no mistake of history. Treatment-era San Quentin, like America's very first prisons, the Walnut Street Jail and Eastern State Penitentiary in Philadelphia, bore the clear stamp of its origin in evangelical reform ideology. And like its early predecessors, San Quentin prison's rehabilitation technology functioned as much as a mechanism of benevolent social control for the community outside the prison as it did as a machine of coercive correction for the prisoners directly under its care. Modifying the language behavior of San Quentin convicts thus played an important, sometimes a crucial, role in keeping public order in the San Francisco Bay Area. This is at bottom the most profound reason why at treatment-era San Quentin it came to matter so very much whether the convict class learned to read from a simplified text of *The Communist Manifesto* or from an elite diet of literary "masterpieces" and why it came to matter such a great deal, as well, whether a convict-written autobiography celebrating crime against the state escaped the attention of prison censors and became a best-seller outside the walls. At San Quentin it came to matter so much, in fact, that the prison's perceived need to crush radical inmates' reading and writing in the 1970's accelerated its turn away from treatment back to simple repressive custody. San Quentin did this for a reason.

Prison reading becomes prison writing, and prison-written texts can become the public's reading. The construction of the convict "self" in inmates' writing therefore directly affects the surrounding community's model of itself and its corresponding model of criminal deviancy. For this reason, the ownership of a prisoner's written self, the control over the production of the inmate's autobiography, or the right to determine how the collective story will be recorded of what "criminals" are in the culture can be an issue of intense controversy. Who owns the prisoner's self? Who will control the terms of that definition? Will the prisoner be remembered as his or her life was recorded in the prison's cumulative file? Will the convict be known as he or she is reflected in a prison-written autobiography, heavily censored by the prison librarian and designed to please the Adult Authority? Or will the inmate's self be the one remembered from a text smuggled out to the Left, or the Right, designed to urge others to secure his or her release? More than in the case of any other autobiographer, the convict's self is in doubt. This is the written self that is struggled over in prison strikes and agitations, the self that is rewritten in covert study groups and prisoner union meetings, and the self that can become dangerously fantastical through long months of isolation. This self is, then, a product of a linguistic struggle, and at certain tragic times in prison a convict's very blood-and-bones life may fall victim to a written construction, as George Jackson's came sadly to be trapped at the juncture of the various discourses that owned him.

As Foucault pointed out, the historical appearance of the notion of criminal reform which produced the prison in the late eighteenth century and laid the foundation for treatment made the inmate a juridically paradoxical creature. In treatment eras the paradox is that guilt is no longer a simple matter of the prisoner's having committed a crime. Establishing guilt becomes secondary to finding the origins of the crime in its psychological or socioeconomic settings. Assigning the causal processes that produced the crime thus replaces a simple determination of guilt. It then also becomes a major part of the prisoner's cure. What is more, in treatment eras convicts' stories as literature—convicts' origins, descent into crime, capture, and reform through imprisonment—must become a source of moral instruction for others outside the prison and a model of penitence. When this is not the case, it is a sign that something has gone seriously wrong in the functioning of the rehabilitative prison. Faced with exactly this situation in the late 1970's, San Quentin chose to turn away from even the pretense of rehabilitation and to merely repress.

By the time of Eldridge Cleaver's 1967 *Soul on Ice*, it was clear that the California rehabilitative prison was malfunctioning. Readers in the Bay Area Left eagerly seized upon the book as a radical conversion narrative, but whereas traditional conversion narratives had served to reaffirm the moral consensus of the community, for the Left reading Cleaver became a form of moral witness against the American state. The story of this angry convict's individual transgression against society, politicized by his written text, became an expression of the Left's similar collectively willed political transgression.

The Bay Area Left was by no means univocal in its attitude toward crime and prisoners in these years. Like the San Quentin administration and staff and the inmates themselves, it, too, was full of contentious groups and contradictory voices. Not all Left radicals even recognized the prisons as an issue. Following the 1969 SDS meeting in Austin, Texas, however, when splinter groups would form the pro-Chinese Progressive Labor party faction of the SDS, the Palo Alto–based Revolutionary Union, the Revolutionary Youth Movement, and Venceremos, the voices of these groups increasingly dictated the political atmosphere of the Bay Area Left. During the height of their influence in 1970–71, a simplified form of Marxist/Maoist class analysis endorsed by these particular groups led the Left more and more to fix upon American prisons as a microcosm of the state. These forces within and without San Quentin converged in the person of George Jackson, first as written and received in *Soledad Brother* and then as rewritten in *Blood in My Eye*. The prison's Adjustment Center, touted at its opening in 1960 as a site of intense rehabilitative counseling and education, thus instead became the locus of its most intense linguistic battle and book suppression as well as the location of its most violent convict insurrection.

But by 1975 the moral and ideological fissures in the Bay Area between the Left and Right were beginning to close up; or, more accurately, the moral discourse of the Right on crime and the criminal had come to dominate. Afterward, convict writing rarely escaped the prison's censors, and the Left's alternative vision of the convict as cultural hero and revolutionary savior, or even as cultural victim, was effectively silenced. The most salient proof of this may be found, once again, in the evidence of a convict text.

In November 1975, Eldridge Cleaver made his return to the United States, not as he had dreamed, by sweeping northward from the Mexican mountains accompanied by foco units of armed guerrillas, but in the custody of two FBI agents. He and his wife and children had spent the previous year in Paris, after leaving in disgust both Cuba, which he had found to be a "San Quentin with palm trees," and Algeria, where, despite their "Russian machine guns, and plenty of fresh-air macho,"[32] he and other exiled Panthers had resorted to hustling stolen cars and falsified passports for their livelihood. After a run-in with the Algerian government over the issue of who was to keep the hijack ransom money fellow Panthers were bringing into the country, Cleaver had felt it best to leave that nation. Soon he was ousted from the Black Panther party. In France, alone and forsaken, Cleaver had finally made the hard decision to turn himself in. He arrived in New York in handcuffs, accompanied by two agents. A warrant for his arrest was read to him, on six felony charges of assault and assault with intent to kill stemming from his April 6, 1968, shoot-out with the Oakland police. He was also arraigned on a fugitive warrant and immediately extradited to San Diego Metropolitan Correctional Center, then to the Alameda County Jail in Oakland. In a book he was soon to publish about this odyssey of his return, which would appear just before his plea bargain of guilty on three assault counts and his final gift of freedom on probation in 1979, Cleaver wrote of the profound Christian conversion he had experienced one night before leaving France:

It was a beautiful Mediterranean night—sky, stars, moon hanging there in a sable void. I was brooding, downcast, at the end of my rope. I looked up at the moon and saw certain shadows . . . and the shadows became a man in the moon, and I saw a profile of myself. . . .

As I stared at this image, it changed, and I saw my former heroes paraded before my eyes. Here were Fidel Castro, Mao Tse-tung, Karl Marx, Frederick Engels, passing in review—each one appearing for a moment of time, and then dropping out of sight, like fallen heroes. Finally, at the end of the procession, in dazzling, shimmering light, the image of Jesus Christ appeared. That was the last straw.

I just crumbled and started crying. I fell to my knees, grabbing hold of the banister; and in the midst of this shaking and crying the Lord's Prayer and the 23rd Psalm came into my mind. . . .

Then I jumped up and ran to my bookshelf and got the Bible.[33]

In the Alameda County Jail, Cleaver's Christian transformation became complete when the prisoner joined an inmate Bible circle.[34] While Cleaver was at San Diego, special arrangements had been made to permit him to visit Billy Graham in his hotel room during a crusade the evangelist was conducting there. The reborn Eldridge Cleaver's reading in his subsequent nine months in the Alameda County Jail would include Watergate conspirator Charles Colson's *Born Again*. The two authors were soon to become close friends as Cleaver courted the Christian power brokers.[35] When he was released on bail in August 1976, he traveled, among other places, to Lynchburg, Virginia, where Pastor Jerry Falwell invited him to speak to his national Sunday morning television audience.[36]

In *Soul on Fire* (1978), Cleaver renounced his former radical prison persona, taking for his own the eighteenth-century evangelical rhetoric of reformative incarceration. Concurring in his book with the opinions of Stanton E. Samenow and Samuel Yochelson that a "total destruction of the criminal's personality" is the only cure for criminal deviancy, Cleaver went on to state his own new prison politics: "I believe nothing short of Christian conversion can truly reshape and redirect the professional gangster."[37] Cleaver's decision to maneuver his formerly radical prison person into the Christian evangelical fold by means of this book just before his impending trial did not endear him to what little remained of the Bay Area Left. Appeals for donations to a Cleaver Defense Fund fell on deaf ears. It didn't help matters any that the defendant now personally closed his letters of appeal for financial support with the words,

> Yours In the Precious Keep
> of Jesus Christ Our Lord
> and Savior,
>   Eldridge Cleaver[38]

Of *Soul on Fire* a reviewer for the *Los Angeles Times* would write that "the story doesn't wash, and I suspect Cleaver knows it. . . . His conversion to Christianity . . . begins with . . . a scene so palpably false it defies criticism."[39]

But Cleaver had better friends. Perhaps the most powerful religious leader in California at the time, Robert H. Schuller, made a personal appeal for Cleaver's pardon. Like Jerry Falwell, Schuller had invited Cleaver to speak at a Sunday telecast aired on more than 150 television stations in the United States, Australia, and Canada. The show had been a resounding success. Ruth Stapleton had happened to see it and requested a videotape of the program to show to her brother, President Jimmy Carter. In a February 1977 letter to Governor Edmund G. Brown, Jr., Schuller wrote:

February 16, 1977

Dear Governor Brown:

I have fond memories of the dinner we shared as we sat around the table at the Balboa Bay Club a few months ago. Now, I am writing to you to make my first request ever to a governor or prominent elected official. . . .

The purpose of this letter is to respectfully request that you grant Eldridge Cleaver a pardon. So many years have elapsed since the alleged crime that one might question whether in fact authentic truth could be uncovered.

And, unquestionably, the Eldridge Cleaver who was involved in the act for which he is now to be tried is not the same Eldridge Cleaver who is alive today. Unquestionably, he is a *new* person and a *different* person.

Respectfully and sincerely yours,
Robert H. Schuller[40]

Cleaver's decision to cast himself in the image of the Penitent Thief, to bear the brand of rehabilitation and become a model treatment-era regenerated convict, may or may not have been sincere. But it was a wise choice. By the late 1970's prisoners could no longer successfully argue that the system was wrong. The struggle for the prisoner's self had been won by the Right. And for Cleaver, the penitent pose worked. In granting the repatriated Cleaver his freedom on condition of five years' probation, Judge Winton McKibben in 1980 expressed his conviction that the prisoner had made "a change for the better."[41]

After Cleaver, what voice might the San Quentin inmate choose to take on? For the moment, it would be best for California prisoners to learn from Cleaver's example. Even now, long after the dust of the prison movement has settled and the California New Left is in its grave, those on the powerful Right are still embittered by the memory of the handful of prisoner rights victories. As crime rates continue to soar, the state seeks solutions that have failed for 200 years. Prospects for even moderate prison reform are dim, and California prisoners have fallen warily silent.

In California, despite the persistence in some quarters of the rhetoric of rehabilitation (as at the final Cleaver trial), all that is left of convict reform through reading and writing is a brazen attempt at near total repression of reading and writing. In the early 1980's at San Quentin the communication crackdown went forward, with more education classes eliminated, more teachers released, and additional guards hired in their place.[42] In 1981 prison authorities were forced to admit that two of the attorney-client visiting rooms were bugged.[43] And in 1982 Warden Reginald Pulley suspended publication of the inmate-written *San Quentin News* after it had attempted to print an article on capital punishment that he had censored.[44] That same year the Department of Corrections put an abrupt end to inmate newspapers at all California prisons. Only protests from the ACLU and California legislators brought the department to reverse its decision and begrudgingly to allow the papers to resume publication, providing rigid censorship guidelines were observed.[45] By devices such as this, throughout the 1980's the voice of the California inmate remained firmly the property of the prison keepers.

And there were to be many more silent prisoners in California. All across the nation in the 1980's, while spending on an unneeded military buildup rocketed out of sight, funding for programs that might have improved the quality of life for America's underclass dwindled to nothing. What was California's response to the social disintegration that ensued? California doubled the number of its prisons in the 1980's. Funding for the state prison system soared 359 percent from 1982 to 1990. In the decade from 1980 to 1990 the percentage of the state's population in prison tripled. In its stern resolve to put all lawbreakers behind bars, California leads the nation. And yet there has been no slowdown in the rate of crime in the Golden State. Even in spite of this phenomenal failure of its prisons either to deter or reform, the state is engaged in "the largest prison construction program ever attempted by any governmental entity." [46] For small-town Chambers of Commerce throughout the dusty California hinterlands, the Department of Corrections now publishes an attractive four-color brochure: "California State Prisons—Good Neighbors, Good Employers, Good Community Partners." [47] And the prisons continue to blossom everywhere, the small town's dream come true of guaranteed full employment in harsh economic times—in Corcoran, Madera, Wasco, Delano, Chowchilla—in a hundred California backwater towns, where the underclass can be put to crop and become more silenced voices in the California carceral fold.

In December 1989, near the California-Oregon border at Crescent City, the California Department of Corrections unveiled its premier, state-of-the-art "maxi-maxi" secret weapon, a bleak gray concrete high-tech prison referred to as the prison of the future. At a cost to the taxpayers of a quarter of a billion dollars, Pelican Bay State Prison was built to house 2,080 prisoners. It is already overcrowded. More "maxi-maxi" prisons are planned or under construction in California and across the nation. The centerpiece of this new prison, the Security Housing Unit (SHU), is designed to warehouse the "worst of the worst" among California inmates. Surprisingly, this refers not to the heinousness of the inmate's original crime but to his disciplinary record while in prison. Pelican Bay is a prison designed to quell inmate anarchy inside the corrections system. Historically, the prison would appear to be a nightmarish fulfillment of CCOA president Moe Comacho's and Governor Reagan's 1971–72 calls for special high-security prisons for revolutionary inmates. In a supreme twist of irony, the space-age dungeons are actually modeled on the Adjustment Center, a place originally designed, it was said, to deliver intensified treat-ment. Here at last is the AC stripped of its pretense of rehabilitation. Though the "troublemakers" the new prison houses are said to be prison gang members and those who have assaulted guards or other prisoners, interviews conducted with 54 inmates in October 1991 by the Pelican Bay Information Project, a group loosely affiliated with the California Prisoners' Union, reveal that the population of the SHU also includes jailhouse lawyers, political activists, and those simply found "associating" with gang members.[48]

In a stark departure from the treatment prison of the past, this new institution has been designed expressly to minimize human con-tact, turning the men who most need to learn to be humane further away from humanity and the world. Half of Pelican Bay's roughly 2,000 inmates sit absolutely idle in windowless cells behind thick, steel-plated doors in the SHU for 22.5 hours a day. They are moni-tored by electronic surveillance and rarely see even the face of a guard. The full effects of this sensory deprivation imprisonment are yet to be felt, but preliminary reports are troubling. The California public should consider well the end product of this new form of im-prisonment, given that some 90 percent of convicts will one day be paroled back to the state's streets. With the commitment to rehabili-tation taken out of the California prison system, only a dangerous remnant of the treatment model remains, a valueless behavior modi-fication of sorts, intended merely to break "bad" convicts. It is as if at Pelican Bay the bankrupt end of the road for the treatment-era prison had been reached, now thoroughly stripped of its belief in convict reform and an instrument of pure, hostile coercion.

Behind the thick door to his cell the SHU inmate sits out his sen-tence. No human contact is allowed, no communal activities are per-mitted. Speech is possible only in whispers with the prisoner in an ad-joining cell. No wall decoration is permitted. No work is permitted. No hobbies are allowed to pass the time. No education class, religious wor-ship, counseling, or psychiatric care is available. Guards view the cell corridors from control booths and communicate with inmates through speakers. Doors are opened and closed by remote control. At meal-times a tray of food is passed through the cell door. Once a day the prisoner is strip-searched, handcuffed, and bellycuffed, then escorted by two guards to the "dog walk," a bare concrete yard without sports equipment, toilet, or water, where he may exercise alone. Pelican Bay prison's SHU cells are places of pure psychological destruction. When he was asked to comment on the new prison, even one of the correction system's own, former San Quentin associate warden James Park, confesses, "It is not a hallmark of a civilized, humane system."[49]

The California Department of Corrections claims that Pelican Bay is reducing violence in the prisons. That remains to be seen, though there are early indications that the prison may actually be having exactly the opposite effect. Inside the prisons, violence continues and at times appears to have worsened. Though the official Department of Corrections figure on assaults on staff shows a drop of 6 percent from 1988 to 1990,[50] fighting among inmates has not abated. In fact, the B yard at Pelican Bay, where SHU inmates are released into the general prison population before parole to the streets, is renowned throughout the system as the "sticking yard." Guards interviewed in the summer of 1992 report close to a stabbing a day in this yard.[51] This is happening for a reason. The only way to get out of the SHU is to "debrief," or name names of inmates in the gangs. SHU prisoners are told the only way they can get out is to debrief or die. Because any inmate coming out of the Pelican Bay SHU onto B yard or into any of the other prisons is automatically suspected of having "snitched," retaliatory strikes on these inmates have skyrocketed. The prison gangs have also learned to turn the SHU into their own superweapon. Gang members in the SHU name enemies who are not truly gang members to get them sent to the Pelican Bay SHU. Or they name someone they *want* in the gang who has been resisting them. After he has a "gang jacket," he has little choice but to join. Not just a place of state torture, then, the SHU has also become a sinister weapon of gang recruitment and revenge.

Much of the violence in our prisons, now as in the past, is perpetrated by uncontrolled gangs of guards. Some degree of physical force may be necessary at times to subdue or restrain a violent prisoner, but guards should be kept within strict, professional limits on the amount of force to be used and the situations in which it is called for. A class action suit filed on behalf of Pelican Bay SHU inmates in San Francisco's U.S. District Court charges the prison with the abuse of guard force.[52]

Prison guards are alleged to have beaten inmates. A team of usually six to eight guards in combat gear with face visors and riot shields has regularly entered the cells of inmates for "cell extractions," sometimes for the mere offense of the inmate's refusal to return his dinner tray. These guard teams have "extracted" prisoners using taser stun guns and weapons that fire rubber bullets, wood blocks, and gas. One infraction alleged in the suit occurred when prisoner Michael Contreras asked for new batteries for his hearing aid. SHU guards refused, then brutally beat him for failing to obey orders he didn't hear. When prisoner Alejandro Madrid clanged on his cell door to complain of a lack of law materials, the suit also claims, he and four other inmates were shackled in the fetal position for 22 hours.

The prison is also alleged to have denied medical care to prisoners. Despite his cries for medical help, the complaint continues, prisoner Bernard Hughes's burst appendix went untreated for days, until he almost died of gangrene.

These abuses are not slipups at Pelican Bay SHU, the class action suit alleges. This is a prison that was designed on a principle of grossly inhumane treatment. Prisoners on "sheet restriction" routinely get no bedding. Those on "cup restriction" cannot drink. Inmates left in their cells with their hands cuffed behind their backs must lap up food from their plates like dogs.[53]

Reports of physical abuse at Pelican Bay are also appearing in the local press. In the summer of 1992 the *Sacramento Bee* reported that a SHU prisoner was thrown fully shackled into a hot water bath, suffering third-degree burns.[54]

Not surprisingly, abuses are also alleged in the area of communication rights. Pelican Bay prisoners claim they are routinely denied lawful access to their attorneys and the courts. Legal mail is read by guards, use of the inadequate law library is severely limited, and telephone conversations with attorneys are monitored. It is a rule at Pelican Bay that no one may speak in the law library. One SHU convict said in an interview that he received a disciplinary write-up with heavy penalties "for asking a question" of another convict in the prison's law library.[55] Another said he had gotten a "115" disciplinary report, although he had not said anything, just for listening to another convict who was speaking in the law library. Another complained that SHU prisoners must sit in cages in the library. A self-professed jailhouse lawyer complained he had sent for but never received the local rules of court. Prisoner Larry Del Bucchia alleges that he looked on while a guard read a letter he had addressed to his attorney. Guards also failed to deliver to him an opinion on his appeal mailed to him by the court. Prison officials have also, he claims, demanded that he recount to them his conversations with attorneys.[56] Of opportunities for in-cell reading, Pelican Bay SHU prisoners have said they are permitted up to ten books or magazines but can get reading only from "a book cart that comes around every few weeks containing about half religious books." Newspapers are permitted, but local news items are censored out. Pelican Bay inmates are permitted in-cell televisions, provided they purchase them, but instead of local stations six Colorado ones are received, making it impossible to stay abreast of California news. Of supposedly private telephone conversations for non-SHU prisoners, one man stated that every time he complained about the prison by telephone his counselor talked to him about the complaints, quoting long sentences out of his conversations verbatim.[57]

What can be left of a prisoner after such treatment? From inmates who are paroled from Pelican Bay's SHU and future prisons like it we can expect only an increase in violent, irrational crimes. Inmates in the SHU are understandably developing severe psychiatric problems. Interviewers from the Pelican Bay Information Project reported after a visit to the prison in 1991 that some prisoners had smeared themselves with their own feces. Others had mutilated themselves or cried and shouted for hours. Some talked nonsensically.[58] Most of these prisoners will someday be paroled to our streets. In February 1992, a parolee who had been released the day before from Pelican Bay was arrested and charged with raping a young woman and viciously beating her with a tire iron in the East Bay near Berkeley. Before his Pelican Bay incarceration this prisoner had been a small-time car thief. After Pelican Bay he was a monster.[59]

We need prisons. We may even need special facilities to break up the gang system. But the Pelican Bay SHU is not meeting that goal. Prisoners are sent to prison for punishment, yes, but they should at least be treated like human beings while they are there. That means acknowledging that they have rudimentary rights. They should be guaranteed opportunities to get help as well—educational, counseling, and religious opportunities that stop well short of the coerced participation of the treatment era.

In the 1940's, 1950's, and 1960's, California's treatment-era prison was touted nationwide as a model plan for reformative incarceration. Visitors came from far and wide to witness the miracles of correction being worked on the lives of the Golden State's criminal class. But the treatment-era prison shared a vulnerability with the prison movement it spawned, which explains why the two died away roughly at the same time. One in particular of the California rehabilitative prison's many flaws proved fatal for both treatment imprisonment and the prison movement. In the treatment prison's view, the best way to change convict culture was through the force of ideas, by means of programs in counseling, bibliotherapy, religion, and education. The problem was that the California system believed it could work this miracle without at the same time substantially improving the material conditions of imprisonment or redressing inequities in its justice system. While the California treatment system privileged ideas inside the prison, it staunchly resisted any reforms in the labor and living conditions for inmates or in the terms of their sentencing and parole. In this way California treatment prisons privileged the ideal over the real. By doing so, the treatment prison, of course, was only being true to its origins in the idealism of the earliest American evangelical penology, which fed its convicts on a steady diet of Bible reading and urged them to publish conversion narratives. The logic of the California treatment era owed a considerable debt, too, to the medieval legal tradition of acknowledging a defendant's ability to read and to write as a proof of innocence, or at least immunity to state prosecution.

It should have been no surprise to anyone when both California prisoners and the public in the 1950's began adopting these same terms of the rehabilitative discourse and then turned them to their own use. Like their keepers, convict authors, beginning with Caryl Chessman, also privileged the ideal over the real and were able to convince readers that, regardless of the issue of their guilt or non-guilt, their sheer ability with words and ideas was powerful proof of their rehabilitation. This notion became the central, shared article of faith of the treatment-era prison, its inmates, and its adversary prison movement. It was also their common weakness. Prison writers were drawing more and more public acclaim. Some became lionized as local heroes. Increasingly as the movement progressed, celebrated convict writing formed its vital energizing center. Chessman was replaced by Cleaver, who was displaced by George Jackson. Soon the center of the movement sprang not so much from substantive attacks on specific material conditions of prison life such as those the Prisoners' Union made. Rather, the critique widened and became more abstract, encrusted in ideology, until in the minds of groups like the Symbionese Liberation Army and the Black Guerrilla Family the last abstractions of George Jackson's *Blood in My Eye* utterly abandoned the real for dangerous political fantasy.

Like the treatment-era prison, then, the prison movement seems to have failed because it privileged the ideal over the real, because its catalytic center became convict writing rather than organizing inmates around real, material issues. The California Prisoners' Union provided the single brief exception to this pattern. It is interesting to speculate what might have happened had the union produced a popular convict writer. But the union lacked a charismatic prison author; it lacked a convict text that might have interwoven its calls for specific, practical, material changes at the prison with themes California readers seem in the period to have wanted discussed. This book might have been one that took up and developed in some compelling way the trope of the outlaw, a crucial topic for Bay Area counterculture readers in the 1960's. It might also have attempted to provide its readers with an alternative male role model, in the way that convict writing provided in the supremely vengeant convict a psychosexual model of male masculinity for its middle-class white readers. And it might have given its readers a new movement hero, a union organizer, perhaps, rather than a suicidal guerrilla warrior. Above all else, it would have downplayed ideology and kept a firm, pragmatic focus on practical changes badly needed in the material conditions of California imprisonment. It is tempting to conclude that, if the union had had such a voice and such a text, it might have regained the center of the movement and brought both the Right and the Left from their ideological squabbles back to consideration of real conditions inside California's prisons. Imagining further, if the extreme Left might then have been convinced to put aside its reductionist two-class model of the American state and the extreme Right been persuaded to put aside its red-baiting, a more rational path to a just prison might have been found. Unfortunately, that did not happen.

So, now, with the treatment era a part of the past, the prison movement in its grave, and prison unionism a lost cause, what can we expect from California's cruel new prisons?

We should remain aware of at least two facts. First, since the early 1960's California's ethnic minority inmates, primarily black and Chicano convicts, have *reversed* the race domination pattern of the American culture at large by coming to control the prison yard and also, crucially, covert prison education inside. Thus the state prisons have become minority-dominated enclaves and universities of the poor. Political organizing and gang activity apparently continue to be possible among inmates even at the highest security levels of these prisons, even at Pelican Bay. The upcoming trial in Santa Clara County of 21 members of La Nuestra Familia on multiple charges of conspiracy to commit murder, extortion, and other crimes should reveal how true this is. The grand jury indictment in the case alleges that coded messages, including hit lists, have been passed from gang leaders inside the highest security cells at Pelican Bay to gang members on the streets. If this is revealed to be true, we can conclude that covert inmate organizing goes on even in "maxi-maxi" prisons. Second, we should take it as a principle that the crueler California prisons get, the more violent the prison yard will likely become, and the more violent prisoners will be when they are finally released to the public streets. Taking into account both these factors, we can expect California's unprecedented boom of prison construction and skyrocketing rate of incarceration to produce, even in high-tech "maxi-maxi" prisons, more, not less, covert political and gang education and organizing among the ethnic minority underclasses. This will mean more outbreaks of violence against the state, possibly in the form of organized domestic terrorism directed outward from the prisons. Now as in the 1960's and 1970's, despite sharp increases in suppression and control of reading at San Quentin and other California prisons, many underclass California prisoners continue to attain their literary skills and political ideology from smuggled, nonelite texts in covert study groups, largely subverting the state's attempts to achieve ideological-moral domination through prison education. As a result, the tremendous expansion of the use of imprisonment in California is likely to bring more, not less, class antagonism into an already deeply fissured social order.

What will the California culture's response be to a new wave of prison revolution? Will Californians finally have the compassion and the common sense to seek real, lasting reforms in their prison and criminal justice systems? Will they this time keep their focus on the real prison and the real prisoners? And how will the texts of convict writers, sure to be again swept into the powerful discourses of opposing groups outside the prison, function in the crisis? The goal of lasting prison reform still eludes us. We should be mindful, as the fires spread outward from our prisons into the California ghettos, to resist this time the mistake made in the 1960's of revering ordinary street criminals as revolutionary freedom fighters. Some observers, dredging up the old, failed language of the 1960's, have already begun to refer to the Los Angeles riot of 1992 as an antistate rebellion. Its looters, murderers, arsonists, and brawlers, they whisper, are our front-line warriors. To go down that path once more is a serious mistake. Despite the obvious injustices and horrible conditions of life in the ghettos of Los Angeles and in other pockets of racism and poverty across California, it is just plain dangerous to call street crime political crime, making street criminals automatically antistate revolutionaries. California convicts of the 1990's will be only too easily convinced to see themselves as guerrilla heroes. Sadly, if it comes to that, these California prisoners will likely become ideological pawns in another cultural crossfire, this time perhaps in a race and class war of which they will be the first victims.

REFERENCE MATTER

Notes

Chapter 1

1. Quoted in *San Francisco Chronicle*, Aug. 21, 1950.
2. For an overview of 1950's-era intellectual repression at California universities, see Rorabaugh.
3. For a good treatment of America's first penitentiary—Philadelphia's Walnut Street Jail—touching on the subject of language management and communication control, see Meranze. More generally, on the topic of early American prisons and asylums as instruments of social control, see Rothman, *Discovery of the Asylum*; Masur; and Alexander. For a general treatment of the history of penal reform, see Eriksson. For a view of the prison against the background of evangelical Protestantism and the benevolent society movement, see Griffin.
4. Rush, *Medical Inquiries*, p. 124. For a discussion of Benjamin Rush's prison reform efforts and language management in early Pennsylvania prisons, see Cummins.
5. See Williams; Slotkin; and Weimerskirch.
6. Wines, pp. 102–3.
7. See Foucault.
8. For a short history of prison education programs, see Roberts.
9. See Sullivan. See also Coyle; MacCormick; and Roberts.
10. For a discussion of the earliest development of the convict reform movement in California, see Bookspan. A general treatment of the history of San Quentin can be found in Lamott.
11. California legislative committee report of 1861, quoted in Lamott, p. 113.
12. Quoted in Lamott, p. 114.
13. Quoted in Mitford, p. 33.
14. Duffy, p. 250.
15. Ibid., pp. 217–18.
16. Foucault, pp. 16, 19.
17. Filreis, p. 307.

18. See U.S. Congress, Committee on Un-American Activities.

19. Chambers, p. 21.

20. California Department of Corrections, Classification Bureau.

21. California Department of Corrections (ca. 1946), quoted in Yee, p. 7.

22. Quoted in Lamott, p. 199.

23. See Flynn.

24. See, for example, Cloward and Ohlin; and Merton.

25. Quoted by Gene Kassenbaum, David N. Ward, and Danile Wilner, *Prison Treatment and Parole Survival*, p. 59, cited in Berkman, p. 27.

26. Quoted in Mitford, p. 100.

27. James Park, int., Feb. 1989.

28. Berkman, p. 70.

29. Ibid., p. 61.

30. Louis Nelson, int., Apr. 1989.

31. Byron Eshelman, telephone int., June 1989.

32. Herman Spector died in 1988 before he could be interviewed. Edna Spector, his widow, provided this information in an interview, January 1989.

33. California Penal Code, Section 5075, quoted in Davidson, p. 37.

34. Henry W. Kerr, chairman, California Adult Authority, in U.S. Congress, House of Representatives, Committee on the Judiciary, p. 30.

35. Ibid., pp. 130, 131–32.

36. Walter Burckhard, quoted in Minton, p. 145.

37. Anonymous San Quentin inmate in the *San Francisco Chronicle*, Feb. 25, 1971.

38. Minton, p. 319.

39. Joe Morse, int., Jan. 1989.

40. Irwin, *Prisons in Turmoil*, p. 64.

41. On Malcolm X's reading and prison education, see Malcolm X, chap. 10, "Satan."

42. See U.S. Congress, Select Committee on Crime.

43. Berkman, p. 39.

Chapter 2

1. Floch, p. 454.

2. Quoted in American Prison Association, pp. 453–55.

3. C. V. Morrison, quoted in ibid., p. 466; James A. Quinn quoted in ibid., p. 471.

4. Floch, p. 454.

5. California Department of Corrections, *Director's Rules*.

6. Braly, p. 297.

7. *Ruffin v. Commonwealth*, 62 Va. (21 Gratt.) 790, 796 (1871).

8. Cal. Pen. Code Sec. 673, 674 (Deering), 1886.

9. 1919 Cal. Stat. c. 28.

10. Cal. Pen. Code Sec. 2600–2601 (Deering), 1949.

11. American Prison Association, Committee on Institution Libraries, pp. 106–7.

12. Spector, "Library Program of the California State Department of Corrections," p. 10.

13. Spector, "Men and Books."

14. Spector, "The Prison Librarian's Responsibility to the Public Library."

15. Spector, comp., "Reading Is the Key."

16. Spector, "Public Library Aspects of the Prison Library," pp. 11–12.

17. Spector, "Library Program of the California State Department of Corrections," pp. 8–9.

18. Spector, comp., "Reading Is the Key."

19. Ibid.

20. Unfortunately, these individual inmate reading and writing records and files and much of Herman Spector's own writings were destroyed when he retired from his post as prison librarian in 1967. The little that remains of Spector's voluminous data on San Quentin readers and writers is in the possession of his widow, Edna Spector.

21. Spector, comp., "Reading Is the Key."

22. Spector, "Library Statistics," p. 84.

23. Ibid., p. 89, quoting from Paul Wiers, "Economic Factors in Michigan Delinquency."

24. Spector, "Library Statistics," pp. 90–91.

25. California Department of Corrections, *Institutional Libraries*.

26. Spector, "Library Program of the California State Department of Corrections," p. 11.

27. Spector, "Men and Books."

28. Spector, ". . . Nor Iron Bars a Cage."

29. Spector, comp., "Reading Is the Key."

30. Spector, ". . . Nor Iron Bars a Cage," p. 106.

31. Joe Morse, int., Jan. 1989.

32. Spector, comp., "Reading Is the Key."

33. Braly, pp. 157, 246, 252, 258, 307.

34. Ibid., p. 307.

35. Ibid., p. 314.

Chapter 3

1. Louis Nelson, int., Apr. 1989. Subsequent quotes from Louis Nelson are from this interview.

2. Freeman, pp. 38–39.

3. Eshelman, p. 189.

4. Ibid., p. 96.

5. Anonymous Death Row inmate, quoted in Freeman, p. 138.

6. Eshelman, pp. 96–97.

7. Chessman, quoted in ibid., p. 192.

8. Louis Nelson int.

9. Freeman, pp. 168, 167.

10. Chessman, quoted in Eshelman, p. 188.

11. Louis Nelson int.

12. Leibert, p. 147.

13. *San Francisco Chronicle*, May 2, 1954.

14. Negley K. Teeters, quoted in "I'm All Ready. . . ," *Newsweek*, May 24, 1954, p. 28; *New York Herald Tribune Book Review*, May 2, 1954, p. 11; *New York Times*, May 2, 1954, p. 28; *Kirkus*, 22 (Apr. 1, 1954): 257.

15. Quoted in "Proud Author at Quentin . . . ," *San Francisco Chronicle*, Apr. 20, 1954.

16. Joe Morse, int., Jan. 1989.

17. Chessman, *Cell 2455*, p. 359.

18. Freeman, p. 178.

19. Quoted in Chessman, *Trial by Ordeal*, p. 45.

20. Ibid., pp. 251–52.

21. Quoted in "State Bars All Death Row Authorship," *San Francisco Chronicle*, Aug. 15, 1954.

22. Morse int.

23. "Chessman Tells About New Book," *San Francisco Chronicle*, Nov. 14, 1954.

24. Louis Nelson int.

25. Eshelman, p. 199.

26. Louis Nelson int.

27. Braly, p. 299.

28. Louis Nelson int.

29. *New York Herald Tribune Book Review*, July 10, 1955, p. 9.

30. "Caryl Chessman's Second Book, *Trial by Ordeal*," *San Francisco Chronicle*, July 17, 1955.

31. Chessman, *Trial by Ordeal*, p. 92.

32. Braly, p. 300.

33. Petition for Writ of Prohibition, No. 26355, Bart Caritativo, Caryl Chessman, and Robert Pierce, by their next best friend, George T. Davis, Petitioners, vs. Harley O. Teets, Louis Nelson, and Doe One through Doe Ten, Respondents, in the Superior Court of the State of California, County of Marin, filed Oct. 11, 1955, Marin County Courthouse.

34. *San Francisco Chronicle*, Dec. 22, 1955.

35. Chessman, *Face of Justice*, p. 110.

36. Petition for Writ of Habeas Corpus, No. 28118, Caryl Chessman, in the Superior Court of the State of California, County of Marin, filed Feb. 20, 1957, Marin County Courthouse.

37. Louis Nelson int.

38. "Prison Escapade: Chessman Defiant About Smuggling," *San Francisco Chronicle*, Feb. 22, 1957. See also "Futile Plea by Chessman Smuggled Out," ibid., Feb. 21, 1957.

39. "Prison Escapade," see n. 38.

40. Complaint No. 26183, Rosalie S. Asher, individually and on behalf of

Caryl Chessman, plaintiff, vs. Richard A. McGee, Director of the Department of Corrections of the State of California; Harley O. Teets, Warden of the California State Prison at San Quentin; Louis Nelson, Associate Warden, defendants, in the Superior Court of the State of California, County of Marin, filed March 12, 1957, Marin County Courthouse.

41. "Warden Refuses to Give Papers to Chessman" and "Some Seized Papers Go Back to Chessman," *San Francisco Chronicle*, Apr. 10, 11, 1957.

42. "3rd Manuscript: Chessman's Book Turns Up," *San Francisco Chronicle*, Mar. 3, 1957.

43. Eshelman, p. 200. See also "Exclusive Report: Chessman Tells How He Wrote His Banned Book," *San Francisco Chronicle*, Aug. 5, 1957.

44. Chessman, *Face of Justice*, pp. 249–251.

45. Ibid., p. 250.

46. Morse int.

47. Freeman, pp. 172–73.

48. Quoted in "Death Row Smuggling: Quentin Staff Takes Lie Tests on Chessman," *San Francisco Chronicle*, Apr. 14, 1957.

49. *New York Times*, Oct. 6, 1957, p. 35.

50. *Saturday Review* 40 (Oct. 5, 1957): 32.

51. "San Quentin Report: Death Row Guards Moved," *San Francisco Chronicle*, Mar. 8, 1957.

52. Quoted in "Death Row Smuggling: Quentin Staff Takes Lie Tests on Chessman," *San Francisco Chronicle*, Apr. 14, 1957.

53. Interview with Caryl Chessman, in Eshelman, p. 197.

54. Biskind and Ehrenreich, pp. 201–15.

55. Kerouac, p. 11.

56. See Warshow.

57. Quoted in *San Francisco Chronicle*, Feb. 18, 1960, p. 1.

58. Quoted in "A Calm Chessman Says Good-by," *San Francisco Chronicle*, Feb. 18, 1960.

59. "Chessman Movie Opens—'Objective,'" *San Francisco Chronicle*, Feb. 23, 1960.

60. "New Folk Song—'Chessman Ballad,'" *San Francisco Chronicle*, Feb. 24, 1960.

61. *New Republic*, 142 (Mar. 28, 1960): 3–4; *Nation*, 190 (Mar. 26, 1960): front cover and following editorial.

62. Caryl Chessman, "Letter from Death Row," reprinted in *Psychology Today*, 2 (Feb. 1969): 39–41.

63. "Chessman Still Talking About Future Books," *San Francisco Chronicle*, Apr. 30, 1960.

64. For a general discussion of the worldwide movement to save Chessman, see Freeman, pp. 190–92.

65. Eshelman, pp. 70, 187–88.

66. Louis Nelson int.

67. Rossman, p. 42.

68. George T. Davis, quoted on "Crimes of the Century: Caryl Chessman,

The Redlight Bandit," produced by Don Ohlmeyer OCC Productions, ABC, Los Angeles, 1987–88.

69. Quoted on ibid.

70. Quoted in the *San Francisco Chronicle*, May 3, 1960.

71. Rossman, p. 41.

72. Irwin, *Prisons in Turmoil*, p. 43.

73. Rossman, p. 44.

74. H. R. Kaye, *A Place in Hell* (London: New English Library, 1972), quoted in Harris, pp. 13–14.

75. Ken Kesey, quoted in Leeds, p. 8.

Chapter 4

1. Byron Eshelman, quoted in "Chessman's Ironic Quentin Legacy," *San Francisco Chronicle*, Jan. 23, 1967.

2. Marable, p. 60.

3. California Department of Corrections, *Summary Statistics of Prisoners and Parolees*, 1951–80.

4. California Department of Corrections, *Characteristics of Resident Population of California State Prisons by Institutions*, 1948–80.

5. Fox, p. 3.

6. Staples, p. 18.

7. See Pope.

8. Staples, p. 18, citing a report by Evelle Younger, attorney general of California, quoted in the *Los Angeles Sentinel*, Aug. 10, 1972, p. A2.

9. McNeely and Pope, p. 13.

10. Koch and Clarke, pp. 84, 87.

11. See Staples, p. 20.

12. From Stuart Nagel, "The Legal Process from a Behavioral Perspective," cited in Staples, p. 20.

13. See Carroll and Mondrick.

14. Charles Garry, int., June 1989.

15. Marable, pp. 20, 29, 47.

16. Harlan Washington, int., summer 1989.

17. Malcolm X, p. 169.

18. Harlan Washington, int., fall 1989.

19. Cleaver, "Prisons: The Muslims' Decline," in Browning, pp. 100–103.

20. Interview with Lawrence Bennet, Sacramento, Sept. 1975, in Berkman, p. 52.

21. William Hankins, int., summer 1989. Subsequent quotes from Hankins are from this interview.

22. "Segregated Dining Ends at San Quentin," *San Francisco Chronicle*, Mar. 8, 1960.

23. "San Quentin 'Adjustment Center' Open," *San Francisco Chronicle*, Aug. 16, 1960.

24. Cleaver, "Prisons: The Muslims' Decline," in Browning, p. 100.

25. *San Francisco Chronicle*, Aug. 23, 1963.

26. Ibid., Feb. 26, 1963.

27. Ibid., Feb. 27, 1963.

28. "Writ Refused for Black Muslim Rites," *San Francisco Chronicle*, Mar. 7, 1963.

29. "New Muslim Outbreak at Quentin" and "Ten More Black Muslims in Isolation at SQ," *San Francisco Chronicle*, Aug. 5 and 7, 1963.

30. *San Francisco Chronicle*, Aug. 11, 1965.

31. "Muslim Religion OKd for Prisoners," *San Francisco Chronicle*, July 9, 1970.

32. Cleaver, quoted in John Pallas and Robert Barber, "From Riot to Revolution," in Wright, p. 245.

33. Cleaver, "Prisons: The Muslims' Decline," in Browning, p. 103.

34. 1959 Cal. Stat. c. 1473.

35. William Malin, former San Quentin teacher, int., spring 1989. Subsequent quotes from Malin are from this interview.

36. Keith Hayball, former San Quentin music instructor (1956–61), then education administrator, int., spring 1989. Subsequent quotes from Hayball are from this interview.

37. Anonymous former San Quentin instructor, int., summer 1989.

38. Robert Minton, int., summer 1989.

39. Spector, ". . . Nor Iron Bars a Cage," pp. 107–8.

40. Ibid., pp. 113–14.

41. Ibid., pp. 114–15.

42. *San Francisco Chronicle*, Oct. 29, 1963.

43. Ibid., Apr. 29, 1964.

44. See Larsen.

45. "Con Lawyers Bloom All Over Quentin," *San Francisco Examiner*, Jan. 16, 1966.

46. Ibid.

47. "Convicts' Plea for Law Books," *San Francisco Chronicle*, Oct. 28, 1966.

48. "Jail Lawyers Get Reprieve for Books," *San Francisco Chronicle*, Mar. 15, 1967.

49. *California Department of Corrections Rules*, Chapter II, article 6, Rule D-2601 (1967).

50. Larsen, p. 348.

51. Ibid., p. 358.

52. Spector, "A Prison Librarian Looks at Writ-Writing," p. 367.

53. Quoted in "A 'Golden Era': Quentin Literary Scene," *San Francisco Chronicle*, Nov. 15, 1967.

54. Hankins int.

55. Joe Morse, int., Spring 1989.

56. Officer Phillip Carter, quoted in *San Francisco Chronicle*, Dec. 6, 1961.

57. Davidson, pp. 14–15.

58. California Department of Corrections *Administrative Manual*, quoted in Mitford, pp. 204–5.

59. LeDonne, p. 46.

60. Blue Ribbon Committee, p. 11.

61. Fred Persily, former San Quentin assistant librarian, int., summer 1989.

62. Terry Cuddy, int., fall 1989.

63. James McHenry, int., spring 1989. Subsequent quotes from McHenry are from this interview.

64. Quoted in the *San Francisco Chronicle*, Jan. 19, 1967.

65. Anonymous San Quentin Nazi inmate, quoted in the *San Francisco Chronicle*, Jan. 21, 1967.

66. Anonymous black San Quentin inmate, in a letter to teacher Robert Minton, late 1960's, in possession of Robert Minton.

67. Davidson, p. 167. The author was a University of California, Berkeley, anthropology student doing inmate interviews at the time of the disturbance. For his account of the incident, see pp. 164–68.

68. Anonymous inmate, quoted in Davidson, p. 167.

69. Stang, pp. 25–40.

70. John Irwin, int., fall 1988. For a brief treatment of the 1967 incident, see Irwin, *Prisons in Turmoil*, pp. 85–86. For a detailed retelling of the disturbance from the viewpoint of a black inmate, see G. Saladin, "Racism III," in Minton, pp. 96–111.

Chapter 5

1. Berkman, pp. 2–3.

2. Harlan Washington, int., summer 1989.

3. Cleaver, *Soul on Fire*, p. 74.

4. Cleaver, "Prisons: The Muslims' Decline," in Browning, pp. 100–103.

5. Breitman, p. 20.

6. Ibid., p. 31.

7. Ibid., p. 33.

8. Louis Nelson, int., April 1989.

9. Marine, p. 52.

10. Quoted in Jacobs.

11. Scheer, p. ix.

12. Geismar, in Cleaver, *Soul on Ice*, p. 9; Cleaver, ibid., pp. 16–19, 12–14.

13. Ibid., pp. 164, 181, 175, 167, 185, 181, 177, 154, 161.

14. This term is Charles Perry's. Material for the following paragraphs on the Haight-Ashbury and Bay Area communes is drawn, in large part, from his *Haight-Ashbury: A History*, and from the *Berkeley Barb*, the *San Francisco Oracle*, and various other underground newspapers of the period.

15. Perry, p. 108.

16. Ibid., p. 147.

17. Ibid., p. 163.

18. Lavigne, p. 20.

19. Wolfe, p. 158.

20. Thompson, p. 313.

21. For the full text of Sonny Barger's telegram offering support to President Johnson, see Lavigne, pp. 33–34.

22. Lavigne, pp. 44–45.

23. The *Berkeley Barb*, Sept. 1–7, 1967.

24. Perry, pp. 114–16.

25. *Berkeley Tribe*, Aug. 15–21, 1969.

26. Leamer, p. 112.

27. Quoted in Leamer, p. 49.

28. George Paul Csicsery, "Stones Concert Ends It: America Now Up for Grabs," *Berkeley Tribe*, Dec. 12–19, 1969.

29. Berkeley Commune, "An Open Letter to the Prophets and Their Apostles."

30. Fred Gordon, "Politics of Violence," *New Left Notes*, Sept. 23, 1968, in Unger, p. 166.

31. Cleaver, *Soul on Fire*, p. 80.

32. Anonymous inmate, int., fall 1989.

33. John Spain, int., summer 1989.

34. Nate Harrington, int., spring 1989.

35. For a discussion of the Panthers' "armed invasion" of California's capitol, see Marine, pp. 62–65.

36. Huey Newton, "The Correct Handling of a Revolution," *Black Panther*, May 4, 1968.

37. *Black Panther*, July 3, 1967.

38. In Scheer, pp. 18–20.

39. Nate Harrington, int., summer 1989.

40. *Berkeley Barb*, Nov. 4, 1966.

41. Ibid., Feb. 25, 1967.

42. "Mobilization Just a Schizoid Scene," *Berkeley Barb*, Apr. 21–27, 1967.

43. Huey Newton, as quoted by Marine, p. 40.

44. Exhibit F, filed in *Black Panther Party* v. *Donald C. Alexander, Commissioner of the IRS*, No. C-74-1247 (N.D. Cal. 1974).

45. Quoted in U.S. Congress, Senate, p. 187.

46. *Newsweek*, Feb. 1969, quoted in Newton, p. 12.

47. See Newton.

48. In Minton, pp. 154–55.

49. Ted Davidson, telephone int., fall 1989.

50. Ernie Bradford, int., winter 1989.

51. Joe Morse, int., Jan. 1989.

52. *San Francisco Chronicle*, Sept. 26, 1967.

53. See Minton and Rice.

54. Davidson int.

55. "From the Inside Out: The Truth About San Quentin," *Berkeley Barb*, Jan. 26–Feb. 1, 1968.

56. "At San Quentin: 700 Cons Strike," *Berkely Barb*, Feb. 16–22, 1968.

57. Davidson int.

58. Ibid.

59. For a more detailed discussion of this strike, see Davidson, pp. 184–88. See also Irwin, *Prisons in Turmoil*, pp. 86–87.

60. *Berkeley Barb*, Feb. 23–29, 1968.

61. In Minton, pp. 16–17.

62. *Berkeley Barb*, Mar. 1–7, 1968.

63. For coverage of the Peace and Freedom party convention, see the *Berkeley Barb*, Mar. 16–22, 1968.

64. From Eldridge Cleaver, Affidavit #1, taken at Vacaville Medical Facility following the parolee's April 6, 1968, shootout with Oakland police, in Scheer, pp. 3–10.

65. Ibid., in Scheer, p. 7.

66. Charles Garry, int., June 1989.

67. *Berkeley Barb*, Apr. 12–18, 1968.

68. For an example, see "Police Shooting of Oakland Negro," letter to the editor, *New York Times*, May 1, 1968.

69. "Letter from McGraw Hill Book Company" and "From Bertrand Russell," Apr. 18, 1968, reproduced on handbill "Getting Eldridge Cleaver."

70. "Prison Decision: Cleaver Running for President," *San Francisco Chronicle*, May 14, 1968.

71. *Saturday Evening Post*, Nov. 11, 1968.

72. "San Quentin and You: Cons Cry for Help," *Berkeley Barb*, July 12–18, 1968.

73. *Berkeley Barb*, July 19–25, 1968.

74. Davidson, int.

75. John Irwin, int., fall 1988.

76. Fred Persily, int., summer 1989.

77. *Berkeley Barb*, Aug. 2–8, 1968.

78. *San Francisco Chronicle*, Aug. 3, 1968.

79. Working paper of the California Department of Corrections, Dec. 1968, in possession of James Park.

80. "A Rights Group for San Quentin," *San Francisco Chronicle*, Aug. 3, 1968.

81. *Berkeley Barb*, Aug. 16–22, 1968.

82. Ibid.

83. Ibid., Oct. 4–10, 1968.

84. Ibid., Oct. 11–18, 1968.

85. Quoted in Pell, p. 13.

86. *Berkeley Barb*, Nov. 29–Dec. 5, 1968.

Chapter 6

1. John Irwin, int., fall 1988.

2. Unidentified San Quentin convict, quoted in Minton, pp. 204–5. The reference is to case studies later published by John Irwin under the title *The Felon*.

3. Unidentified San Quentin convict, quoted in Minton, pp. 206–7.

4. For the Convict Grievance Report and a detailed discussion of it, see Minton, pp. 202–72.

5. See Chapter 2 for a discussion of the civil death statute.

6. Alan Sieroty, telephone int., May 23, 1989.

7. 1968 Cal. Stat. c. 1402.

8. Rowan Klein, telephone int., May 28, 1989.

9. *Gilmore* v. *Lynch*, 319 F. Supp. 105 (N.D. Cal.), *Younger* v. *Gilmore*, 404 U.S. (1971).

10. *Van Geldern* v. *Eli*, 5 Cal. 3d 832, 489 P. 2d 578 (1971).

11. *Harrell* v. *McKinney*, 2 Cal. 3d 675, 470 P. 2d 640 (1970). For a summary of court cases relating to inmate reading and writing in California in the 1960's and 1970's, see LeDonne, pp. 80–88.

12. *Jordan* v. *Grady*, 7 Cal. 3d 930, 500 P. 2d 873 (1972), and *Jordan on Habeas Corpus*, 12 Cal. 3d 575, 526 P. 2d 523 (1974).

13. Wright, p. 85.

14. Stender, "Violence and Lawlessness at Soledad Prison," in Pell, p. 227.

15. *Los Angeles Free Press*, July 24, 1970.

16. Berkman, p. 9.

17. James McHenry, int., spring 1989.

18. James Park, int., Feb. 1989.

19. *San Francisco Chronicle*, Mar. 2, 1971.

20. U.S. Congress, House of Representatives, Committee on the Judiciary, p. 160.

21. Richard Nelson, int., spring 1989.

22. *San Francisco Examiner / Chronicle*, May 2, 1971.

23. Reproduced in Wright, pp. 96–97, and, in part, in *San Francisco Examiner / Chronicle*, May 2, 1971.

24. Richard Nelson, int., spring 1989.

25. See Wright, p. 134.

26. Nate Harrington, int., summer 1989.

27. Dorsey Nunn, int., summer 1989.

28. Anonymous former Soledad inmate, int., spring 1989.

29. John Spain, int., summer 1989.

30. For a history of California prison gangs and gang alliances, see Zinn. See also Kahn and Zinn.

31. Information on the educational department of La Nuestra Familia is from confiscated NF documents now in the personal papers of William Hankins, formerly of San Quentin's Special Investigations Unit.

32. Records of the Black Guerrilla Family education system, in possession of William Hankins.

33. Quoted in Marable, p. 107.

34. Julius Nyerere, from *Ujamaa: Essays on Socialism*, quoted in Marable, pp. 119–20.

35. Giovanni, p. 212.

36. Marable, p. 111.

37. Poll of Vietnam-era GIs conducted by Wallace Terry II, Vietnam correspondent for *Time*, published in the *San Francisco Chronicle*, June 30, 1970.

38. Cleaver, "An Aside to Ronald Reagan," Oct. 26, 1968, in Scheer, pp. 108–11.

39. Cleaver, *Soul on Fire*, pp. 101–2.

40. David McReynolds, letter to Eldridge Cleaver, July 31, 1968, Cleaver file, Data Center, Oakland, California.

41. Don A. Schanche, "Burn the Mother Down," *Saturday Evening Post*, Nov. 11, 1968.

42. Cleaver, "Playboy Interview with Nat Hentoff," Oct. 1968, in Scheer, p. 179.

43. See Drumgo.

44. Cleaver, "An Address on Prisons."

45. Cleaver, "Farewell Address."

46. "A Fugitive Voice Speaks Out," *Saturday Review*, Mar. 1, 1969.

47. Betsy Carr, "Afterword," in James Carr, p. 209.

48. Charles Garry, int., summer 1989.

49. Leamer, p. 59.

50. Unger, p. 182.

51. Information on the Beaty escape attempt was provided in personal interviews with John Irwin and former sergeant William Hankins of San Quentin's Special Investigations Unit, winter 1989. For a discussion of the escape attempt from the perspective of the radical Left, see Wald. For the state's version, see U.S. Congress, House of Representatives, Committee on Internal Security, pp. 76–79.

52. John Irwin, int., fall 1988.

53. Even after his death, few would discuss Huey Newton's darker side. One of the few printed sources for details on Newton's post-prison years is *This Side of Glory: The Autobiography of David Hilliard and the Story of the Black Panther Party*, by David Hilliard. Another, more opinionated and overly negative source is "Baddest," by Collier and Horowitz, pp. 141–167.

54. For a catalog of COINTELPRO actions against the Panthers, see Marable, pp. 124–25, 142–43.

55. Spain int.

56. A letter from "Black Dan," in possession of Robert Minton.

57. Cleaver, *Revolution and Education*.

Chapter 7

1. Marx, p. 109, quoted in Davis, Magee, et al., p. 27.

2. Yee, pp. 124–25.

3. Yee, p. 124.

4. Berkman, p. 58.

5. California Senate, p. 14.

6. Reproduced in Durden-Smith, pp. 196–98.

7. In ibid., pp. 197–98.

8. Luis Talamantez, int., summer 1989. Subsequent quotes from Talamantez are from this interview.

9. Durden-Smith, p. 200.

10. Jackson, *Blood in My Eye*, p. xi.

11. Quoted in Armstrong, p. 237.

12. Durden-Smith, p. 198.

13. James Park, int., summer 1989.

14. Jackson, *Blood in My Eye*, pp. 108–9.

15. Quoted in Durden-Smith, p. 271.

16. John Irwin, int., fall 1988.

17. John Spain, int., summer 1989. Subsequent quotes from Spain are from this interview.

18. William Hankins, int., summer 1989.

19. Anonymous former *San Francisco Chronicle* reporter, int., spring 1989.

20. Reproduced in Pell, pp. 239–40.

21. "Ex-Con Testifies: Racial Hate at Soledad," *San Francisco Chronicle*, Mar. 26, 1975.

22. Anonymous former Soledad North inmate, int., summer 1989.

23. Anonymous former Soledad inmate, int., spring 1989.

24. Armstrong, p. 44.

25. Davis, p. 5.

26. Irwin int., fall 1988.

27. "Con Says He Saw Soledad Guard Slain," *San Francisco Chronicle*, Jan. 7, 1972.

28. For excerpts from these depositions, see Armstrong, pp. 47–49.

29. Quoted in ibid., p. 199.

30. Ibid., pp. 98, 102.

31. Nate Harrington, int., summer 1989.

32. Anonymous former Soledad North inmate, int., summer 1989.

33. Dorsey Nunn, int., summer 1989.

34. Harrington int., summer 1989.

35. Yee, pp. 153–54.

36. Ibid., pp. 153–55.

37. *Berkeley Monitor*, June 24, 1970.

38. John Irwin, int., winter 1988.

39. Armstrong, dust jacket copy.

40. From a Soledad Brothers Defense Committee handbill, Oct. 1970.

41. *Berkeley Monitor*, Sept. 19, 1970.

42. Harrington int., summer 1989.

43. Durden-Smith, p. 102.

44. Ibid., p. 103.

45. Frank L. Rundle, "The Roots of Violence at Soledad," in Wright, p. 167.

46. Armstrong, pp. 133–34.

47. *Times Literary Supplement*, May 28, 1971, p. 605.

48. Durden-Smith, pp. 203–4.

49. Jackson, *Soledad Brother*, pp. 233–34.

50. Durden-Smith, pp. 215–16, xxi.

51. Armstrong, pp. 204, 14, 150.

52. Ibid., pp. 138, 156–57, 161–65.

53. Ibid., p. 167.

54. See Durden-Smith, pp. 203–5.

55. For a discussion of the early genre conventions of criminal narrative, see Cummins.

56. Armstrong, p. 183.

57. Ibid., pp. 11, 43, 74.

58. Ibid., pp. 17–18.

59. Ibid., p. 121.

60. Quoted in Durden-Smith, p. 271.

61. Armstrong, pp. 168–69, 191.

62. Yee, p. 169.

63. Ibid., p. 155.

64. Ibid., pp. 171–72.

65. Armstrong, p. x.

66. See Szulc.

67. See "'Private Gas Chamber' Charge," *San Francisco Chronicle*, June 5, 1970.

68. See ibid., and "Settlement in San Quentin Death Saga," *San Francisco Chronicle*, June 14, 1978.

69. "Quentin Cons Sue—'Brutality,'" *San Francisco Chronicle*, Sept. 17, 1970.

70. "Lawyers' Inspections Wanted: Judge's Order on Quentin," *San Francisco Chronicle*, Oct. 30, 1970.

71. Davis, Magee, et al., p. 199.

72. For accounts of the Marin County Courthouse shootout see Yee, pp. 157–74, and the *San Rafael Independent Journal*, Aug. 8, 1970.

73. Quoted in the *San Francisco Chronicle*, Aug. 15, 1970.

74. Armstrong, p. 133.

75. *San Francisco Chronicle*, Aug. 20, 1970.

76. Quoted in *San Francisco Chronicle*, Aug. 20, 1970.

77. Governor Ronald Reagan, quoted in the *San Francisco Chronicle*, Aug. 13, 1970.

78. Quoted in Davis, Magee, et al., p. 176.

79. For a discussion of the Angela Davis trial, see Ashman.

80. *San Francisco Chronicle*, Aug. 14, 1970.

81. Ibid., July 22, 1971.

82. Ibid., June 23, 1973.

83. Davis, Magee, et al., p. 6.

84. Ibid., p. 197.

85. *San Francisco Chronicle*, Aug. 12, 1970.

86. Ibid., Aug. 11, 1970.

87. Richard Nelson, int., spring 1989.

Chapter 8

1. Davis, "Political Prisoners, Prisons and Black Liberation," written in Marin County Jail, May 1971, in Davis, Magee, et al., pp. 26–27.

2. Davis, Magee, et al., p. 3.

3. Quoted in ibid., p. 13.

4. Carr, pp. 202–3.

5. *San Francisco Chronicle*, Aug. 12, 1970.

6. See University of California, Berkeley, Bancroft Library, Social Protest Collection, carton 4, folder 17.

7. *San Francisco Chronicle*, Aug. 25, 1970.

8. Wright, p. 100.

9. Inmate demands of Aug. 25, 1970, reproduced in the *San Francisco Chronicle*, Aug. 26, 1970.

10. *San Francisco Chronicle*, Aug. 27, 1970.

11. Ibid., Aug. 28, 1970.

12. Ibid., Sept. 2, 1970.

13. Ibid., Sept. 30, 1970.

14. Ibid., Oct. 2, 1970.

15. See Berkman, p. 102.

16. From an interview with Huey Newton by Mark Lane, *Los Angeles Free Press*, Aug. 1, 1970.

17. Quoted in Davis, Magee, et al., p. 138.

18. Kasirika and Muntu, p. 7.

19. Paul Comiskey, California Prisoners' Union attorney, int., summer 1989.

20. California Department of Corrections, *Administrative Manual*, 1974, Section 195.02, cited in Berkman, p. 81.

21. William Hankins, int., summer 1989.

22. Anonymous former Soledad North inmate, int., spring 1989.

23. Luis Talamantez, int., summer 1989. Subsequent quotes from Talamantez are from this interview.

24. Richard Nelson int., spring 1989. Subsequent quotes from Richard Nelson are from this interview.

25. *Black Panther*, May 1968.

26. Debray, pp. 106, 109–10, 114, 116.

27. See Taber, *M-26*.

28. Taber, *War of the Flea*, pp. 17, 19, 27–28, 60, 55, 166–67.

29. James Smith, int., summer 1989. Subsequent quotes from Smith are from this interview.

30. John Irwin, int., fall 1988.

31. From "Folsom Prisoners Manifesto of Demands and Anti-Oppression Platform," in Pell, pp. 191–201. For a discussion of the demands, see Berkman, pp. 62–67.

32. John Irwin, int., winter 1988.

33. "Folsom Prisoners Manifesto of Demands and Anti-Oppression Platform," in Pell, pp. 191–201.

34. "Message from a Brother in Folsom," in Pell, pp. 201–2.

35. Brown, pp. 87–88.

36. Irwin int., winter 1988.

37. For a version of the strike from the point of view of one of Folsom prison's correctional officers, see Brown, pp. 87–88.

38. Reproduced in American Friends Service Committee, pp. 160–61.

39. Irwin int., winter 1988.

40. Michael Snedeker, int., summer 1989. Subsequent quotes from Snedeker are from this interview.

41. Irwin int., fall 1988.

42. *San Francisco Chronicle*, Oct. 9, 1971.

43. Jackson, *Blood in My Eye*, pp. 17–19.

44. Ibid., pp. 23, 30.

45. Ibid., p. 31.

46. Ibid., pp. 32–33.

47. Ibid., p. 55.

48. John Spain, int., summer 1989. Subsequent quotes from Spain are from this interview.

49. Jackson, *Blood in My Eye*, p. 74.

50. See Durden-Smith, pp. 48, 273.

51. Jackson, *Blood in My Eye*, p. 124.

52. Ibid., pp. 60, 69, 67.

53. In possession of William Hankins.

54. Jackson, *Blood in My Eye*, p. 181.

55. *San Francisco Chronicle*, Aug. 21, 1971.

56. Ibid., Aug. 22, 1971.

57. James McHenry, int., winter 1989.

58. Durden-Smith, p. 80.

59. Ibid., p. 35.

60. See United Prisoners Union.

61. James Park, int., summer 1989.

62. San Quentin spokesman, quoted in the *San Francisco Chronicle*, Aug. 23, 1971.

63. Jay Halford, telephone int., fall 1989.

64. Irwin int., fall 1988.

65. Anonymous former Soledad North inmate, int., spring 1989.

66. Nate Harrington, int., summer 1989.

67. Irwin int., winter 1988.

68. Harlan Washington, int., fall 1989.

69. Mitford, p. 296.

70. Snedeker int.

71. Berkman, pp. 87–92.

72. *Midnight Special: Prisoners News* 3 (Nov. 1973): 12. This issue was among those intercepted in San Quentin's mail room.

73. *San Francisco Chronicle,* Aug. 27, 1971.

74. Ibid., Oct. 9, 1971.

75. See National Lawyers Guild.

76. Los Angeles Guild Prison Committee, National Lawyers Guild, San Diego conference position paper, 1972, in possession of William Hankins.

77. National Lawyers Guild, 1973 position paper, in possession of William Hankins.

Chapter 9

1. For a list of prison riots across the nation in the fall of 1971, see U.S. Congress, House Select Committee on Crime, pp. 6–8.

2. See "Prison Action Conference."

3. *San Francisco Chronicle,* Aug. 25, 1971.

4. Luis Talamantez int., summer 1989.

5. Edwin T. Caldwell, Esq., testimony in U.S. Congress, House of Representatives, Committee on the Judiciary, pp. 72–76.

6. *San Francisco Chronicle,* Aug. 27, 1971.

7. Ibid., Sept. 25, 1971.

8. Ibid., Aug. 24, 1971.

9. Ibid., Sept. 25, 1971.

10. Ibid., Aug. 25, 1971.

11. Ibid., Aug. 28, 1971.

12. Ibid., Aug. 23, 1971.

13. Letter sent to the *San Francisco Chronicle,* reported Aug. 25, 1971.

14. *San Francisco Chronicle,* Aug. 26, 1971.

15. James Park, int., Feb. 1989.

16. William Hankins, int., summer 1989.

17. *San Francisco Chronicle,* Aug. 29, 1971.

18. Ibid., Aug. 29, 1971.

19. Durden-Smith, p. 245.

20. See ibid., pp. 121–25. See also Tackwood.

21. Carr, pp. 223, 229–30.

22. See "They Are Innocent."

23. See "Frame-Up."

24. See "Trial Dates."

25. *San Francisco Chronicle,* July 21, 1973.

26. Weather Underground, p. 151.

27. For further information on police infiltration of the California Left, see Durden-Smith and also Tackwood.

28. For details on this attempt at surveillance, see Yee, pp. 177–85.

29. Quoted in Mitford, p. 292.

30. See U.S. Congress, House of Representatives, Committee on Internal Security, p. 3.

31. *San Francisco Chronicle,* Aug. 30, 1971. See also Aug. 5, 1971.

32. *San Francisco Chronicle,* Sept. 20, 1971.

33. From the "Keldgord Report," reported in the *San Francisco Chronicle*, Oct. 9, 1971.

34. Quoted in U.S. Congress, House of Representatives, Committee on the Judiciary, p. 143.

35. *San Francisco Chronicle*, Apr. 30, 1971.

36. Ibid., Dec. 2, 1971.

37. Ibid., Dec. 5, 1971.

38. Ibid., Sept. 16, 1972.

39. U.S. Circuit Court judge Ben C. Duniway, and U.S. District judges Albert C. Wollenberg and Alfonso J. Zirpoli, quoted in the *San Francisco Chronicle*, Feb. 6, 1973.

40. Quoted in Mitford, pp. 238–39.

41. Wynne, p. 25.

42. Task Force to Study Violence, "Report and Recommendations," California Department of Corrections working paper, May 1974, Table 1, in possession of James Park.

43. Ibid., pp. 4, 27.

44. *San Francisco Chronicle*, Dec. 6, 1973.

45. American Correctional Association, pp. 34, 38.

46. Ibid., p. 42.

47. Ibid., p. 46.

48. Ibid., p. 54.

49. *San Francisco Chronicle*, Jan. 22, 1972.

50. Ibid., June 27, 1972.

51. Ibid., Jan. 3, 1973.

52. Ibid., Jan. 3 and 4, 1973.

53. Ibid., Jan. 9, 1973.

54. For example, see ibid., Dec. 21, 1973.

55. Letter in possession of Luis Talamantez.

56. Nate Harrington, int., summer 1989.

57. Black Guerrilla Family, "Our Family's Role and Ideology," 1973, in possession of William Hankins.

58. Anonymous former BGF member, int.

59. U.S. Congress, House of Representatives, Committee On Internal Security, pp. 1, 3, 76.

60. Ibid., p. 106.

61. Ibid., pp. 6–10.

62. Harrington int., summer 1989.

63. Harlan Washington, int., summer 1989.

64. Dorsey Nunn, int., summer 1989. Subsequent quotes from Nunn are from this interview.

65. I thank Michael Zuckerman for pointing this out to me.

66. Vernel Crittendon, information officer, San Quentin telephone int., spring 1990.

67. Quoted in Payne and Findley, p. 21.

68. Quoted in ibid., p. 42.

69. Unnamed BCA political science tutor, quoted in ibid., p. 48.

70. For details on BCA tutors and Berkeley's Peking House, see ibid., pp. 68–100.

71. Quoted in ibid., p. 87.

72. From the San Quentin prison register of visitors, in possession of William Hankins.

73. Hankins int., summer 1989.

74. Payne and Findley, p. 117.

75. Jackson, *Blood in My Eye*, quoted in ibid., p. 151.

76. *San Francisco Chronicle*, Dec. 17, 1973.

77. Payne and Findley, p. 183.

78. Ibid., p. 213.

79. Ibid., p. 216.

80. Harrington int., summer 1989.

81. Payne and Findley, pp. 223–24.

82. Ibid., pp. 236–37, 244.

83. Ibid., pp. 290, 286.

84. Nate Harrington int., spring 1989.

85. John Spain, int., summer 1989.

86. See August 21 Mobilization Committee.

87. Quoted in Payne and Findley, p. 317.

88. *San Francisco Chronicle*, May 20, 1975.

89. Anonymous former BGF member, int., summer 1989.

90. Charles Garry, int., June 1989.

91. Harrington int., summer 1989.

92. Former Soledad inmate, int., spring 1989.

93. San Quentin inmate, int.

94. *San Francisco Chronicle*, Jan. 7, 1972.

95. U.S. Congress, House of Representatives, Committee on Internal Security, pp. 106–7.

96. California Assembly Bill 1181 (1971), quoted in Wright, p. 268.

97. Wright, pp. 274–75.

98. Richard Nelson, int., spring 1989.

99. William Malin, int., spring 1989.

100. James McHenry, int., spring 1989.

101. Joe Morse, int., Jan. 1989.

102. McHenry int.

Chapter 10

1. Luis Talamantez, int., summer 1989.

2. Jay Halford, telephone int., summer 1989.

3. John Irwin, int., fall 1988.

4. Payne and Findley, pp. 316–17.

5. *San Francisco Chronicle*, Apr. 9, 1976.

6. Harlan Washington, int., summer 1989.

7. California Prisoners' Union, "Proposal to the Department of Corrections for a Prisoners' Union Inside," Oct. 14, 1975, Exhibit P, *Richard Price et al. on Habeas Corpus*, 25 Cal. 3d 448, 600 P. 2d 1330 (1979).

8. Memorandums from Nelson Kempsky to J. J. Enomoto, June 27, July 15, and Sept. 11, 1975, papers of the California Department of Corrections, State Archives, Office of the Secretary of State, Sacramento.

9. For the complete text of the accepted union proposal, see Exhibit P, *Richard Price et al. on Habeas Corpus*, 25 Cal. 3d 448, 600 P. 2d 1330 (1979).

10. Michael Snedeker, int., summer 1989. All subsequent quotes from Snedeker are from this interview.

11. For the text of this charter, see *Richard Price et al. on Habeas Corpus*, Exhibit A.

12. Ibid., Exhibit D.

13. *Richard Price et al. on Habeas Corpus*.

14. *Jones v. North Carolina Prisoners' Union*, 433 U.S. 119 (1977).

15. *Reynolds on Habeas Corpus*, 25 Cal. 3d 131, 599 P. 2d 86 (1979).

16. Harlan Washington, int., fall 1989.

17. *Brandt on Habeas Corpus*, 25 Cal. 3d 136, 599 P. 2d 89 (1979).

18. Washington int., fall 1989.

19. *San Francisco Chronicle*, Feb. 24, 1971.

20. *San Francisco Chronicle*, Mar. 26, 1975.

21. Ibid., Mar. 23, 1975.

22. Quoted in ibid., Mar. 28, 1975.

23. Ibid., Mar. 28, 1975, and Apr. 9, 1976.

24. Ibid., Mar. 29, 1975.

25. Ibid., July 29, 1975.

26. Ibid., June 2, 1975.

27. Ibid., Sept. 9, 1975.

28. Ibid., June 24, 1976.

29. Quoted in ibid., June 30, 1976.

30. See Wald.

31. *San Francisco Chronicle*, July 25, 1980.

32. Cleaver, *Soul on Fire*, pp. 143, 150.

33. Ibid., pp. 211–12.

34. Ibid., pp. 223–24.

35. Ibid., p. 232.

36. Ibid., p. 236.

37. Stanton E. Samenow and Samuel Yochelson, in *The Criminal Personality*, quoted in Cleaver, *Soul on Fire*, p. 68; Cleaver, ibid.

38. Eldridge Cleaver Legal Defense Fund letter to Paul Jacobs, Mar. 10, 1977, Data Center, Oakland, Calif.

39. Morton Kamins, "Eldridge Cleaver's Journey: From Communist to Christian," review of Cleaver's *Soul on Fire*, in *Los Angeles Times*, Oct. 29, 1978.

40. Schuller to Brown, Feb. 16, 1977, Data Center, Oakland, Calif.

41. Quoted in the *Oakland Tribune*, Jan. 4, 1980.

42. *San Rafael Independent Journal,* Mar. 6, 1981.

43. Ibid., Oct. 31, 1981, and *San Francisco Chronicle,* Oct. 31, 1981.

44. *San Rafael Independent Journal,* Aug. 23, 1982.

45. "California Reverses Decision to Shut Prison Papers," *New York Times,* Aug. 28, 1982, p. 6.

46. "More Prisons Don't Create a Safer Society," *San Jose Mercury News,* Feb. 8, 1990.

47. "Prison Vaults Valley Backwater into an Oasis of Respectability," *San Jose Mercury News,* June 30, 1990, p. 4F.

48. See Pelican Bay Information Project.

49. *Bay Area Recorder,* Sept. 19, 1991.

50. Ibid.

51. Pelican Bay Information Project minutes, Aug. 27, 1992, Pelican Bay Information Project.

52. Class action complaint *Madrid* v. *Gomez,* case no. C-90-3094 [TEH], filed in 1992 in U.S. District Court for the Northern District of California, by the law firm Wilson, Sonsini, Goodrich, and Rosati.

53. Ibid., p. 30.

54. *Sacramento Bee,* June 24, 1992.

55. Inmate interview, Oct. 1991, Pelican Bay Information Project.

56. Class action complaint *Madrid* v. *Gomez,* p. 22.

57. Inmate interview, Oct. 1991, Pelican Bay Information Project.

58. Ibid.

59. Roemer, p. 16.

References

Interviews

Ernie Bradford, San Quentin vocational education supervisor, winter 1989

Paul Comiskey, California Prisoners' Union attorney, summer 1989

Vernel Crittendon, San Quentin information officer telephone ints., 1988–1990

Terry Cuddy, former San Quentin inmate, fall 1989

Ted Davidson, former University of California, Berkeley, graduate researcher at San Quentin, fall 1989

Byron Eshelman, former San Quentin chaplain, June 1989

Charles Garry, former attorney for the Black Panthers, June 1989

Jay Halford, former Deuel Vocational Institution and Soledad inmate, then early Prisoners' Union board member, telephone ints., summer, fall 1989

William Hankins, former San Quentin sergeant, Special Investigations Unit, winter, summer 1989

Nate Harrington, former Deuel Vocational Institution and former San Quentin inmate, spring, summer 1989

Keith Hayball, former San Quentin music instructor and education administrator, spring 1989

John Irwin, former Soledad inmate and early Prisoners' Union organizer, winter, fall 1988

Rowan Klein, former aide to state assemblyman Alan Sieroty, telephone int., May 1989

William Malin, former San Quentin teacher, spring 1989

James McHenry, former San Quentin librarian, spring 1989

Mary Mims, San Quentin chief librarian, summer 1990

Robert Minton, former San Quentin teacher, summer 1989

Joe Morse, San Quentin inmate, January 1989, spring 1989

Louis Nelson, former captain of Death Row, associate warden of custody, and warden of San Quentin, April 1989

Richard Nelson, former San Quentin Adjustment Center lieutenant, then associate warden, custody, spring 1989

Dorsey Nunn, former San Quentin inmate, summer 1989
James Park, former San Quentin associate warden, February 1989, summer 1989
Fred Persily, former San Quentin assistant librarian, summer 1989
Alan Sieroty, former California state assemblyman, telephone int., May 1989
James Smith, former California Prisoners' Union attorney, summer 1989
Michael Snedeker, former California Prisoners' Union attorney, summer 1989
John Spain, former Soledad Central and San Quentin inmate, summer 1989
Edna Spector, widow of former San Quentin librarian Herman K. Spector, January 1989
Luis Talamantez, former San Quentin inmate, summer 1989
Harlan Washington, former San Quentin inmate, summer, fall 1989
Several former inmates and staff members who wish to remain anonymous

Works Cited

Alexander, John K. *Render Them Submissive: Responses to Poverty in Philadelphia, 1760–1800.* Amherst: University of Massachusetts Press, 1980.
American Correctional Association, Committee on Riots and Disturbances. *Causes, Preventive Measures, and Methods of Controlling Riots and Disturbances in Correctional Institutions.* Washington, D.C.: American Correctional Association, 1970.
American Friends Service Committee. *Struggle for Justice.* New York: Hill & Wang, 1971.
American Prison Association. *Proceedings of the Seventieth Annual Congress, Cincinnati, Ohio, October 21–25, 1940.* New York: American Prison Association, 1940.
———. Committee on Institution Libraries. *Library Manual for Correctional Institutions.* New York: American Prison Association, 1950.
Armstrong, Gregory. *The Dragon Has Come.* New York: Harper & Row, 1974.
Ashman, Charles. *The People vs. Angela Davis.* New York: Pinnacle Books, 1972.
August 21 Mobilization Committee. Handbill, 1974. University of California, Berkeley, Bancroft Library, Social Protest Collection, Carton 4, Folder 17.
Barnes, Harry Elmer. *The Evolution of Penology in Pennsylvania.* Indianapolis: Bobbs-Merrill, 1927.
Berkeley Commune. "An Open Letter to the Prophets and Their Apostles," 1968. Berkeley Commune File, Social Protest Project, Bancroft Library, University of California, Berkeley.
Berkman, Ronald. *Opening the Gates: The Rise of the Prisoners' Movement.* Lexington, Mass.: Lexington Books, 1979.
Biskind, Peter, and Barbara Ehrenreich, "Machismo and Hollywood's Working Class." In Donald Lazere, ed., *American Media and Mass Culture: Left Perspectives.* Berkeley: University of California Press, 1987.
Blue Ribbon Committee on Correctional Library Services. *Report to the Director*

of the California Department of Corrections. Sacramento: California Library Association, 1973.

Bookspan, Shelley. *A Germ of Goodness: The California State Prison System, 1851–1944.* Lincoln: University of Nebraska Press, 1991.

Braly, Malcolm. *False Starts: A Memoir of San Quentin and Other Prisons.* Boston: Little, Brown, 1976.

Breitman, George. *The Last Year of Malcolm X: The Evolution of a Revolutionary.* New York: Merit, 1967.

Brown, Michael. "History of Folsom Prison, 1878–1978." Folsom: Folsom Vocational Graphics Arts Students, 1978. In the papers of the California Department of Corrections, State Archives, Office of the California Secretary of State, Sacramento.

Browning, Frank, and *Ramparts* Editors. *Prison Life: A Study of the Explosive Conditions in America's Prisons.* New York: Harper & Row, 1972.

California Department of Corrections. *California Department of Corrections Rules.* Sacramento: California Department of Corrections, 1967.

————. *Characteristics of Resident Population of California State Prisons by Institutions.* Sacramento: California Department of Corrections, 1948–80.

————. *Director's Rules.* Sacramento: California Department of Corrections, 1954.

————. *Institutional Libraries: Selected Data.* Sacramento: California Department of Corrections, 1956.

————. *Summary Statistics of Prisoners and Parolees.* Sacramento: California Department of Corrections, 1951–80.

————. Classification Bureau. *Manual of Procedures for the Institutional Library.* Sacramento: California Department of Corrections, 1949.

California Senate. *Black Caucus Report on California Prisons.* Sacramento: California State Legislature, 1970.

Campbell, W. Reason. *Dead Man Walking: Teaching in a Maximum Security Prison.* New York: Richard Marek, 1978.

Carr, James, with Dan Hammer and Isaac Cronin. *BAD: The Autobiography of James Carr.* New York: Herman Graf, 1975.

Carroll, Leo, and Margaret E. Mondrick. "Racial Bias in the Decision to Grant Parole." *Law and Society Review* 2 (Fall 1976): 93–109.

Chambers, Whittaker. "What Is a Communist?" *Reader's Digest* (Oct. 1953): 19–22.

Chessman, Caryl. *Cell 2455 Death Row.* New York: Prentice-Hall, 1954.

————. *The Face of Justice.* Englewood Cliffs, N.J.: Prentice-Hall, 1957.

————. *Trial by Ordeal.* New York: Prentice-Hall, 1955.

Cleaver, Eldridge. "An Address on Prisons Delivered at a Rally in His Honor a Few Days Before He Was Scheduled to Return to Jail." In Frank Browning and *Ramparts* Editors, *Prison Life.* New York: Harper & Row, 1972, pp. 140–42.

————. Cleaver Legal Defense Fund Letter to Paul Jacobs, Mar. 10, 1977. Cleaver File, Data Center, Oakland, California.

————. "Farewell Address." Nov. 22, 1968. In Robert Scheer, ed., *Eldridge*

Cleaver: Post-Prison Writings and Speeches. New York: Random House/Ramparts Books, 1969, pp. 147–59.

———. "The Guru of San Quentin," *Esquire* 67 (Apr. 1967): 88.

———. "Prisons: The Muslims' Decline." In Frank Browning and *Ramparts* Editors, *Prison Life.* New York: Harper & Row, 1972, pp. 100–103.

———. Review of Frantz Fanon's *The Wretched of the Earth.* In Robert Scheer, ed., *Eldridge Cleaver: Post-Prison Writings and Speeches.* New York: Random House/Ramparts Books, 1969, pp. 18–20.

———. *Revolution and Education.* Pamphlet. June 28, 1969. Special Collections, University of California, Santa Cruz.

———. *Soul on Fire.* Waco, Texas: Word Books, 1978.

———. *Soul on Ice.* New York: Dell, 1968.

Cloward, Richard A., and Lloyd E. Ohlin. *Delinquency and Opportunity.* Glencoe, Ill.: Free Press, 1960.

Collier, Peter, and David Horowitz. "Baddest." In *Destructive Generation: Second Thoughts About the Sixties.* New York: Summit Books, 1989, pp. 141–67.

Cook, Allen. "The Correctional Institution Looks at Educational Needs." Paper delivered at the Annual Conference of the Adult Education Association, Oct. 24, 1951. In the papers of the California Department of Corrections, State Archives, Office of the California Secretary of State, Sacramento.

Coyle, William J. *Libraries in Prisons: A Blending of Institutions.* New York: Greenwood Press, 1987.

Cummins, Eric. "'Anarchia' and the Emerging State." *Radical History Review* (Fall 1990): 33–62.

Davidson, R. Theodore. *Chicano Prisoners: The Key to San Quentin.* New York: Holt, Rinehart and Winston, 1974.

Davis, Angela. "The Soledad Brothers." *Black Scholar* (Apr.–May 1971): 2–7.

Davis, Angela, Ruchell Magee, the Soledad Brothers, and Other Political Prisoners. *If They Come in the Morning: Voices of Resistance.* New York: Third Press, Joseph Okpaku, 1971.

Debray, Regis. *Revolution in the Revolution? Armed Struggle and Political Struggle in Latin America.* New York: Grove Press, 1967.

Drumgo, Fleeta. "We Are All Prisoners." *Black Scholar* (Apr.–May 1971).

Duffy, Clinton. *The San Quentin Story.* Garden City, N.Y.: Doubleday, 1950.

Durden-Smith, Jo. *Who Killed George Jackson?* New York: Knopf, 1976.

Eriksson, Torsten. *The Reformers: An Historical Survey of Pioneer Experiments in the Treatment of Criminals.* New York: Oxford University Press, 1976.

Eshelman, Byron. *Death Row Chaplain.* Englewood Cliffs, N.J.: Prentice-Hall, 1962.

Filreis, Alan. "Words with 'All the Effects of Force': Cold-War Interpretation." *American Quarterly* 39 (Summer 1987): 307–11.

Floch, Maurice. "Correctional Treatment and the Library." *Wilson Library Bulletin* 26 (Feb. 1952): 452–55.

Flynn, Frank T., Jr. "Behind the Prison Riots." *Social Service Review* 27 (Mar. 1953): 73–86.

Foucault, Michel. *Discipline and Punish: The Birth of the Prison*. Translated by Alan Sheridan. New York: Vintage, 1979.

Fox, James G. *Organizational and Racial Conflict in Maximum-Security Prisons*. Lexington, Mass.: Lexington Books, 1982.

"Frame-Up." Handbill, spring 1972, University of California, Berkeley, Bancroft Library, Social Protest Collection, Carton 4, Folder 17.

Freeman, Bernice, with Al Hirshberg. *Assignment San Quentin*. London: Peter Davies, 1962.

"Getting Eldridge Cleaver." Handbill, spring 1968, Cleaver File, Data Center, Oakland, California.

Giovanni, Nikki. *Black Feeling, Black Talk, Black Judgement*. New York: William Morrow, 1970.

Griffin, Clifford S. *Their Brothers' Keepers: Moral Stewardship in the United States, 1800–1865*. Westport, Conn.: Greenwood, 1960.

Harris, Maz. *Bikers: Birth of a Modern Day Outlaw*. London: Faber and Faber, 1985.

Hilliard, David, and Lewis Cole. *This Side of Glory: The Autobiography of David Hilliard and the Story of the Black Panther Party*. Boston: Little, Brown, 1993.

Irwin, John. *The Felon*. Englewood Cliffs, N.J.: Prentice-Hall, 1970.

———. *Prisons in Turmoil*. Boston: Little, Brown, 1980.

Ives, George. *A History of Penal Methods: Criminals, Witches, Lunatics*. 1914. Reprint. Montclair, N.J.: Patterson Smith Reprint Series in Criminology, Law Enforcement, and Social Problems, 1970.

Jackson, George. *Blood in My Eye*. New York: Random House, 1972.

———. *Soledad Brother: The Prison Letters of George Jackson*. New York: Coward, McCann, 1970.

Jacobs, Paul. Cleaver interview notes dated Soledad, Feb. 23, 1966. Working papers of the *Ramparts* editorial staff, Data Center, Oakland, California.

Kahn, Brian, and Neil Zinn. "Prison Gangs in the Community." *Journal of California Law Enforcement* 13 (Jan. 1979): 105–14.

Kasirika, Kaidi (Kenneth Divans), and Maharibi Muntu (Larry M. West). "Prison or Slavery?" *Black Scholar* 3 (Oct. 1971).

Kerouac, Jack. *On the Road*. New York: Signet, 1955.

Koch, Gary G., and Stevens H. Clarke, "The Influence of Income and Other Factors on Whether Criminal Defendants Go to Prison." *Law and Society Review* 2 (Fall 1976): 57–93.

Lamott, Kenneth. *Chronicles of San Quentin*. 1961. Reprint. New York: Ballantine, 1972.

Larsen, Charles. "A Prisoner Looks at Writ-Writing." *California Law Review* 56 (Apr. 1968): pp. 342–64.

Lavigne, Yves. *Hell's Angels: Three Can Keep a Secret If Two Are Dead*. New York: Carol, 1987.

Leamer, Laurence. *The Paper Revolutionaries: The Rise of the Underground Press*. New York: Simon and Schuster, 1972.

LeDonne, Marjorie. (Institute of Library Research, University of California,

Berkeley.) *Survey of Library and Information Problems in Correctional Institutions. Vol. 1: Findings and Recommendations.* Project No. 2-0847, Grant No. OEG-0-72-2531. Washington, D.C.: U.S. Department of Health, Education and Welfare, Office of Education, 1974.

Leeds, Barry H. *Ken Kesey.* New York: Frederick Ungar, 1981.

Leibert, Julius A. *Behind Bars: What a Chaplain Saw in Alcatraz, Folsom and San Quentin.* New York: Doubleday, 1965.

MacCormick, Austin H. "A Brief History of Libraries in American Correctional Institutions." Paper delivered at the American Correctional Association's Centennial Congress of Correction, Cincinnati, Ohio, Oct. 12, 1970. In Albert R. Roberts, ed., *Readings in Prison Education.* Springfield, Ill.: Charles C. Thomas, 1973.

Malcolm X, with Alex Haley. *The Autobiography of Malcolm X.* New York: Ballantine, 1964.

Marable, Manning. *Race, Reform, and Rebellion: The Reconstruction in Black America, 1945–1982.* Jackson: University of Mississippi Press, 1984.

Marine, Gene. *The Black Panthers.* New York: Signet, 1969.

Marx, Karl. "The Class Struggle in France." In *The Handbook of Marxism.* New York: International Publishers, 1935.

Masur, Louis P. *Rites of Execution: Capital Punishment and the Transformation of American Culture, 1776–1865.* New York: Oxford University Press, 1989.

McNeely, R. L., and Carl E. Pope, eds. *Race, Crime and Criminal Justice.* Beverly Hills, Calif.: Sage Publications, 1981.

Meranze, Michael. "Public Punishments, Reformative Incarceration, and Authority in Philadelphia, 1750–1835." Ph.D. diss., University of California, Berkeley, 1987.

Merton, Robert K. *Social Theory and Social Structure.* London: Free Press of Glencoe, 1957.

Minton, Robert J. *Inside: Prison American Style.* New York: Random House, 1971.

Minton, Robert J., and Stephen Rice. "Using Racism at San Quentin." *Ramparts* (Jan. 1970): 19–24.

Mitford, Jessica. *Kind and Usual Punishment.* New York: Knopf, 1973.

National Lawyers Guild. "Street Sheets Greatest Hits: Legal First Aid." 1970? Data Center, Oakland, California.

Newton, Huey P. "War Against the Panthers: A Study of Repression in America." Ph.D. diss., University of California, Santa Cruz, 1980.

Pallas, John, and Robert Barber. "From Riot to Revolution." In Erik Olin Wright, *The Politics of Punishment: A Critical Analysis of Prisons in America.* New York: Harper & Row, 1973, pp. 241–60.

Palmer, Forrest C. "Prison Renaissance." *Library Journal* 82 (Jan. 1, 1957): 37–40.

Payne, Les, and Tim Findley, with Carolyn Craven. *The Life and Death of the S.L.A.* New York: Ballantine, 1976.

Pelican Bay Information Project. "Pelican Bay Prison Inmate Interviews." Summer 1992. Pelican Bay Information Project, San Francisco.

Pell, Eve, and Members of the Prison Law Project, eds. *Maximum Security: Letters from California's Prisons*. New York: E. P. Dutton, 1972.

Perry, Charles. *The Haight-Ashbury: A History*. New York: Random House, 1984.

Pope, Carl E. "Race and Crime Revisited." *Crime and Delinquency* (Summer 1979): 347–57.

"Prison Action Conference." Handbill, Jan. 28–30, 1972. University of California, Berkeley, Bancroft Library, Social Protest Collection, Carton 4, Folder 17.

Prison Law Collective. *The Jailhouse Lawyer's Manual: How to Bring a Federal Suit Against Abuses in Prison*. San Francisco: Prison Law Collective, 1973.

Roberts, Albert R. *Sourcebook on Prison Education: Past, Present, and Future*. Springfield, Ill.: Charles C. Thomas, 1971.

Roemer, John. "High-Tech Deprivation." *San Jose Mercury News West*, June 7, 1992, pp. 16–17.

Rorabaugh, W. J. *Berkeley at War: The 1960s*. New York: Oxford University Press, 1989.

Rossman, Michael. *The Wedding Within the War*. New York: Doubleday, 1971.

Rothman, David J. *The Discovery of the Asylum: Social Order and Disorder in the New Republic*. Boston: Little, Brown, 1971.

Rush, Benjamin. "The Influence of Physical Causes upon the Moral Faculty." In Dagobert D. Runes, ed., *The Selected Writings of Benjamin Rush*. New York: Philosophical Library, 1947.

———. *Medical Inquiries and Observations upon the Diseases of the Mind*. 1812. Reprint. New York: Hafner, 1962.

Saladin, G. "Racism III." In Robert J. Minton, *Inside: Prison American Style*. New York: Random House, 1971.

Scheer, Robert, ed. *Eldridge Cleaver: Post-Prison Writings and Speeches*. New York: Random House / Ramparts Books, 1969.

Schuller, Pastor Robert H. Letter to Governor Edmund G. Brown, Jr., Feb. 16, 1977. Data Center, Oakland, California.

SLA. Handbill, Oct. 4, 1975. University of California, Berkeley, Bancroft Library, Social Protest Collection, Carton 17, Folder 21.

Slotkin, Richard. "Narratives of Negro Crime in New England, 1675–1800." *American Quarterly* 25 (Mar. 1973): 3–31.

Soledad Brothers Defense Committee. Handbill, San Francisco, Oct. 1970. University of California, Berkeley, Bancroft Library, Social Protest Collection.

Spector, Herman K. "Library Program of the California State Department of Corrections." *Special Libraries* 48 (Jan. 1957): 7–11.

———. "Library Statistics: Their Meaning and Significance to the Librarian and to the Administrator." In American Prison Association, Committee on Institution Libraries, *Library Manual for Correctional Institutions*. New York: American Prison Association, 1950, pp. 83–100.

———. "Men and Books: Books and Men." Feb. 24, 1960. Papers of the San Quentin Museum Association, San Quentin.

———. ". . . Nor Iron Bars a Cage." *California Librarian* (Apr. 1963): 105–15.

―――. "A Prison Librarian Looks at Writ-Writing." *California Law Review* 56 (Apr. 1968): 365–70.

―――. "The Prison Librarian's Responsibility to the Public Library." Lecture to the Friends of the Burlingame Public Library, Feb. 17, 1963, pp. 27–28. In possession of Edna Spector.

―――. "Public Library Aspects of the Prison Library." Paper delivered to the California Library Association, Golden Gate District, May 3, 1958. In possession of Edna Spector.

―――, comp. "Reading is the Key: I Read Because . . ." Apr. 12–18, 1964. Papers of the San Quentin Museum Historical Association, San Quentin.

Stang, David P. "The Inability of Corrections to Correct." In James S. Campbell, Joseph R. Sahid, and David P. Stang, *Law and Order Reconsidered: A Staff Report to the National Commission on the Causes and Prevention of Violence*. Washington, D.C.: U.S. Government Printing Office, n.d., pp. 25–40.

Staples, Robert. "White Racism, Black Crime, and American Justice: An Application of the Colonial Model to Explain Crime and Race." *Phylon* 36 (March 1975): 14–23.

Stender, Fay. "Violence and Lawlessness at Soledad Prison." In Eve Pell and Members of the Prison Law Project, eds., *Maximum Security: Letters from California's Prisons*. New York: E. P. Dutton, 1972, pp. 224–30.

Sullivan, Larry E. "The Big House Is Also a Home: Reading and the Development of Prison Libraries in the United States, 1840–1940." Lecture delivered at the Strong Museum, Rochester, N.Y., spring 1987.

Sykes, Gresham. *The Society of Captives*. Princeton: Princeton University Press, 1958.

Szulc, Ted. "George Jackson Radicalizes the Brothers in Soledad and San Quentin." *New York Times Magazine*, Aug. 1, 1971, pp. 10–11.

Taber, Robert. *M-26: The Biography of a Revolution*. New York: Lyle Stuart, 1961.

―――. *The War of the Flea: A Study of Guerrilla Warfare Theory and Practice*. New York: Lyle Stuart, 1965.

Tackwood, Louis. *The Glass House Tapes*. New York: Avon, 1973.

Teeters, Negley K. *The Cradle of the Penitentiary: The Walnut Street Jail, 1773–1835*. Philadelphia: Pennsylvania Prison Society, 1955.

"They Are Innocent." Handbill, 1973. University of California, Berkeley, Bancroft Library, Social Protest Collection, Carton 4, Folder 17.

Thompson, Hunter S. *Hell's Angels: A Strange and Terrible Saga*. New York: Ballantine, 1966.

"Trial Dates." Handbill, fall 1972. University of California, Berkeley, Bancroft Library, Social Protest Collection, Carton 4, Folder 17.

Unger, Irwin. *The Movement: A History of the American New Left, 1959–1972*. New York: Dodd, 1974.

United Prisoners Union. Handbill, Nov. 6, 1971. University of California, Berkeley, Bancroft Library, Social Protest Collection, Carton 14, Folder 17.

U.S. Congress. House of Representatives. Committee on Internal Security,

93d Cong., 1st sess. *Revolutionary Target: The American Penal System.* Washington, D.C.: U.S. Government Printing Office, 1973.

———. Committee on the Judiciary, 92d Cong., 1st sess., *Prisons, Prison Reform, and Prisoners' Rights: California.* Washington, D.C.: U.S. Government Printing Office, 1971.

———. Committee on Un-American Activities, 86th Cong., 1st sess., "Language as a Communist Weapon: Consultation with Dr. Stefan T. Possony," Mar. 2, 1959. Washington, D.C.: U.S. Government Printing Office, 1959.

———. Select Committee on Crime. *Reform of Our Correctional Systems: A Report by the Select Committee on Crime.* Washington, D.C.: U.S. Government Printing Office, 1973.

——— Senate. *Book III: Final Report of the Select Committee to Study Governmental Operations with Respect to Intelligence Activities,* 94th Cong., 2d sess. Washington, D.C.: U.S. Government Printing Office, 1976.

Wald, Karen. "The San Quentin Six Case: Perspective and Analysis." *Crime and Social Justice* (Fall/Winter 1976): 58–68.

Warshow, Robert. "The Gangster as Tragic Hero" and "Movie Chronicle: The Westerner." In *The Immediate Experience: Movies, Comics, Theatre and Other Aspects of Popular Culture.* New York: Doubleday, 1962.

Weather Underground. *Prairie Fire: The Politics of Revolutionary Anti-Imperialism. Political Statement of the Weather Underground.* San Francisco: Communications Co., 1974.

Weimerskirch, Philip J. "Benjamin Rush and John Minson Galt, II: Pioneers of Bibliotherapy in America." *Bulletin of the Medical Library Association* 53 (1965): 510–26.

Williams, Daniel E. "'Behold a tragic scene strangely changed into a theater of mercy': The Structure and Significance of Criminal Conversion Narratives in Early New England." *American Quarterly* 38 (Winter 1986): 827–47.

Wines, Enoch C. *The State of Prisons and of Child-Saving Institutions in the Civilized World.* 1880. Reprint. Montclair, N.J.: Patterson Smithe, 1968.

Wolfe, Tom. *The Electric Kool Aid Acid Test.* New York: Bantam, 1968.

Wright, Erik Olin. *The Politics of Punishment: A Critical Analysis of Prisons in America.* New York: Harper & Row, 1973.

Wynne, John M., Jr. *Prison Employee Unionism: The Impact on Correctional Administration and Programs.* Washington, D.C.: National Institute of Law Enforcement and Criminal Justice, Law Enforcement Assistance Administration, U.S. Department of Justice, 1978.

Yablonsky, Lewis. *The Hippie Trip.* New York: Pegasus, 1968.

Yee, Min S. *The Melancholy History of Soledad Prison: In Which a Utopian Scheme Turns Bedlam.* New York: Harper's Magazine Press, 1970.

Zinn, R. Neil. *Prison Gangs in the Community: A Briefing Document for the Board of Corrections.* Sacramento: California Department of Corrections, 1978.

INDEX

In this index an "f" after a number indicates a separate reference on the next page. A continuous discussion over two or more pages is indicated by a span of page numbers, e.g., "pp. 57–58." *Passim* is used for a cluster of references in close but not continuous sequence. SQ is an abbreviation for San Quentin.

Adjustment Center: radical inmates in, 71, 91; and communication control, 196, 266; revolt in, 209–12, 224, 226, 262; censorship in, 225, 266; and contemporary prison design, 270–71. *See also* Jackson, George; Muslims; Revolutionaries; San Quentin Six

Adult Authority: under McGee, 11–12; composition of, 17–18; abolition of, 192, 253, 257

American Correctional (formerly Prison) Association, 22, 25, 233–34

Armstrong, Gregory, 167, 172–73, 174–76

Asher, Rosalie, 41–42, 48, 50

Assembly Committee on Criminal Procedure, 129

Attica Correctional Institution, 222, 230, 237

Attorneys, prison movement: 98, 131–32, 231. *See also* Asher, Rosalie; Bingham, Stephen; Davis, George; Garry, Charles; National Lawyers Guild; Prison Law Collective; Snedeker, Michael; Soladay, Salle S.; Stender, Fay; Thorne, John

Atwood, Angela, 241, 244

August Seventh Guerilla Movement, 229, 242

Axelrod, Beverly, 98

Baldwin, James, 189

Barger, Sonny, 105. *See also* Hell's Angels

Beaty, Ronald, 147

Behavior modification, *see* Bibliotherapy; Counseling; Pelican Bay State Prison; Rehabilitation

Berkeley Barb: on Black Panthers, 112, 114, 118; and celebrity outlaw, 117, 126; and calls for inmate strike, 117–18, 122; prison censorship of, 118; prison articles in, 119, 121, 125. *See also Outlaw*

Berkeley Tribe, 107, 147

Bible, 5, 19

Bibliotherapy: in criminal reform, 4–5, 22; at SQ, 12, 17, 21, 24–32, 63, 78–79, 96; measuring success of, 23; techniques of, 23, 27; and Malcolm Braly, 29–31; inmate faith in, 32; and Caryl Chessman, 63; and Eldridge Cleaver, 78–79, 96. *See also* Censorship; Rehabilitation; Spector, Herman

Billingslea, Fred, 180–82

Bingham, Stephen, 209

Black Culture Association, 239–40. *See also* Symbionese Liberation Army

Black Guerrilla Family: political education of, 136, 140; origins and constitution of, 223, 236; political gangsterism in, 236, 241, 246. *See also* Revolutionaries; Symbionese Liberation Army

Black Muslims, *see* Muslims

Black Panther, 110–12, 134

Black Panthers: "Panther Bill," 110; early program of, 110–14; and weapons, 110–14, 120; as celebrity outlaws, 112, 115; counterinsurgency against, 114–15, 261; SQ chapter, 136; and George Jackson, 136, 171; and plans to attack prisons, 144; convict cult of, 146–47; and in-prison court sessions, 191–92; in Folsom strike, 201–2; in Algiers, 266–67. *See also* Cleaver, Eldridge; Foco theory; Newton, Huey

Blood in My Eye, see under Jackson, George. *See also* Foco theory

Board of Prison Terms, 257

Booker T. X, 72

Braly, Malcolm, 29–31

Brando, Marlon, 53, 104

Brown, Edmund G., 50, 55

Caldwell, Patricia, 87

California Correctional Officers Association, 230–31, 256

California Prisoners' Union, *see* Prisoners' Union, California

Carr, James: and critique of Left, 128, 189–90, 228; and George Jackson, 157, 178, 208; death of, 228

Castro, Fidel, 197–98

Cell 2455 Death Row (Chessman), 38–40, 51

Censorship: of private citizens, 2–3, 264; anticommunism and, 3, 9; court opinions on, 3, 9, 24, 132; of inmate mail, 8, 24, 83, 131, 133, 196, 231–32; of *San Quentin News*, 8, 83–84; of inmate reading, 10, 25, 43, 81, 134, 137, 196, 231–32, 235–36, 253, 269; Calif. Dept. of Corrections guidelines on, 24; of inmate writing, 24, 30–31, 40–50, 63, 82–83; and Herman Spector, 24–25, 29–31, 82; American Prison Association guidelines on, 25; of Malcolm Braly, 30–31; of Caryl Chessman, 41–48 *passim*; on Death Row, 43, 63–64; at Pelican

Bay, 53; antisubversion laws, 68; in SQ Education Department, 75; in SQ library, 80–81, 133; of access to media, 83–84, 118, 238–39; of telephone calls, 84, 238–39; of parolees, 119–20, 122, 144; of Eldridge Cleaver, 119–21, 143–44; and Ronald Reagan, 122, 143, 184; Penal Code 2600 and, 131–33; House Committee on Internal Security and, 219, 223, 230, 237, 248; in Adjustment Center, 225, 266; social unrest and, 263–64; treatment ideology and, 263–64

Chambers, Whittaker, 9

Chandler, Raymond, 53

Chessman, Caryl Whittier: early prison years of, 2, 33–34; "Red Light Bandit" trial of, 34–35; character of, 34–36, 40; Death Row law office of, 36–38, 43, 50, 51, 63–64; censorship of, 41–48 *passim*; and death penalty, 52; as celebrity outlaw, 52–54; and rehabilitation rhetoric, 55, 57f; execution of, 59–61; and prison movement, 60–62

——— Works: *Cell 2455 Death Row*, 38–40, 51; *The Face of Justice*, 46–48, 50–51; *The Kid Was a Killer*, 43, 45, 51, 57; *Trial by Ordeal*, 41–43

Christmas, William, 157, 182

Civil death, 24–25, 31, 42, 44; Calif. Penal Code amendment, 130

Class analysis, *see* Marxism

Cleaver, Eldridge: as Black Muslim, 71–74, 95–96; as teacher, 76, 96, 149; in bibliotherapy, 78–79, 96; and Left readership, 93, 99f, 109, 125; on parole, 93, 119, 143–44, 146; on crime and oppression, 94, 112, 125, 145; early prison years of, 95; reading of, 95–97, 99, 267; sexual politics of, 99, 109–10, 112, 114; and conversion genre, 99, 267–69; as celebrity outlaw, 102, 122, 125; as Black Panther, 111, 136, 171, 267; censorship of, 119–21, 143–44; and police shootout, 120–21, 127, 143, 146; presidential candidacy of, 125–26; trial of, 267–69; *Soul on Fire*, 268

——— *Soul on Ice*: smuggled manuscript

of, 98, 100; publication and sales of, 99, 144; content of, 99–100; as read by prisoners, 109, 112, 134; and romanticization of prisoners, 120, 126; as conversion narrative, 265
Clutchette, John, 165, 194, 220
COINTELPRO, 258, 263
Comacho, Moe, 231, 270
Committee for the Rights of the Imprisoned, 123
Communication control, see Bibliotherapy; Censorship; Education; Library; Spector, Herman
Communist Control Act of 1954, 3
Contraband: of Caryl Chessman, 36, 42–48 passim; literature, 77, 89, 98, 116–18; weapons, 210. See also Censorship; House Committee on Internal Security
Conversion genre, criminal, 99, 172, 176, 264–65, 267–69
Convict Bill of Rights, 131–33, 203
Convict cultism: of Black Panthers, 146–47; of Huey Newton, 147–48; of George Jackson, 167–74 passim, 179, 220–21; of Soledad Brothers, 169–70; destructiveness of, 187–88
Convict Grievance Report, 129–30
Convict Unity Holidays, 117–24
Coordinating Council of Prisoner Organizations, 200
Counseling, group, 14–17. See also Bibliotherapy
Court sessions, in-prison, 188, 191–93
Craven, Walter, 201–2
Criminal conversion genre, 99, 172, 176, 264–65, 267–69
Criminality: in early medical theory, 5–6; Eldridge Cleaver on, 94, 112, 125, 145; capitalism as cause of, 141, 188–89, 193; Angela Davis on, 153, 187–89; George Jackson on, 153–54, 158, 179; in Mao, 199

Davidson, Theodore, 116–17, 122–23
Davis, Angela: on political crime and revolution, 153, 187–89; and Soledad Brothers, 165, 172; trial of, 170, 184–85, 188; and San Quentin Six, 261
Davis, George, 43–45, 50, 59

Dean, James, 53
Death penalty, 34, 36, 51–52, 55–60, 67, 165, 232
Death Row, 36–37, 43, 50, 63–64
Debray, Regis, 196–98
DeFreeze, Donald, 239–40, 241–44
Determinate Sentence Law, 253
Drumgo, Fleeta, 162–63, 165, 220–21
Du Bois, W. E. B., 68
Duffy, Clinton: as warden of SQ, 1–2, 8, 12–14; as prison reformer, 8, 10–20

Eastern State Penitentiary, 6
Education, inmate: SQ Education Department, 68, 74–77, 140; secret study groups, 134–40, 156–57, 167; inmate self-improvement groups, 135; at Pelican Bay, 271. See also Black Culture Association; Chessman, Caryl; Cleaver, Eldridge; Jackson, George; Library
Edwards, Cleveland, 164
Eisenhower, Dwight D., 56
Eshelman, Byron, 35, 48, 58
Execution, see Death penalty

Face of Justice, The (Chessman), 46–48, 50–51
Fact-Finding Committee on Un-American Activities, 2
Falwell, Jerry, 267
Foco theory, 153, 197–98, 203, 205, 250–51
Folsom prison strike, 199–202
Foster, Marcus, 242
Foucault, Michel, 9, 265
Freeman, Bernice, 35, 38, 41, 49
Free speech, see Censorship
Fricke, Charles, 34

Gangs, prison: Black Guerrilla Family, 136–37, 241; La Nuestra Familia, 139–40, 276–77; and prison power relations, 140, 154, 199; George Jackson and, 155–56, 159, 164; at Pelican Bay, 271–72
Garry, Charles, 66–67, 120, 200, 246
Ginsberg, Allen, 54, 104
Guards, assaults on, 165, 185, 219, 232

Haley, Alex, 97
Haley, Joseph, 182–83
Hammett, Dashiell, 53
Harriet Tubman Prison Movement, 228
Harris, Emily, 241, 246
Harris, William, 241, 246
Hayden, Tom, 191, 202
Hearst, Patricia, 242–46
Hell's Angels, 103–8
Hilliard, David, 171
Ho Chi Minh, 153
Holliday, James "Doc," 241
Hoover, J. Edgar, 9, 115, 258
House Committee on Internal Security, 219, 223, 230, 237, 248
House Committee on Un-American Activities, 9
Hutton, Bobby, 120

Indeterminate Sentence Law, 11, 15, 123, 130, 253
Inmate case files, 64, 234
Irwin, John, 123, 200, 202, 216, 254

Jackson, George: as Black Panther, 136, 171, 227; as teacher, 138, 160–61, 172, 179; as celebrity outlaw, 153, 170, 188, 221; on criminality and revolution, 153–54, 158, 179; early prison years of, 155; in prison gangs, 155–56, 159, 164; reading of, 156–57, 159, 196–98; Marxism of, 156–62 passim, 179; recruiting techniques of, 158, 160, 162; and white convicts, 158–59, 180; military tactics of, 164, 205–7; in "Soledad Incident," 164–67; defense committee of, 166, 168–69, 175; leftist supporters of, 167, 169, 173, 176–77, 212; convict cult of, 167–74 passim, 179, 220–21; isolation of, 168, 171–73, 179, 186, 207, 212–13; in mass media, 170–71, 178; mythification of, 171–72, 174, 179, 213, 220–21; death of, 209, 225–27, 262; and Soledad Trial, 220, 258–62
———— Works: Blood in My Eye, 153, 204, 250–52; Soledad Brother: The Prison Letters of George Jackson, 134, 153, 170–80 passim
Jackson, Jonathan, 182–83, 185–86, 205

Jackson, "Popeye," 215–17, 245, 253–55
Jefferson Airplane, 61
Johnson, David, 261–62
Johnston, James A., 22

Kerouac, Jack, 54
Kesey, Ken, 62, 101
Kid Was a Killer, The, see under Chessman, Caryl

Leftists: and challenge to social mores, 100–109; and romanticization of prisoners, 126–27, 142, 146, 169, 186; infiltration of, by government, 229–30. See also August Seventh Guerilla Movement; National Lawyers Guild; New World Liberation Front; Outlaws, celebrity; Peace and Freedom party; Symbionese Liberation Army; Venceremos; Weather Underground
Library, San Quentin, 8, 10, 17, 22, 26, 77–79, 80–81, 86–87, 133, 249–50. See also Bibliotherapy; Censorship; Spector, Herman
Little, Malcolm, see Malcolm X
Little, Russell, 242
Loyalty oaths, 2–3

McClain, James D., 182
McGee, Richard A., 11, 38, 41
McHenry, James, 86–87, 133–34
Magee, Ruchell, 182
Mail, inmate, see under Censorship
Malcolm X, 20, 69, 96–97
Mao Tse Tung, 113, 199
Marin County Courthouse shootout, 182–85. See also Davis, Angela; Jackson, Jonathan
Marxism: of Malcolm X, 96–97; class analysis, 103, 203, 266; of Eldridge Cleaver, 112, 142; prison as two-class state, 124, 142–43, 199, 223; inmate study of, 136–38; capitalism as cause of crime/racism, 141, 189, 193; of George Jackson, 156–57, 159, 162, 179; of Huey Newton, 204; and the Right, 229–30
Masculinity, construction of, 52–54, 61, 103, 112, 120–22, 125, 170, 176
Miller, Alvin, 164

Minority prisoners, 65–66, 154, 276. See also Gangs; Muslims
Mitford, Jessica, 194
"Moral instructors," 6
M'tume, Cinque, 239–40, 241–44
Muslims, 65, 69–74, 76, 89, 95–96, 218. See also Minority prisoners

National Lawyers Guild, 187, 207–8, 219, 221
National Prison Association, Congress of the, 11
Nation of Islam, 65, 69–70. See also Muslims
Nazis, inmate, 89
Nelson, Louis, 43, 47, 97, 129, 135, 192
Nelson, Richard, 210–12
Newton, Huey: early Panther days of, 95, 110–11, 113; as political prisoner, 114; "Free Huey!" movement, 118–19, 171; conviction and imprisonment of, 125, 144; on prison censorship, 133; and party purges, 136, 171; convict cult of, 147–48; death of, 148; and George Jackson, 171, 227; on prison economy, 194; and Regis Debray, 196; Marxism of, 204; and drugs, 247–48
New World Liberation Front, 245
Nixon, Richard, 115, 184, 204, 230, 259
Nolen, W. L., 156, 163
Nuestra Familia, La, 139–40, 276–77

Olsen, Culbert, 10
Outlaw, 115–19, 122, 214, 219, 257
Outlaws, celebrity: Caryl Chessman, 52–54; and the Beats, 54; Hell's Angels, 54, 103–4, 107, 112; in rock music lyrics, 61, 104, 107–8; Eldridge Cleaver, 103, 122, 125; Black Panthers, 112, 115; and Mao, 113–14, 199; in Berkeley Barb, 117, 126; Huey Newton, 148; George Jackson, 153, 170, 188, 221

Park, James, 89, 134, 212
Peace and Freedom party, 118–26 passim, 144
Pelican Bay Information Project, 271
Pelican Bay State Prison, 270–74, 277.

See also Adjustment Center; Rehabilitation
Penal Code 2600, 131–33, 203
Perry, Nancy Ling, 241
Pinell, Hugo, 261–62
Political prisoners: Eldridge Cleaver on, 94, 112, 145; convicts as, 103, 127, 152, 161, 182–83; Huey Newton as, 114; Berkeley Barb on, 117; capitalism and crime/racism, 141, 188–89, 193; Ho Chi Minh on, 153; Angela Davis on, 153, 187–89; George Jackson on, 153–54, 158, 161–62, 179; Mao on, 199. See also Revolutionaries
Pratt, Geronimo, 136, 171
Prison construction boom, 270
Prisoners, romanticization of, 126–27, 221. See also Convict cultism; Outlaws, celebrity
Prisoners' Union, California: and Convict Unity Holidays, 117–24; unionism, 118, 124, 200–202; class analysis and, 152, 187, 191, 193–94, 203; and Folsom strike, 199–202; factional split of, 215–17, 253–54; organizing tactics of, 217–19, 255, 276; membership size of, 219; battle for legality of, 255–57; present-day union, 257. See also Convict Grievance Report; Outlaw
Prisoners Union, United: under Popeye Jackson, 213–17, 225, 243, 245; split of, from Calif. Prisoners' Union, 215–17, 253–54; demise of, 255
Prison Law Collective, 187
Prisons, early, 4–7
Pulley, Reginald, 269

Radio, inmate, 1, 83
Reading, inmate, see Bibliotherapy; Censorship; Education; Library; Revolutionaries
Reagan, Ronald: and social unrest, 114, 242; and censorship, 122, 143, 184; on prisons, 131, 248, 270
Reform, inmate, see Rehabilitation
Rehabilitation, inmate: at SQ, 1–20, 22, 35, 64, 71, 74; origins of, 4–6; communication control and, 4–6, 16, 263–64; and Congress of the Na-

tional Prison Association, 7; inmate response to, 15, 19–20, 68, 90, 94, 253; results of, 15, 19–20, 74; and death penalty, 52, 58, 60; end of, 63, 85, 92, 249–50, 253, 275; at Pelican Bay, 271. *See also* Adjustment Center; Bibliotherapy; Counseling

Remiro, Joseph, 241, 244

Revolutionaries, inmate: ideology of, 103, 198; turn to terror of, 148, 187, 189–90, 236, 245, 247; misperceptions of, 167–68, 172–73, 186f, 192, 206–7, 212–13, 221; contraband literature of, 188, 195–96, 219; demands of, 192, 200–201. *See also* Adjustment Center; Black Guerrilla Family; Contraband; Foco theory; Jackson, George; Political prisoners; San Quentin Six; Symbionese Liberation Army

Right, political: attacks of, on prison reform, 188f, 223, 229–30; and crackdown on prisoners, 229, 230–31, 237, 248, 266; and Marxism, 229–30; opposition of, to inmate unions, 256; and domestic spying, 258–59, 263

Riots, *see* Strikes

Rubin, Jerry, 125

Rush, Benjamin, 4–5

San Quentin News, 8, 83–84

San Quentin Six, in Adjustment Center revolt, 209–12, 224, 226, 262; public support for, 228, 259, 261; trial of, 253–63 *passim*. *See also* Adjustment Center; Revolutionaries

San Quentin Twenty-Six, 224, 234

Savio, Mario, 119

Schuller, Robert H., 268

Seale, Bobby, 95, 110, 113, 119, 227, 260

Sieroty, Alan, 131

Sinclair, John, 127

Smith, Court, 10

Smuggling, *see* Contraband

Snedeker, Michael, 203, 218, 255

Soladay, Salle S., 181

Soledad Brother: The Prison Letters of George Jackson, see under Jackson, George

Soledad Brothers: in "Soledad Incident," 163–67; and Angela Davis, 165, 172; as teachers, 168; public support for,

169, 178–79; convict cult of, 169–70; trial of, 186, 220–21, 224; inmates' demands of release of, 192, 200

"Soledad Incident," 163–67

Soledad Seven, 109n, 168

Soltysik, Patricia, 241, 244

Soul on Fire (Cleaver), 268

Soul on Ice, see under Cleaver, Eldridge

Sousa, Martin, 199

Spain, Johnny, 160, 209, 261–62

Spector, Herman: background of, 17; and bibliotherapy, 21, 24, 26–27, 77; as censor, 24–25, 29–30, 82; research of, 27–29; and Malcolm Braly, 30–31; and Caryl Chessman, 35, 37; and Eldridge Cleaver, 78–79, 96

Stender, Fay, 127, 166, 169, 187, 196, 246

Strikes, inmate: in SQ (1950), 1–2, 8; 1950's wave of, 20; Black Muslims in, 72–73; of 1963, 79; SQ yard riot (1967), 87–89, 91; response to, 91, 124, 230–34; Convict Unity Holidays, 117–18, 122–23, 129; outsider involvement in, 117–18, 123; demands of, 123; in-prison court sessions, 191–93; at Folsom (1970), 199–202; effectiveness of, 215; American Correctional Association on, 233–34; in SQ (1972), 234–35

Subversive language, 9, 68. *See also* Censorship; Supreme Court

Sumner, George W., 256

Supreme Court, U.S.: on subversive language, 3, 9; on civil death, 24; on prison unionism, 256–57

Symbionese Liberation Army, 198, 208, 239–45, 246

Taber, Robert, 198–99

Tackwood, Louis, 261

Teeters, Negley K., 39

Teets, Harley O., 20, 37, 41

Telephones, inmate, 84, 238–39

Television, inmate, 83–84, 238–39

Tenney, Jack, 2

Thomas, Gary, 182–83

Thorne, John, 175, 221

Treatment model: at SQ, 1–20, 35; rhetoric of, 3–4; origins of, 4–6; communication control in, 4–6, 16, 263–64. *See also* Rehabilitation

Treatment staff, 16, 19, 63, 90–91
Trial by Ordeal (Chessman), 41–43
Trials, in-prison, 188, 191–93
Turner, Nat, 154, 179

United Prisoners Union, *see* Prisoners
    Union, United
University of California, 2–3, 55, 143,
    146

Vanguard groups, *see* Foco theory;
    Revolutionaries
Venceremos, 147

War of the Flea (Taber), 198–99
Warren, Earl, 11
Weather Underground, 147, 227–29
Wells, Robert Wesley, 2–3, 67–68
White Panthers, 127
Wilson, Lawrence, 88
Wolfe, Willie, 241, 244
Writing, inmate, *see* Bibliotherapy; Cen-
    sorship; Education; Library
Writ-writing, 64, 72, 80–82

Library of Congress Cataloging-in-Publication Data

Cummins, Eric.
  The rise and fall of California's radical prison movement / Eric
Cummins.
      p.   cm.
  Includes bibliographical references and index.
    ISBN 0-8047-2231-5 (cloth) :   — ISBN 0-8047-2232-3 (pbk.)
    :
    1. California State Prison at San Quentin.   2. Prisoners—
California.   3. Prisoners' writings—California.   4. Prison riots—
California.   5. Prison sentences—California.   6. Prisons—
California.   I. Title.
HV9475.C3C83   1993
365'.9794—dc20   93-17831

∞This book is printed on acid-free paper